LARA CROFT TOMB RAIDER™

the angel of darkness

PRIMA'S OFFICIAL STRATEGY GUIDE

PRIMA GAMES
A Division of Random House, Inc.
3000 Lava Ridge Court
Roseville, CA 95661
1-800-733-3000
www.primagames.com

Prima Games is a division of Random House, Inc.

Associate Product Manager: Jill Hinckley

Project Editor: Teli Hernandez

Acknowledgements

Prima would like to thank everyone at Core Design, Eidos UK, and Eidos US who helped in the creation of this book. In particular, this guide would not have been possible without the help and support of Mike Schmitt and Corey McCracken. Thank you!

David S. J. Hodgson would like to thank his wife, Melanie; Mum, Dad, Ian; Bryn G. Willia; Jennifer, Jill, and Teli from Prima for their help, support, and merriment; Bryan Stratton for accidentally picking the difficult levels to write; Carl McCoy and the real Nephilim (Blessed Be); and the letter "E", for Ernest, who choked on a peach.

Bryan Stratton would like to thank Jill Hinckley, Teli Hernandez, and everyone at Prima who put in the necessary long hours to get this book into your hands. Thanks also to David Hodgson, with whom I enjoyed losing my mind, and Steve Stratton and Holly Hannam for reminding me to shower and eat occasionally.

ISBN: 0-7615-4039-3

Library of Congress Catalog Card Number: 2002114069

Printed in the United States of America

03 04 05 06 GG 10 9 8 7 6 5 4 3 2

Contents

Return of the Monstrum

CENTRAL NATIONAL BUREAU, PARIS

COMMISSIONER MIREPOIX,
SPECIAL CRIMES INVESTIGATION FORCE

TO THE PREFECTURE DE POLICE

REPORT ON RECENT SERIAL ATROCITIES WITHIN THE CAPITAL

As yet no significant arrests have been made for this latest spate of "Monstrum" killings in the capital; seventeen have been reported so far. A woman was seen leaving the apartment of the latest victim, Professor Werner Von Croy. Described as Caucasian, brunette, about 1.8m, and of slim build, she was wearing jeans, a denim jacket, and sported a pony tail. She is dangerous and probably armed. Officers are being advised to use extreme caution when apprehending the suspect.

The press have sensationalized this latest outbreak of killings as "The Monstrum's Dark Renaissance," referring to similar atrocities in the capital over the last decade, and possibly as far back as the 1950s. There are definite links to atrocities in other European cities going back at least 50 years.

Forensics have made no headway regarding the bizarre metallic eruptions found on the bodies of all victims. At present, nothing appears to link any of the individuals involved. There have been significant numbers of casualties within Parisian gangland factions.

It would all appear to be the work of a single, highly psychotic perpetrator. The bodies were desecrated and all crime scenes daubed with unintelligible graffiti, indicating some ritualistic fixation. There are no known survivors of these attacks so far.

The suspect's apprehension should be made top priority.

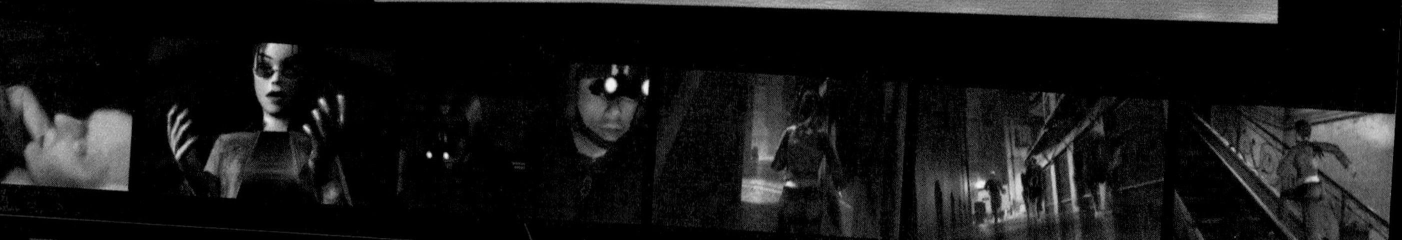

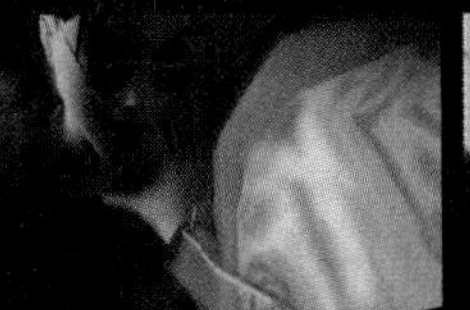
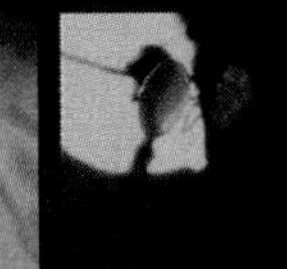

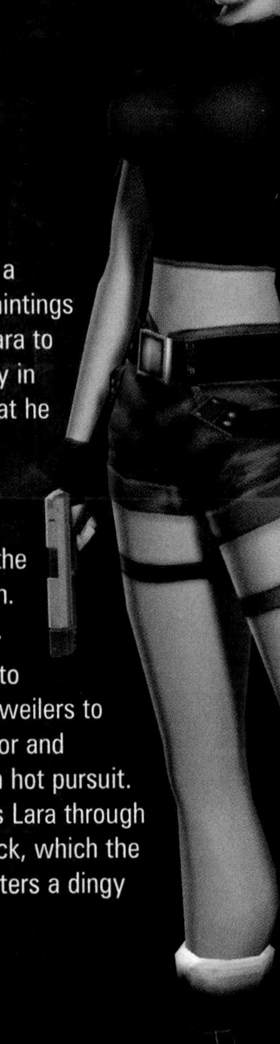

Flashback: Two Days Earlier

Lara and Von Croy are sitting in the professor's apartment study during a thunderstorm. Werner asks Lara for help; he is tracking five Obscura Paintings for a client named Eckhardt. Fearful for his life, Von Croy pleads with Lara to help him deal with the psychotic client. After her treatment by Von Croy in Egypt, Lara is less than enticed at this prospect and informs Werner that he should handle it himself.

Seconds after Von Croy hands Lara a piece of paper with a colleague's name on it, there is a flash of light. Gunfire echoes through the pattering rain. Someone is slumped on the ground. There's a faint gurgle. Against the backdrop of an open window, Lara bends down to inspect the prone form. The professor has been murdered—and Lara has his blood on her hands.

Against the beating rain, a tactic K9 unit of French police screeches to a halt near the apartment and unleashes a duo of specially trained Rottweilers to apprehend the supposed murderess. Lara runs, slamming through a door and fleeing to a ramshackle apartment complex with the growling beasts in hot pursuit. She reaches the end of the corridor. There's no time to run. A dog rams Lara through the window, and she lands outside, unscathed but missing her backpack, which the hound is slobbering. Through a maze of connecting courtyards, Lara enters a dingy back alley and begins the quest to free herself from this nightmare.

How to Use this Guide

Welcome to *Lara Croft Tomb Raider: The Angel of Darkness—Prima's Official Strategy Guide*. Contained within these hallowed pages are expansive hints, tips, and detailed answers to the many puzzles Miss Croft faces during her expedition through Paris, Prague, and beyond.

CAUTION It is important to remember that this guide contains gameplay-sensitive information, and revelations of shocking plot twists abound. We recommend a little self control in the perusing of this guide, as it reveals every single puzzle and gameplay trait in detail. If you don't want to know what waits for you during your journey through the Hall of Seasons, keep your finger from turning those pages. You have been warned.

Introduction and Training

The "Introduction" details the shocking commencement of Miss Croft's European vacation. The "Training" section shows you how Miss Croft's upgrades are awarded, gives tips on utilizing all of her moves, offers hints on completing leaps, shows combat tips, reveals the mysterious Kurtis Trent and his anthology of movements, and gives general advice on surviving and thriving.

NOTE It is important that you familiarize yourself with the game manual prior to reading the "Training" section, as it shows you the basics of tomb raiding. "Training" gives specific examples of putting Lara's moves into practice.

The Book of Monsters

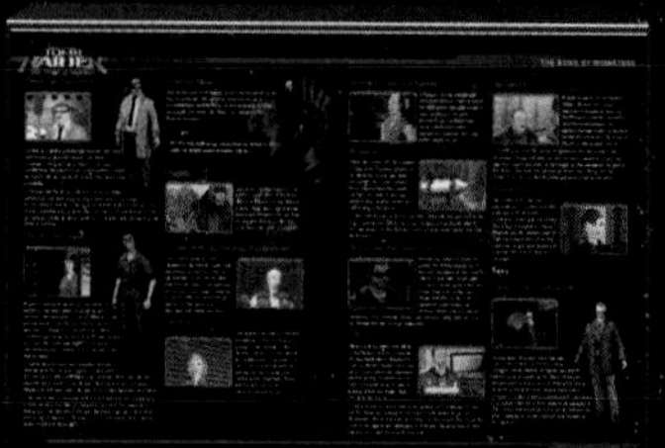

This section of the guide details Miss Croft and Kurtis Trent, the main protagonists in this adventure. It then gives detailed accounts of every entity you encounter in the game, from the hapless French gallery guard to the ferocious and freakishly powerful abominations later into your outing. Where appropriate, takedown tactics for the regular enemies are shown. Strategy for defeating boss beings are shown in the walkthrough.

Items and Weapons

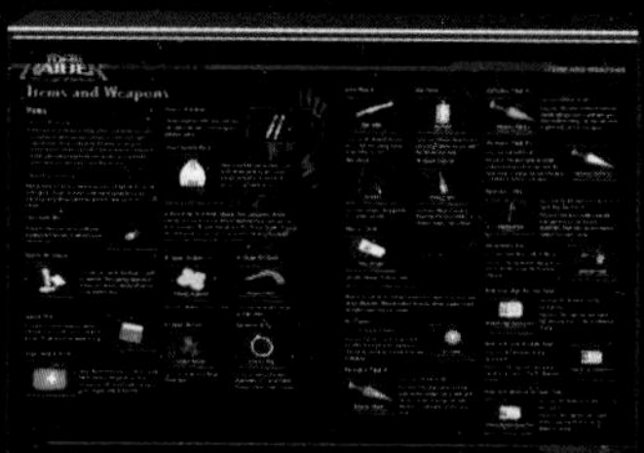

As you'd expect, both Lara and Kurtis keep a large collection of items, arcane materials, and health items for use in a variety of situations. This section of the guide attempts to list every item available in the game. There are weapons (each with detailed information on ammunition type and usage), health (the various medicines and items to pick up), and unique items (available in specific locations and important to the the quest).

Walkthrough

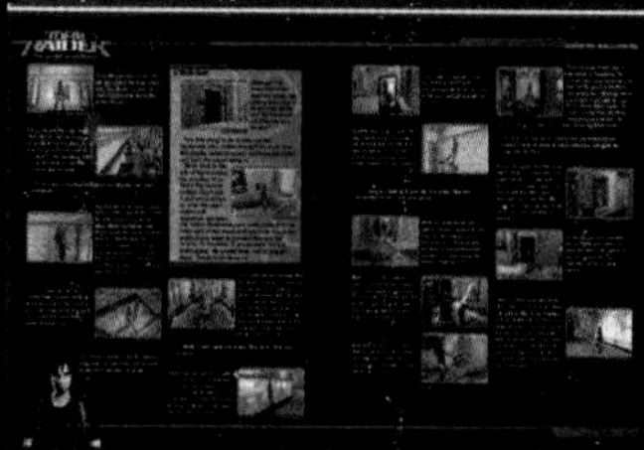

This section details the dozens of locales visited by both Miss Croft and Mr. Trent during the course of their adventure. The walkthrough is segmented into specific areas, each with an overview and notes on items, entities, and upgrades found. The walkthrough shows the preferred method for completing each level. Where the walkthrough deviates from linearity (that is, where there is more than one path to follow), this is mentioned, along with tips and notes. Delve into this section if you're after a quick fix of information on an area you're stuck in, but don't venture too long or you'll complete the zone without trial and error.

Lara's Notebook and Upgrades

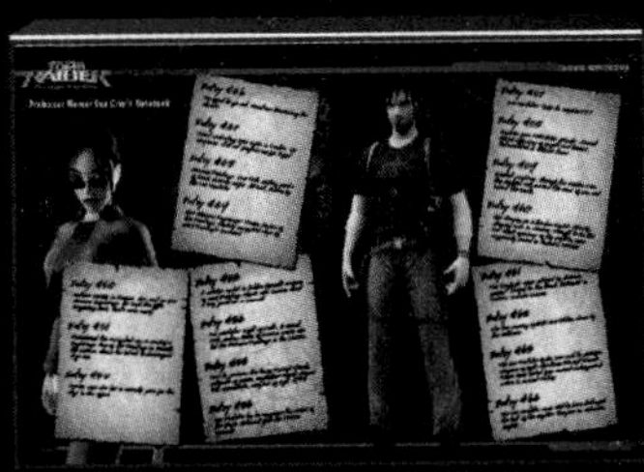

This section of the guide shows fragments of notes from Lara, Von Croy, and another more secretive scribe. These are designed to act as a cryptic series of notes to refer to as the game progresses. After this is a chart showing all 20 of Lara's upgrades, both to her upper and lower body. There is also a visual description of where each upgrade is available, as well as information on how to achieve the upgrade in the easiest manner.

Training: The Craft of Croft

This "Training" section deals with Lara and Kurtis's many maneuvers. Note that every move, with the exception of sneaking, applies to both adventurers.

NOTE The following strategies incorporate the analog stick for better handling and maneuvering. If you are a PC gamer and you don't have an analog controller, maneuver with the Forward, Backward, Left, and Right arrows, and use the mouse to adjust the view.

Walking, Jogging, and Sprinting

The walk is ideal for narrow or unfamiliar ledges.

The jog is excellent for moving at higher speed.

The sprint is the only way to travel when you need real speed.

If you are using an analog joypad, you know that incrementally pressing harder in a certain direction causes Lara to accelerate from a walk to a jog. You don't need to press the Walk button in order to jog; just control Lara with moderate pressure on the analog stick. Walk (without needing the Walk button) when you're positioning Lara near a context-sensitive area, such as a ladder or pipe. Jog at all other times.

Later into her expedition, Lara upgrades her legs to allow her to sprint (but only when you hold Sprint button). As soon as Lara receives this upgrade, use it continuously to cover large distances with ease. Only stop sprinting when you're negotiating tight platforms or corners, as Lara doesn't turn well when running at full tilt.

Making Turns

Tight turning helps in tighter spots.

A quick 180-degree spin is perfect for positioning yourself easily. The skid and turn is less useful, as you slide instead of stopping.

Jogging or sprinting increases your turning radius. Only attempt in large areas.

Once you've mastered the art of pressing forward on your joypad, you're probably ready to start turning as you move. At walking speeds, pressing Right or Left allows a tight turn, which is preferred on all narrow surfaces. At jogging speed, Lara's turning radius is elongated slightly, but she can still turn with some degree of stability. Jog and turn in areas you have already explored. Finally, when you're sprinting down a corridor, your turning radius is extremely wide, and your stopping distance is long. So make sure you've already dealt with any hazards—or react quickly to them.

In addition to turning while moving, Lara can also execute two types of 180-degree turns. The first is a spin, which is achieved by stopping and then pressing your analog stick in the opposite direction. Use this for precise rotating on narrow platforms. The second is a skid and turn. Travel at full speed and stop Lara by letting go of the directional control. Wrench the control in the other direction, and she skids and turns around. This is dangerous if attempted by the edge of a ledge, so employ the stop and spin unless you're in an area without danger or that you know well.

You must walk on this narrow ledge with slow steps and spin turns, not sliding ones.

The Walk Button

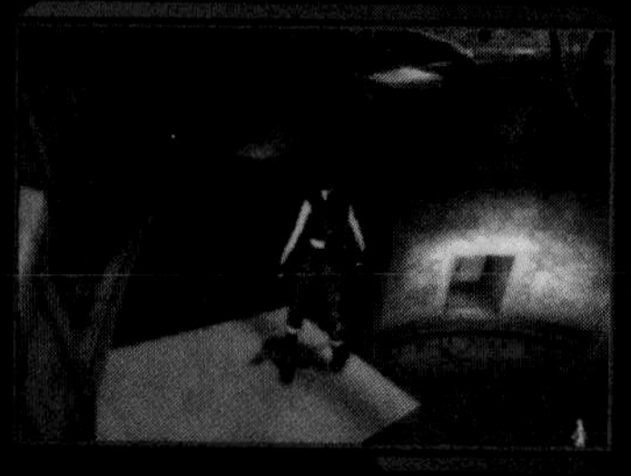

Press and hold the Walk button until the blue man appears. Press again to remove him. Now never fall off platforms.

The Walk button is the new friend of any Lara novice. Simply press this button, and Lara cannot fall off the platform she is on, unless you move her onto a slope. Then all bets are off. Use this exclusively until you've competently figured out her maneuvering repertoire. You can hop from the walk stance. Note that walking with the button and walking by not pressing the analog stick hard enough are not the same moves; the Walk button doesn't allow you to drop or fall.

360-Degree View

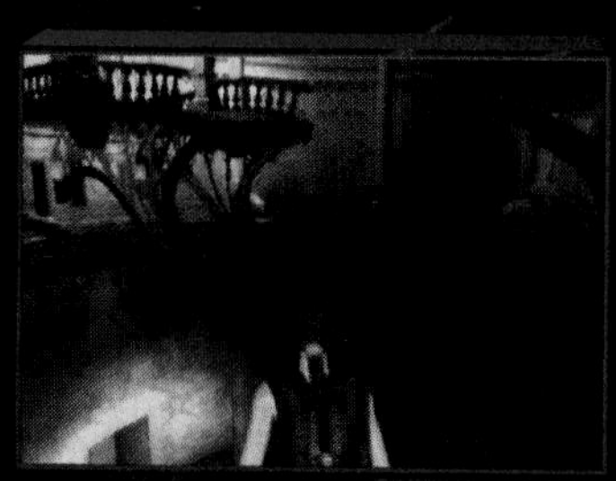

Sprinting was already covered earlier. This technique is for looking around.

We've explored the benefits of sprinting. If you want an over-the-shoulder view of the action, press the Sprint button while Lara is standing still. Then use the right analog stick to look around, but don't move or you revert to normal camera. Use this to check heights and depths.

NOTE **Stealth. Walking. Sprinting. Each dominates another. If you're in Stealth mode, you won't walk or sprint unless you release the Stealth button. If you're walking, you can't sprint unless you release the Walk button, then press the Sprint button. If you're sprinting, you'll move to a Walk or Stealth mode.**

The Stealth Button

Lara strikes a stealth pose in an appropriate locale.

From the stealth pose, you can track an enemy in silence. Don't let him see you.

When an enemy stops and doesn't see you, you can then lay him out with the Action button. This is a great alternative to weapon and health expenditure.

If you're near a wall, you can press Action and hug it. You are now "stuck" to the wall.

Finally, while hugging a wall, you can come to a corner and peek around to view the areas beyond (and any incoming enemies).

Early in her adventure, Miss Croft's ability to silence her footfalls and hunch her shoulders enables her to maneuver along guarded areas without resorting to combat. This is important at the beginning of her outing, as she has no armaments. Pressing the Stealth button allows Lara to move at a half pace without giving away her location. If an enemy cannot see her, she is effectively invisible.

From this stealth pose, Lara can attempt one of three additional moves. First, she can move silently. This is effective when creeping through areas of heavily armed enemies without attracting undue attention. Next, she can bring down a stopped adversary (don't try it on a moving one) with an Action button flurry. Lara grabs the goon by the neck, flips him onto his back, and punches him with a critical strike. This saves on ammo. Finally, she can hug a wall with the Action button, then peer around a corner. This has the added benefit of keeping you close to an exterior wall if you're on a narrow ledge, and you won't fall off when you reach the end.

You can only emerge from the stealth pose after laying out a victim, pressing the Stealth button again, or drawing your weapon.

Unfortunately, Lara cannot carry a weapon while in Stealth mode—or bring down a moving foe from behind. These are two points to consider before employing the stealth crouch.

Kurtis's Farsee Ability

Kurtis Trent does not have the ability to sneak around like a covert operative. Instead, his Stealth button is a Farsee ability (also known as Scrying), which allows him to remotely view areas of the level he is about to move into. This is only utilized during specific periods and during cutscenes; it cannot be attempted in real time. Kurtis's stealth abilities aren't necessary to his survival either, as the entities he encounters are more difficult to remove than a French policeman.

Roll

Use the roll when you want to show off.

The Roll button has but a single use—to make Lara roll forward, then stand up in the opposite direction. This is very similar to the skid and turn, but has the added benefit of working every time you attempt it. It is excellent for changing direction during a fight, or in an area you know well. You can also fire any drawn weapon at the same time as rolling (Weapon button, then Roll and Action at the same time). This can fend off attackers approaching from disparate directions.

Camera View

Repositioning Lara's camera behind her is helpful in enclosed areas.

Remember to change the direction you're moving in when turning the camera to keep it pointing the same way.

It's the only way to travel. Expert Lara handlers should turn her using the camera.

Before moving on to more complex maneuvers such as combat and jumping, you should find the nearest large area and practice utilizing the camera. Most of the time (with the exception of some hanging or jumping areas of the game), you have full control over the camera. If you're stuck behind a shrub, it's the fault of your camera work, not the game. So remember, to keep Lara pointed in the same direction as the camera turns (or you turn the camera), adjust your analog stick's direction. This is achieved by turning both analog sticks in the same direction.

If you want to run down a corridor but view the action from the left side, rotate the right analog stick clockwise and press Left on the left analog stick. Lara will continue to run in the same direction. This is useful if you're being attacked and quickly need to look all around you but keep moving. Practice rotating both analog sticks (one moves Lara, the other moves the camera) until you understand this move. Finally, press the right analog stick inwards to reposition the camera behind Lara. This is a godsend when you're attempting fine and precise leaping.

Crawling

Ducking is only useful for getting into the crawl position.

Being on all fours is exciting for those wishing to avoid head-level problems.

The Commando Crawl is the one-move-fits-all crawling maneuver.

Lara's three techniques using the Duck button are rarely employed, and are only used to avoid obstacles. The first is the crouch. This leaves Lara on her haunches and shouldn't be used. (Duck then Weapon, or Weapon then Duck, and Action). The other two moves cannot be used with a weapon. The first is a crawl. Although amusing to view, there's no real reason to use it over the Commando Crawl (hold Duck, then hold Stealth until the move starts), which is your all-purpose technique for shifting under gaps. You don't need to continue holding Stealth either; just keep pressing Duck, or Lara stands up. Otherwise, let go during a crawl under an object, and Lara rises up as soon as possible—great for getting her into position for combat quickly.

TIP Don't press Stealth then Duck, as nothing happens. Press Duck first, then Stealth.

Combat

Hand-to-hand combat is for when you're high on health, or fighting someone bulky.

Gun combat is the preferred and healthiest method.

Stealth tactics—the grab, flip, and punch—are discussed in the "Stealth" portion of this section.

Both guns blazing, Lara showcases a perfect melding of capabilities and dual pistols.

Kurtis's Chirugai is a unique armament. It is only used in cutscenes.

Hand-to-Hand Combat

Combat can be divided into two categories—armed and unarmed. Unarmed combat is to be waged against weak or bulky enemies with limited armaments of their own. Depending on how close (or high) you are to your enemy, repeatedly pressing the Action button results in a number of aggressive actions.

If you're fighting an opponent that is shorter than you, such as a dog, you employ kicks.

If you're very close to an adversary, you fight with punches. Vary the speed of the Action button tapping for a series of single punches (slow taps) or two-hit combo attacks with a punch, then overhand right (fast taps).

If you're fighting a larger opponent or are farther away, you employ kicks. These are usually single kicks unless you fiercely tap Action. You can score a three-hit combo with two kicks and a roundhouse to finish.

Ranged Combat

The alternate (and safer) way to dispose of your enemies is to utilize the Weapon button. Note that this isn't necessary for hand-to-hand combat, only for ranged attacking. When you unhook your weapon from its holster (or your back if it is a shotgun or machine gun), you can fire single shots with a press of the Action button. During this time, your ammo is displayed near your health in the top-left corner of the screen. You can keep firing until you holster your weapon, down your foe, or decide to stop fighting. Perform the following techniques to ensure combat supremacy. Note that you automatically face and aim at the enemy until you either step too far away, another enemy comes closer (then your aim switches), or you put away your gun.

The Circle Strafe

The classic, and easiest, way to confuse foes while whittling them down is to circle strafe. Naturally, you must be able to run around your enemy (if you can't, move quickly from side to side or in a semicircle). During that time, continuously fire as your foe attempts to strike you. Normally, you come out ahead.

The Jump and Rotate

You can flummox an enemy if you start side somersaults as you fire. Although you can't fire as you jump, you are more difficult to attack. Try a jump and rotate (circle strafing, but leaping around as well) for the ultimate in humiliating takedowns.

Firing through Scenery

Obviously, walls and scenery can't be blasted through, but mesh walls and other partially transparent objects can. This is no substitute for getting up close. But if you have a lot of ammunition, or cannot reach your enemy, try firing from cover or through plants.

Point-Blank Blasting

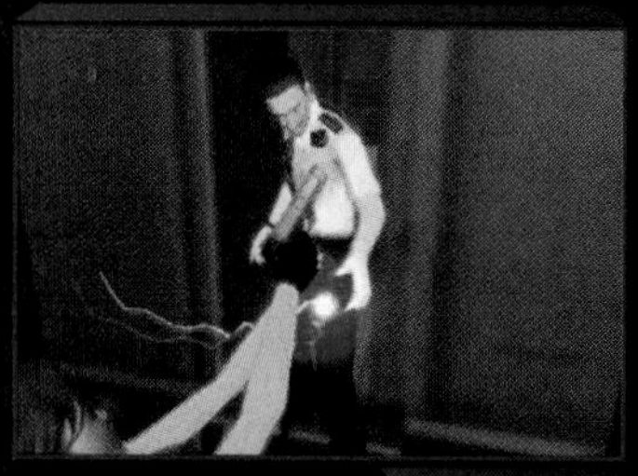

You'd be surprised what a point-blank shotgun blast to the skull can do. With this in mind, if your health and bravery are large enough, pop caps into foes as close to them as possible. You inflict more damage, and you save on ammo.

NOTE You can fire your weapon while stationary, crouching, jogging, and walking, but not while crawling, sprinting, and in Stealth mode. When you're jumping, your weapon is drawn but not fired.

TIP For continuous fire, keep your finger held down on the Action button. You unleash the maximum number of bullets and fire immediately after a jumping move.

NOTE The full complement of ordinance available to Miss Croft and Mr. Trent is detailed in the subsequent "Inventory" section.

Fleeing Combat

Some foes are invincible, and some are just not worth wasting ammo. Enemies without carried items should be ignored or avoided to save ammunition. Humans who drop items when killed should be targeted. Don't overstay your fighting welcome unless you must defeat your foes. The walkthrough refers to specific examples when fleeing is necessary.

Combat Examples

Here are two examples of inventive ways to deal with skilled entities. The Knight refuses to give up and revives countless times. You can coax him into a trap, activate it (in this case, a trapdoor), watch him fall in, then avoid him for the rest of the game.

You can also kick an enemy off a ledge. In this example, a Cabal soldier receives a sharp slap to the helmet and staggers off a ledge. He isn't coming back from that fall, and neither will a Knight if you employ this tactic on him.

Rennes' Gun Emporium

You find ranged weapons on the bodies of certain foes (such as policemen and guards) and lying on the ground. However, the Parisian Ghetto has Daniel Rennes' Pawn Shop, which comes fully stocked with ordinance for every occasion. It is imperative that you locate valuables (such as Vintage Cognac, Antique Doubloons, and jewelry) to hawk at the shop in return for weaponry. Sell everything, as there's no more shopping after this.

Jumping

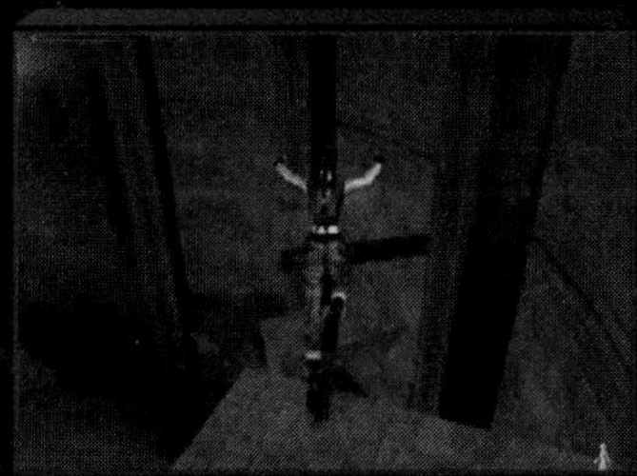

Use the vertical jump when you need to grab a ledge, rope, or object above you.

The hop (walking and jumping) is used to cover short gaps and fissures.

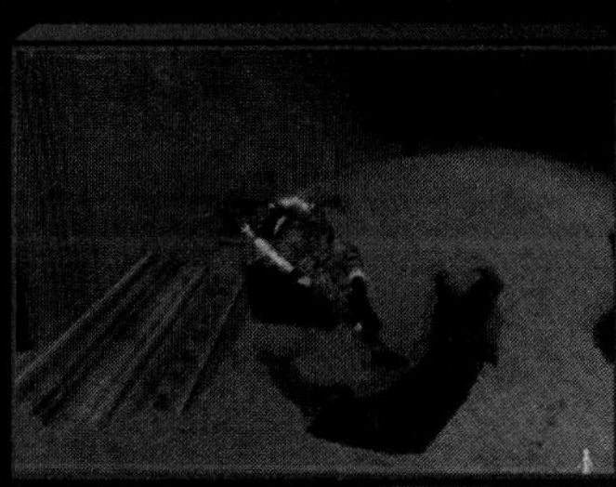

Use the side jump when you're stuck behind objects.

Do the back-flip to confuse an enemy, or get down from a ladder in style.

The standing forward jump (press the Jump button) allows you to leap crevasses with six feet of air.

The running jump (jog and press the Jump button) hurls you 10 feet.

The sprinting jump (press Sprint, then Jump) is ideal for covering huge gaps.

The swan dive to a forward roll is a great alternative to a heavy landing. Press Sprint when jumping (after upgrade).

Jumping up stairs saves time. Avoid accidentally side jumping.

Jump at an exterior wall that's above the platform you want to land on. You hit the wall and slide down it without damage. This is easier than judging distances.

The key elements to Lara's continued success are her incredibly powerful legs. As you can see from the previously detailed jumping types, there is a leap for every situation—although the standing and running jumps, not to mention the vertical jump followed by a grab, are utilized most extensively. Sometimes it is incredibly difficult to gauge how far you are from a platform separated by a chasm, so it is important to time each jump and stretch out for a grab after each launch. Finally, you may sometimes execute a side jump when the camera is turning or you're pointing just slightly off center, and this usually ends in disaster. You can't rush jumps, so make sure you're facing directly ahead (with the camera directly behind) to avoid any anomalous results.

> *TIP* **If you want a quick glimpse of Lara's many jumping techniques, find a large, flat area, keep tapping the Jump button, and press different directions on your joypad. She leaps from spot to spot. Impressive!**

Hanging Around

Hanging from a ledge, maneuver yourself out of this predicament post haste.

The vault is a simple hop over an obstacle. This can be used to bound over balconies, but look before you leap.

The hand-over-hand is useful for maneuvering along ledges using only your hands to grip. Extremely narrow platforms are no match for Lara's nimble and muscular fingers.

Climbing pipes and ivy-covered walls takes more skill than a ladder. There are no grip problems with the ladder.

Certain rock walls (note the rock texture) can be climbed, but be wary of venturing too far without a rest.

Clambering on sloping ceilings can induce vertigo. You may auto-turn at the top of these slopes and begin the next technique.

The monkey swing is perhaps the most terrifying move of all, requiring you to maneuver with only your hands. Complete these moves quickly.

Pressing Duck while monkey swinging allows you to place your feet on the wire or chain and continue moving. Unless your feet are dangling dangerously close to an obstacle, this technique isn't recommended, as it takes a second to perform, meaning a second less grip time for Miss Croft.

Hanging from various objects and scenic features is a staple of Lara's incredible array of moves. This time, she has the added bonus of rock climbing, clambering up slopes and ceilings, and even monkey swinging across ropes. These techniques involve your grip bar and turning corners. There are many occasions where you should shimmy around a rock wall or ledge turn. Always check that there are no upper-body upgrades in your area before you climb, or you could fall.

TIP **Remember that you cannot grab everything. This mesh wall at grab height proves too problematic for Lara. In these cases, look elsewhere for the solution to your maneuvering.**

Falling

Some of the jumps are pretty difficult, so falling is common. Remember that the farther you fall, the more damage you take. Over 20 feet, and you lose a half of your health. Much farther, and you land with a sickening thud (complete with a grotesque rag doll animation for our heroine). With this in mind, heed the following advice and utilize the following techniques to minimize the pain and suffering.

The Walk button prevents you from falling on everything, but a slope. Without it, you usually fall when you come to an edge and keep moving. Afterwards, you auto-turn and grab the ledge you were just on. Decide to drop or clamber back up from this point.

If you approach the same ledge with speed, you'll fall off and won't grab the ledge. Remember that the auto-grab only works if you don't leap from the ledge or run off it at great speed.

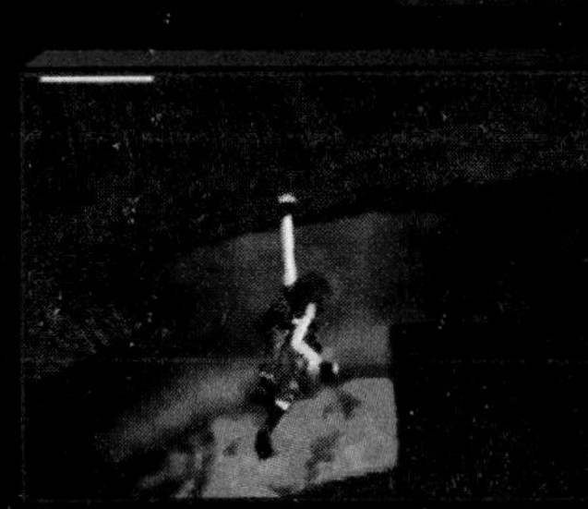

The dangle and drop is used to quickly descend. Don't fall too far.

Dangle and drop, then dangle when ladders aren't quick enough to descend platforms directly underneath each other. Note the word, "directly."

When you leap for a ledge and don't make it, use the jump and grab. Press Action to stretch out your arms and you grab the ledge.

A variant of the jump and grab is to leap for a platform, hit it with your waist, then slide down and grab it. This is easier than landing on top of the platform.

Finally, grab onto a ladder if you're falling past it, just like the lip of a ledge.

Swimming

Treading water allows you to cross the surface of water without losing oxygen. When you reach a ledge, pull yourself out of the water with the Action button.

Diving underwater allows quick breast strokes as Lara swims like a fish. Unfortunately, she doesn't breathe like one, so always be on the lookout for the surface.

Usually there are holes to swim through. Gauge your available air before swimming too far down these passages.

With the appropriate upgrade, instead of jumping and landing feet-first in the water, you can gracefully swan-dive.

Swimming is part of the tomb-raiding experience, and holding your breath while dodging spear traps is all part of the fun. Lara's breath eventually runs out, so look for an air hole before venturing too far into the unknown depths. It is better to take a couple of breaths and backtrack instead of reaching your final location and drowning. Simply tap Action to dive and swim underwater. Landing in water keeps you alive, even after a plummet from a high platform. Aim for water if you can.

Scenery

Stairs are always climbed at walking pace. Avoid this laborious technique by jumping up stairs six at a time.

Ladders are part of the scenery, and most are complete. However, some end in midair, forcing you to jump off or climb back up to seek a different area. Unlike pipes, you can stay on ladders indefinitely. Back-flips from ladders serve as shortcuts to climbing if you know how far you'll fall.

There are various environmental hazards during the course of your adventure. The walkthrough details how to complete these difficult areas.

When you're sliding down a slope, you cannot stop. All you can do is leap from the bottom of the slope to safety. If you can't jump, tap Action to turn and grab the lip of the slope before you slide off it. Then, you can shimmy to safety.

The final piece of scenery involves puzzles—such as feeding a tendril tree trunk a poison concoction, or tapping in a five-digit pass code. The walkthrough details all the puzzles to complete.

The Hand Icon

A hand icon on the screen means something needs to be pushed, pulled, activated, or opened. Try all of these techniques, just in case you don't understand exactly what to do. For example, when checking wall sections, don't just tap Action. Pull and push as well to ensure the entire section can't be shoved back and forth. Look for the hand, as this is the key to completing tasks or receiving clues. There's something on the floor, in a cupboard, or nearby that looks interesting.

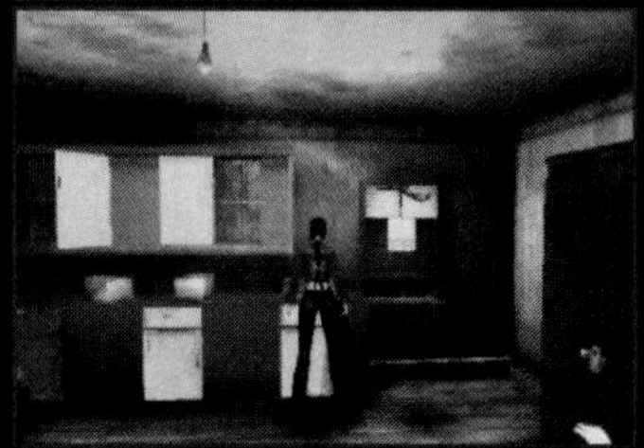

That door looks like it can be opened, or at least rattled.

Doors that don't have a hand near them are either sealed or opened with a lever.

Levers, switches, valves, and buttons all feature the hand and should be pressed.

There are levers underwater. They work in the same way as land-based levers.

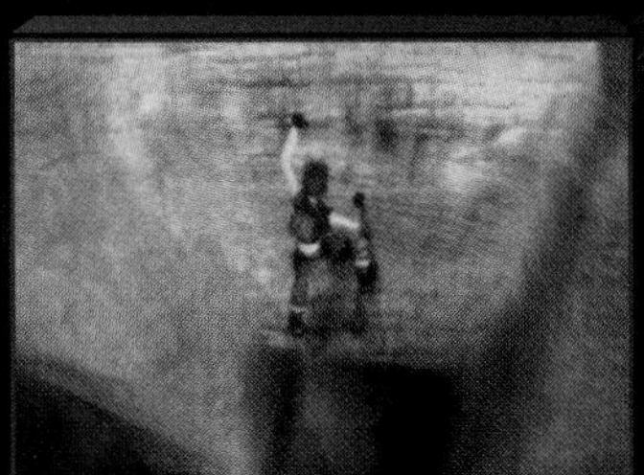

This wall doesn't show you a hand, but you can still interact with it. Check everything.

Leap for hanging chains and wire above you. You automatically grab on.

Pulling boxes and pushing crates is routine for any aspiring archaeologist. Remember that some pieces of wall can be pushed or pulled in the same way.

Kicking doors is another way of entering areas, usually after collecting an upgrade.

The Inventory Screen

The Inventory screen is fully explained in the game manual. However, it is wise to continuously check your Inventory for items you pick up and notes Lara made that can help you with a puzzle. Finally, only utilize ammunition, weapons, and health with manual button tapping.

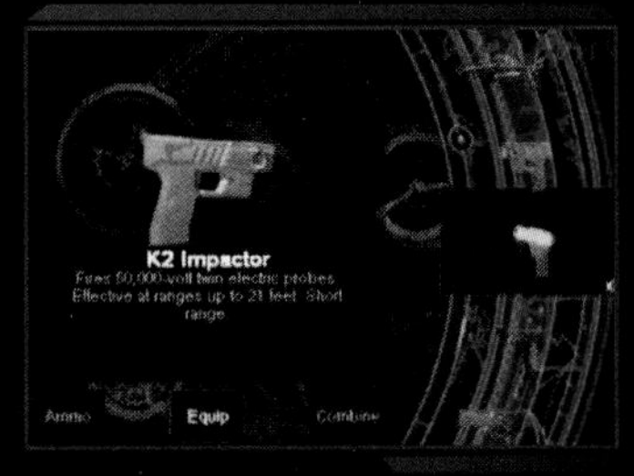

Puzzle items are used automatically and do not need to be accessed.

Upgrades

Although Lara doesn't change physically, during the game she receives 20 separate upgrades. There are 10 upgrades to her upper body and 10 to her lower body. Upper-body upgrades are awarded after pulling or pushing an object or scenery. Lower-body upgrades are awarded for lengthy jumps or kicking doors open. Upgrades serve to increase Lara's grip, award her with the sprint move, and allow her to open doors she previously couldn't open.

TIP Stuck at a door you're not strong enough to open? Can't cross a gap because of your weak legs? Then fear not—there is a place nearby to upgrade Lara's body. Go find it, then return to the area you couldn't access.

NOTE The complete list of upgrades, what they do, and where they are, is located in the "Lara's Upgrade Chart" section at the back of this guide. You will be surprised at how bulked up Lara becomes. At the start of the game, Lara only has enough grip to hang off a ledge for 14 seconds. At the conclusion, she can hang for an amazing 30 seconds.

Top Ten Tips for Surviving and Thriving

10: Let the Camera Turn You

Instead of using the left analog stick to turn, press the Forward button continuously in this direction, then maneuver the camera (and Lara) with the right analog stick. This way, you see everything, can quickly pan or tilt without losing control, and have a much better grasp of how Lara handles.

9: Jump and Hit Walls

The technique of leaping at a wall, hitting it, and sliding down onto a ledge is the easiest method of maneuvering around platforms of indeterminate distance. This saves hours of trial-and-error jumping.

8: Close in for the Kill

Don't waste time with a ranged weapon, attempting to whittle an enemy down to size. Once you've realized what offensive strategy the enemy possesses, sprint into close quarters and fire. You save on ammo, spend less time fighting, and generally feel better about yourself.

7: Entity Bemusement

You'll be amazed at how close you can get to enemies without them taking offensive measures. Enemies aren't bright, don't react well to you circling them, and have restricted vision. Use this to your advantage.

6: Avoid Five-Digit Disasters

Pass codes with five digits are the choice of the Cabal, and every number puzzle you solve involves the input of five separate figures. If you see a five-digit number, jot it down— you'll be using it soon. All the digits are revealed in the walkthrough, if you aren't close enough to a pen.

5: Talk to Everyone

Individuals who aren't trying to kill you have something incredibly important to say. Talk to everyone and always save your game before you do. Margot Carvier has a notebook that she'll only give you if you answer her questions to her satisfaction. Saving before talking to her means you can replay the chat if you insult her.

4: Doors: Sealed, Locked, and Jammed

There are many doors in Paris and Prague, and most of them don't lead anywhere. If a door doesn't offer you the hand icon, ignore it. If it is jammed or sealed, disregard it. The only doors that concern you are those that you aren't strong enough to kick open, or those that are locked; usually a nearby key solves that problem.

3: Items and Adjacent Puzzles

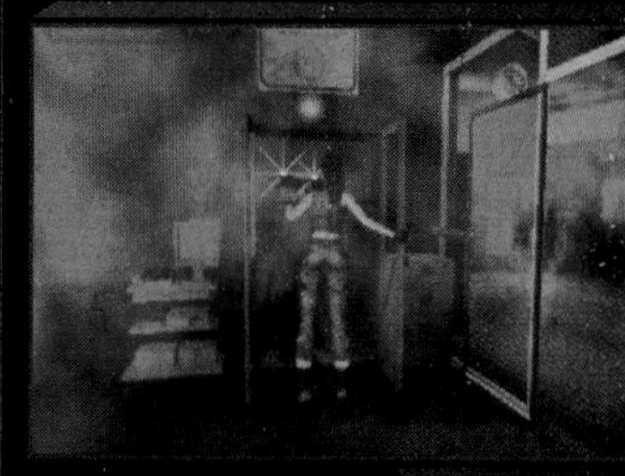

In most puzzles requiring a specific item, the object in question is close by, usually within two or three rooms of the puzzle. With the major exception of the elemental chambers in The Hall of Seasons, if you see a puzzle, check the immediate vicinity.

2: Bring out the Big Guns

Whenever you investigate an area that you haven't explored, or one with enemies yet to be dispatched, always carry your weapons out of their holsters. If foes appear, Lara auto-targets them before you even know they're there.

1: Save Often

Save your game—before you enter a room, prior to engaging an enemy, when you're about to locate a unique item in an unfamiliar area, and most of all, just before a jump of unknown distance.

NOTE Congratulations, Miss Croft. You've completed your training. Be aware that, although the levels to come are varied and vast, they are linear in nature. And more often than not, only one path is available. Utilize the walkthrough completely, and you'll have no trouble locating the real killer of Professor Von Croy, as well as uncovering secrets too terrifying to utter.

The Book of Monsters

Traversing the many traps, puzzles, and dark alleys of this adventure is tough enough, but you're further tested when interacting with the host of misfits, law enforcement patrols, covert soldiers, and terrifying mutations that populate Lara's world. This section details the main players of the game—friends, foes, and fiends. Find out the real story behind some of the game's most freakish participants.

Friends

Lara Croft

Nationality: British

Date of Birth: 14/02/????

Birthplace: Wimbledon, Surrey

Marital Status: Single

Blood Group: AB

Height: 5'9"

Weight: 9st 4

Vital Statistics: 34D 24 35

Hair Color: Brown

Eye Color: Brown

Distinguishing Features: 9mm handgun

Education:

Private Tutoring (3-11)

Wimbledon High School for Girls (11-16)

Gordonstoun Boarding School (16-18)

Swiss Finishing School (18-21)

The Early Years

Lara was independent and outgoing at school, always preferring individual to team sports. While at Gordonstoun, she excelled at rock climbing, canoeing, horseback riding, and archery. A natural athlete, she discovered a passion for firearms but was discouraged by the school authorities. Later, in her Swiss finishing school, she further developed her interest in firearms by charming her way onto the Swiss Armed Forces training range, where she proved to be a natural and qualified markswoman. Later in life she felt drawn to fast vehicles and any form of extreme sports, "just to keep me trim."

Finding Her Calling

As the daughter of Lord Henshingly Croft, Lara was used to the security of an aristocratic background. Predictably, she rebelled against the more confining aspects of her upbringing, and when she moved to Gordonstoun in 1984, the mountains of Scotland gave her an unprecedented degree of freedom. Her world changed further when she came across the work of Professor Von Croy and heard him lecture about his archaeological career. The experience had a profound effect on Lara, triggering a passion for remote locations and adventure.

Her First Field Trip

Lara discovered that Von Croy was preparing for an archaeological expedition to Asia and persuaded her parents to let her accompany him. Von Croy was convinced after being promised financial assistance for the expedition. He was also impressed by the young amazon's enthusiasm and energy. She could obviously take care of herself, and the experience would be a unique and educational opportunity.

This expedition set the pattern for the rest of her life. For the first time, she experienced the hazards and mysteries of the ancient world of antiquities. Terrifying dangers became an accepted part of her life. In the intervening years, she has combated ancient mythical forces, survived a Himalayan plane crash, and outgunned heavily armed opponents, always emerging with the prize.

Lifestyle

Despite inheriting the Croft mansion in Surrey, Lara lives the same way she prefers to work—alone. In her rambling home she has installed a custom-built assault course and shooting range. With her unique physical abilities, Lara could break many world athletic records, but sees no challenge in this for herself. It lacks the necessary ingredient of danger.

The huge rooms of the mansion are useful for storing the many artifacts she has acquired in her adventures. There is also adequate space for her favorite vehicles. Anything on two wheels and over 650ccs is considered acceptable, but she finds both the Triumph Speed Triple and the Harley V-Rod especially attractive.

Apart from her archaeological successes, Lara is proud of her achievements in other areas, too. She drove the dangerous Alaskan Highway from Tierra del Fuego in record time. This escapade resulted in worldwide headlines confirming the opinion of the established antiquities community that she was a loose cannon. She loves this profile, but generally shuns the media spotlight, as it interferes with her tomb-raiding activities.

And Now

Events in recent times have cast a shadow over Lara's life. She went missing, presumed dead, after a disastrous field trip to the Egyptian tombs with Von Croy. She refuses to confirm or deny rumors about time spent among obscure North African tribes. But whatever happened after Egypt, she has become reclusive since her return to Surrey.

Kurtis Trent

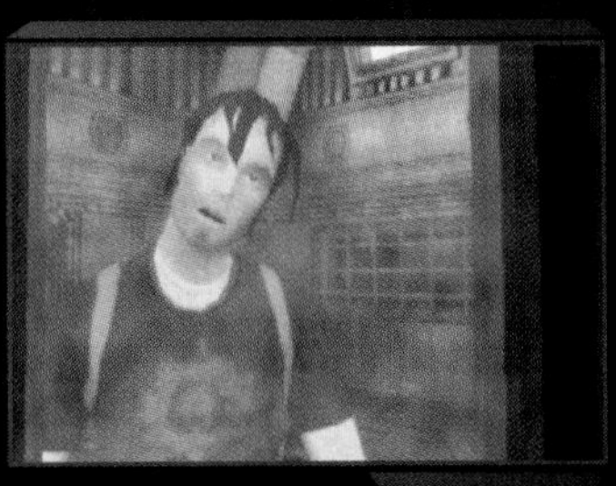

1972: Born on June 26 in Utah Salt Flats, USA

1975: Kurtis, three years old, is trained by his father Konstantin as a Lux Veritatis initiate. The ancient order is being ruthlessly hunted by Eckhardt and the Cabal.

1988: Kurtis, aged 16, undergoes the most intense stages of his Lux Veritatis initiation.

1991: At age 19, Kurtis disappears and joins the Foreign Legion, changing his name to Trent. He remains hidden within the legion for five years, constantly assaulted by bizarre events linked to the occult. In this time, he gets the nickname "Demon Hunter."

1996: Kurtis leaves the legion and begins freelancing with a variety of mercenary and less-than-legal agencies. He hears from his father, but never sees him alive again.

2001: Konstantin is murdered by Eckhardt. This is Kurtis's wakeup call. He receives two talismanic items, the Periapt Shards, and the terrifying Chirugai blade. In a rage of vengeance, he goes after Eckhardt.

2002: Kurtis crosses paths with Lara in Paris, and they team up in Prague to combat the Cabal and Eckhardt. Lara first sees Kurtis tearing away from Le Serpent Rouge on his motorcycle. Their paths cross several times during their adventure, but it isn't until the end of the Maximum Containment Area level that Lara finds out if Kurtis is a friend or foe. Kurtis has several psychic talents, including telekinesis and a Farsee ability that gives him a glimpse of areas he can't physically reach.

Notes on the Chirugai

***Chir-rug-ai:* (Latin) Violent measures involving surgery**

This discus-like blade is an ancient Lux Veritatis weapon, made from ferilium, a rare meteorite alloy. Kurtis inherited it, along with the Periapt Shards, when his father was killed by Eckhardt. Kurtis's ability to control the terrifying weapon comes from his early years of training as a Lux Veritatis initiate.

Professor Werner Von Croy

A world-respected archaeologist and part-time adventurer, Werner was Lara's mentor in her early years. Now in his late 50s, he lives alone, pouring over manuscripts and assorted antiquities in his Paris apartment. Lately he has been troubled by a stranger with an odd-shaped hand, who has instructed him to search for items known as the Obscura Paintings.

Mlle. Margot Carvier

A historian and academic at the Louvre Department of Medieval and Renaissance Studies, Carvier is a stern woman involved in recent archaeological digs beneath the Louvre galleries. She is both a friend and colleague of Professor Von Croy. She lives alone in an apartment near Paris's industrial district.

Thomas Luddick

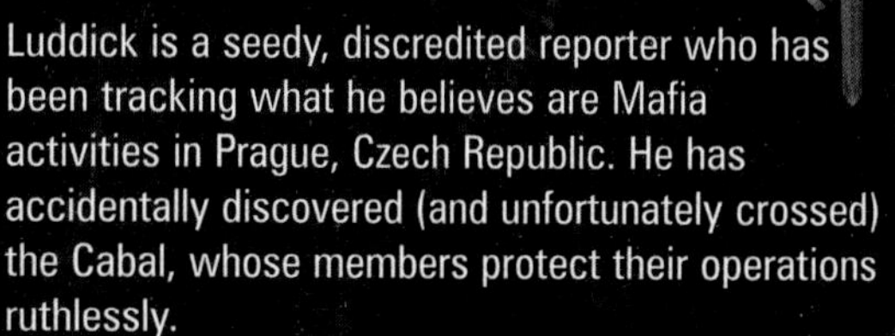

Luddick is a seedy, discredited reporter who has been tracking what he believes are Mafia activities in Prague, Czech Republic. He has accidentally discovered (and unfortunately crossed) the Cabal, whose members protect their operations ruthlessly.

He also has the entry code to Strahov Fortress, which he's only too happy to share with Lara in exchange for her story of events in Paris—plus whatever she uncovers in the future. Unfortunately, Luddick has a bit too much confidence in his journalistic immunity, which gets him in trouble with Eckhardt in the Strahov Fortress.

Daniel Rennes

A gaunt Frenchman suffering from delusions including (but not limited to) insanity and paranoia, Rennes makes a living hawking underground wares in the Parisian Ghetto. He is a specialist in illegal documentation and black marketeering, using his back street pawnbrokers as a front for these operations. He is also a demolitions expert, thanks to time served in the French Navy.

Daniel Rennes owns and operates Rennes' Pawnshop in the Parisian Ghetto, a place where you can buy or sell "extra-legal" merchandise. Here, Lara can turn valuable items found in the Parisian Back Streets and Le Serpent Rouge into cold hard cash, as well as purchase weapons and items.

Rennes is also in business with Louis Bouchard and is expecting to take delivery of a Wad of Passports. But with the pressure he's feeling from the Monstrum killings, Bouchard has had a hard time getting the passports to Rennes. If Lara could deliver them, Rennes would know that she's legit.

Luther Rouzic

Thin to the point of ill health, Luther Rouzic works at the Prague archives. The Librarian Honorarium, he is acknowledged worldwide to be the authority on dead languages and texts. He is also the keeper of the Strahov archives.

NOTE **The following characters are listed in the order in which you encounter them.**

Hobo

Lara runs into two hoboes in an abandoned section of the Paris Metro at the start of the Parisian Ghetto. They claim not to know who Louis Bouchard is, but they do suggest that Lara visit the Café Metro for more information.

Enterprising Young Salesman

This friendly chap is rather insistent in his efforts to sell Lara something to take her mind off her troubles during the Parisian Ghetto level. Being a straightedge tomb raider, Lara doesn't take him up on his offer, but she does get plenty of information about Bouchard and Pierre from him.

Janice

This scarlet lady has an intimate knowledge of the comings and goings of the citizens of the Parisian Ghetto, and the streets she walks keep no secrets from her. If Lara converses with her politely, Janice reveals information about Bouchard, Pierre, and Bernard that is of tremendous help to Lara.

Willowtree Herbalist

A Parisian Ghetto shopkeeper who specializes in healing herbs, the Willowtree Herbalist doesn't have anything to do with Bouchard, but he does have some information about Bouchard's doorman that may prove helpful to Lara.

Boxers

There isn't much call for a house of God in the Parisian Ghetto, so St. Aicard's Church has been converted into a gym, where three boxers hone their skills. Zak and Carl spar in the ring while a third pugilist works the heavy bag in the corner.

Their trainer, also a bit of a gambler, observes Zak and Carl in the ring. If you've got 200 Euros to put up against his Golden Watch, you can wager on the fighters. Carl's a much better boxer than Zak, by the way.

Bouchard's Doorman

Bouchard's unnamed doorman guards the entrance gate to St. Aicard's Graveyard in the Parisian Ghetto. If you want to get past him, you'd better have either the Trinket Box from Le Serpent Rouge and 800 Euros, or a password given to you by Bernard. While he's not overtly menacing, Lara probably couldn't just force her way past him and his Rottweilers and emerge unscathed.

Pierre

Pierre currently owns Café Metro in the Parisian Ghetto, but his last job was bartender in Bouchard's club, Le Serpent Rouge. He left the job in a hurry when his coworkers started getting murdered left and right, but he still kicks himself for leaving behind the Trinket Box in the club's lighting rig.

Pierre is one of Lara's options for getting into Le Serpent Rouge and St. Aicard's Graveyard. Find him in Café Metro to get the Bartender's Key to the club, and bring him the Trinket Box to get the code to the apartment belonging to Francine, his ex-girlfriend. She can get Lara past Bouchard's doorman.

Bernard

A surly ex-janitor at Le Serpent Rouge, Bernard left Louis Bouchard's employ as soon as the Monstrum started murdering Bouchard's employees. He spends his days sitting in the park across the street from St. Aicard's Church in the Parisian Ghetto.

If Lara gives him 160 Euros, he gives her the Ex-Janitor's Key to Le Serpent Rouge and tells her that he has a password to get her past Bouchard's doorman. In exchange for the password, he wants the Trinket Box from the lighting rig of the club. Bring him the Trinket Box, and you find that Bernard is as good as his word.

Francine

The entrance to Francine's apartment is in an alley near the entrance to St. Aicard's Graveyard. If you give the Trinket Box to her ex-boyfriend, Pierre, he gives you the access code to Francine's apartment. Enter the apartment to get past Bouchard's doorman and into St. Aicard's Graveyard.

Foes

Pieter Van Eckhardt

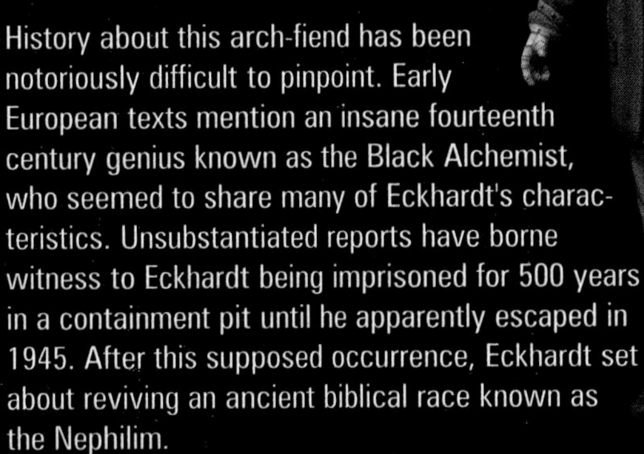

History about this arch-fiend has been notoriously difficult to pinpoint. Early European texts mention an insane fourteenth century genius known as the Black Alchemist, who seemed to share many of Eckhardt's characteristics. Unsubstantiated reports have borne witness to Eckhardt being imprisoned for 500 years in a containment pit until he apparently escaped in 1945. After this supposed occurrence, Eckhardt set about reviving an ancient biblical race known as the Nephilim.

The Sleeper

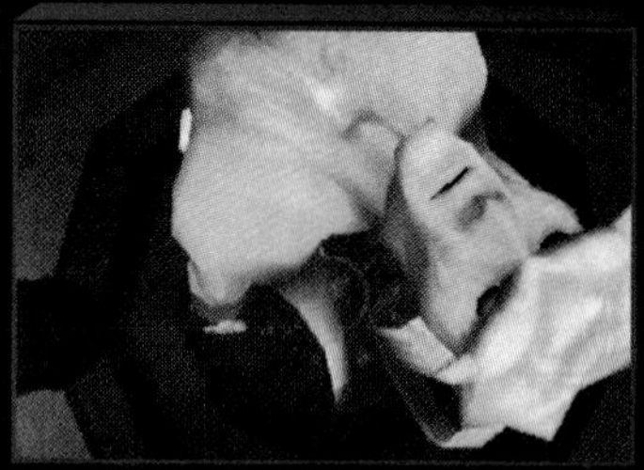

Said by legend to be the last intact specimen of the biblical Nephilim race, this creature is in a permanent stasis field, supposedly buried in a state of "death, but dreaming" in one of the subterranean cities of central Cappadocia in Turkey.

The Cabal

The Cabal is one of those inscrutable organizations that operates from the shadows, manipulating events for its own unfathomable purposes. Based in the Strahov Fortress in Prague, the Cabal is so dangerous and powerful that it uses the Mafia as a front for its activities, which currently involve recovering the five Obscura Paintings and using their power to revive the ancient Nephilim race. Eckhardt and Gundersen are senior members of the Cabal.

Joachim Karel

With a shock of white cropped hair, and a corporate legal mastermind within his furrowed brow, Joachim Karel's Paris office oversees the investments of a new world order known as the Cabal, as well as its recruitment drives. In addition, he takes particular delight in protecting his client's interests in the worldwide arena, and is a legal scholar not to be trifled with.

RESEARCHING THE NEPHILIM MYTH

Scholars from the Louvre archives have been pouring over ancient texts and biblical tomes in order to present a little background to the race of Nephilim. The following information has been gathered to provide a necessary backdrop to the hideous machinations that Pieter Van Eckhardt is said to be undertaking.

"There were giants in the earth in those days; and also after that, when the sons of God came in unto the daughters of men, and they; bare children unto them, the same became mighty men which were of old, men of renown."
—*Genesis 6:4* (King James Version)

The root of Nephilim is *nephel*, which means "untimely birth, abortion, miscarriage." The biblical tradition says the Nephilim were on the earth before the great flood and afterwards, but they appear to be missing during the flood.

"The Nephilim were upon the Earth in those days and thereafter too. Those sons of the gods who cohabited with the daughters of the Adam, and they bore children into them. They were the Mighty Ones of Eternity, the People of the Shem."
—*Genesis 6:4*

"The *Book of Giants* was another literary work concerned with Enoch, widely read (after translation into the appropriate languages) in the Roman empire.... The 'giants' were believed to be the offspring of fallen angels (the Nephilim; also called Watchers) and human women."
—Robert Eisman and Michael Wise, *The Dead Sea Scrolls Uncovered*

"The Hebrew word for *giants* (nephilum) literally means the *fallen-down-ones* because these tall celestial beings fell from the sky. Their half-breed progeny and their descendants are often mentioned in the early books of the Old Testament until the last of them were finally killed off. They were known as the Rephaim (Hebrew for 'phantoms'), Emim, Anakim, Horim, Avim, and Zamzummim. Some scholars speculate that this tradition of giants born from the union of gods and humans formed the basis for the demigod of Greek mythology."
—Raymond E. Fowler, *The Watchers*

"And there we saw the Nephilim, the sons of Anak, which come of the Nephilim: and we were in our own sight as grasshoppers, and so we were in their sight."
—*Numbers 13:33*

Louis Bouchard

Looking every inch the gangland czar he claims to be, the wide-collared, slightly paunchy (but nevertheless imposing) Louis Bouchard is responsible for running illicit operations throughout the French capital. His jovial nature can snap into rage at the click of a synapse, and he has a reputation for large scale ruthless and opportunistic violence, despite never being convicted of a crime.

Arnaud

Arnaud is one of Bouchard's most capable men, but an attack by the Monstrum has left him critically injured and severely deformed. Still, he's lucky compared to the three of Bouchard's employees who were killed by the Monstrum prior to his injury. Lara encounters him in Bouchard's Hideout in the Parisian Ghetto.

Anton Gris

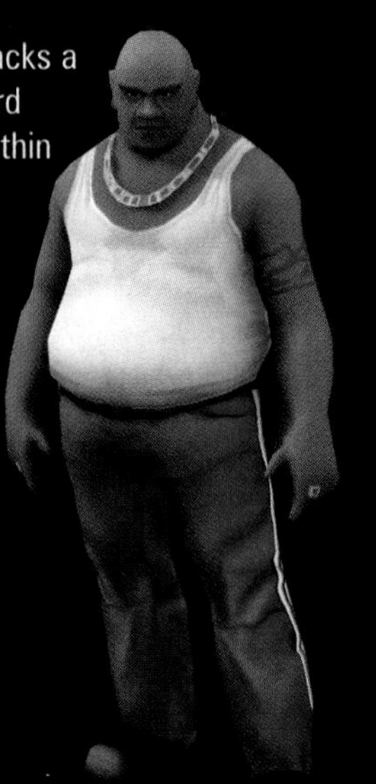

The massive physique of Anton Gris packs a considerable punch, and Louis Bouchard employs him as a coach and trainer within Bouchard's organization. Originally recruited in Marseilles, Bouchard encouraged him to relocate to Paris when illegal operations expanded into the capital.

Marten Gundersen

The chiseled cheekbones and broad shoulders of this veteran soldier allow him to impose his will on his underlings without uttering a word. A veteran of countless conflicts around the world, Gundersen is now fully committed to running a clandestine organization known as the Agency. His organization, a thinly disguised mercenary recruitment service, provides specialized forces for anything from basic security to all-out invasions. He has been spotted in the company of Eckhardt.

Kristina Boaz

Originally based in Argentina, Boaz became the head of corrective and remedial surgery at the Strahov Psychiatric Institute in Prague—a facility of which very little is known. Subjects have been reported entering the building complex, but none have been seen or heard from since. One item to note: Boaz's already grimacing visage was horribly disfigured from scars she suffered after a horrific plane crash in 1987.

Dr. Grant Muller

This portly and once-jocular man now has little time for amusement. Running the research programs for the dubious World Pharmaceuticals Commission takes up all his available time. Based in Rome, Muller also heads the botanical research wing of the Strahov Complex in Prague and has been seen conversing with Marten Gundersen on more than one occasion. Muller's considerable talents are currently giving local authorities cause for more than a little concern.

Fiends

Rottweiler

Located: Parisian Back Streets, Industrial Roof Tops, Parisian Ghetto

Strengths: Ferocious, fast-moving

Weaknesses: Doesn't jump, easy to avoid

Dispatch With: Kicking, any pistol

Remarks

When they're not chained to a wall (presenting an easy target), Rottweilers are vicious attack dogs sent to tear you apart. Prevent this from happening by moving your limbs away from their powerful jaws. Employ a series of jumps around the hounds while firing at them to confuse and finally dispatch them. Kicking is an alternative, if you don't mind the bite marks. Otherwise, it's easiest to simply leap onto higher ground, or over a fence, then tackle the dog or ignore it.

Gendarme

Located: Parisian Back Streets, Derelict Apartment

Strengths: Automatic surrender by Lara if she's spotted

Weaknesses: Slow to react, easy to dispatch

Dispatch With: Stealth attack

Remarks

The bumbling French police have sent two types of Gendarme your way, and one is much less of a threat than the other. The regular Gendarme poses little risk to you physically, but if you're spotted by one, Lara automatically surrenders, as she has no weapons. Therefore, wait until the Gendarme has stopped and is looking away from you, then sneak up behind and grab him to pull him down and knock him out.

Gendarme Riot Soldiers

Located: Derelict Apartment, Margot Carvier's Apartment

Strengths: Well armed, invincible

Weaknesses: None

Dispatch With: N/A

Remarks

When the Gendarme locate you (as they suspect you in the murder of Von Croy), they send officers in riot gear, usually carrying tear gas, to flush you out and block entrances. These officers stand at an exit, preventing your escape. And when you reach them, your lack of weaponry forces you to surrender. Run away from them.

Police Helicopter

Located: Industrial Roof Tops

Strengths: Automatic weaponry, invincible

Weaknesses: Poor accuracy

Dispatch With: N/A

Remarks

The Paris Special Branch is pulling out all the stops to catch you. Subsequently, you're ambushed along the rooftops by a police helicopter. Alas, rocket-propelled grenade launchers are in short supply, so quickly flee from the roof. The helicopter can't be downed, but the machine gunner is a lousy shot. Venture into hiding when you see this piece of hardware arrive.

Le Serpent Rouge Guard

Located: Le Serpent Rouge

Strengths: Patrol in twos or threes

Weaknesses: Slow rate of fire, low stamina

Dispatch With: Any gun, hand-to-hand combat, stealth attack

Remarks

There are a dozen guards in Le Serpent Rouge following the Monstrum killings, and they shoot first and ask questions later. Move in Stealth mode to avoid alerting them to your presence, and take them out from behind with a stealth attack if possible. If not, get in close and attack them directly. They are drawn by loud noises, so if you fire a gun near one, expect him to turn and investigate.

Rat

Located: Louvre Storm Drains

Strengths: Takes three bullets to down

Weaknesses: Not aggressive

Dispatch With: Any pistol

Remarks

For those adventurers that wish to cause the maximum amount of pain, waste the most ammunition, and paint the floor of the Louvre Storm Drains in red specks of rodent offal, shoot any rats you see. Most won't harm you; in fact, they scurry along, stop to sniff the air, then continue. A few bite you on the ankle, inflicting minimal damage. Brandish a weapon, and three bullets later, you have an incredibly embarrassing "small game hunt" to add to your manor house's collection of stuffed critters. The best plan? Ignore them unless they attack you.

Museum Guard

Located: Louvre Galleries, Archaeological Dig, Galleries Under Siege

Strengths: Fast to react, good hearing

Weaknesses: Weak weaponry, little armor

Dispatch With: Fists or any pistol

Remarks

Clad in a white shirt, and sometimes armed with a taserlike device, the guard isn't prepared to stop a professional tomb raider such as Miss Croft. His lack of ranged weapons means all you need to do is pepper the guard at a distance. You can also get in quick and start your kick or punch combinations before the electrocution starts. You receive a nasty jolt if the guard connects, so dart in and out.

Gendarme Security

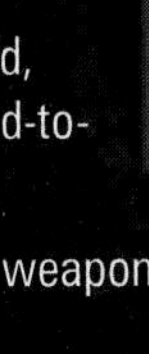

Located: Louvre Galleries, Archaeological Dig, Galleries Under Siege

Strengths: Powerful handgun, reasonable shot

Weaknesses: Lightly armed, pathetic hand-to-hand skills

Dispatch With: Fast-firing weapon, fists

Remarks

As you enter the Louvre, but before the Agency soldiers arrive, you may come across special agents clad in light body armor and sporting baseball hats. They have been dispatched to help locate those infiltrating the Louvre. These guards always spot you, or appear in front of you, negating your stealth tactics. Therefore, charge straight in and strike them unconscious before they can fire a shot, or attack with a weapon while circle-strafing them.

The Knight

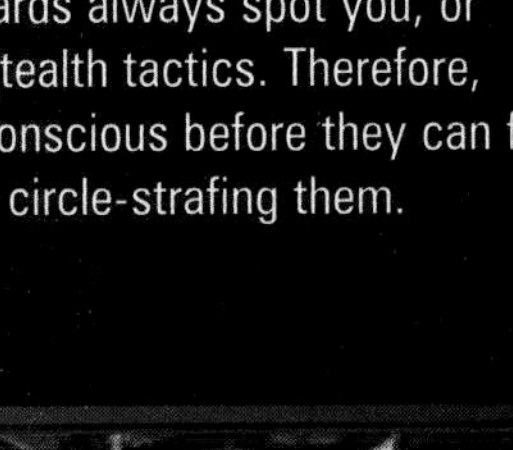

Located: Tomb of Ancients, The Hall of Seasons, Neptune's Hall, Wrath of the Beast, Eckhardt's Lab

Strengths: Indestructible, relentless

Weaknesses: Slow and cumbersome

Dispatch With: Kick off a precipice

Remarks

Warrior of a bygone age, the Knight is a resurrected entity, awakened when strangers enter the nearby vicinity. Knights carry a long sword and shield and are sometimes ablaze. Without ranged weaponry, Knights are no match for your guns and fall after five or six shots. However, they don't stay down. Give them a wide berth, blasting them only in close quarters (hand-to-hand attacks do work, but you'll take damage), or coax them to ledges and kick them off.

Bat

Located: Tomb of Ancients

Strengths: Flying ability, swoop in-and-out attacks

Weaknesses: Extremely weak

Dispatch with: Any ranged weapon

Remarks

Congregating at the ceiling of a gigantic cylindrical chamber, various nocturnal Bats have set up home in the crumbling fissures, ancient ruins, and other decaying matter in this long-forgotten place. One Bat in particular isn't happy with Lara infiltrating its air space, and swoops in to nibble on her before flying away. A simple drawing of a pistol, and three well-placed shots, dispatches this bothersome pest.

Brother Obscura

Located: The Hall of Seasons

Strengths: Indestructible, fast moving, a fearful sight

Weaknesses: No ranged attacks, easy to escape

Dispatch With: V-Packer shotgun or fast-firing weapon

Remarks

Neither living in this world nor dead in the next, a hooded and frightening specter lurks in an old ceremonial chamber hidden in a distant tomb under the Louvre. Attacking with a sweeping charge, this floating horror only activates in the presence of grave robbers. Brother Obscura can be driven back, but never dispatched by ordinary weapons. Force him back and take the item you've endangered your life for, then flee.

Agency Soldiers

Located: Galleries Under Siege, Strahov Fortress

Strengths: Fast rate of fire, appear in pairs, extremely observant

Weaknesses: Especially vulnerable to stealth kills, as you can see where they're looking

Dispatch With: Any gun, hand-to-hand combat, stealth attack

Remarks

Hired by the Cabal, these are the Agency's foot soldiers. Dressed from head to toe in urban combat gear, they patrol the Louvre and the Strahov Fortress and are sent to various locations to do the Cabal's dirty work. Although they're highly skilled fighters, they tend to telegraph their movements by shining their flashlights in the direction that they're looking. As long as you can avoid being seen by them, you can take them out quickly and quietly with stealth attacks.

The Cleaner

Located: Von Croy's Apartment

Strengths: Endurance, multiple weapons, explosives training

Weaknesses: Specific attack pattern

Dispatch With: Rigg 09 pistol, fast-firing weapon

Remarks

A mercenary for hire, the Cleaner works for the Agency under Marten Gundersen. He is part weapons specialist, part demolitions expert, chosen to dispatch unwanted subjects. To this end, he can rig environments with bombs and explosives laced to laser trip wires. Avoid these. When in a firefight, the Cleaner moves to specific locations (noted in the walkthrough) as he takes more and more of your ranged weapon fire. Unload on him while stepping out from cover only after he finishes firing.

Czech Policemen

Location: Monstrum Crimescene

Strengths: Fast rate of fire, hard to sneak up on

Weaknesses: Low stamina

Dispatch With: Any gun, hand-to-hand combat, stealth attack

Remarks

Normally, Lara's much more respectful of local authorities. But these policemen are in the pocket of the Cabal, and they're not looking to arrest Lara when she shows up in Prague—they'll gladly shoot her and claim self-defense. Don't be shy about shooting first.

Abomination Phase II

Located: Bio-Research Facility

Strengths: Nasty spearlike arms

Weaknesses: Slow, without ranged attacks

Dispatch With: V-Packer shotgun, any ranged weapon

Remarks

Dripping humanoids drenched in amniotic fluids, these degenerates are early specimens in Doctor Grant Muller's continuing mission to create host forms for the coming of the Nephilim. The beasts stagger around in a state of confusion, homing in on living humans and attempting to swipe them with large, needlelike claws. Back away from them, and plant well-aimed shots into their hides until they fall. Close combat isn't favored.

Abomination Grub

Located: Bio-Research Facility

Strengths: Hardy, quick, low lying, ranged poison attack

Weaknesses: Easy to avoid

Dispatch With: Any ranged weapon

Remarks

Abomination Grubs are malformed pupae from Doctor Muller's more hideous experiments, usually kept in long pods encased in a feeding solution. Recently, the creatures (which come in three colors) have escaped through maintenance ducts. They attack by spitting brightly colored, poisonous spores clouds at you, then rolling up to charge. React by backing off and plugging them from a few feet away, or move to higher ground as they cannot climb stairs. Alternatively, leave them to their own devices.

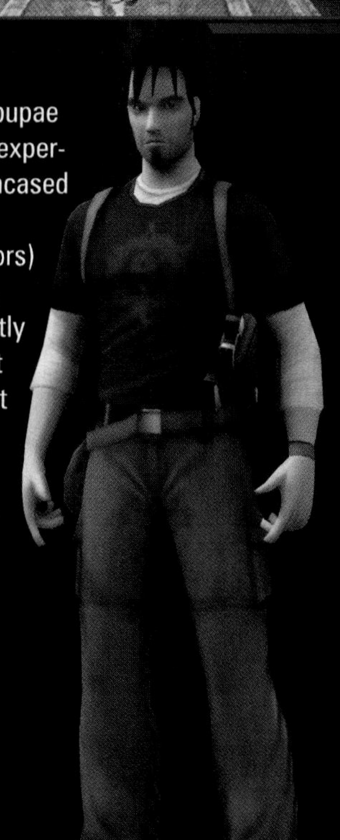

Leviathan

Located: Bio-Research Facility, Aquatic Research Facility

Strengths: Indestructible, fearsome

Weaknesses: Unable to exist out of water

Dispatch With: N/A

Remarks

Grotesque, as well as powerful, the shark-sized Leviathan is a monster that prowls the waters of the Strahov Fortress. A gaping maw sits at the end of its sinewy body and tail, its yellow-and-black color scheme inflicting a sense of danger before the being attacks. If you are in water when you see one, remove yourself as quickly as possible. One speeding thrust and it will lacerate you to death. Stay on dry land (where the creature cannot follow). Do not move near these creatures, and if you are caught near one, swim directly to the nearest ledge to climb out.

Cabal Soldier

Located: Bio-Research Facility

Strengths: Excellent endurance, impressive armor

Weaknesses: Bulky, witless, easily duped

Dispatch With: Kicks or V-Packer shotgun

Remarks

The Cabal soldier is a biohazard-suited version of the Agency soldier. However, stealth takedowns from behind are not recommended, as you encounter these guards in large, open environments. Instead, you can use a ranged weapon at distance, but the toughness of the Cabal soldiers' protective clothing makes them hard foes to topple. Kick them to the ground, or off a balcony ledge, to take them out.

Tendril Trunk

Located: Bio-Research Facility

Strengths: Impervious to weapon fire

Weaknesses: Susceptible to poisoned feed

Dispatch With: Poisoned feed

Remarks

The vast botanical gardens, tendered lovingly by the psychotic Dr. Grant Muller, are full of countless gigantic flora and fauna. Muller's experimentation with DNA and the dark arts has yielded intelligent, but vicious, plant life, which in turn provides valuable test data for the construction of the Nephilim. One of the doctor's more useful creations is the Tendril Trunk—a pustule-ridden tree with protruding appendages that wrap and hold with great force. It cannot be defeated by ordinary ordinance; pump poisoned feed into its trunk so its tentacles recede.

Carnivorous Horror

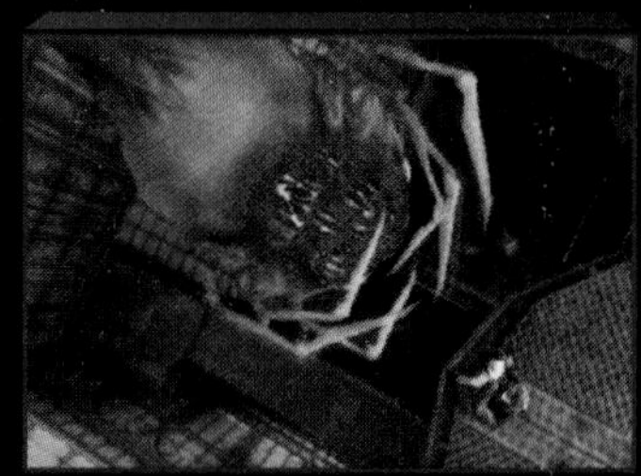

Located: Bio-Research Facility

Strengths: Close proximity to keeper

Weaknesses: None

Dispatch With: N/A

Remarks

Doctor Grant Muller is responsible for testing and perfecting a variety of secret "projects" inside the Bio-Research Facility of the Strahov Fortress. Of course, these "projects" often result in mangled creatures too hideous not to immediately shoot and dissect. One of the doctor's pet projects is a ceiling-dwelling entity with a gaping maw and a penchant for human flesh. The doctor is currently keeping this deviant alive as a kind of "guard dog" more than anything else. This becomes apparent when Lara witnesses it swallow Kristina Boaz whole (thankfully, Miss Croft doesn't have to fight this form of the creature). Later, the mutation utilizes Boaz's DNA and transforms into a frightful beast (detailed later).

Sanitarium Zombie

Location: Sanitarium

Strengths: Freaky looking

Weaknesses: Mostly harmless

Dispatch With: Any gun, hand-to-hand combat

Remarks

Kurtis finds these poor devils in the Sanitarium. Kidnapped by the Cabal and subjected to unholy experiments that destroyed their sanity and humanity, Sanitarium Zombies shuffle along the halls. Their attacks are limited to slapping at Kurtis with the loose sleeves of their straightjackets, or biting him with the teeth they've got left. Do them a favor and put them out of their misery. Shoot them from short range to conserve ammunition.

Proto-Nephilim

Location: Sanitarium

Strengths: Fast, vicious, incredibly resistant to damage

Weaknesses: Predictable attacks, vulnerable to Boran X ammo

Dispatch With: Boran X

Remarks

When she shuts off the power to the Maximum Containment Area in the Strahov Fortress level, Lara inadvertently frees Proto-Nephilim, one of the Cabal's most dangerous alchemical experiments. Resembling a cross between a wolf and a boar, the Proto-Nephilim busts out of its chamber and proceeds to devour most of the staff. Kurtis spends the Sanitarium and Maximum Containment Area levels chasing Proto-Nephilim back to its lair, where he must ultimately destroy it.

The Proto-Nephilim's preferred method of attack is to crawl into rooms through ventilation ducts and leap out at its startled prey. Not only is it unbelievably fast and possessed of sharp teeth and long claws, it's also extremely dexterous, negotiating narrow ledges and swinging from pipes with its five-fingered paws. It can also recover from severe damage quickly, appearing to rise from the dead, which is as psychologically damaging to its prey as it is physically threatening.

Sanitarium Mutant

Location: Sanitarium

Strengths: Fast, powerful close-range attack, usually found in pairs

Weaknesses: Not bulletproof

Dispatch With: Boran X

Remarks

Sanitarium Mutants are Sanitarium Zombies infused with Nephilim DNA, endowing them with huge, sharp claws and a terrifying bloodlust. They tend to appear out of nowhere and quickly rush you. If you don't have your gun drawn when they appear, expect to take some damage before killing them. Fortunately, they're not much more resistant to injury than Sanitarium Zombies, and Kurtis's Boran X pistol dispatches them quickly.

Kristina Boaz

Location: Boaz Returns

Strengths: Incredible stamina, two attack forms, variety of attacks

Weaknesses: Doesn't dodge your attacks

Dispatch With: Boran X

Remarks

Kristina Boaz is a Cabal scientist who makes the mistake of disappointing Eckhardt, resulting in the termination of her employment—and humanity. Fed to the Carnivorous Horror, she is transformed into a mindless hybrid beast of great power.

Kurtis needs to kill Boaz once and for all in the Boaz Returns boss fight level. Boaz falls after Kurtis shoots her more than a dozen times, but she crawls out of the carcass of the Carnivorous Horror in a new form that has razor-sharp claws, bioelectric energy blasts, and insectlike wings, which give her great speed and agility. Shoot her repeatedly to destroy her.

Items and Weapons

Items

Spoiler Warning

Since you're reading a strategy guide, you probably expect to find some game secrets, and you're absolutely right. This section tells you about all the items in the game, where they're found, and what they're used for. However, it also gives away important plot points, so if you don't want them revealed, don't read this section.

Healing Items

Healing items are found in several locations throughout the course of the game. They're all stored in the Health subsection of your Inventory; using them replenishes some of Lara's (or Kurtis's) health energy.

Chocolate Bar

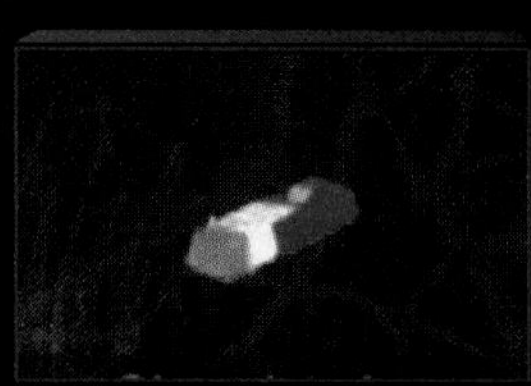

Chocolate Bars give Lara a quick burst of energy and recover 10 percent of her health energy.

Health Bandages

Lara can use Health Bandages to patch up wounds. Their healing capacity is limited, but they do restore 40 percent of her health energy.

Health Pills

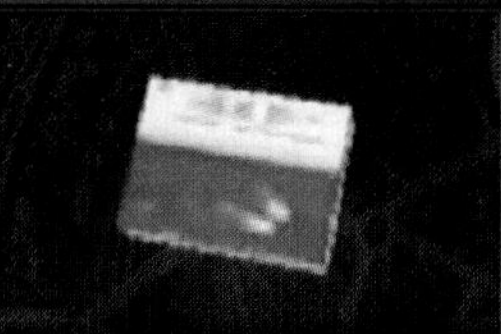

A miracle of modern science, Health Pills give Lara a quick stamina boost and recover 20 percent of her health energy.

Large Health Pack

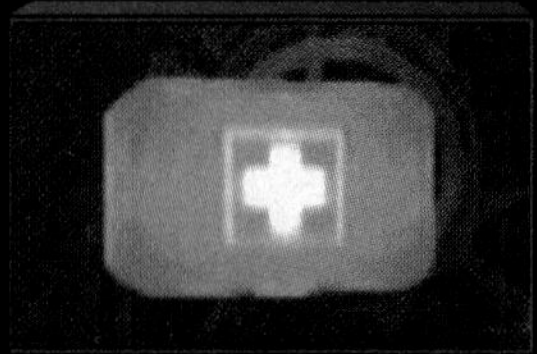

Large Health Packs are among the rarest health items in the game, but they completely refill Lara's health energy, so go out of your way to find them.

Small Health Pack

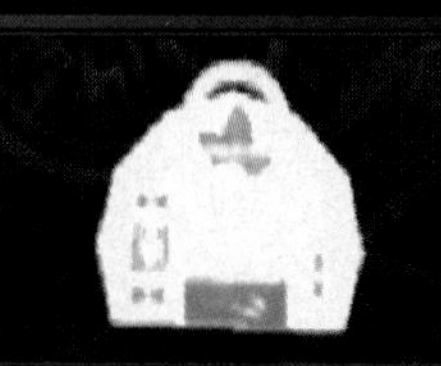

These attractive little satchels match Lara's shoes perfectly and contain enough medication to recover 60 percent of her health energy.

Valuable Items

In the first two Paris levels (Parisian Back Streets and Parisian Ghetto), Lara comes across several items that have only one use—to be pawned at Rennes' Pawnshop in the Parisian Ghetto. Pawning the items gives Lara enough Euros to bribe Bernard, Bouchard's doorman, and Luddick later in the game.

Antique Doubloons

Location: Several places in Paris

Antique Flintlock

Location: Le Serpent Rouge (garage locker)

Antique Record

Location: Le Serpent Rouge (dance floor)

Diamond Ring

Location: Margot Carvier's Apartment (on a small table), Parisian Ghetto (metro tunnels)

Gold Watch

Location: St. Aicard's Church (win it from the boxing trainer by gambling on Carl)

Vintage Cognac

Location: Margot Carvier's Apartment (in the kitchen), Le Serpent Rouge (two bottles)

Necklace

Location: Parisian Back Streets (in a locked cabinet)

Wad of Cash

Location: Several places in Paris

Mission-Critical Items

Mission-critical items must be discovered in order to continue past certain obstacles. Mission-critical items are almost always unique items that have only one purpose.

Air Crystal

Location: Breath of Hades

Purpose: The Air Crystal is used with the other three elemental crystals to activate the elemental furnace in the Hall of Seasons.

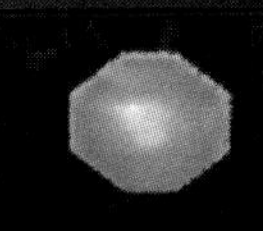

Alchemic Phial #1

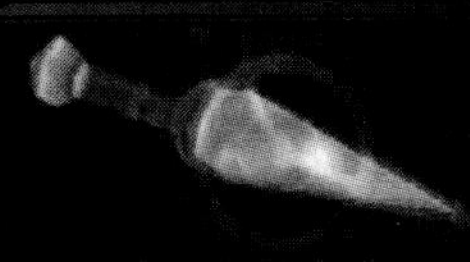

Location: Eckhardt's Lab

Purpose: This phial contains alchemically purified oxygen and is used with the other phials to change the toxic elements in Eckhardt's Lab into pure water.

Alchemic Phial #2

Location: Eckhardt's Lab

Purpose: This phial contains alchemically purified hydrogen and is used with the other phials to change the toxic elements in Eckhardt's Lab into pure water.

Alchemic Phial #3

Location: Eckhardt's Lab

Purpose: This phial contains alchemically purified salt and is used with the other phials to change the toxic elements in Eckhardt's Lab into pure water.

Apartment Key

Location: Derelict Apartment Block (in a fourth-floor apartment)

Purpose: This key unlocks a second-floor apartment in the Derelict Apartment Block that contains several optional but useful items.

Bartender's Key

Location: Café Metro (talk to Pierre)

Purpose: The Bartender's Key gets Lara into Le Serpent Rouge via the stage entrance.

Botanical High Access Pass

Location: Bio-Research Facility (on a guard)

Purpose: This magnetic card opens high-security doors in the Bio-Research Facility.

Botanical Low Access Pass

Location: Bio-Research Facility (on a guard)

Purpose: This magnetic card opens low-security doors in the Bio-Research Facility.

Botanical Medium Access Pass

Location: Bio-Research Facility (on a guard)

Purpose: This magnetic card opens medium-security doors in the Bio-Research Facility.

Café Owner's Contact

Café Owners Contact
Francine, 17 Rue Dominique - Gate Code 15328

Location: Café Metro (trade Pierre the Trinket Box for it)

Purpose: Return to Café Metro with the Trinket Box and threaten Pierre to get him to exchange the box for the Café Owner's Contact, which has the pass code (15328) to the apartment belonging to his ex-girlfriend, Francine. Her apartment overlooks St. Aicard's Graveyard; Lara can use her balcony to enter the graveyard.

Carvier's Security Pass

Location: Louvre Galleries (in Mlle. Carvier's office)

Purpose: Carvier's Security Pass is a high-level pass that unlocks any locked door in the Louvre with a card reader next to it, including the door to the archaeological dig.

Carvier's Security Pass
Carvier's Personal High Level Louvre Pass

Cellar Key

Cellar Key
For exit from Vasileys premises

Location: Monstrum Crimescene (on Bouchard's corpse)

Purpose: The Cellar Key unlocks a door in the basement of Vasiley's apartment that lets Lara return to street level and proceed to the Strahov Fortress.

Crowbar

Location: Parisian Back Streets (on a rooftop), Louvre Galleries (in a utility closet on the roof)

Purpose: Use the Crowbar to pry padlocks off a shed on a rooftop in the Parisian Back Streets, and off a storage area on the rooftops of the Louvre.

Crowbar
Useful for heavy leverage

Earth Crystal

Earth Crystal
Resonates to the element Earth

Location: Wrath of the Beast

Purpose: The Earth Crystal is used with the other three elemental crystals to activate the elemental furnace in the Hall of Seasons.

Eckhardt's Glove

Location: Eckhardt's Lab

Purpose: Eckhardt wore this glove as the Monstrum and used it to leave his victims horribly disfigured. Lara takes it from his corpse after killing him at the end of the game, then uses it to energize the chamber with the Sleeper in it.

Eckhardt's Glove
Glove Of Immeasurable Power, In The Right Hands

Ex-Janitor's Key

Ex-janitor's key
For Access Into The Serpent Rouge

Location: Parisian Ghetto (speak to Bernard in the park and pay him 160 Euros)

Purpose: This key gets Lara into Le Serpent Rouge via the garage entrance.

Explosives

Location: Rennes' Pawnshop (in the vault in the back of the shop)

Purpose: Lara plants these on the boiler at the end of the Louvre Storm Drains to blast open a passage to the Louvre basement.

Explosives
High powered explosives pack with timer
Ideal for large obstacles

Farsee Code 06289

Farsee Code
Door Code 06289

Location: Sanitarium (at a locked gate)

Purpose: Kurtis gets this virtual "item" at a locked gate in the Sanitarium. It's not a physical item, but rather a reminder of a five-digit code (06289) that he saw in his vision. This code unlocks the door he's standing in front of when he gets the vision.

Farsee Code 17068

Location: Maximum Security Area (at a locked door)

Purpose: Kurtis gets this virtual "item" at a locked cell door in the Maximum Containment Area. It's not a physical item, but rather a reminder of a five-digit code (17068) that he saw in his vision. Enter the code at a nearby security console to unlock the cell door.

Farsee Code
Door Code 17068

Fire Crystal

Fire Crystal
Resonates to the element Fire

Location: Sanctuary of Flame

Purpose: The Fire Crystal is used with the other three elemental crystals to activate the elemental furnace in the Hall of Seasons.

First Ancient Symbol Tracing

Location: The Archaeological Dig (on the printer next to the scanner)

Purpose: The First Ancient Symbol Tracing shows the image of one of the four symbols that you need in order to open the lock that seals the Tomb of Ancients.

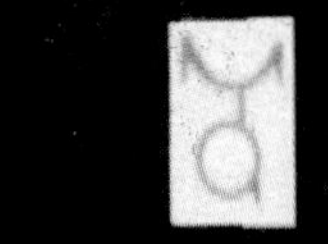

First Ancient Symbol Copy
Print Out Of Buried Symbol

First Obscura Painting

First Obscura Painting
One Of The Five Paintings Originally Created By The Black Alchemist In The 1400's

Location: Tomb of Ancients (during fight with Brother Obscura)

Purpose: This is one of the five Obscura Paintings originally created by the Black Alchemist in the 1400s. Scan the First Obscura Painting in the Louvre X-ray room during Galleries Under Siege to see the secret symbol embedded in it. Lara attempts to keep the painting out of the hands of Eckhardt and the Cabal, but she doesn't have much luck doing so.

Gantry Gate Key

Location: Parisian Back Streets (on a ledge just below a rooftop)

Purpose: The Gantry Gate Key is guarded by a Gendarme. You must grab it to unlock a gate at the end of the ledge where it's found in order to progress to the Derelict Apartment Block.

Gantry Gate Key
An Old Iron Key

Jackal Walking Stick

Jackal Walking Stick
Von Croy's Walking Stick

Location: Von Croy's Apartment (just behind your starting location)

Purpose: An ancient cane; Von Croy's favorite, and one with emotional attachment. Check your Notebook.

Last Obscura Engraving

Location: Monstrum Crimescene (in Vasiley's secret office)

Purpose: The fifth and Last Obscura Engraving contains a hidden map of the location of the Vault of Trophies, which contains the Last Obscura Engraving.

Last Obscura Engraving
5th and last Engraving with a hidden map of the Vaults location

Last Obscura Painting

Last Obscura Painting
The 5th And Final Painting

Location: Vault of Trophies (behind a bookcase)

Purpose: Without all five Obscura Paintings, Eckhardt can't use their power to awaken the Sleeper and revive the Nephilim. Lara's goal is to keep this final painting out of his hands.

Lift Maintenance Key

Location: Derelict Apartment Block (on the floor of a fourth-floor apartment)

Purpose: This key allows Lara to access the elevator maintenance area on top of the Derelict Apartment Block. It's an essential item for proceeding to the Industrial Roof Tops.

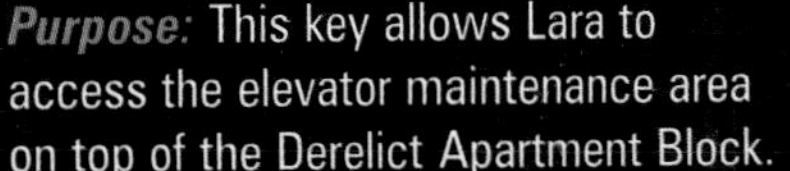

Lift Maintenance Key
Access Rooftop

Louvre Guard's Key

Louvre Guard's Key
Access Maintenance Areas

Location: Louvre Galleries (on a guard)

Purpose: This key unlocks a maintenance room on the rooftops of the Louvre that contains a Crowbar.

Louvre Low Level Security Pass

Location: Louvre Galleries (on a Louvre Guard)

Purpose: The Louvre Low Level Security Pass allows Lara to temporarily deactivate the laser trip wires around the Mona Lisa, giving her access to the air-conditioning vent above it that leads to the Louvre rooftops.

Louvre Low Security Pass
Access Low Security Areas

Map of Archaeological Dig

Map of Archaeological dig
Up To Date Maps Of The Louvre Archaeological Digs

Location: Rennes' Pawnshop (in the vault at the back of the shop)

Purpose: This is an up-to-date map of the archaeological digs in progress under the Louvre, which Rennes was holding for Von Croy. When Lara finds it, it provides the necessary inspiration for her to visit the dig site.

Map of Sewers Around Louvre

Location: Rennes' Pawnshop (in the vault at the back of the shop)

Purpose: This tiny map tells Lara where to place the explosives in the Louvre Storm Drains that blow open a hole to the Louvre basement, getting her inside without having to get past the Gendarmes on the streets.

Map Of Sewers Around Louvre
The Storm Drain System Beneath The Louvre

Rennes' Wallet

Rennes' Wallet
Old Leather Wallet

Location: Rennes' Pawnshop (after Bouchard's Hideout, at the back of the shop)

Purpose: Rennes' Wallet lies next to its late owner after Lara speaks to Bouchard in Bouchard's Hideout. Pick it up and use it in your Inventory to find the Scrap of Paper.

Respirator

Location: Galleries Under Siege (in X-ray room cabinet)

Respirators
Protects against dangerous fumes during restoration processes

Purpose: The Respirator was originally for Louvre staff members to protect themselves from hazardous fumes during the restoration of artworks. But Lara gets two advantages from it. First, it protects her against the gas that the Agency soldiers fire into the Louvre. Second, it gives her a lower-body upgrade (Upgrade Dash Enable: Lower Body Level 6) that allows her to dash for short periods of time.

> ***NOTE*** **You must view the Respirator in your Inventory and choose "Use" for Lara to actually put the Respirator on her face and filter out the gas.**

Scrap of Paper

Scrap Of Paper
Code Number

Location: Rennes' Pawnshop (in Rennes' Wallet)

Purpose: The Scrap of Paper in Rennes' Wallet contains the five-digit code (14529) required to open the vault at the back of the pawnshop.

Sanitarium Low Access Pass

Sanitarium Low Access Pass
Access Low Security Areas

Location: Maximum Containment Area (on the corpse of a guard)

Purpose: This pass unlocks a door in the Maximum Containment Area.

Sanitarium Medium Access Pass

Sanitarium Medium Access Pass
Access Medium Security Areas

Location: Maximum Containment Area (on the corpse of a guard)

Purpose: This pass unlocks the door to the fight with the Proto-Nephilim in the Maximum Containment Area.

Second Ancient Symbol Tracing

Second Ancient Symbol Tracing
Print Out Of Symbol Tracing

Location: The Archaeological Dig (in an office at the surface level of the dig)

Purpose: The Second Ancient Symbol Tracing shows the image of one of the four symbols you need to open the lock that seals the Tomb of Ancients.

Shard

Location: Eckhardt's Lab

Shard
Crystal Shard of unknown origin

Purpose: There are three of these crystal Shards. Lara receives two of them from Kurtis just prior to the boss fight with Boaz, and she finds the third Shard in Eckhardt's Lab. Eckhardt has a good reason for locking it away in the bowels of Strahov Fortress—these three Shards combined is the only thing that can truly kill him.

Socket Spanner

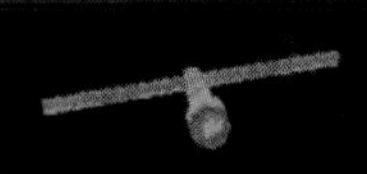
Socket Spanner
Heavy Duty Socket Spanner

Location: Le Serpent Rouge (garage workbench)

Purpose: The heavy-duty Socket Spanner activates a switch in the garage entrance of Le Serpent Rouge. The switch activates a dumbwaiter and draws the attention of a guard, who enters the garage to investigate. He unlocks the door to the dance floor, allowing you to enter it.

Stage Door Key

Location: Le Serpent Rouge (stage entrance)

Stage Door Key
Access To Dance Floor

Purpose: The Stage Door Key unlocks the door between the club's stage entrance and its dance floor.

Strahov Assistant's Pass

Strahov Assistants Pass
Access Medium Security Areas

Location: Sanitarium (on a researcher's body)

Purpose: This magnetic key card opens the door to the Sanitarium kitchen, which allows Kurtis to open a door that leads into the Maximum Containment Area.

Strahov High Security Pass

Location: Strahov Fortress (on an Agency soldier)

Strahov High Security Pass
Access High Security Areas

Purpose: The Strahov High Security Pass opens the door to the power room, which allows Lara to disarm all of the Strahov security systems and proceed to the Bio-Research Facility.

Strahov Low Security Pass

Location: Strahov Fortress (on an Agency soldier)

Purpose: The Strahov Low Security Pass opens a door that allows Lara to proceed deeper into Strahov Fortress.

Ticket Office Key

Location: Le Serpent Rouge (control room above dance floor)

Purpose: This old steel key unlocks the door to the ticket office in Le Serpent Rouge.

Trinket Box
Valuable and mysterious. Contents unknown

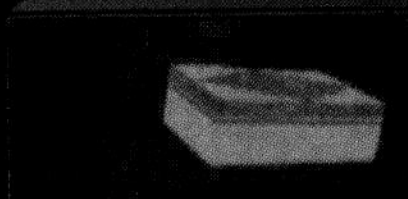

Location: Le Serpent Rouge (in a nonfunctioning light above the dance floor)

Purpose: Bernard and Pierre both want the Trinket Box, each claiming that the box is his. If you give it to either one, they'll give you something that will get you into St. Aicard's Graveyard. You can also give it (and 800 Euros) to Bouchard's doorman to enter the graveyard.

Vasiley Full Fax

Location: Monstrum Crimescene (in Vasiley's secret office)

Purpose: This fax from Vasiley to Mlle. Carvier contains the five-digit code (31597) to open the vault behind the painting that contains the Last Obscura Engraving.

Vasiley Full Fax
Mlle Carvier, Please Refer To Website
SHADOWWHISTORIES PR To Access
Restricted Information Type Code 31597

Von Croy's Notebook
Von Croy's Field Notes And Clues. Notes
Are Added As The Game Proceeds

Location: Margot Carvier's Apartment

Purpose: Werner Von Croy gave Margot Carvier his notebook for safekeeping shortly before his untimely demise. It contains all of the information he accumulated regarding the Obscura Paintings, the Nephilim, and the various shady characters he came across prior to his death. Lara will need his information to complete her quest. If Lara is honest and polite to Mlle. Carvier, she'll get Von Croy's Notebook in Margot Carvier's Apartment.

Wad of Passports

Location: Bouchard's Hideout (speak politely to Bouchard to get them)

Purpose: Bouchard needs someone to deliver a handful of fake passports to Rennes' Pawnshop, but the Monstrum has left him with a lack of capable couriers. If Lara delivers them for him, she'll earn Rennes' trust.

Water Crystal

Location: Neptune's Hall

Purpose: The Water Crystal is used with the other three elemental crystals to activate the elemental furnace in the Hall of Seasons.

Weapons

All of the weapons you find in the game are firearms, and each has its own unique form of ammunition. A weapon without ammo is useless. Some weapons have more than one type of ammunition; select "Ammo" on the Weapons section of the inventory to equip different types of ammo for the weapon.

Boran X

Boran X

Boran X Ammo
High Impact 9mm Ammo

Location: Kurtis is always equipped with this weapon

Ammo Type: Boran X Ammo

Rate of Fire: Semiautomatic

Employed by: Kurtis Trent

Wielded: Single handed

The Boran X is a unique pistol created by Kurtis Trent, and it is the only weapon he can use. Although it's semiautomatic, it fires as fast as you can press the button, and it's extremely powerful, especially at close range. Kurtis begins his Sanitarium level with plenty of ammo, and he finds more as he goes, so don't be shy about using this weapon.

Dart SS

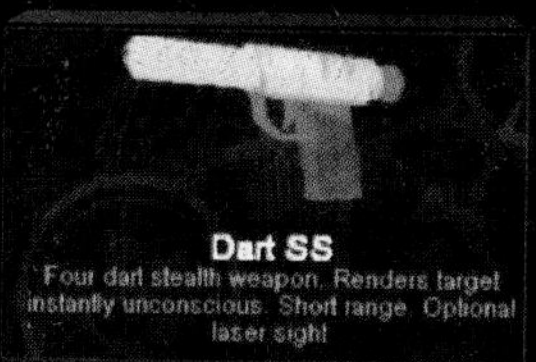

Dart SS
Four dart stealth weapon. Renders target instantly unconscious. Short range. Optional laser sight

Dart SS

Dart SS Tranq Darts

Location: Rennes' Pawnshop (in a locked vault at the rear of the store)

Ammo Type: Dart SS Tranq Darts (four-dart packs)

Rate of Fire: Single shot

Employed by: Lara Croft

Wielded: Single handed

The Dart SS is the ultimate in non-lethal stealth weaponry. Although its range is limited, and ammunition for the Dart SS is rare, the gun makes almost no sound when fired, and a successful shot drops your target almost instantly with no alarm raised. Use it only when you absolutely cannot afford to be detected.

K2 Impactor

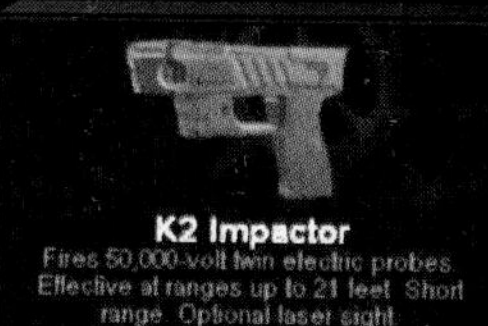

K2 Impactor
Fires 50,000-volt twin electric probes. Effective at ranges up to 21 feet. Short range. Optional laser sight

K2 Impactor

K2 Impactor Battery

Location: Rennes' Pawnshop (in a locked vault at the rear of the store)

Ammo Type: K2 Impactor Battery (3-charge power packs)

Rate of Fire: Single shot

Employed by: Lara Croft

Wielded: Single handed

The K2 Impactor is great for non-lethal self-defense. Used by the Louvre guards to discourage intruders, it sends 50,000 volts into a target within 21 feet, shocking him or her into unconsciousness. However, it's not at all effective at long ranges, and batteries for it are few and far between.

M-V9

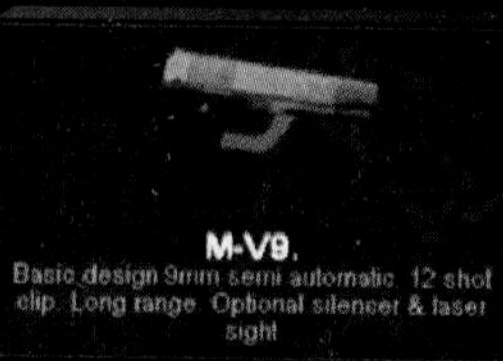

M-V9.
Basic design 9mm semi automatic. 12 shot clip. Long range. Optional silencer & laser sight

M-V9

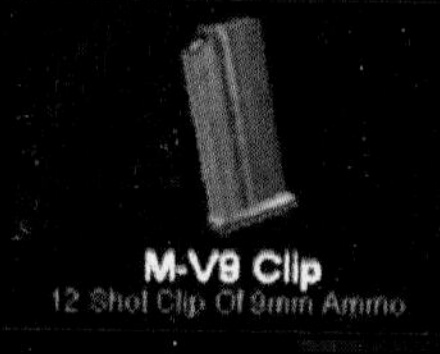

M-V9 Clip

Location: Parisian Back Streets (in a locked shed on a rooftop), Parisian Ghetto (taken from fallen Le Serpent Rouge guards)

Ammo Type: M-V9 Clip (12-round clips)

Rate of Fire: Semiautomatic

Employed by: Lara Croft

Wielded: Single handed

The M-V9 is Lara's first and most basic weapon. A commonly-used weapon by Parisian street thugs, it is easy to conceal and has a fairly quick rate of fire. It doesn't have much stopping power at a distance, but it's a deadly weapon when used up close. Most of Bouchard's Le Serpent Rouge guards carry these weapons, so you don't lack for M-V9 Clips in the club.

Mag Vega

Mag Vega
9mm, 30 Round Clip. Three Modes - Single Action, Semi Automatic And Fully Automatic Long Range Weapon. Optional Silencer & Laser Sight

Mag Vega

Mag Vega Clip

Location: Galleries Under Siege (on Agency soldier)

Ammo Type: Mag Vega Clip (30-round clips)

Rate of Fire: Single shot, semiautomatic, and full auto

Employed by: Lara Croft

Wielded: Two handed

This baby is possibly Lara's best all-around weapon. It fires a lethal hail of 9mm lead at a blazing rate of fire, it's got a generous 30-shot clip, and it's extremely accurate at long distances. Considering that just about every Agency soldier Lara takes out in the Strahov Fortress leaves behind ammunition for the Mag Vega, there's no reason not to go hog wild with it when storming the Cabal's lair.

Rigg 09

Rigg 09

Rigg 09 Clip

Location: Von Croy's Apartment

Ammo Type: Rigg 09 Clip (9-round clips)

Rate of Fire: Single shot

Employed by: Lara Croft

Wielded: Single handed

We don't want to disparage the Rigg 09. Back in the day, it might have been a reliable sidearm, but that day was years ago. This single-action 9mm pistol is incredibly inaccurate at distances, and it probably has more value as an antique than it does as a weapon. Pick it up as a backup weapon, but it should be used only as a last resort.

Scorpion X

Scorpion X

Scorpion X Clip

Location: Strahov Fortress (interrogation room)

Ammo Type: Scorpion X Clip (30-round clips)

Rate of Fire: Full auto

Employed by: Lara Croft

Wielded: Single handed

The Scorpion X machine pistol is one of the most versatile weapons in Lara's arsenal. With a 30-round clip and fully automatic fire, Lara can squeeze off a volley of rounds single-handedly. Designed as a medium-range weapon, the Scorpion X doesn't lose much accuracy at long ranges, and it's not too unwieldy to use at point-blank range either.

V-Packer

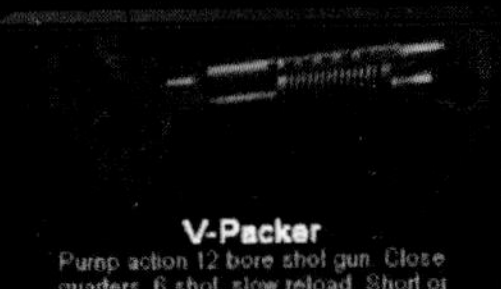

V-Packer
Pump action 12 bore shot gun. Close quarters. 6 shot, slow reload. Short or medium range effectiveness depending on whether using standard shot or spreadshot

V-Packer

V-Packer Spread Cartridges

V-Packer Standard Cartridges
25 Cartridges Of Limited Shot

V-Packer Standard Cartridges

Location: Tomb of Ancients

Ammo Types: V-Packer Spread Cartridges (25-shell boxes), V-Packer Standard Cartridges (25-shell boxes)

Rate of Fire: Single shot

Employed by: Lara Croft

Wielded: Two handed

The V-Packer pump-action 12-bore shotgun is Lara's best short-range weapon. While it's almost useless from a distance, the V-Packer takes out just about any enemy with one or two shots at close range. Using the Spread Cartridges shortens the weapon's already limited range, but it improves its accuracy, as the shot flies in a wider arc. The weapon's only disadvantages are its fairly short range and slow reload times.

Vector-R35

Vector-R35

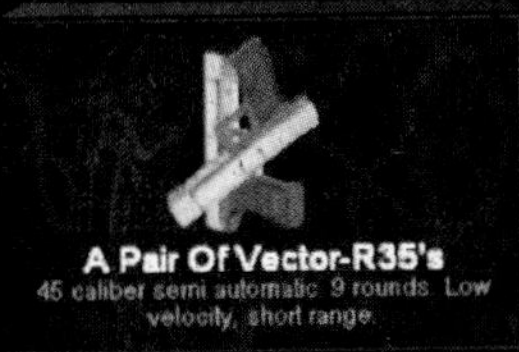

Vector-R35 Ammo

Location: Derelict Apartment Block (in a locked second-floor apartment), Von Croy's Apartment (second R-35 dropped by the Cleaner)

Ammo Type: Vector-R35 Clip (9-round clips)

Rate of Fire: Semiautomatic

Employed by: Lara Croft

Wielded: Single handed

A punchy weapon with excellent penetration power, the Vector-R35 is a fine pistol for any tomb-raiding adventuress. It's best when used at short ranges. There aren't many of the 9-round Vector-R35 Clips lying around, though, so save this bad boy for special occasions.

Once you face the Cleaner in Von Croy's Apartment, you can pick up the R-35 that he drops and turn Lara into a double-fisted engine of vengeance. Not only does wielding a pair of Vector R-35s double her rate of fire, she can also shoot at two different enemies simultaneously.

Viper SMG

Viper SMG.
Automatic and semi-automatic fire. Holds 70 rounds. Long range weapon. Optional laser

Viper SMG

Viper SMG Clip

Location: Von Croy's Apartment (dropped by the Cleaner)

Ammo Type: Viper SMG Clip (70-round clips)

Rate of Fire: Full auto, semiautomatic

Employed by: Lara Croft

Wielded: Two handed

The Viper SMG is guaranteed to take your breath away, as well as the breath of anyone who so much as looks at you funny. With a 70-round clip and a blistering rate of fire, the Viper is ideal for taking out troublesome enemies—by the platoon. It's very accurate at long range, but it's too big to wield effectively at short range.

Parisian Back Streets

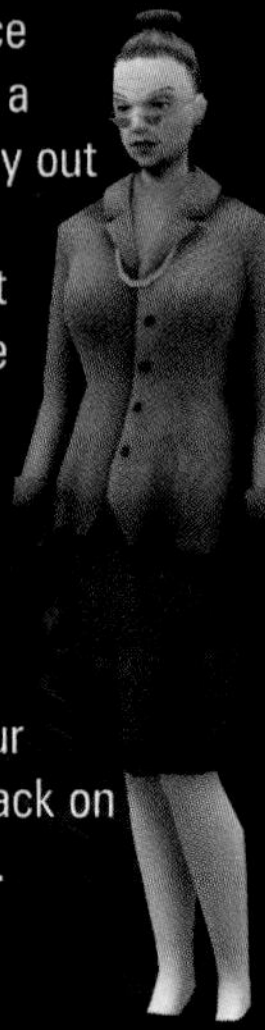

Escaping Paris's elite police units, Lara finds herself in a gloomy alley. The only way out is up. You'll quickly learn some of Miss Croft's most useful maneuvers, and the reason why the Walk button is crucial. You'll climb up to a second balcony, up a ladder, pause to ransack an apartment, then work your way onto an apartment roof. Here lies a Crowbar (useful for locating your first weapon and for powering up your arms). You then a shimmy to a balcony, execute a stealth attack on a policeman, and descend to the nearby apartment courtyard.

ENTITIES ENCOUNTERED

- Rottweiler
- Gendarme

CRITICAL ITEMS TO LOCATE

- Crowbar
- Necklace
- Gantry Gate Key

AVAILABLE UPGRADES

- **Upgrade Grip: Upper Body Level 2**
  A brief wrestle with a Crowbar to open a padlocked roof hut results in increased arm strength—perfect for hanging and shimmying!

After landing in a dank Parisian alley, Miss Croft must complete one overriding task—locate and rendezvous with Margot Carvier. Her apartment is over a number of rooftops, and your backpack is being chewed by an overzealous Rottweiler. You need weapons and items first, as well as a plan to stay out of the shadows.

NOTE With the Gendarme on your tail, make sure you aren't spotted; otherwise, you'll be at the receiving end of a French baton. Stay stealthy if you see the police in your vicinity.

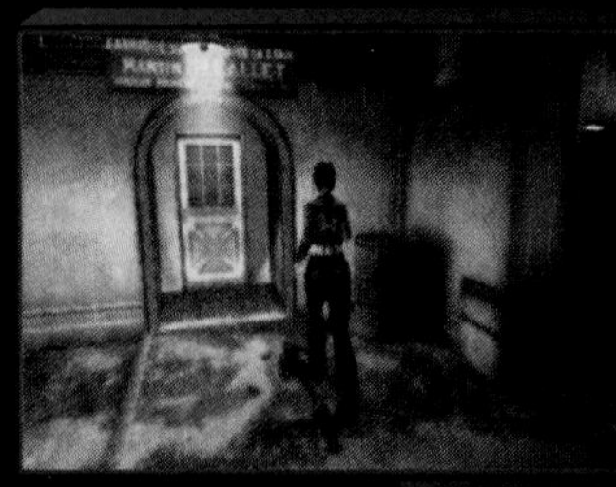

Walk forward, following Lara's maneuvering advice, and step under the door marked "Martin Meallet" to pick up the Chocolate Bar (an energy boost). The door in front of you is locked. Turn and investigate the alley.

The ground floor alley houses a tethered Rottweiler. Ignore it, or use the Action button to kick it until it keels over. A door at the end of the alley is locked.

Climb onto the bin in the corner, near the "Martin Meallet" door. Turn right and jump to grab the balcony. Pull yourself up. Once you're standing on the balcony, take a look at the gap in front of you.

Run to the edge of the gap and jump it (with the Jump button). You can even make it from a stationary position. Once on the other side of the gap, move past the door with the round window in it, to the ladder, and continue along to a sealed gate. You cannot progress further.

Before you climb the ladder, there's a Large Health Pack on the doorstep of the door you slammed behind you just before this adventure began.

Reach this item by running, then leaping over the railing and across the alley. Land on the other side of the metal door and pick up the Large Health Pack. Leap down to the alley, or across to the balcony railing, back to the ladder.

TIP **Keep falling off? Then make sure your Walk button is pressed firmly when you're on a platform you want to stay on. This saves you countless minutes of accidental plummeting.**

The only way to gain entrance to the Derelict Apartment Block involves the ladder climb.

Climb the ladder, move left onto the upper balcony, and walk around until you see a second ladder and the open window.

Enter the empty apartment and ransack the cupboards. You find a Wad of Cash in a cabinet, a Chocolate Bar in a drawer, and Antique Doubloons on the ground near the bed (walk to the camera). The armoire is locked and requires a Crowbar to open it. Return with a Crowbar and obtain the Necklace.

Exit the apartment, back onto the balcony, and climb up the second ladder riveted to the wall. At the top, turn right and step onto the balcony. The door next to you is locked.

Follow the wooden ledge so you can see the opposite rooftop. Claim the second set of Antique Doubloons to the left of the gap, then position yourself at the edge and jump.

You land on the jutting roof of the opposite building. Turn left, then walk to the railing and stop. Push forward to vault over the rail to a small balcony next to a witch's hat roof. Take the Chocolate Bar.

Leap over the railing and back onto the roof ledge. Walk forward to the end of the ledge and make a right turn. Lara tells you about the "hop" jump (a jump with the Walk button held down). This is great for leaping across treacherous terrain, but make sure you're facing the ledges to your right before you launch.

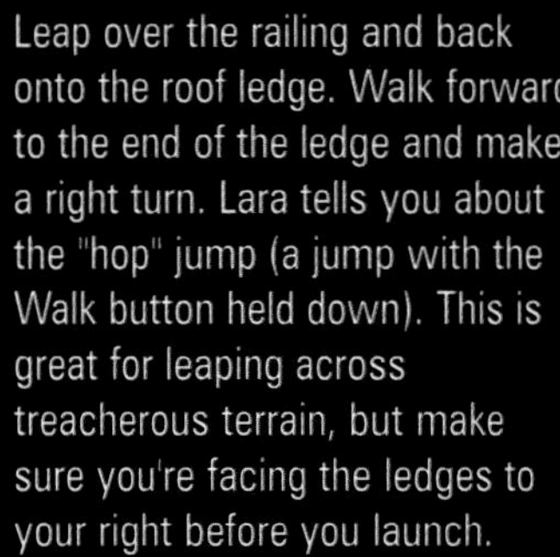

With the Walk button held down, move across the ledge, over the wooden plank, and walk into the drainpipe so you grab hold of it. As you climb, maneuver the camera to look right so you can see where you need to go.

At the top of the drainpipe, make sure Lara moves to the right and grabs the rooftop ledge. Her grip is failing, so quickly shimmy to the right until the pattern of the wall changes. Then press Action or let her drop onto the tile roof.

Watch out. Even walking on this tile roof can cause you to slide off the edge to your death. Instead, turn right and grab the roof ledge. Shimmy to the right, around the corner, and pull yourself up onto the roof of the apartment building.

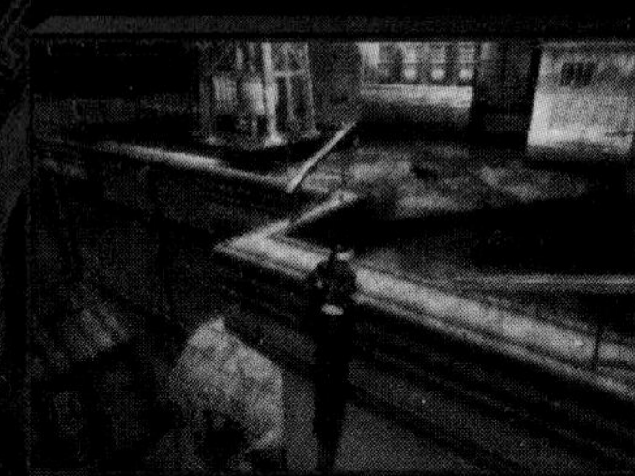

As the crows flap away, climb and walk on the roof. You pass a locked hut to your right (you must open the door with a Crowbar), as well as the large scaffolding holding the water supply for the apartment. Follow the instructions for moving the barrel away from the edge of the roof.

Head to the gap in the wire fence diagonally opposite the area of the roof where you started. Peer over the edge to spy a Crowbar on a roof ledge below. Drop with the Action button to claim it, then jump back onto the roof.

You can now move to the hut atop the roof and force the lock with the Crowbar. Lara feels stronger (Upgrade Grip: Upper Body Level 2) when the door opens. Inside are a couple of barrels and a red cabinet. Open the cabinet and take the M-V9 9mm semiautomatic.

NOTE **Don't get too cocky with this new weapon yet, Miss Croft. There's no ammunition for it.**

The gate is your next area of interest; it requires a key to open. Press the Stealth button, then the Action button, and hug the wall. Carefully edge left and peer around the corner. There's a Gendarme guarding the walkway ahead. Creep around the corner.

Continue with your stealth stoop, moving past the Gantry Gate Key that Lara spies and up the three steps to position yourself behind the guard. Quickly press the Action button, and Lara grabs the Gendarme by the neck, flips around, and brings him to the ground with a knockout punch.

Unlock the gate and watch your step. Sidestep onto the long ladder and descend it. Ignore the lower balcony and drop to the courtyard.

Return to the roof ledge where you grabbed the Crowbar, drop onto it, then jump and grab the roof. Shimmy to the left, quickly. If you're quick enough (and received your Upper Body upgrade), you'll have enough strength to drop and land on the other side of a locked gate. Remember to return for the Necklace inside the cupboard before you start the shimmy, or you won't be able to return for it.

You can simply take the Gate Key without bothering with the guard (as long as you're stealthy). Don't wander up to him nonchalantly, or he'll swing around, draw his pistol, and force you to engage in combat, ending your rooftop escapades. Take the key and return to the gate.

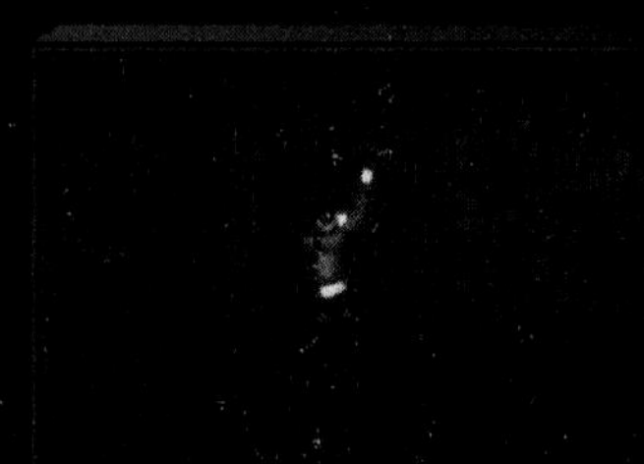

Derelict Apartment Block

The race is on! After moving a wardrobe to impede the oncoming forces, Lara climbs to the central elevator landing. As she descends, there are numerous obstacles to avoid, such as a small hole in the stairs, a larger landing gap, and a wardrobe that needs yanking out of her path. Once at the top of the landing, she shoves a crate in place to leap to the elevator maintenance room, where two keys of interest are found. One key opens the exit onto the roof, while the other unlocks a lower apartment. Switching the lift on, she rides it down, taking care not to descend too far into enemy territory, and claims some more regular items. Then it's back to ascending to the roof.

ENTITIES ENCOUNTERED

- Gendarme
- Gendarme Riot Soldiers (x2)

CRITICAL ITEMS TO LOCATE

- Lift Maintenance Key
- Apartment Key

AVAILABLE UPGRADES

- **Upgrade Push Object: Upper Body Level 3**
  Using a little legwork and pushing power to maneuver a crate at the top of the stairs, Lara can now shoulder certain doors open.

A team of special French police agents and a helicopter corner Lara, but she quickly kicks open the building door and slams it shut behind her. The police try to break open the door, but Lara quickly strengthens it with a metal beam. It'll hold—for now.

TIP It's best not to punch a heavily armed Frenchman, let alone a policeman with backup. Lara will auto-surrender if the police draw a weapon. Avoid them; do not engage.

Now in the abandoned apartment building, you can turn and pull the green wardrobe next to the door so that it blocks the door. Hopefully, this will stave off your French foes for a little while. Climb the stairs.

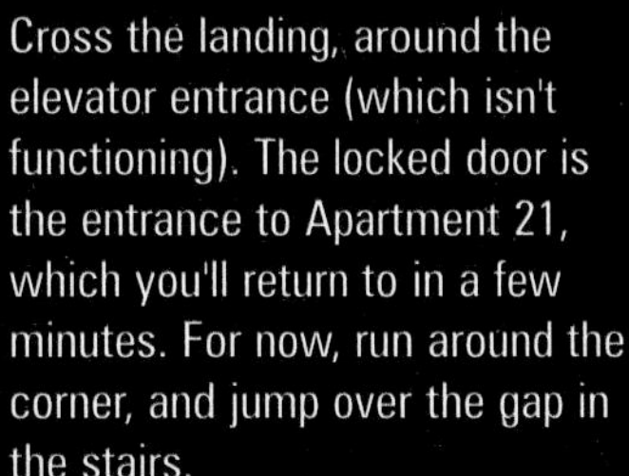

The police kick through the barricades, and while two riot guards lob in tear gas from the door, a third Gendarme runs in after you. Continue with your progress to the landing above. Ignore the boarded-up doors to your left, and continue running around the elevator.

Cross the landing, around the elevator entrance (which isn't functioning). The locked door is the entrance to Apartment 21, which you'll return to in a few minutes. For now, run around the corner, and jump over the gap in the stairs.

Make sure you leap the gap, as the Gendarme is on your tail. Continue to climb the steps until you reach the next floor's landing. Falling masonry tears through the remaining flooring just ahead of you, leaving a gaping hole and bursting gas pipes in the walls.

You can leap over the gaping hole in the floor, grabbing the opposite side of the hole if you come up short. Check the next alcove for Health Pills.

Instead, move to the wardrobe blocking the continuation of the stairs. Pull the wardrobe out, then run around it, up the steps, and to the next landing. Here you'll find a Small Health Pack and a door that you can actually open, although you have to shoulder-barge it to enter the room beyond.

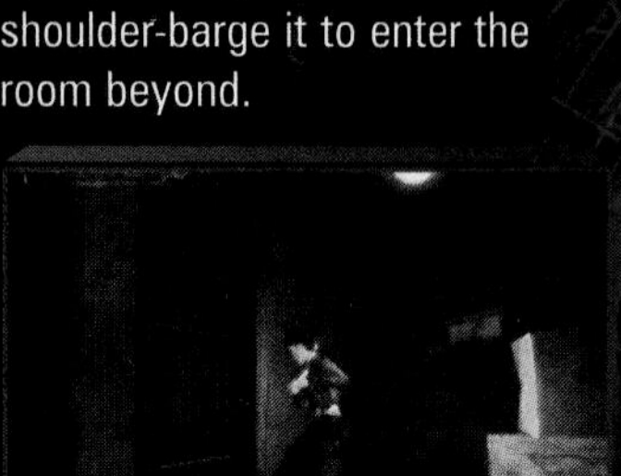

You enter Apartment 31B with a renewed sense of vigor (Upgrade Pull/Push: Upper Body Level 2). Ransack the place, opening the wardrobes to reveal V-Packer Spread Cartridges and a K2 Impactor Battery. Then go back into the elevator landing.

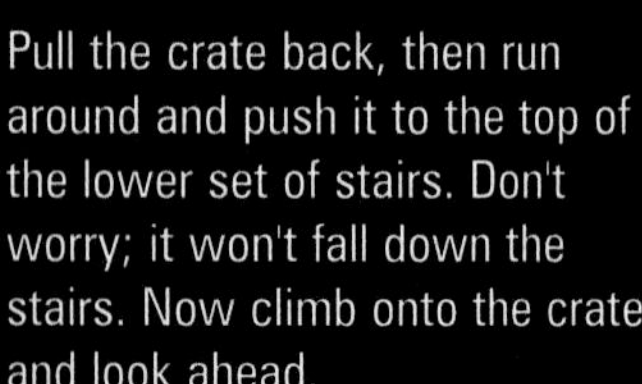

Sprint around the landing, collect the Health Bandages, and head up the steps. If you turn right, you reach an impassable blockade of beams, mattresses, and other assorted debris. Move to the small landing between the two sets of steps with the crate on it.

Pull the crate back, then run around and push it to the top of the lower set of stairs. Don't worry; it won't fall down the stairs. Now climb onto the crate and look ahead.

Leap and grab the railing above you, pull yourself over, and alight on the top floor landing. From here, you can inspect a door with a semicircular window above it (locked permanently) and the other side of the barricade. Now open the sliding door.

You enter the elevator maintenance room. On the ground is a Lift Maintenance Key, and on the wall hook of keys is the Apartment Key. Pick both of these up, then activate the heavy, green lever that winches the elevator to the top floor.

Use the Apartment Key to open the door, and go through the desk and wardrobe. The wardrobe holds Health Bandages, while the top desk drawers on either side of the smashed chair yield a Chocolate Bar and a Large Health Pack. Pocket these and head upward.

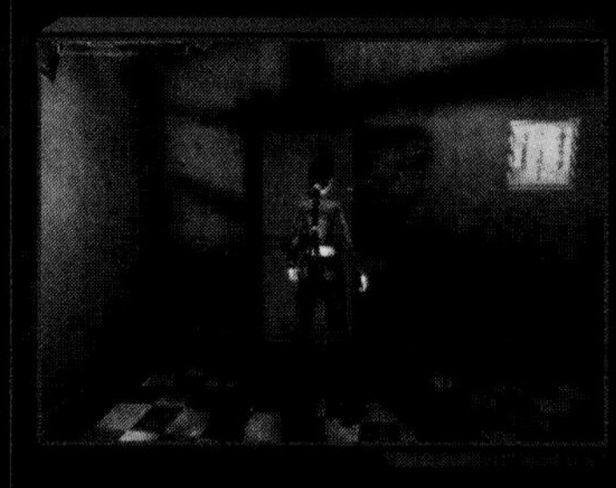

Enter the elevator, picking a floor (choose any except one or zero, as the police are patrolling the lower sections). Exit and descend until you're back at the large hole in the landing. Leap the hole, and move to the apartment door (the only other one not boarded up.

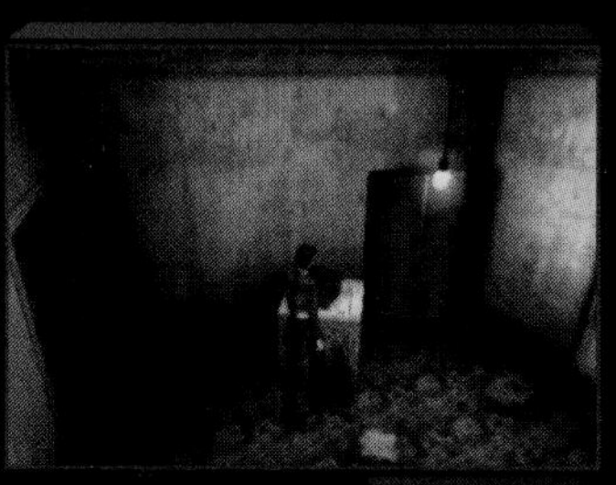

Move to the top of the elevator landings again, either using the lift or leaping across the crate once more. Head for the blue steel door that is opened with the Lift Maintenance Key, and step onto the rooftops. Make sure you've picked up all desired items first.

Industrial Roof Tops

Once on the roof, Lara proceeds by climbing onto the rooftops, shimmies across a wire (flipping her legs to avoid a mesh wall), and reaches the other side, hopefully before she runs out of grip. Once across the buildings, Lara needs to descend to the grimy streets below to shove a heavy crate near a flaming barrel. With this new-found strength, she can leap across the interior of a warehouse, winding her away across gantries and fire-escapes to a rooftop near Margot Carvier's apartment. Note that there are two ways across this roof once the crate is shoved, depending on whether you exit off the main ladder or not.

ENTITIES ENCOUNTERED
- Police Helicopter
- Rottweiler

CRITICAL ITEMS TO LOCATE
- There are no critical items to locate on this level.

AVAILABLE UPGRADES
- **Upgrade Jump Level: Lower Body Level 2**
  Pushing a large crate with a generator inside it may not seem like a rewarding exercise (especially when under chopper fire), but the workout does allow Lara to leap further.

Now on the roof, the only way to continue is to leap onto the metal ledge and up the ladder to the upper roof ledge. Carefully position yourself under the electrical wire (use the Walk button), and before you begin your shimmy, save your game.

As you move hand-over-hand, with only slippery wire and the rain separating you from a 200-foot plummet, the French authorities' helicopter appears and circles you. Don't get rattled—keep moving hand-over-hand.

Lara comes to a jutting wire fence that blocks her legs. Immediately swing her legs up and continue moving along the wire. You must continue to *hold* the Duck button, or Lara will drop to her hand-over-hand pose and waste valuable time.

Continue to shimmy until you reach the narrow rooftop on the other side. If you lose your grip and fall on your way to this rooftop, Lara will slide down the roof to a nasty demise.

TIP If Lara starts to drop before you reach the other roof, steer her to the foreground or the left roof, and as she slides, press the Action button so she grabs the gutter of the roof. If you're quick enough, you can shimmy left to the metal platform between the two buildings.

Shrug off the machine-gun fire and run around the right side of the stacked boxes, picking up the Health Bandages. Bring the camera around so you're looking down the gap in the fence at the left rooftop. Slowly, walk down the narrow gripped strip of roofing.

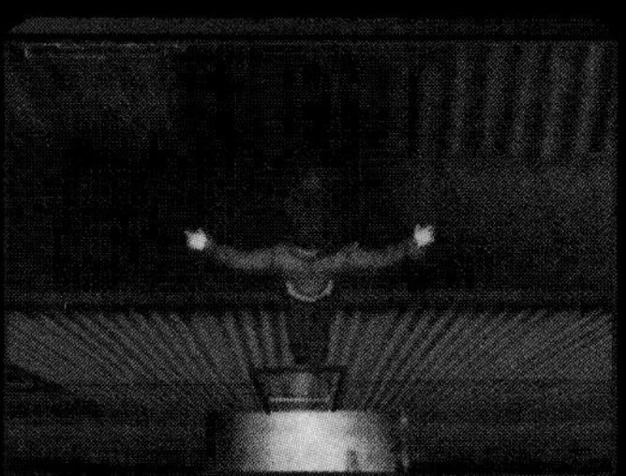

If you stray off this strip, you'll slide down the roof. Grab the gutter to avoid a deadly fall (Action button), then shimmy to the metal platform between the two buildings. This is where you should aim for eventually.

With careful treading, you can walk down the roof, then jump across to the small, flat rooftop balcony on the other side (you can't grab the side of it if you fall short). Duck on all fours, enter the open crate, and secure the Health Bandages inside.

Turn around, drop between the roofs, and enter the metallic door to the next building (the one you stood on to claim the Health Bandages inside the crate). Or you can stand atop the second building, slide onto the skylight, and fall through it into the second building.

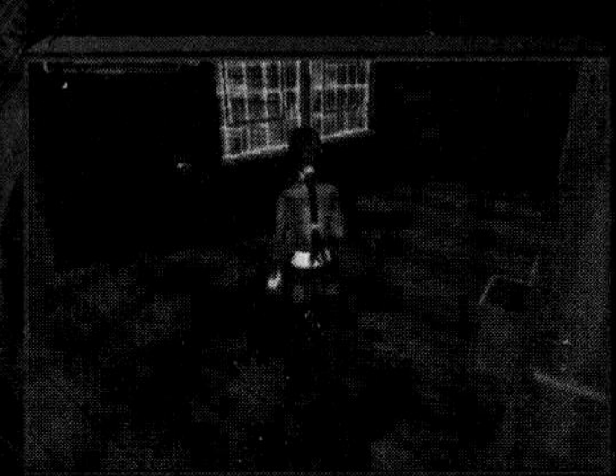

If you fall through the skylight, you can't run through the claustrophobic passages to the main room. On the ground are Antique Doubloons. Enter the main room and locate the M-V9 Clip (12 shots) in one corner and Chocolate Bar on the chest.

Kick open the next metal door to find yourself between two more warehouse buildings. Ahead of you is a metal door and a ladder riveted to the side of the third building.

Climb down and drop off the end of the ladder. There's no point in entering the interior of the warehouse, as you'll reach a ledge halfway down the warehouse that you can't jump across yet. Instead, drop down by the flaming barrel and turn right.

Run along the passage, around a corner, and pick up an M-V9 Clip. Two thirds of the way down this alley is a mesh fence that can be scaled (jump vertically). It is near the half-open garage door leading to the base of the warehouse you need to leap across. On the other side is a vicious Rottweiler. Ignore the Rottweiler.

You can run into the main alley area, but all directions are blocked by mesh fences with barbed wire at the top. These cannot be accessed. You can run along the alley below the ledge between warehouses one and two; there's a Large Health Pack at the far end.

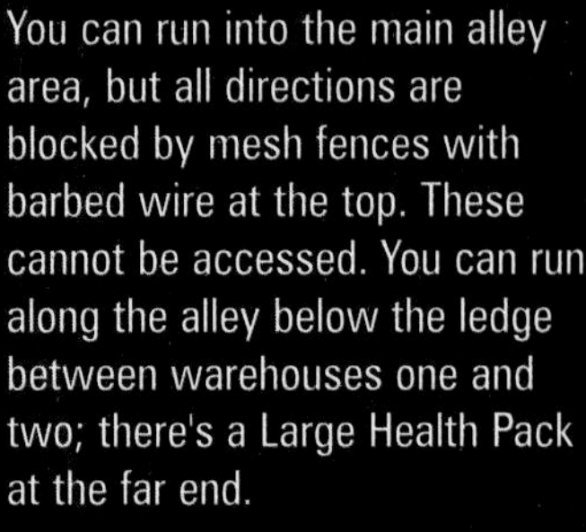

When you're finished lurking about, return to the crate with the generator in it and rest. Push the crate toward the broken ladder near the locked doors to the third warehouse. Push it until it hits the immovable barrel. Move to the other side and finish pushing the crate.

Lara exclaims that her legs are now sturdier (Upgrade Jump: Lower Body Level 2). She can now leap the gap in the third warehouse. Either run around to the half-open garage door and climb up inside the warehouse, or stand on the crate you just pushed, jump, and grab the ladder. Climb it to the ledge you descended from earlier.

You now have two choices on how to exit this area. One is via the rooftops, and the other is through the interior of the third warehouse. The interior method is detailed first (enter the warehouse door instead of continuing up the ladder).

Method #1: Warehouse Workout

Once inside the warehouse, move to the lower-level ledge. This is done in one of two ways. The first involves a heavy landing and a slight health loss. Turn left, walk down the steps to the broken edge of the walkway, and drop to the floor below.

The other way is to turn right, hang off the broken walkway, then shimmy to the drainpipe. Once on the drainpipe, shimmy to the lower ledge. Drop to the floor, pick up the Large Health Pack at the base of the drainpipe, and shimmy back to the lower ledge.

Climb on the ledge, and attempt a running jump over the gap with Lara's now-strengthened legs. Use Action to grab the ledge on the other side if you fall short. Pull yourself up to a walkway on your left where you can snag V-Packer Spread Cartridges.

Jump the gap in the walkway over the ladder, and open the metal door on the far side. Run down the enclosed corridor, ignoring the sealed door on your left, and open the one to the right. You're on a tiny ledge overlooking a fire escape. There's a drop to the passage where the Rottweiler is.

Leap the gap, then descend the fire escape, ignoring the doors but grabbing the Antique Doubloons at the end of the ledge. Retrace your steps to the top of the structure, open the door, and climb the small interior ladder to emerge inside a hut. Open the door; you're on the final rooftop.

Method #2: All Along the Rooftops

The other way to exit this area is to continue up the ladder, past the entrance to the warehouse, and onto the roof of the third building. When you reach the water barrel ledge, run around and climb a second ladder next to the barrel.

NOTE You can climb this area and exit this zone without dropping down or moving into the interior of the third warehouse. However, it is wise not to, as you won't get your increased Jump skill if you miss the pushing of the crate on the ground.

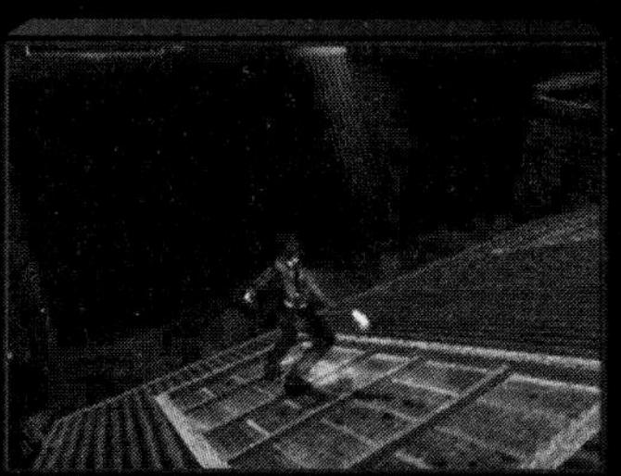

Clamber onto the very top perch of the third warehouse, claim the V-Packer Spread Cartridges, worry a crow, then turn and slide down toward a final set of rooftops. There are Health Pills at the left side of the flash gutters between the two buildings.

Run right, along the flash gutters, to the ladder up to a final rooftop area. Once at the top, turn right, ignoring the machine-gun fire, and look ahead. There's a gap in the railing and a drop between the buildings. Run and jump the drop. Don't fall!

Land on the roof of the opposite building (the gap you leapt was directly above the alley where you pushed the crate to the broken ladder), and run around the left side of the hut to obtain more Antique Doubloons. Now make your escape to Margot Carvier.

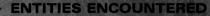

Margot Carvier's Apartment

At Margot Carvier's apartment, you'll find that the Mademoiselle gives you a rather chilly reception. The conversation becomes strained as Carvier realizes that not only was Lara at the scene of Von Croy's grisly demise, but she cannot account for her actions during that time! To Carvier, Croft is the prime suspect, and Lara must employ a mixture of cunning and persuasion before Carvier hands over Von Croy's Notebook. There's just enough time after the conversation ends for Lara to search the apartment, taking a couple of items that will fetch a good price, then escape through an open window before the police arrive.

ENTITIES ENCOUNTERED
- Margot Carvier
- Gendarme Riot Soldiers (x2)

CRITICAL ITEMS TO LOCATE
- Von Croy's Notebook
- Diamond Ring
- Vintage Cognac

AVAILABLE UPGRADES
- There are no available upgrades on this level.

With only a 20-foot jump between her and a military helicopter, Lara takes the risk and leaps across to grab a piece of gutter. It can't take the impact and tears off the wall, taking Lara with it and plunging her into a dunpster.

Emerging bruised but nearing her goal of locating Mademoiselle Carvier's apartment, Lara retrieves the address from her back pocket, notes it, and walks to the flats nearby. Carvier's buzzer sounds. She lets Lara in to explain herself.

NOTE **The conversation between Lara and Mademoiselle Carvier has two different outcomes. Therefore, save the game just before completing Industrial Roof Tops so you can be sure to obtain the better outcome.**

Lara and Carvier talk curtly. It seems Werner feared for his life and in recent weeks had been babbling about a commission from a client named Eckhardt. The research was on five medieval Obscura Paintings said to be linked to Alchemy and the Dark Arts.

Fearing he was being stalked, Werner left a package with Carvier in case something happened to him—a Notebook. After Lara explains what happened, Carvier either is too shocked to give you the book, or is bewildered and frightened enough to hand it over before she disappears.

In order to retrieve Werner Von Croy's Notebook, you must be truthful and a little firm with Mademoiselle Carvier. Make sure that your conversation ends with you telling her you were a good friend of Werner, and firmly suggest that the Notebook be handed your way.

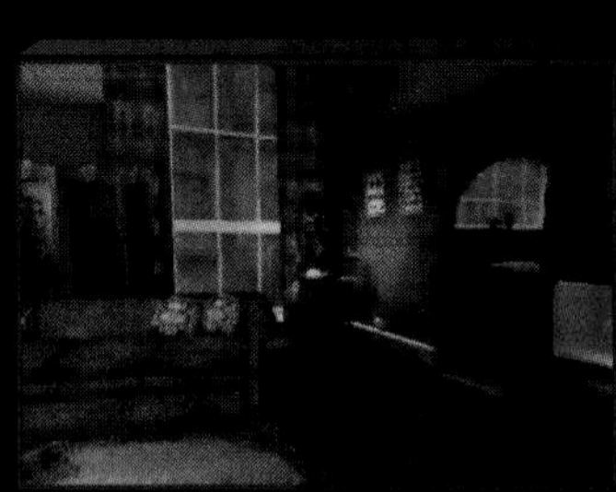

Carvier then abruptly departs her apartment, leaving you with Von Croy's Notebook and only a minute to check the place for valuables before the French police find you. Snag the Diamond Ring on the small table in the corner of the room, near the fish tank.

NOTE **The content of Von Croy's Notebook is revealed in "Lara's Notebook" at the end of this guide.**

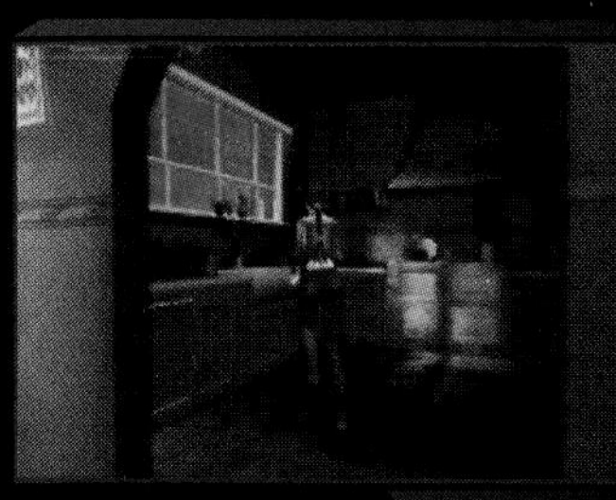

Head into the kitchen, taking the Vintage Cognac by the sink. If Carvier didn't hand you the Notebook, it appears in the cupboard on the right. Venture back into the living room and open the ornate desk drawer for Health Pills. The doors in the room are firmly locked.

Exit to the hallway to the right of the fireplace, and pass the potted plant on the side drawer. Open the door, and you'll automatically run to a window, leap out of it, and flee into the night. You seek sanctuary and refuge. You'll find it in the Parisian Ghetto.

Parisian Ghetto

Having been chased relentlessly through the back streets of Paris, Lara finds herself in the Parisian Ghetto, a hub level with several smaller areas in it. Life is cheap here, but the information that Lara needs about Von Croy's death is very expensive. You must recover a valuable item from Le Serpent Rouge, a club owned by crime lord Louis Bouchard. You must then deliver it to one of Bouchard's ex-employees in order to gain access to St. Aicard's Graveyard, which is the secret entrance to Bouchard's Hideout. If you play your cards right, Bouchard will take Lara into his confidence and share some valuable information in exchange for her services.

ENTITIES ENCOUNTERED

- Hobo (x2)
- Enterprising young salesman
- Mysterious motorcyclist (Kurtis Trent)
- Janice, a streetwalker
- Bernard, an ex-janitor
- Rottweiler
- Bouchard's doorman
- Zak, a boxer
- Carl, a boxer
- Boxer (unnamed)
- Boxing trainer
- Pierre, an ex-bartender

CRITICAL ITEMS TO LOCATE

- Bartender's Key
- Ex-Janitor's Key
- Gold Watch
- Café Owner's Contact (upon returning the Trinket Box)

AVAILABLE UPGRADES

- **Upgrade Jump: Lower Body 2**
  If you didn't get this in the previous chapter, you can power-up Lara's legs by pulling or pushing the stone altar in St. Aicard's Church.

After Lara's daring escape from the local Gendarmes, she winds up in an abandoned metro car in the seedy Parisian Ghetto. Exit the metro car through the only open door.

Make a U-turn after leaving the metro car, and approach the two hoboes near the train. Press the Action button to strike up a conversation with them.

The hoboes either don't know Bouchard, or they don't feel like sharing any information. The only advice they offer is that you visit the Café Metro in the Place d'Arcade. The owner might have some information to share. After finishing the conversation, it's time to get out of the abandoned metro tunnel.

Climb onto the broken section of pipe next to the metro car.

Face the metro car and jump to grab the edge of the roof, then pull yourself up.

Crawl under the pipes that run over the metro car's roof to get the Large Health Pack, then crawl back under the pipes.

Walk toward the vertical strip of fencing that leads up from the top of the metro car. Lara automatically climbs the fencing.

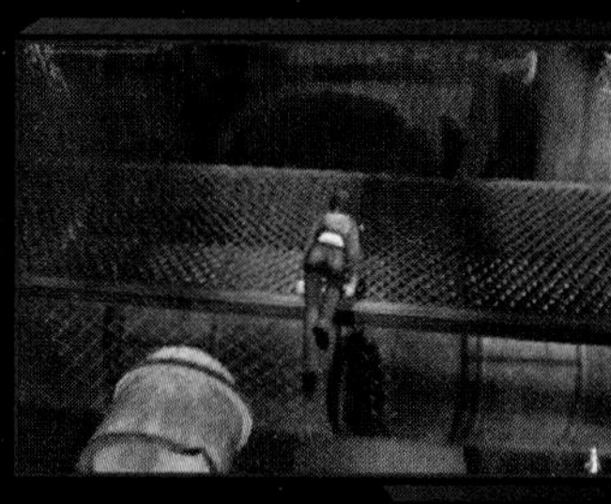

Climb up the fencing until you reach the top of the large pipe you crawled under, then pull yourself up onto the grating above it. From here, speak to a young "salesman" near the exit, or take a quick detour for an optional secret (see sidebar).

Want Some Candy, Little Girl?

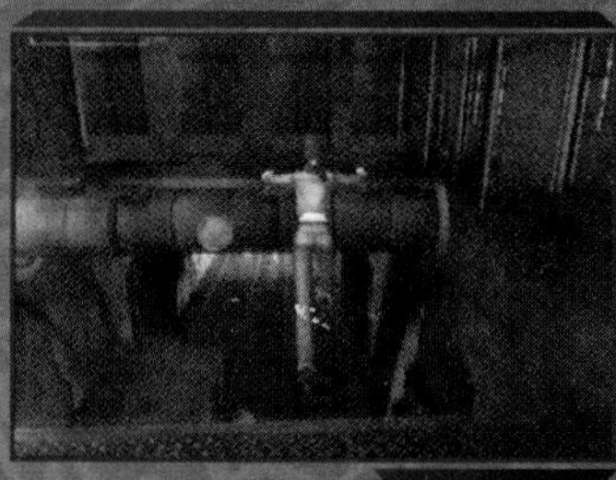

From the top of the large pipe, turn toward the hobos below you, run toward the edge of the grating, and jump just before you run off. Press the Action button in the air to grab the lip of another grating above large pipe. Pull yourself up onto it.

Now make a second jump in the same direction and press the Action button in mid-air to grab the ledge in front of you. Shimmy along the ledge to the right.

Shimmy around the corner of the ledge and pull yourself up through a hole in the fence above you. There's a Chocolate Bar on this ledge.

Walk to the other end of the grating to find a hole in the fence that runs around the perimeter of the tunnel. Jump through the hole to land safely on a dirt pathway.

There's a young fellow waiting next to a door near where you just landed. If you speak to him, he tries to get Lara to buy some of his illicit wares. Lara asks for information about Bouchard instead. The man tells Lara that she's looking for some dangerous information.

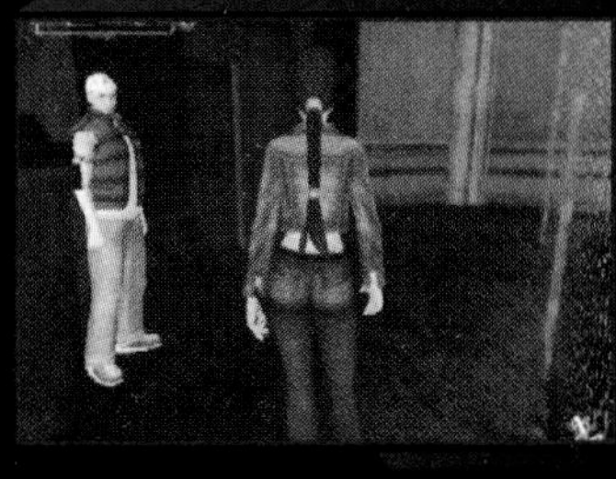

He also mentions that Paris is being stalked by a serial killer dubbed "the Monstrum." No one in Paris is safe from the Monstrum's grisly murders, even Bouchard. Bouchard, it turns out, runs a club called "Le Serpent Rouge," but he's been having some trouble with his staff. Many have been murdered, and the killings have shaken the normally unflappable Bouchard. Like the hoboes, the young man suggests that Lara visit the Café Metro. Once you've finished talking to the young man, enter the Parisian Ghetto proper through the door right next to him.

NOTE **It doesn't matter which choices you make during your dialogue with the young man; you get the same information regardless.**

Lara's ultimate goal is to find Louis Bouchard, and to do that she must retrieve an object from Le Serpent Rouge, Bouchard's club. The front entrance to the club is just to your right as you enter the ghetto streets, but the doors are firmly shut and sealed. You must find a way into the club; you should also visit several other areas of the Parisian Ghetto before going in.

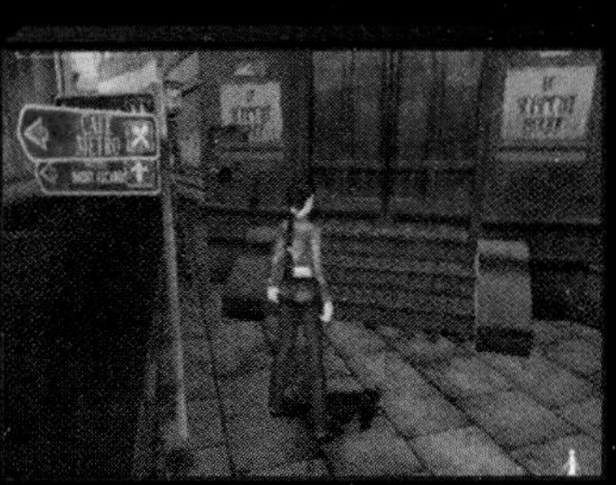

Janice

Standing in front of Le Serpent Rouge is Janice, a "lady of the night," with information to share.

Janice isn't happy to see Lara approach, figuring that she probably isn't a prospective client. However, if you say the right things, Janice will provide you with valuable clues.

TIP To get the maximum amount of useful info from Janice, make the following choices in conversation with her:

- "Have you worked in this neighborhood for long?"
- "[illegible] trouble?"
- "What makes this café owner so [illegible]"

Janice says that Bouchard had to leave Le Serpent Rouge after the murders at the club, and he's lying low for the time being. She doesn't know where he is, but if he's trying not to be found, he won't be easy to contact. No one knows why Bouchard has been targeted, and the Monstrum has everyone too afraid to discuss the matter openly.

She tells Lara about two men who used to work at Le Serpent Rouge. The first is the club's former janitor, Bernard, who can be found in the park. The second is Pierre, a former bartender at the club, who now runs Café Metro. Apparently, Bouchard held back money or other valuables from Pierre. Janice then drops a bombshell on Lara. She just heard on the radio that Mlle. Carvier was murdered. There are a lot of sickos on the streets.

Willowtree Herbalist

The Willowtree Herbalist is a small shop specializing in medicinal herbs and other beneficial flora. Although its proprietor keeps to himself, no one who lives or works in the Parisian Ghetto can be ignorant of Bouchard's ever-present influence.

After speaking with Janice, run down the street past Le Serpent Rouge, take a left when it ends, and head uphill until you reach a walkway to the right. Make a U-turn onto that walkway and enter the door to the Willowtree Herbalist at the end of it.

The elderly Asian proprietor doesn't know Bouchard, but he shares what little information he has with Lara. He knows that there is a doorman nearby who serves as Bouchard's bodyguard. If Lara had enough money and the proper password, the bodyguard might take her to Bouchard. The herbalist doesn't know the password, nor does he know who might have it.

St. Aicard's Church

This church-turned-gym doesn't hold many answers for Lara, but if she knows what she's doing, she can get a lower-body strength upgrade and a Gold Watch to pawn at Rennes' Pawnshop.

St. Aicard's Church is near the Willowtree Herbalist. To reach it, keep walking along the street, away from Janice and the herbalist. You can't miss its imposing gothic architecture (or the fact that a crosswalk in the street leads right to the front door).

The church isn't being used as a house of worship anymore. It's been turned into a gym, complete with heavy bags and a boxing ring. Two boxers spar as their burly trainer looks on.

Appropriately enough, Lara can strengthen her legs in this church turned gymnasium. Push the white stone altar at the front of the church to improve Lara's lower-body strength. This enhances her jumping distance.

If Lara has 200 Euros, she can bet on the fighters in the ring. Approach the hefty trainer as he observes the boxers, and press Action to talk to him. After a bit of sassy talk, Lara convinces the trainer to bet his watch against her cash. Pick a fighter (Zak or Carl), and the fight begins. If you choose wisely, Lara wins the trainer's pawnable Gold Watch. If not, she's 200 Euros lighter. Either way, you can only bet once.

NOTE **Unfortunately, neither one of the fighters is a sure bet to win the fight. You've got a 50-50 chance of winning!**

▶ The Doorman

Bouchard's doorman guards the entrance to St. Aicard's Graveyard. To get past him, you need one of the following items:

- *The Trinket Box from Le Serpent Rouge and 800 Euros*
- *The password from Bernard*

Since you don't have either of those at the moment, make a mental note to return to this area after you complete Le Serpent Rouge.

TIP If you can get [illegible] apartment from [illegible] boyfriend), you can bypass the doorman altogether.

Francine's Apartment

Just past Bouchard's doorman and the gate to St. Aicard's Graveyard is a locked door with a numeric keypad next to it. If you can find the code, you can open the door to Francine's apartment and enlist her assistance in getting into St. Aicard's Graveyard, without having to deal with Bouchard's doorman at all.

TIP To get the code, find the Trinket Box in Le Serpent Rouge and return it to Pierre, who then gives you the four-digit code to Francine's apartment.

Rennes' Pawnshop

Rennes' Pawnshop is a no-questions-asked, one-stop shop for buyers and sellers of all sorts of merchandise. The proprietor, Daniel Rennes, is justifiably skeptical of anyone who comes through the door. To access his entire catalog of wares, prove that you're not trying to bust him.

To reach Daniel Rennes' Pawnshop, return to the locked front entrance to Le Serpent Rouge, and run down the street (past Janice and away from Le Serpent Rouge). Rennes' Pawnshop is the last doorway on the right side of the street, just before the red-and-orange-striped barricade.

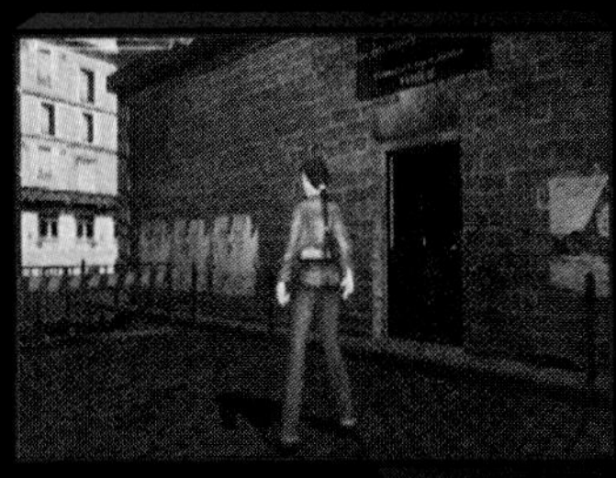

At Rennes' Pawnshop, you can sell valuable items that you collect for a fat stack of Euros. Don't worry that you're going to accidentally sell any mission-critical items—you can only sell items meant to be sold at the pawnshop. Sell every item you can, and return here if you find more valuable items. This is your only opportunity to do so, and you can never have too many Euros.

Key to Le Serpent Rouge

You must meet either Pierre at Café Metro or Bernard in the park to get a key to Le Serpent Rouge. Visit both of them if you desire access to both club entrances and all of the hidden goodies.

Both of them want the same thing: an item hidden in a nonfunctioning stage light. Giving the item to either of them gives you something that gets you into St. Aicard's Graveyard, which is the entrance to Bouchard's Hideout.

NOTE **Pierre gives you the entry code to Francine's apartment; the apartment overlooks the graveyard and can be used to enter it. Bernard gives you a password that gets you past Bouchard's doorman at the gate to the graveyard.**

Café Metro

Café Metro might not have the best food or friendliest service, but it is owned by Pierre, Le Serpent Rouge's ex-bartender. Perhaps he can help you find his old boss, Louis Bouchard....

To reach Café Metro, return to the front entrance of Le Serpent Rouge and climb the stairs across the street.

In the courtyard beyond the stairs, look for the charcuterie (butcher) and the street beyond it that is closed off by three short, concrete pillars.

The café is to the right, just beyond the concrete pillars. A motorcycle sits in front of the café.

Approach Pierre's counter and speak to him. He's not willing to give information away for free, but he is willing to help Lara find Bouchard if she'll do a favor for him. He left something of value behind in a nonfunctioning stage light at Le Serpent Rouge. He can't go back to get it, as he left Bouchard on less than ideal terms, and the club is no doubt staked out due to the Monstrum attacks. He gives Lara the Bartender's Key, which opens the back door to the club.

TIP **To get the optimal results from your conversation with Pierre, make the following dialogue choice.**

- **"No, I don't, but I do deal with problems. Sort them out."**

There's a customer sitting in the café, but he's not talking at the moment. After getting the Bartender's Key, leave the café.

Parisian Ghetto Park

The entrance to the park is directly across the street from St. Aicard's Church—follow the crosswalk to the iron gate and open it to enter the park.

NOTE **You need to have spoken to Janice, and have 160 Euros, to get any information out of Bernard.**

Approach Bernard and begin speaking with him. He seems more than a little paranoid, but if you make the correct dialogue choices he says that 160 Euros might jog his memory.

If you've got the cash, Bernard tells Lara that he wants a box he had to leave behind in a broken lighting rig in Le Serpent Rouge. If Lara gets it for him, he'll tell her the password to get past Bouchard's doorman. He gives Lara the Ex-Janitor's Key, which unlocks the garage entrance to Le Serpent Rouge.

TIP **To get the information you need from Bernard, make the following choices in conversation with him:**

- **"Your name's Bernard. Janice said I might find you here."**
- **"I'm trying to find someone."**
- **"Here. Now, how do I find Bouchard?"**

Le Serpent Rouge

Le Serpent Rouge ("The Red Serpent") is a nightclub that the crime boss uses as a front for his illegal activities. Since the Monstrum started killing Bouchard's men, Bouchard has fled Le Serpent Rouge, but he's still got a dozen of his foot soldiers staking it out. Once you have a key from Bernard or Pierre, you can enter Le Serpent Rouge. Both entrances lead to the dance floor, but you must overcome an obstacle or two at each entrance before you can reach it.

ENTITIES ENCOUNTERED

- Le Serpent Rouge guards (x9)

CRITICAL ITEMS TO LOCATE

- Antique Doubloons (x3)
- Socket Spanner
- Antique Flintlock
- Vintage Cognac (x2)
- Wad of Cash
- Stage Door Key
- Antique Record
- Trinket Box
- Ticket Office Key

AVAILABLE UPGRADES

- **Upgrade Jump: Lower Body 2**
  If you didn't get this in the previous chapter, you can power-up Lara's legs by pulling a crate in Le Serpent Rouge.
- **Upgrade Kick Door/Wall: Lower Body 3**
  When Lara kicks down the catwalk bridge in the rafters of Le Serpent Rouge, her leg strength is powered up.
- **Upgrade Shoulder Barge: Upper Body 4**
  This upper-body upgrade can be acquired by pulling a lever in Le Serpent Rouge's garage.

Garage Entrance (Bernard's Key)

The garage entrance (which you can open with Bernard's Ex-Janitor's Key) is on the side of Le Serpent Rouge facing the street. It's a green door to the left of a corrugated metal garage door. Press Action near the door to automatically use the Ex-Janitor's Key and open the door.

Pull the lever on the yellow lift to raise the car.

As the hydraulic lift raises the car, the camera moves inside of the garage office to show you some Antique Doubloons sitting inside.

There don't seem to be any passageways from the garage to the club's dance floor, but there is a hidden passage that you can open. Follow these steps to do so.

There's another lever next to the desk. Pull it to open a secret passage under the hydraulic lift.

NOTE **Pulling the lever that opens the secret passage upgrades Lara's upper-body strength, allowing her to shimmy along ledges for greater distances.**

After enhancing her upper-body strength by pulling the second lever, Lara can break open the door to the garage office with a well-placed shoulder thrust. Inside, you can pick up some Antique Doubloons.

TIP **Before going down the secret passage to the club's dance floor, you should pick up the following items in the garage:**

On the desk, grab the Socket Spanner.

In the lockers, you find a K2 Impactor Battery, a Desert Ranger Clip, Health Bandages, and an Antique Flintlock.

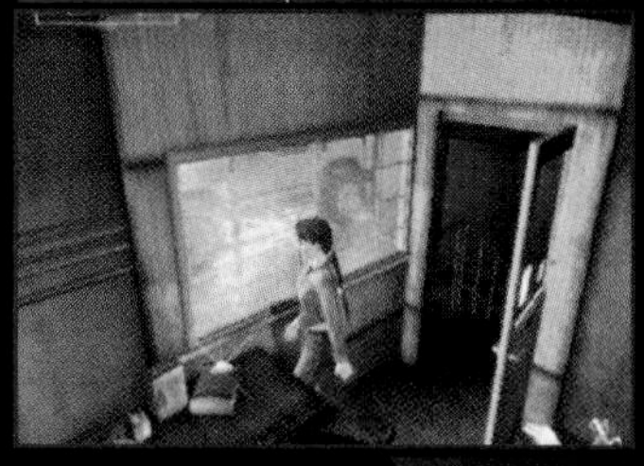

In the office, pick up the aforementioned Antique Doubloons from the garage office desk.

TIP **After grabbing all of the items in the garage, drop through the secret passage under the hydraulic lift and head along the hallway until you reach a ladder that leads up into a storage area.**

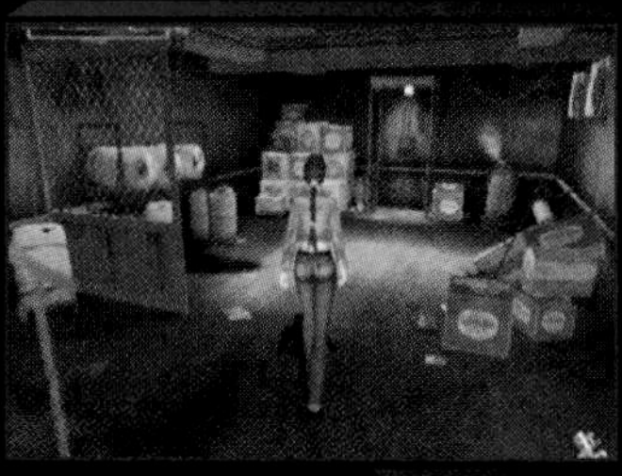

At one end of the room is a locked door that you don't have a key for, and at the other end is a lever. Pick up the Vintage Cognac on the floor near the lever. Use the Socket Spanner on the lever to activate a malfunctioning dumbwaiter near the door.

Activating the dumbwaiter draws the attention of a guard, who runs down to the storage room from the dance floor. As soon as you see him coming, switch into Stealth mode and duck behind the short wall by the kegs.

The guard pokes his head in, shines his flashlight around, and leaves—but he doesn't lock the door behind him. Go through it to reach the dance floor (and skip to the "Dance Floor" section of this walkthrough).

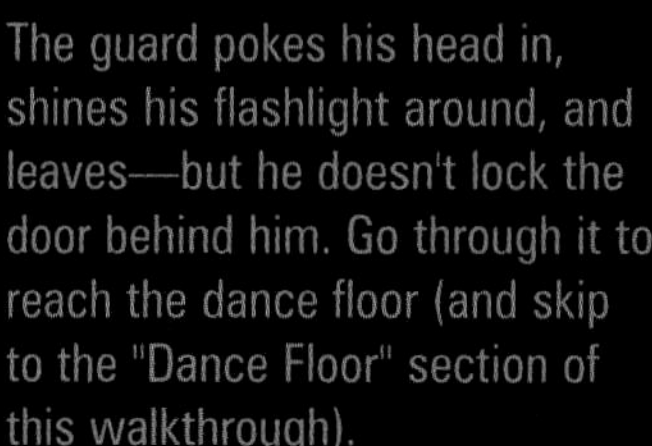

TIP **If you're quick and crafty, you can take out the guard, leaving you one less guard to deal with on the dance floor. However, it's actually much easier to take him out on the dance floor.**

Stage Entrance (Pierre's Key)

The stage entrance to Le Serpent Rouge is in the alley around the corner from the garage entrance. As you enter, you see a quick cutscene of the club's office area. There are several items in the back office, but there's also a guard there.

Instead of heading directly for the office, head down the opposite hallway and pull the lever in the middle of the hallway to kill the lights outside the office.

This causes the guard to walk out of the office and head for the light switch to see what's going on. If you duck into the room between the office and the light switch, you can watch the guard pass by and sneak up behind him (in Stealth mode) to take him out without firing a shot or drawing any unnecessary attention to yourself.

TIP **Once you take out the guard, don't forget to grab his pistol to add an M-V9 Clip to your inventory.**

With the guard disposed of, go into the office to pick up the Stage Door Key, some Antique Doubloons, and a Wad of Cash. Once you've picked up all of the items, head back down the hallway with the light switch to find the door to the dance floor. Open it with the Stage Door Key and enter the dance floor area.

NOTE **Regardless of which entrance you use to reach the dance floor, you appear in the same area. The doors leading from the back entrance and garage entrance are right next to each other in the same corner of the dance floor.**

As soon as you enter the dance floor, switch into Stealth mode and hide behind the nearby stacks of amplifiers and crates to avoid detection by the guard near the door. Sneak up on him and take him out.

With the guard downed, sneak onto the stage and pull the lever on the wall. This turns on the dance floor music and lights. Although it draws a lot of attention, it also starts the upper light rigging moving up and down, which is exactly what you need it to do.

CAUTION **As soon as you start up the lights and music, two more guards appear on the floor. Stay in Stealth mode.**

TIP **There's an Antique Record on the stage that you should grab. You can pawn it later.**

Leave the stage by climbing over the railing opposite the stairs you climbed up. This drops you right near a pack of Health Pills.

If you're feeling daring, check out the bar on the dance floor. You should probably sneak up on and take out most of the guards on the dance floor before you try it, or you're almost certain to be seen. The only guard you shouldn't go after is the one in the corner of the dance floor near the yellow room, as another guard pops out from a nearby door if you attack him.

Pull the lever on the wall to activate the dumbwaiter You'll get some V-Packer Spread Cartridges from it for your troubles.

You should also grab the Vintage Cognac and the Antique Doubloons from the bar before you leave it. Both of these can be fenced at Rennes' Pawnshop.

Sneak along the wall to the first set of stairs leading up from the dance floor.

CAUTION **Watch out for the guard who appears at the top of the stairs once you start climbing. You can either rush him and take him out (which causes another guard to come out of the door at the top of the stairs) or try to draw him down the stairs and sneak past him.**

Walk around the catwalk to the other side of the room, where you find a moveable crate and a pile of junk blocking the foot of the next set of stairs.

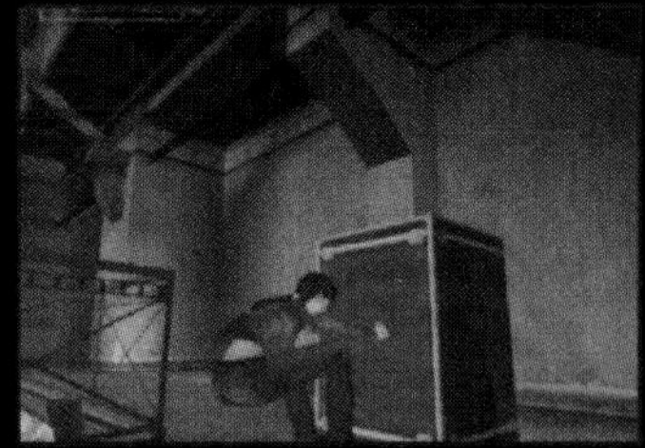

Pull the moveable crate away from the wall and onto the small landing on the catwalk. Line it up so that it's under the overhead lighting rigging.

NOTE Pulling the crate gives Lara Upgrade Jump: Lower Body Level 2.

Climb onto the crate and jump to grab the edge of the lighting rig. Pull yourself up and walk along it toward the center of the room.

Walk to the edge of the lighting rig and jump toward the walkway on the other side of the room. You should be able to leap easily without grabbing the edge of the walkway.

CAUTION Once you land on the catwalk, a guard comes out of a door in the corner of the room to investigate. Take him out quickly and quietly.

Grab the Large Health Pack from the area of the catwalk you pulled yourself up to, as well as the Health Bandages near the guard in the corner of the room.

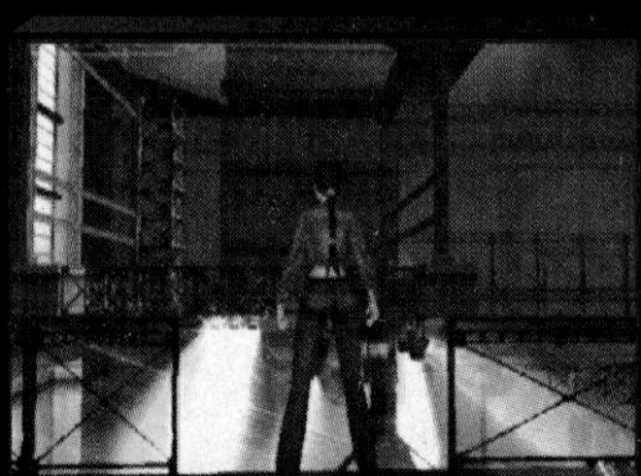

There's a gap in the catwalk railing near the guard in the corner and the Health Bandages. Leap from it onto the moving lighting rig when the rig is at its lowest point. Don't hold down the Forward button after you jump, or you may overshoot the rigging and fall off to your death.

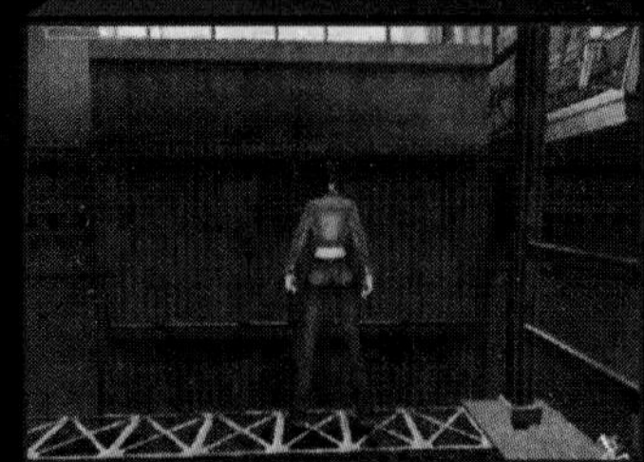

Make another hop in the same direction to land on the other side of the lighting rig. Again, don't hold the Forward button after you jump, or you might overshoot the rig and fall.

From the far side of the rig, turn left and climb onto the scaffolding. Move 90 degrees counterclockwise around it and climb up it to reach the top of the moving lighting rig.

Make one more nerve-wracking jump across the lighting rig to reach the other side of the top. It's best to try and jump to the wider corner of the other side of the rig, as it's a bit more forgiving.

TIP If you overshoot the rig, press Action immediately. If you're lucky, you'll grab the catwalk that you leapt from onto the lighting rig.

Wait for the lighting rig to rise to its highest position, then leap from it onto the green catwalk against the wall. Once you land on the green catwalk, climb the nearby ladder to reach the highest point of the room.

At the top of the ladder is a short section of catwalk pointing toward the center of the room. At the end of that catwalk is a small box that hangs from the highest lighting rig. You can open it (with the Action button), but there's nothing in it at the moment. Remember this location, though; you'll find Pierre/Bernard's Trinket Box here in a few minutes.

From the top of the ladder, walk along the wall to slide down an angled section of catwalk. Quickly jump off of the catwalk to leap to a small platform in the corner of the room.

From that small platform, continue moving counter-clockwise around the perimeter of the room by jumping to the next platform, then leaping off of the end of that platform. Press Action while in the air to grab the rig beyond it.

There are some pipes running over the rig, and you can't pull yourself up until you're beyond them. So quickly shimmy to the left to get past the pipes before Lara's stamina gives out and she falls to her death.

From the top of this lighting rig, leap down to the catwalk next to the control room below you.

As soon as you land safely on the catwalk, approach the raised section and hit Action to kick and lower it. You can now walk over to the area with the ladder leading to the box in the lighting rig.

NOTE Kicking down the catwalk bridge also upgrades Lara's lower-body strength and lets her break open the door to the control room.

Once the catwalk bridge is down, kick in the door to the control room. There's a control console inside that lets you move the lights around overhead. Although it looks like it's all one control panel, the console actually has *two different* controls. If you stand at the left side and hit Action, you can rotate the four overhead lights counterclockwise. If you stand at the right side and hit Action, you can move the light closest to the box at the top of the ladder into that box.

Pull the left lever twice to move the sparking light close to the box at the top of the ladder, then pull the right lever to move it into the box. (Remember, both Pierre and Bernard said the object they wanted was in the light that didn't work.)

Once the light is in position, exit the control room, cross the lowered catwalk bridge, climb the ladder, and open the box to get the Trinket Box. Mission complete. Now you just have to get out in one piece.

Runback across the catwalk, take out the guard who appears in the control room, and grab the Ticket Office Key from the floor.

Before leaving Le Serpent Rouge, climb down the ladder in the control room to find a delicious Chocolate Bar at the bottom of it. Grab it, go back up to the control room, and use the Ticket Office Key to unlock the control room door.

CAUTION Don't go through the door at the bottom of the ladder! This takes you back to the dance floor catwalks, and you can't go back through the door once you're there. This also means you have to go back out through the stage entrance or garage entrance to leave the club!

The control room door takes you to a fire escape outside of Le Serpent Rouge. Descend the fire escape to return to the street level of the Parisian Ghetto.

TIP Before you proceed into St. Aicard's Graveyard, be sure to clear up any loose ends in the Parisian Ghetto. If you want to check out the unused entrance to Le Serpent Rouge, now is the time to do so.

Metro Tunnels

There are several entrances to the metro tunnels that run underneath the Parisian Ghetto. The main entrance is found in the park across from St. Aicard's Church, but it's locked. Fortunately, you can also lift any of the manholes in the Parisian Ghetto to drop into the metro tunnels.

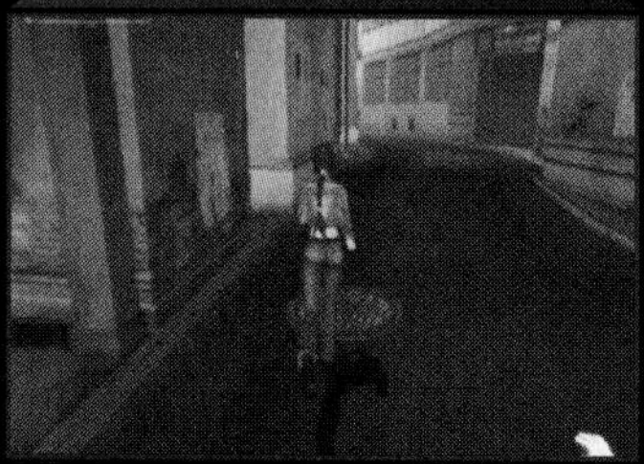

Here's one way (of several) to get all of the items in the metro tunnels: Backtrack to Le Serpent Rouge and press the Action button near the adjacent manhole cover to enter the tunnels.

NOTE **Although the loading screen says "Bouchard's Hideout," you're not actually going to meet the Parisian Crimelord just yet.**

From the manhole entrance to the tunnel, run down the narrow corridor and take a left at the four-way intersection.

Clamber onto the largest box at the end of the tunnel and climb the rough section of wall to reach a small wooden platform.

Jump from that platform to the platform on the other side of the room. Face the wall, jump to grab a ledge, shimmy to the right, and enter a rectangular tunnel between the two platforms.

Crawl to the end of that tunnel and jump up into the lighted, elevated tunnel at the end of it.

This takes you to the other side of the entrance gate at the street level of the Parisian Ghetto. You can unlock the gate from this side, and you can also pick up the V-Packer Spread Cartridges, Health Bandages, and Vector-R35 Clip.

Now backtrack into the tunnels to the four-way intersection. Take a left at the intersection to arrive at a large round vertical room with a broken pathway running across the center of it.

Take a running leap and grab the edge of the other side of the pathway.

Pull yourself up and climb the ladder leading to the other side of the pathway.

Kick down the door at the top of the ladder. On the other side of the door are a Large Health Pack and a hallway that leads out to a catwalk that overlooks the area you just came from. Grab the Wad of Cash on the catwalk before leaving.

Backtrack across the broken pathway (by taking a running leap across it again), then walk to the right edge of the broken pathway to see a rough section of wall that Lara can climb down. To climb onto it, hang from the broken pathway and shimmy over to the wall.

Climb down the rough section of wall and enter the small tunnel below the broken pathway. There's a Diamond Ring in here! Climb back up the wall.

NOTE **Once you have the Large Health Pack, the Diamond Ring, the V-Packer Spread Cartridges, the Health Bandages, the Vector-R35 Clip *and* you've unlocked the main metro entrance, you've done all you can do down here. Head to the surface.**

You should also visit Rennes' Pawnshop to sell your valuable items before proceeding. You won't have a chance to after St. Aicard's Graveyard, and you won't find any pawnable items in the graveyard either.

Now that you've got the coveted Trinket Box, you must trade it for access to St. Aicard's Graveyard, which leads to Bouchard's Hideout. You've got a few options for how to go about it.

Entering the Graveyard with Pierre's Assistance

Return to the Café Metro to find Pierre still behind the bar. Approach him and press Action to begin a conversation. He trades you the Café Owner's Contact for the Trinket Box. The Café Owner's Contact has the numeric key code to Francine's apartment, which overlooks St. Aicard's Graveyard.

NOTE **The code to Francine's apartment is 15329.**

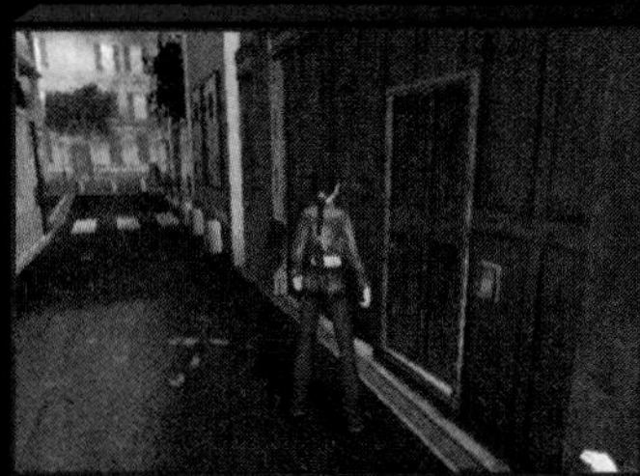

The door to Francine's apartment building is right next to Bouchard's doorman. Punch in the code, enter the apartment building, and go up the stairs to reach Francine's apartment.

Speak to Francine, who tells you that Bouchard's Hideout is in the basement of the old church. You need to enter it via a mausoleum in St. Aicard's Graveyard, which her apartment overlooks. You can enter the graveyard through Francine's window, but you need to watch out for the ledges—they're dangerous.

Press the Action button near the window to the balcony, high above St. Aicard's Graveyard.

Make a running jump off of the edge of the balcony without a railing to grab the edge of the balcony in front of you. Pull yourself up.

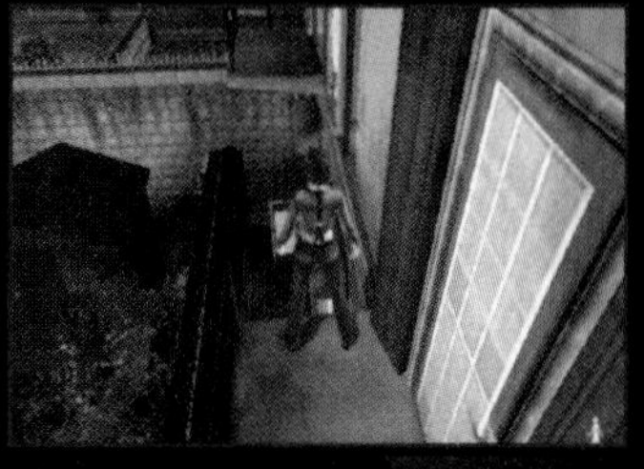

Hop over the railing in front of you to reach a vertical pole that you can climb up. It's easy to miss, as it's the same color as the rest of the building. Press Forward while walking toward it to get Lara up the pole.

Pull yourself up to the ledge above the pole and run along it. Sections of the ledge collapse, so keep running and jump off of them if you need to, but don't run off the end of the ledge!

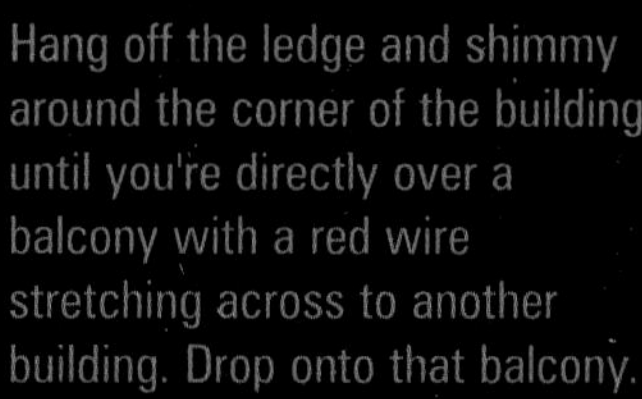

Hang off the ledge and shimmy around the corner of the building until you're directly over a balcony with a red wire stretching across to another building. Drop onto that balcony.

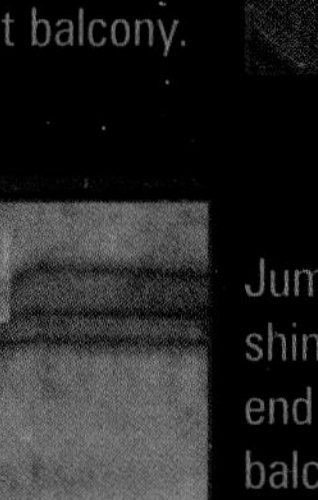

Jump up, grab the red cable, and shimmy all the way to the other end of it. Drop down onto the balcony above the other end of the cable.

Walk to the end of this balcony and hang off the edge that doesn't have a railing. When you drop from this hang, you're in St. Aicard's Graveyard.

Entering the Graveyard with Bernard's Assistance

You find Bernard in the park, exactly where you left him. Give him the Trinket Box, and he tells Lara that the password for the doorman is "Pluit Noir" (black rain). Once you have the password, go and speak to the doorman.

The doorman is satisfied with the password, and he opens the gate to St. Aicard's Graveyard in a gentlemanly manner.

Entering the Graveyard with the Doorman's Assistance

To convince the doorman guarding St. Aicard's Graveyard to open the gate without Bernard's password, you need to give him 800 Euros and the Trinket Box. He opens the gate for you and lets you into the graveyard.

St. Aicard's Graveyard

Two Rottweilers patrol the grounds of St. Aicard's Graveyard. While you can just charge forward and shoot them, there's a much more elegant solution—hopping from mausoleum to mausoleum. That way, you don't waste any bullets, and you don't wind up on PETA's hit list. To reach Bouchard's Hideout from St. Aicard's Graveyard, you must topple a statue into a crypt to reveal the entrance to Bouchard's Hideout.

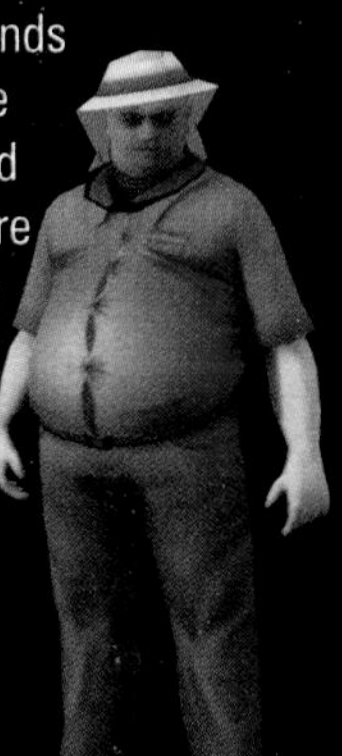

ENTITIES ENCOUNTERED

- Rottweiler

CRITICAL ITEMS TO LOCATE

- None

AVAILABLE UPGRADES

- **Upgrade Shoulder Barge: Upper Body Level 4**
  This upper-body upgrade can be acquired by shouldering down a mausoleum door in St. Aicard's Graveyard.

NOTE **If you got the upper-body strength upgrade by pulling the lever in Le Serpent Rouge's garage, you don't need to get it again to push over the statue. But you forfeit the 9mm ammo you get from doing it here.**

Either pick off the Rottweiler or wait for it to pass, then run up to the mausoleum that overlooks the tomb surrounded by a fence in the corner of the graveyard.

Jump up to grab the roof of the mausoleum, pull yourself up to the roof, and jump down inside the fence of the adjacent tomb.

Stand in front of the tomb door, press Action to shove the door with your shoulder, and boost Lara's upper-body strength. Pick up the two clips of ammo inside the tomb. Once you have the strength upgrade, return to the graveyard entrance.

Climb onto the third crypt from the entrance to the graveyard. If you entered the Graveyard via Francine's apartment, this is where you begin.

Jump toward the tall mausoleum in front of you and grab the edge of it to pull yourself onto the roof.

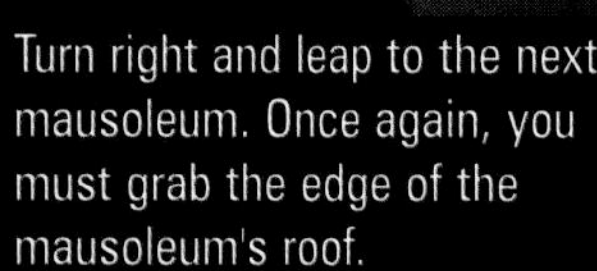

Make another leap forward to catch the lip of the roof of the next mausoleum.

Turn right and leap to the next mausoleum. Once again, you must grab the edge of the mausoleum's roof.

Turn left and leap onto the adjacent mausoleum, grabbing the lip of the roof.

Jump straight ahead to the next mausoleum roof. Make sure to grab the lip of the roof.

Turn right and hop down onto the roof of the tomb in the area enclosed by a fence.

Finally, climb down from the tomb, approach the angel statue, and press Action to send it crashing through the crypt.

Drop into the crypt to enter Bouchard's Hideout.

Bouchard's Hideout

Time to meet the Parisian crime boss himself, and hopefully extract some information from him about Werner Von Croy's final days. Louis Bouchard's subterranean refuge is designed to keep unwanted visitors out, but that's never stopped Lara before.

ENTITIES ENCOUNTERED

- Arnaud, Bouchard's wounded henchman
- Louis Bouchard, Parisian crime lord
- Tall dark stranger (Eckhardt)
- Daniel Rennes

CRITICAL ITEMS TO LOCATE

- Wad of Passports
- Rennes' Wallet
- Scrap of Paper
- Dart SS
- Map of Sewers Around Louvre
- Explosives
- K2 Impactor
- Map of Archaeological Dig

AVAILABLE UPGRADES

- There are no upgrades available in this level.

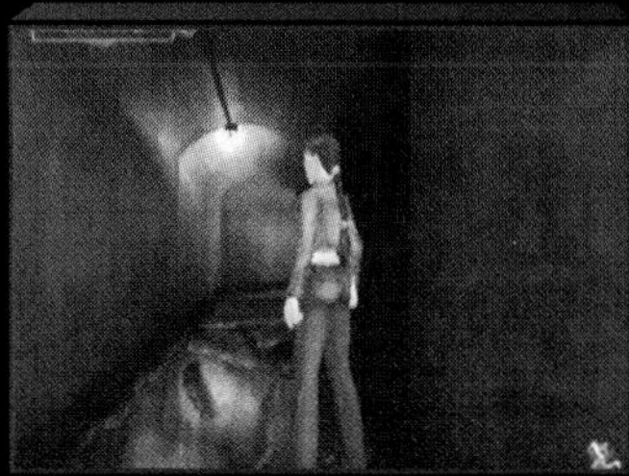

A pile of rubble blocks one of the two ways through this tunnel, so walk forward along the tunnel, past the locked door, until a section of the floor crumbles. Hang from the crumbled edge of the floor and drop to the bottom of the pit.

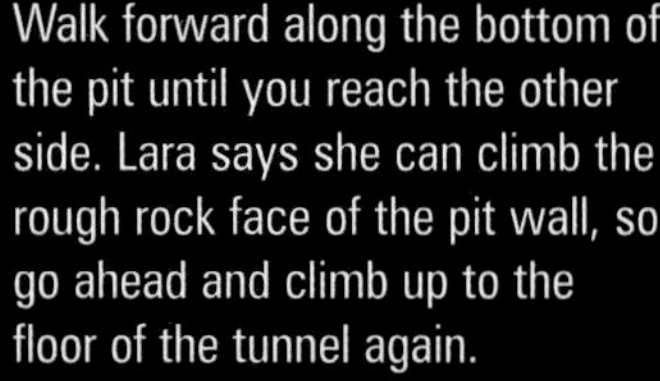

Walk forward along the bottom of the pit until you reach the other side. Lara says she can climb the rough rock face of the pit wall, so go ahead and climb up to the floor of the tunnel again.

There's a second pit immediately following the first. Face the right wall and jump up to grab a pipe that runs along the wall. Shimmy along the pipe to reach the other side of the pit.

TIP **If you fall into the second pit, there's a tunnel at the bottom of it that you can crawl through to reach the bottom of the first pit.**

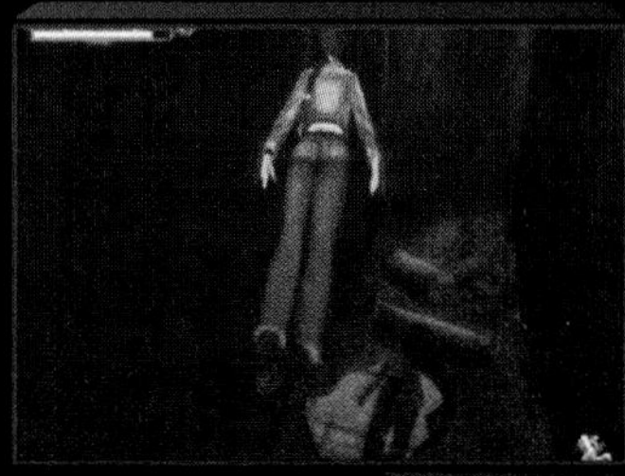

Just after the second pit is yet another pit. This one drops you into a pool of water. Dive under the water (with the Jump button) and swim forward under some rubble to reach the other side of the pit.

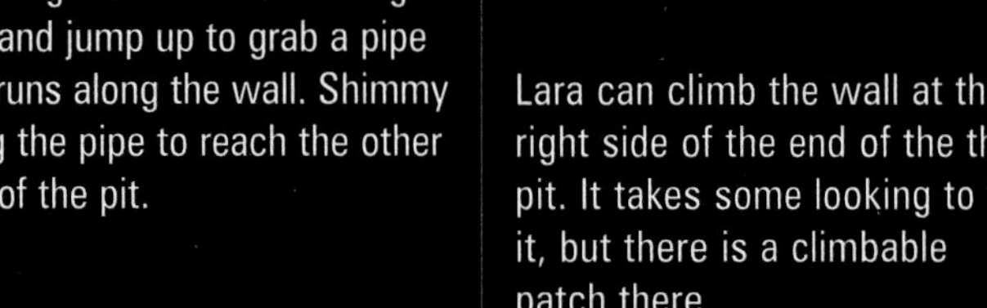

Lara can climb the wall at the right side of the end of the third pit. It takes some looking to find it, but there is a climbable patch there.

Once you climb to the top of the pit, shimmy along the deep crack above you to reach the end of the third pit. Drop onto the solid ground past the third pit to continue.

Continue walking forward until you see a short, metal grate in the wall. Press Action near it to kick it open, then crawl through it.

Follow the doors beyond the grate to return to the beginning of the level. This unlocks the door at the beginning of the level and lets you bypass all three pits. Backtrack to the metal grate you kicked open after the third pit.

Approach the rubble just beyond the metal grate and hold both the Action and Backward button to pull a chunk of the rubble out of the pile. The entire rubble pile shifts, but you still can't get past it.

Use the tunnel beyond the grate you kicked open to return to the beginning of the level. The rubble pile that blocked one end of the tunnel is the same rubble pile you just pulled a chunk out of. You can now move beyond it, so go ahead.

Drop into the pool of water and swim along the surface to the other side. Press Action to pull yourself out of the water and keep going forward.

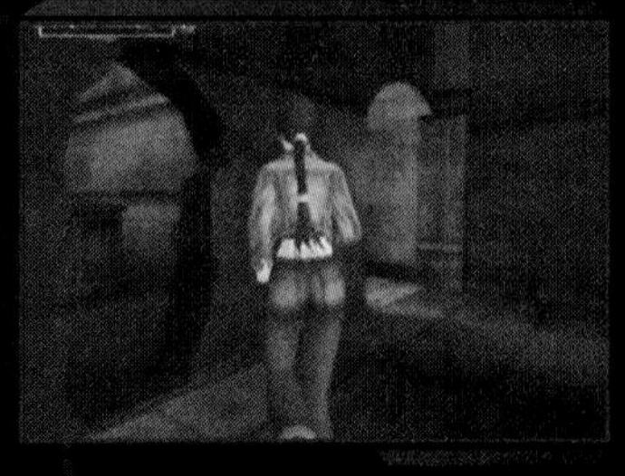

Beyond the pool of water is a small room with a hole in the wall. Go through the hole to reach the next area, an empty cell. There's only one door you can go through in here, so head through it.

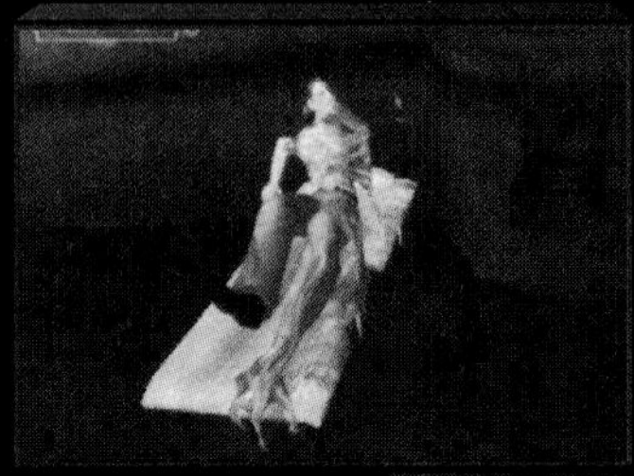

As soon as you enter the next cell, you see a deformed man writhing on a cot. It's hard to tell what sort of injuries he's suffering from; it looks as if half of his body has simply melted.

There's nothing to do in this cell, so exit it through the other open door. There's another empty cell across the hall that you can explore, but there's no reason to do so. Instead, open the door at the end of the hallway.

Bouchard is on the other side of the door. Approach him to engage him in conversation. He tells Lara that what happened to Arnaud, his injured man in the cell, is none of her business. He claims not to recognize the name Eckhardt and professes not to know Werner Von Croy.

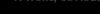

CAUTION Be very careful about how you answer Bouchard. If you offend him, he'll shoot Lara dead. To achieve a positive outcome, give the following answers during the dialogue.

- "Easy, Bouchard. I lost that friend yesterday. Now I'm wanted for his murder."
- "A front, obviously."
- "Passports!"

Bouchard is interested in hearing anything Lara knows about a previous Monstrum killing, but Lara doesn't volunteer any information. After some conversation, Bouchard tells Lara that Von Croy wanted access to recent archaeological finds inside the Louvre, and Bouchard gave him a contact. He offers Lara the same.

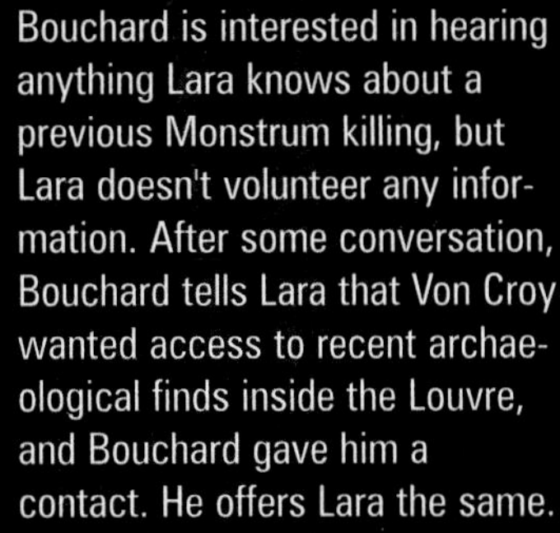

Lara asks for weapons and equipment as well, but Bouchard tells her to go to Rennes' Pawnshop for that. In fact, he tells her that if Lara delivers some Czech passports to Rennes for him, Rennes will know that Lara has Bouchard's confidence.

Bouchard also tells Lara that his man Arnaud was the only survivor out of four attacks so far, and he has no idea who or what is doing the attacking. He thinks it might be the Paris Monstrum, but he's still looking into it. As a result, he can't spare any manpower or firepower for Lara's errand.

After speaking with Bouchard, you must open the exit from his hideout. Pull the lever in Bouchard's office to open a cell door in the hall.

Enter the cell that just opened and pull the moveable crate so it's right next to the doorway. You should be able to climb onto the crate, jump, and grab the edge of a loft above the door.

Pull yourself up to the loft and pull the lever there to open a door in Bouchard's office. Go through this door to exit Bouchard's Hideout and return to St. Aicard's Church.

Rennes' Pawnshop

Leave St. Aicard's Church and head for Rennes' Pawnshop. To get there, go down the street past the entrance to the park, toward Janice. Round the corner near Janice and run all the way down the street until you reach the red-and-orange-striped barricade. Rennes' Pawnshop is to your right.

As Lara enters the pawnshop, a mysterious man wearing dark clothes and sunglasses brushes past her roughly on his way out the door. As Lara approaches the counter, she sees that the pawnshop has been torn apart, and there's no sign of Rennes. She lays Bouchard's passports on the counter.

NOTE **The mysterious man is Eckhardt, leader of the Cabal, but Lara doesn't recognize him yet.**

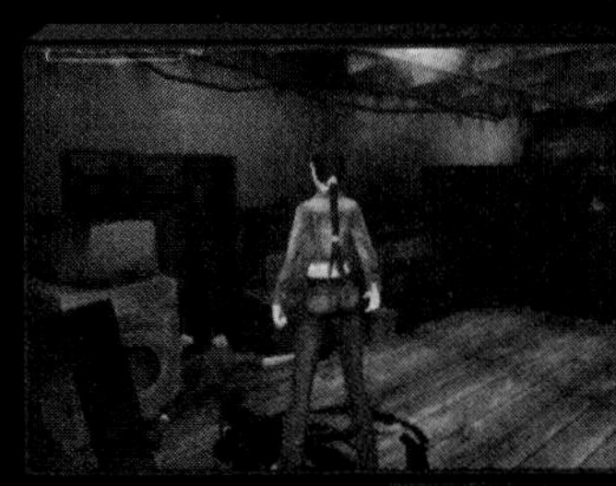

Go into the back room behind the counter to see Rennes' lifeless form in a heap on the floor. The letter "M" is written in blood in front of the body—the mark of the Monstrum. There's nothing you can do for Rennes, but be sure to pick up Rennes' Wallet and examine it in your inventory screen to find a Scrap of Paper inside with the numbers "14529" written on it.

Explore the rest of the back room to find a bundle of timed explosives. There's a wooden trapdoor in the floor that looks like a way out, but it's sealed shut. There's also a locked door in the far wall with a numeric keypad next to it.

Enter the code from the Scrap of Paper (1-4-5-2-9) into the numeric keypad to open the adjacent door. Inside is a virtual treasure trove of items and information. Pick up all of the following items: Dart SS, Dart SS Ammo, Map of Sewers Around Louvre, Explosives, K2 Impactor, K2 Impactor Battery, and the Map of Archaeological Dig.

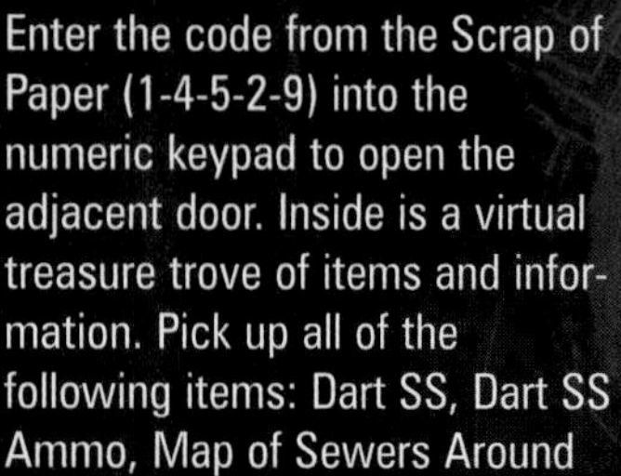

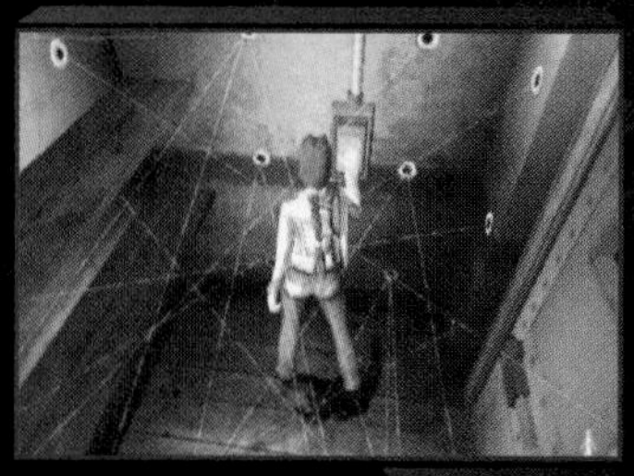

Once you've grabbed everything from the storeroom, an array of security beams activates, locking the door behind you. The camera shows the timer on the explosives is counting down. Don't panic; simply press the large, yellow button in the storeroom to open the door, then exit the storeroom.

Walk to the trapdoor and press Action to open it. Drop into the trapdoor and run down the corridor and into the sewers beyond.

There's only one path you can take through the sewers, and as soon as you run far enough, the game switches into a cutscene.

The explosion from Rennes' Pawnshop propels Lara out of the sewer like a bullet from a gun as the mysterious motorcyclist she saw earlier looks on. Fortunately, Lara was far enough from the blast that she's not injured.

The scene then changes to a meeting of the enigmatic Cabal. Eckhardt, the man that Lara saw in Rennes' Pawnshop, addresses the group on the matter of a series of paintings called the "Obscura Paintings." They found three of them, and Werner Von Croy found the fourth. The fifth is somewhere in Prague.

A man by the name of Gunderson is dispatched to Prague by Eckhardt. Eckhardt places his hand on Gunderson's shoulder, and a strange purple light emanates from it.

Eckhardt tells the Cabal members that once they have the final Obscura Painting, they can try to awaken "the Sleeper." He hopes that they will have more success doing so than they did during a previous attempt.

Louvre Storm Drains

Sliding down to the filthy underbelly of a slowly-decaying Parisian effluent overflow, Miss Croft must now make haste in a watery wade toward the boiler room underneath the Louvre gallery. Once she's familiarized herself with the sights of this unpleasant locale, it's off to locate six valves in order to shut off the water gushing into a central conduit. A propeller fan needs calming and moving to power Lara up to succeed in this task. Once up and down two conduit chambers, and into the boiler room, she must detonate explosives, then dive into the safety of water to avoid being fried to death. After a nimble skedaddle across the burning gantry planks, Lara steps through the hole she created, and finally infiltrates the Louvre.

ENTITIES ENCOUNTERED
- Rats

CRITICAL ITEMS TO LOCATE
- Explosives (carried on you)

AVAILABLE UPGRADES
- **Upgrade Turn Valve: Upper Body Level 5**
  Halting the rotation of a propeller fan, Lara builds her body into a valve-turning machine.

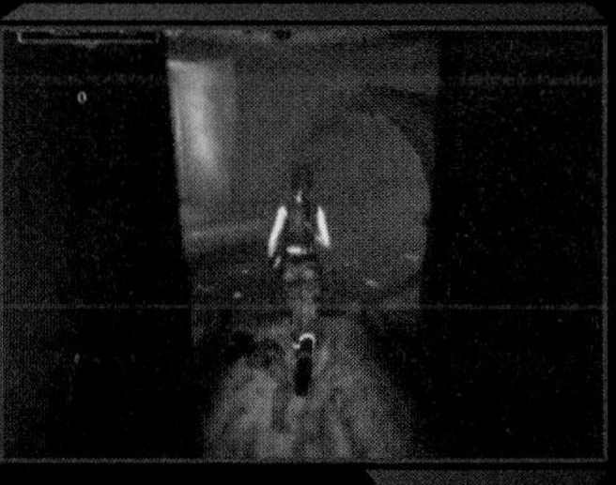

Slide down the overflow pipe at the start of this sewer access and begin your murky investigation. Run to the collecting sewage in the semicircular pool and you see two exits. There is a corridor to the left and a sewer tunnel to the right.

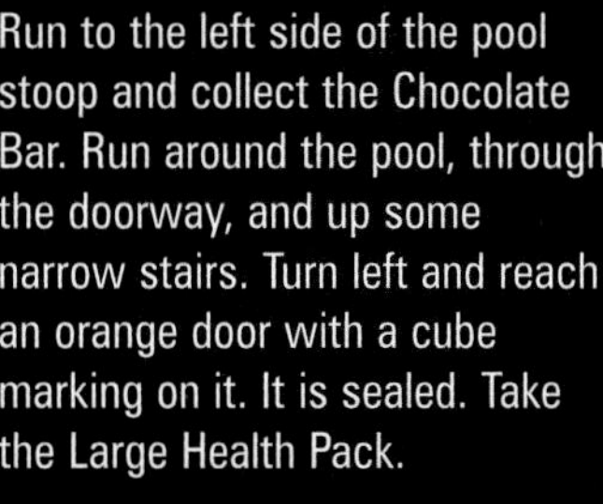

Run to the left side of the pool stoop and collect the Chocolate Bar. Run around the pool, through the doorway, and up some narrow stairs. Turn left and reach an orange door with a cube marking on it. It is sealed. Take the Large Health Pack.

Return to the sewage pool and drop right in. Ignore the bobbing "matter," run into the tunnel, and go over the beam at ankle height. You can hear the sounds of rushing sewage ahead. But first, check out the passage to your left.

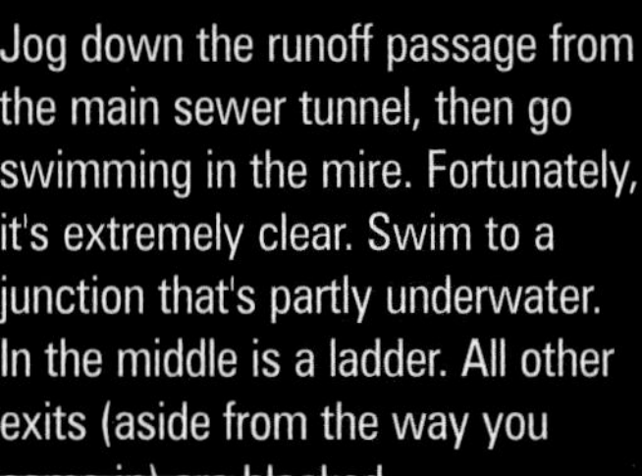

Jog down the runoff passage from the main sewer tunnel, then go swimming in the mire. Fortunately, it's extremely clear. Swim to a junction that's partly underwater. In the middle is a ladder. All other exits (aside from the way you came in) are blocked.

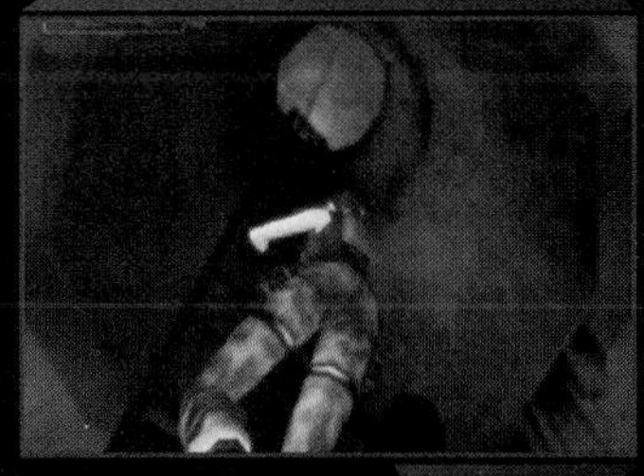

Climb the ladder after diving beneath it to collect a Large Health Pack. Clamber up this rusting ladder to emerge inside a steam valve room. The valve ahead is too tight for Lara to budge.

Run past the valve and down a metal corridor leading to another main sewer tunnel. On the way, stoop to pick up the Vector-R35 Clip.

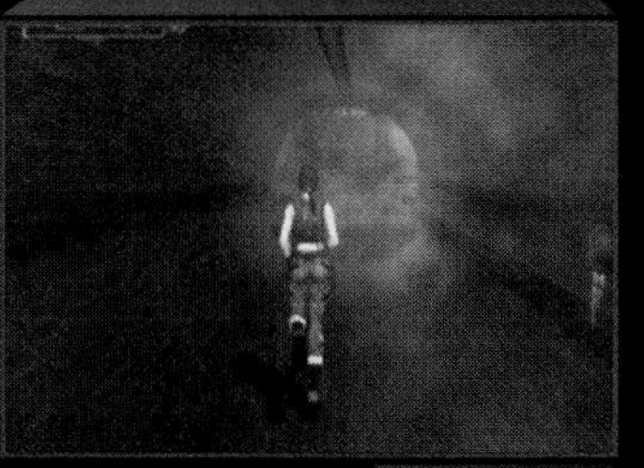

From either exit, the only way is down the sewer tunnel toward the cascade of water and sewage raining from above. To reach the boiler for the Louvre, you must stop that waterfall. Inspect this middle section.

There are three sewage tunnels feeding this central chamber. There's the one that leads back to the level entrance (which you cannot climb). There's also the one that leads to a metal door and passage to the valve (where you just found the ammo).

TIP Although you can step on the funnel-like central ground of this chamber, don't jump into the waterfall—you'll plummet to a horrible demise. Come back here later in your adventure.

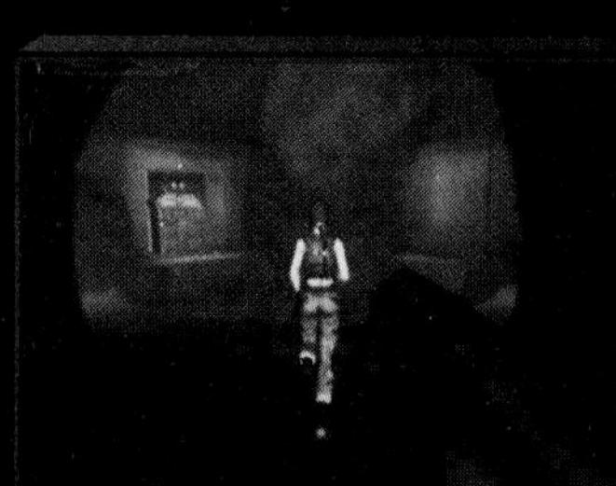

There's also a third tunnel to explore. Head past the large pipe on the left and stop at an opening to your right. Up a small and rusting ladder is a rotating fan. You must stop it to take the item twinkling behind it.

At the end of the tunnel, also on your right, is a steep sewage chute, and there's no way you can climb up it. You'll come here a little later. Head into the main circular sewage chamber and halt that propeller.

There are two areas of interest in this circular chamber. The first is the valve pressure unit, which shows how many valves there are (six), and how many are sealed (none). Your job is to stop the flow of water so you can escape through the upper sewer tunnel where the water is currently falling from.

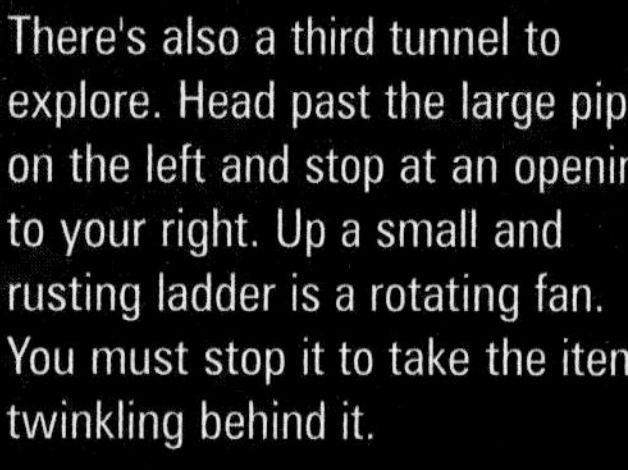

The other area of interest is the narrow platform surrounding the central runoff area. There's a drainpipe that Miss Croft reckons she can scale. Climb up to the dilapidated mesh platform (either hang on it and pull up, or keep climbing, then stand on it).

Run around the gantry platform to the large green lever at the other side. Pull it. This stops the propeller fan downstairs. Retrace your steps to the fan. Ignore the crane pulley that juts from the gantry; you'll come back here in a moment.

Climb the shabby ladder, then look at the propeller and pull down hard on one of the fins. Lara exclaims that she's strong enough to turn the valves. She should be; she just increased her physique (Upgrade Turn Valve: Upper Body Level 5).

Turn the propeller once more, then use the Duck button and crawl between the gaps in the fins. Once inside the metallic tunnel, stoop to claim the V-Packer Spread Cartridges, then run to the end and drop down next to the barrel.

You must now locate all six valves in order to stem the flow of the waterfall. Turn the valve on the pipe in this steam room. This releases pressure in pipe #3. Then enter the small corner alcove with the blocked metal door to claim a batch of Dart SS Tranq Darts.

Head to the barrel, under the propeller, vault over the railing atop the ladder, and go back to the main sewer area. Before you climb that drainpipe again, move past the pressure gauge and enter the sewer to the right of it. Move to the first valve you saw in this level.

This valve is located through the metal door, or all the way back to the flooded area and up the ladder. When you reach here, turn the valve and release pressure to pipe #5. Two of the six lights on the pressure gauge unit are green. Time for the other four.

Run to the central waterfall area and climb that drainpipe. When you reach the gantry plank where you ran to switch off the propeller fan, press the Walk button and carefully move across the yellow and black warning stripes of the gantry crane.

You walk through the falling water without a problem. Stay at a manageable speed and don't fall, and you'll reach the opposite side, where the third valve is located. Turning it releases pressure to pipe #6 and floods the outflow tunnels below the waterfall. You can now enter the tunnels.

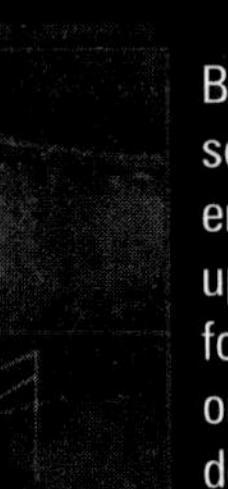

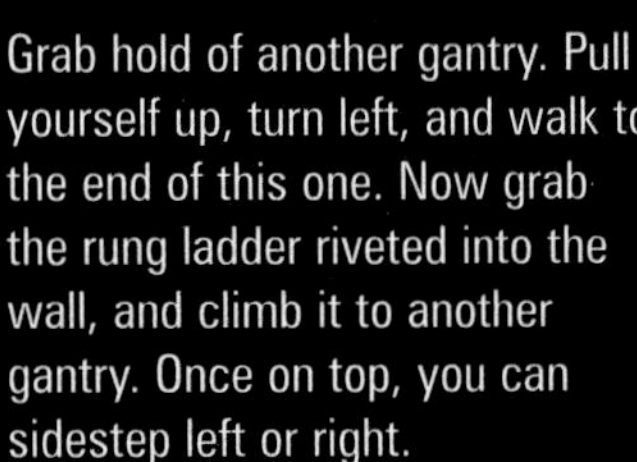

Before you drop down, there's some climbing to do. Walk to the end of this new gantry and pick up the Desert Ranger Clip at the foot of the barrel. Now climb onto the barrel, whip around 180 degrees, and jump up.

Grab hold of another gantry. Pull yourself up, turn left, and walk to the end of this one. Now grab the rung ladder riveted into the wall, and climb it to another gantry. Once on top, you can sidestep left or right.

You cannot reach the very top gantry, as there's a rung missing on the ladder you just moved from. Instead, you can run to the right until fallen mesh floor blocks your path, or (if you sidestepped left) you can hold the Walk button and move onto another gantry crane and walk to the middle.

At either of these two points you can look up and spot a horizontal pipe spanning the diameter of this chamber. Jump and grab it, then shimmy across to your fourth valve. Turn it and pressure is released to pipe #1. Only two more to go.

There's little else to accomplish in this sewage chamber, except to investigate the doorway on the opposite side of the crane girder. Shimmy back to the crane, drop on it, and run through the doorway. Turn left to see a locked door. On the floor is a M-V9 Clip.

You'll enter this corridor later. For now, return to the rung ladder and descend. Run to the edge of the gantry below and drop onto the barrel. Run across the lower crane girder, across the gantry, and shimmy down the drainpipe (or drop from this height).

NOTE **Despite the outflow tunnels being flooded, don't attempt a swan dive from the top of this shaft, or leap past the waterfall when you're at its same level. This simply ends in Lara's demise.**

Once at the base of the waterfall, you see the sewer flood. Quickly swim and dive beneath the waterfall. Follow the route of the tunnel—and don't delay, or you'll drown. Swim downwards.

As the overflow tunnel joins a horizontal tunnel, swim along it, away from a barred area. Continue until you reach another barred area on your left. Turn and swim to the right. Ahead is another barred area. As you reach it, point Lara upwards.

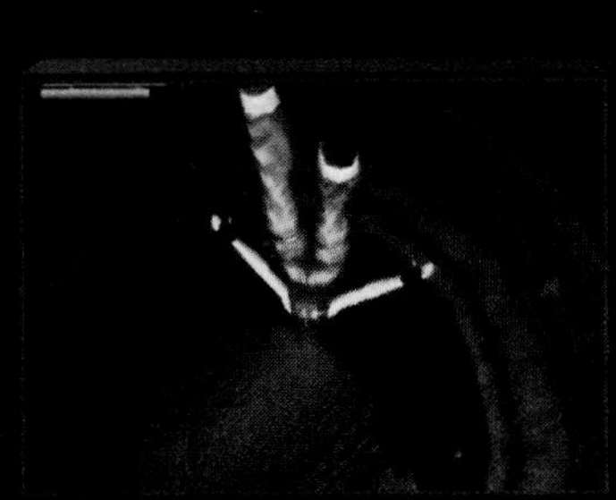

Swim upwards immediately, passing a green area with another barred tunnel. You emerge, spluttering for air, inside a half-filled central chamber. Swim to the fallen gantry platform that hangs into the water.

Clamber up this gantry, pulling yourself onto the mangled remains, and walk onto the section still riveted to the wall. Run around the ledge until you spot a gap in the railings. There's a pipe above your head that you can leap up and grab.

You might want to try something a little more daring. If so, move to the far end of the gantry and check the second gap in the railings. Turn left and make a jump, landing on the yellow and black crane girder. Not up to it? Then shimmy along the pipe and drop onto the girder.

Once on the girder, walk to the left side to find yourself at another valve. This one releases the pressure from pipe #4. One more to go. Now ignore the rung ladder to your right (it leads nowhere), and move to the middle of the chamber.

Leap up from the crane girder and grab the pipe. Now shimmy to another piece of mangled gantry. Climb onto it and ascend to the metal ledge above. Walk onto the ledge, then move around the upper gantry perimeter.

You pass a large sewer tunnel entrance. Move to the edge of the orange gantry next to the sewer tunnel entrance, stop, and look ahead.

There's a gap, and it must be jumped (not hopped). On the other side is a small section of orange gantry leading to an alcove, where the sixth and final valve is located. Turn this so that the pressure is off on all six pipes, and the waterfall stops completely.

There are two ways to retrace your steps to the first tubelike chamber. One involves a scary (but straightforward) jump, while the other has you sliding and backtracking. We'll cover the frightening leap first.

Boiler Room Roaming Method #1

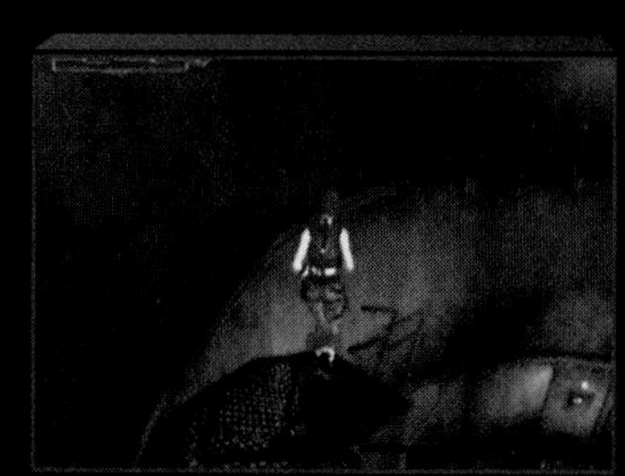

From the gantry you're standing on, turn and leap back to the sewer entrance. Run past it, staying on the length of gantry. Continue running as the gantry begins to sag. Just before the gantry falls away (the area you climbed up on), jump, then press Action.

You reach and grab the edge of a new piece of gantry leading to a familiar door with a broken window pane. Open this door (it couldn't be accessed from the other side), run down the small, metal corridor, and turn right. Remember the M-V9 Clip if you didn't pick it up earlier.

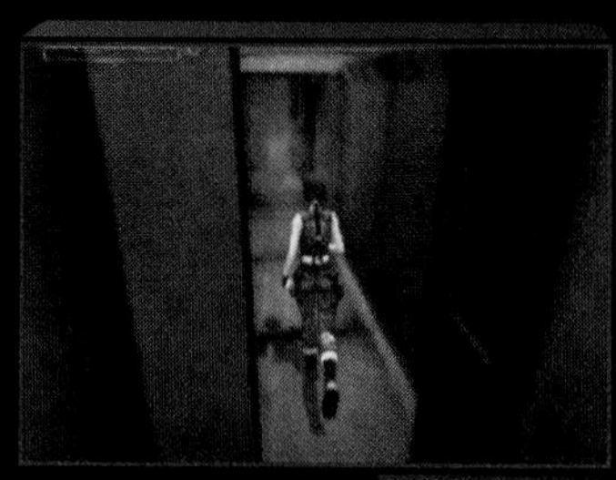

You're back at, and to the right of, the first main tubelike chamber. All that remains is for you to move across the upper crane girder, then jump onto the moss-lined sewer tunnel that the water was flowing from. You made it. Now to the boiler room.

Boiler Room Roaming Method #2

The second method for entering the boiler room is less daring, and more lengthy. From the gantry you're on, turn and leap back to the sewer entrance. Enter this sewer tunnel, duck, and crawl under the railings. Run to the opening on your left.

Slide down the chute, and back down to the sewer tunnel with the propeller fan. Move past the fan to the base of the main chamber, run past the all-green pressure unit, and climb the drainpipe. Follow the instructions to reach the top of this chamber, then leap onto the moss-lined sewer tunnel that the water was flowing from. You made it. Now to the boiler room.

Climb on the large sewer pipe and open the door. You step into a large overflow pool chamber with the boiler. Be wary of that smell of oil.

Enter the chamber by hanging from the pipe and dropping onto a gantry, or dive off the pipe and into the water. There's oil on the surface of this water, but it doesn't damage you—yet.

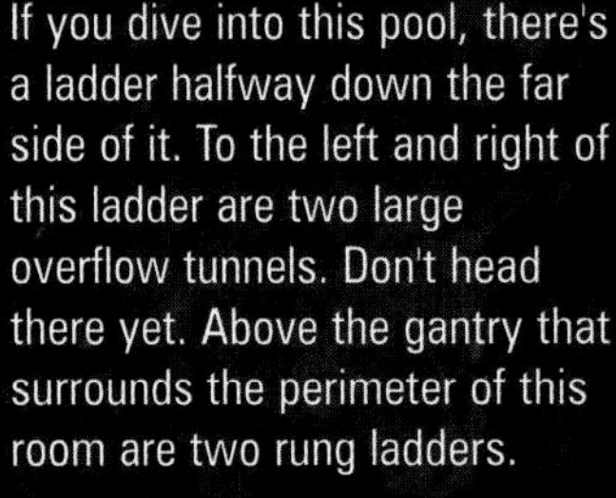

If you dive into this pool, there's a ladder halfway down the far side of it. To the left and right of this ladder are two large overflow tunnels. Don't head there yet. Above the gantry that surrounds the perimeter of this room are two rung ladders.

Each ladder leads to an upper gantry and a valve, but these aren't in use. Drop onto the near gantry (below where you entered this chamber) and run to the far end of it, to the boiler. The walkway is collapsing, but it will take your weight. Grab the V-Packer Spread Cartridges at the far end.

TIP There's going to be an imminent firestorm with a 50 percent chance of frying Lara. Time to save your game.

As you round the corner, Lara mentions that this looks like the place to insert the explosives. Consult the map, then turn and place the explosives on the boiler and on two oil drums. The timer is set for a five-second fuse. Time to dive.

As soon as Lara places the explosives, back flip (press Jump and back on the Control Stick) over the railing and into the water. Or jump in the pool as best you can.

You will die if you're not underwater when the boiler goes up. If you surface, or step in any fire during this time, you'll be dead in three seconds. Avoid the flames.

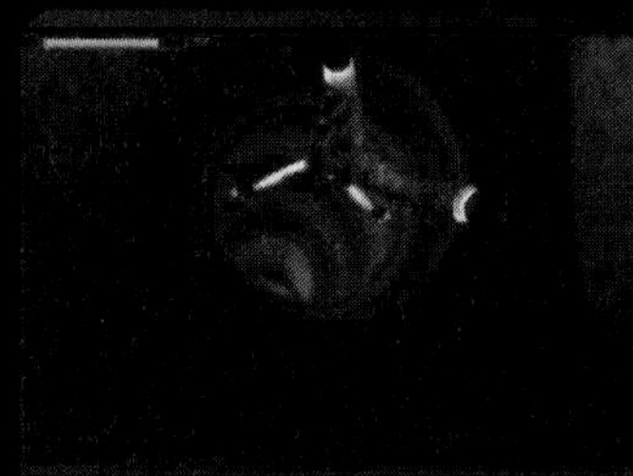

The way out of this predicament is via the underwater tunnel pipes. Swim into the right tunnel, then forward at the first junction. Turn left at the second junction, continue forward, and ignore all junctions until you emerge from the water.

Wade out of the water and make a left, following the two pipes up the large tunnel.

At the next junction, your way is blocked to the right, so turn left to find yourself overlooking the inferno below. Great work. The boiler is no more, and the hole it created leads right under the Louvre. Walk to the edge, then hang off and fall onto the stone ledge.

There is only one safe path to the hole in the wall. Turn and head left, up the ladder, toward the upper stone ledge with the railings on it. Run to the corner, and instead of heading down the other ladder, leap over it and land on the gantry.

TIP If you descend on the ladder instead, an area of fire will burn you. As soon as this happens, make a back flip immediately away from it, landing on the gantry. Watch that gap between the collapsing gantry and railing; it's been specifically designed for you to fall through.

Now on the gantry where you started your chamber exploration, run down the collapsing section, leap over a patch of burning oil on the gantry, round the corner, and move directly through the hole in the wall. Don't stand on the fire.

You are now underneath Paris's most famous art gallery. The gigantic stone buttresses are cordoned off, so turn left at the hole, and run around the stonework in the blue gloom until you reach the double doors on your left. You've made it into the Louvre.

Louvre Galleries

Ah, the Louvre—not only the repository of some of the Western world's greatest cultural treasures, but also a grueling test of skills for tomb-raiding adventuresses. Lara doesn't have a chance to study the works of the great masters—she's too busy avoiding the laser trip wires guarding them. With more than a dozen guards on patrol and the finest security devices in Europe, the Louvre Galleries demand every ounce of stealth and surefootedness Lara possesses, and then some. Her mission is to find Mlle. Carvier's Security Pass to access the subterranean archaeological dig under the museum, and to probe the mysterious circumstances of Werner Von Croy's untimely demise.

ENTITIES ENCOUNTERED

- Museum Guards (x11)
- Gendarmes (x2)

CRITICAL ITEMS TO LOCATE

- Low-Level Security Pass
- Louvre Guard's Key
- Crowbar
- Carvier's Security Pass

AVAILABLE UPGRADES

- **Upgrade Pull/Push: Upper Body Level 4**
  Lara pumps up her arm strength by pushing a small display case near the Mona Lisa.
- **Upgrade Shoulder Barge: Upper Body Level 6**
  After shimmying along a high wire, Lara's upper body is stronger than ever.

After her adventures in the Louvre Storm Drains, Lara appears at the Louvre entrance. From your starting position, switch into Stealth mode and climb the stairs until you see the red light of a security camera above you.

There are two museum guards at the top of this staircase. If you run through the security camera's field of vision, the guards come down the stairs and attack you with K2 Impactor stun guns. If you move quickly and carefully, you can avoid the camera's gaze. Once past the camera, sneak up on the guards and take them out from behind in Stealth mode. You can also intentionally walk through the camera's red light to lure the guards to your position, and ambush them from there.

NOTE **There's a door underneath the camera that Lara can't open because she doesn't have the necessary upper-body strength. We'll remind you to come back when you can get in.**

Double doors to the first gallery are at the top of the stairs past the two guards. Head inside—there are no guards on the other side.

The first gallery tests your jumping and shimmying abilities. Laser trip wires line the entire gallery. If you do cross the trip wires, steel grates drop over the doors and a Gendarme shows up to ruin your day.

TIP **With active laser trip wires in this gallery, always use walk-only mode. It's impossible to achieve the precision required to navigate the obstacles in this room if you run.**

Climb onto the first display case and turn toward the large, stone slab mounted on the wall. Jump toward it and press the Action button to grab it.

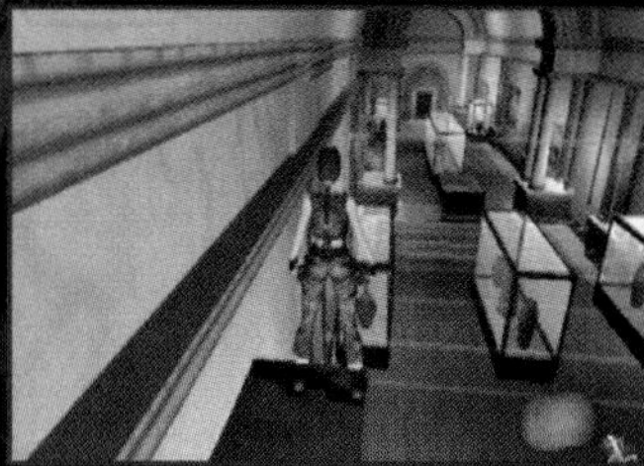

Pull up and grab the Large Health Pack, then turn right so you're facing the end of the gallery. Jump from the top of the stone slab to the top of the display case in front of you. This takes you over the first set of laser trip wires.

TIP As soon as you land safely on the display case, save your game.

The next set of trip wires moves up and down. To pass them, face the wall, jump, and grab the ledge above the display case. Shimmy past the trip wires when they're at their lowest point. Time your moves carefully so your swinging feet don't trigger the trip wire as it moves past you. Move quickly, as Lara's grip won't last forever.

Once you pass the second moving laser trip wire, continue shimmying around the pillars to your right. Drop to the floor once you're past the horizontal trip wires on the ground.

TIP If you've made it this far without triggering any trip wires, pat yourself on the back and save the game.

▶ BUSTED!

Whoops! You break one of the laser trip wires, the steel grates drop in front of the doors, and the alarms go off. What do you do now?

The first thing to do is take out the Gendarme who rushes through the door. Use the display cases as cover; he draws his pistol and isn't shy about using it.

Next, look to the left of the doorway (as you face it) to find a big, square button. Approach it and press Action to raise the steel grates and reactivate the laser trip wires. Remember, you must make it to the other end of the room with all of the trip wires intact if you want to proceed through the Louvre. Fortunately, if you activate the trip wires again, the grates drop, but no trigger-happy Gendarmes show up.

Climb onto the display case after the second moving trip wire and face the end of the gallery. Several horizontal laser trip wires run across the room in front of you, but the top two flicker on and off. Make a carefully timed jump to the display case on the other side of the flickering trip wires as they turn off.

TIP Made it past these trip wires? Nice work. Now save your game.

There's one last set of trip wires to go, and it's one of the easiest sets in the gallery. Walk to the side of the display case and press Action to hang off the end. Shimmy to the end of the case, past the laser trip wires.

To get past the last set of laser trip wires, jump and grab on to the display case on the right side of the room and pull yourself on top of it.

Face the wall, jump to grab the ledge above the display case, and shimmy past the last of the laser trip wires. Drop to the ground, and go through the double doors to the next gallery.

TIP Good job making it past the trip wires. Now you know what to do—save your game.

When you enter the second gallery, you get a panoramic view, including the museum guard in the middle of it. There are laser trip wires in this gallery as well, but there's no way to pass them without triggering them.

Walk in front of the museum guard to lure him to you. If you have a long-range weapon, pick him off before he attacks you with his K2 Impactor. Grab the Low-Level Security Pass the guard drops once you take him out.

Now walk through one of the laser trip wires to drop a metal grate over the door and attract a Gendarme. Quickly take out the Gendarme.

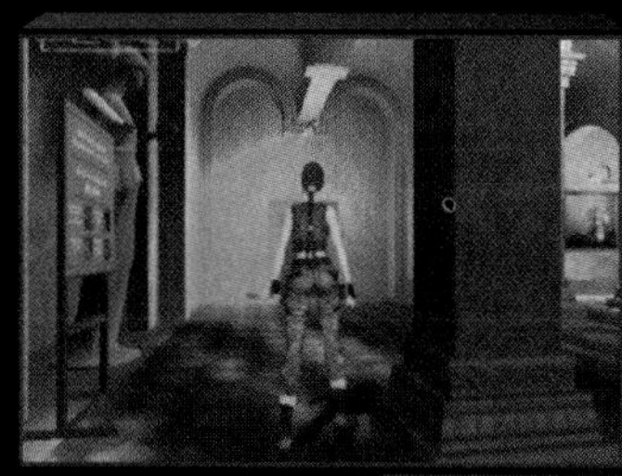

There's a Large Health Pack in one corner of the gallery. It's guarded by a security camera, so take out the guard in the Mona Lisa gallery (see following) before grabbing it. If you walk through the camera's field of vision, the museum guard from the Mona Lisa gallery pursues you. You lose your chance to take him out from behind in Stealth mode.

TIP You can also move quickly and carefully past the camera's field of vision to avoid detection and grab the Large Health Pack.

Across the gallery from the Large Health Pack is a locked door with a card reader. The Low-Level Security Card doesn't open it, but Lara recalls that Von Croy's Notebook mentioned that Mlle. Carvier had a security pass in her office. You need that pass to proceed.

Go through the only unlocked door in the second gallery to reach the Mona Lisa gallery. It's the door next to the one monitored by the security camera.

There's a security camera on the other side of the door to the Mona Lisa gallery. Wait in the doorway until its passes you by, then run along the side of the room to enter the main part of the gallery. As soon as you see the vertical laser trip wires around the Mona Lisa, switch into Stealth mode; there's a museum guard inside the main part of the gallery.

Sneak up and take down the guard from behind while in Stealth mode. You can also punch, kick, or shoot him, but why waste the time, ammo, or health?

Approach the small, glass display case in the corner of the gallery and pull it out of the corner. This powers up Lara's leg strength and reveals a switch that temporarily disarms the laser trip wires around the Mona Lisa.

Pull or push the large display case in front of the Mona Lisa. Get as close to the painting as it will go, but do not cross the laser trip wires. If you do, a choking gas spews from the floor and kills Lara instantly.

Once you've moved the display case, hit the switch to disarm the laser trip wires, climb onto the display case, leap from the case to the ledge above the Mona Lisa, and crawl through the open maintenance tunnel on that ledge. It's very tricky, and it may take you more than one try to do it.

TIP Save your game once you've have everything in position. If you fail to do everything correctly, Lara dies.

NOTE **As long as you're on the ledge above the Mona Lisa, you're safe from the gas when the trip wires turn back on.**

There's only one way to proceed through the maintenance tunnels above the Mona Lisa. Climb the ladder at the end of the tunnels to reach the Louvre rooftops.

There's a grate at the top of the ladder leading up from the maintenance tunnels, and a museum guard patrols the rooftops on the other side of the grate. Watch the museum guard until he's no longer visible from the grate, then press Action to knock out the grate.

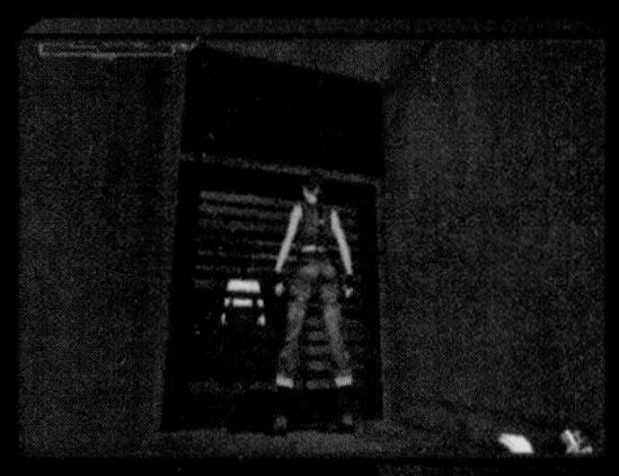

If you wait long enough, the museum guard won't hear you knock out the grate. Switch into Stealth mode and stalk him until he stops, then take him out from behind.

Climb on the air-conditioning unit near the L-shaped air duct in the corner of the upper part of the Louvre rooftop. From there, climb onto the L-shaped duct, face the wall, and jump to grab an overhead ledge.

Pull yourself onto the ledge, turn right, and walk along the ledge (in walk-only mode) until you reach a small obstruction. Press Action to hang from the ledge, shimmy past the obstacle, and pull yourself back up. You must do this again in a few feet, and when you pull yourself back up after the second obstacle, you see a steel cable running overhead.

Jump to grab the steel cable, and shimmy to the end of it. When you reach the end of the cable, Lara's upper-body strength increases.

From the end of the cable, carefully walk along the narrow ledge until you reach a gap in the ledge. You can climb down the pipe that runs through the center of the gap, or you can cross the gap by hanging from the ledge and shimmying to the other side. Climb down the pipe first.

Once you get halfway down the pipe, there's an open window that you can climb through. Wait for the guard on the other side of the window to pass by, then sneak in and take him out from behind in Stealth mode. Pick up the Louvre Guard's Key that he leaves behind.

NOTE **It is not necessary to grab the Louvre Guard's Key (or take out the guard) if you picked up the Crowbar from the Parisian Back Streets and still have it in your inventory.**

None of the doors near the museum guard can be opened, so climb back out the window and continue down the pipe until you reach the lower level of the Louvre rooftop. Unlock the door to the wire-mesh fence.

With the upper-body strength upgrade, Lara can shoulder open the utility doors on each end of the lower level of the Louvre rooftop. Behind one of the doors, are some health bandages; there is nothing behind the other door.

Once you've grabbed the loot from behind the utility doors, return to the pipe, and climb it until you reach the top ledge. Pull yourself up to the ledge to the right of the pipe and walk carefully along it. When you get to the end of the ledge, hang from it, shimmy around the corner, and pull yourself up to the adjacent ledge through the hole in the fence.

Walk along the length of this ledge until you come to a ladder leading down from a wire-mesh storage area. Climb down the ladder to reach the lower level of the Louvre rooftop.

NOTE **If you still have the Crowbar from the Parisian Back Streets level, you don't have to descend the ladder to get a Crowbar from the maintenance room.**

There is a blue utility door to the right of the ladder (as you face the ladder). The Louvre Guard's Key unlocks the door, and there's a Crowbar inside.

NOTE **You can also unlock the door in the wire-mesh fence that runs along this side of the lower level of the rooftop, but it's not necessary to do so.**

After grabbing the Crowbar, climb up the ladder and press Action near the door to the wire-mesh storage area to pop the lock with the Crowbar and open the door.

Climb the metal device on the other side of the door, and use it to enter the maintenance tunnel above it. Climb down the ladder to reach a storeroom in the Louvre offices.

Watch the window for the guard in the hallway. Wait for the guard to pass, then open the door, stalk the guard in Stealth mode, and take him out from behind.

At one end of the hallway is a locked door with a key card reader. At the other end is the locked door to Mlle. Carvier's office; there's a numeric keypad next to the door.

To find the code that unlocks Mlle. Carvier's office, open the closest door to that office and sneak into the security office beyond it. Creep through the circular glass doors, and take out the museum guard near the security monitors.

There are four security monitors you can view in here. The leftmost one views Mlle. Carvier's office. Use the camera to zoom in on a piece of paper stuck to her monitor. There's a five-digit number written on the paper: 14639.

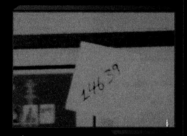

Return to the door to Mlle. Carvier's office and enter 1-4-6-3-9 at the numeric keypad to unlock the door. Press Action at several places in the office to get information on the Obscura Paintings and Pieter Van Eckhardt (see sidebar). Open the cabinet to the right of the desk to get Carvier's Security Pass.

MLLE. CARVIER'S RESEARCH

It seems that Mlle. Carvier was researching the same thing that Werner Von Croy was looking into before he died. By looking at the parchment on the artist's desk, you find that each of the Obscura Paintings contains a secret engraving of an encrypted map that leads to another painting's location.

Take a gander at the painting above the fireplace to read about a fellow named Pieter Van Eckhardt who was the original keeper of the Obscura Paintings, each of which has a metallic symbol of power hidden in it. The five paintings hide something called the Sanglyph ("blood sign"). They were seized by the Lux Veritatis in the 1300's or 1400's and painted over with religious imagery. Could the Eckhardt mentioned be an ancestor of the Eckhardt that Von Croy mentioned? Or...could they somehow be the same person?!

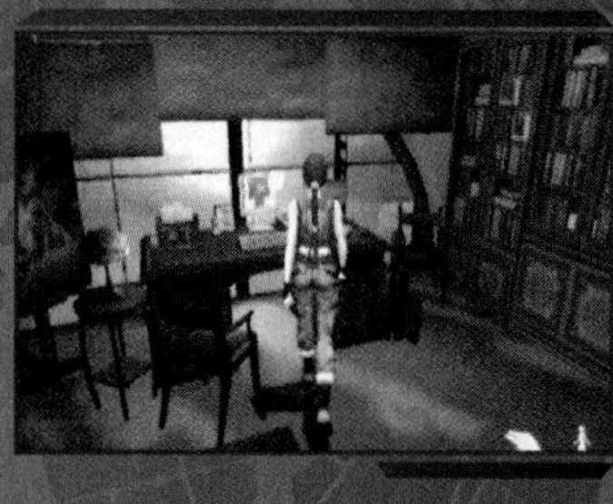

Inspect Mlle. Carvier's computer to find out some information about a fellow named Brother Obscura, who was ordered to paint over the original Obscura images. The paintings were hidden, but Brother Obscura made secret sketches of the paintings, known as the Obscura Engravings, and hid them as well.

Leave Mlle. Carvier's office and walk down the hall. There's a door to an X-ray room near the door to the security office, but there's nothing you can do here right now.

NOTE **Remember this room—you must come back here when you return to the Louvre after visiting the Tomb of Ancients.**

Carvier's Security Pass unlocks the door at the end of the hall near the storeroom (press Action near the door's card reader). Proceed through it to the archaeological dig.

Descend the spiraling stairs, and walk through the open door at the end of the hallway. There are two doors in the room beyond the door. Go through the only one that opens.

There's a lone museum guard in the gallery. If you're in Stealth mode, sneak up on him and take him out.

Lara can unlock the door at the other end of the gallery by using Carvier's Security Pass. The door leads to the second gallery you came through, near the beginning of the level.

Remember that room way back at the beginning of the level that you couldn't open because Lara didn't have enough upper-body strength? Well, thanks to the strength upgrades you got in this level, you can now break it down. Backtrack through the second gallery and use Carvier's Security Pass on the door with the metal grate.

This raises the gate and gives you access to the first gallery, which no longer has any laser trip wires in it. Go through the first gallery and out the door at the end. Head down the hall and stairway until you come to the locked door. Press Action to bust it open. You don't have to worry about the security camera, as you've taken out every guard in the museum by now.

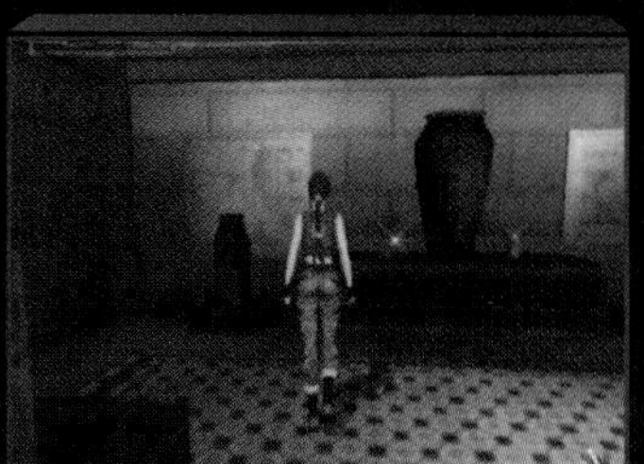

At the far end of this room, you find some Health Bandages and a Small Health Pack.

Use Carvier's Security Pass on the locked door that you couldn't open previously. It has a sign next to it that advertises an archaeological dig site.

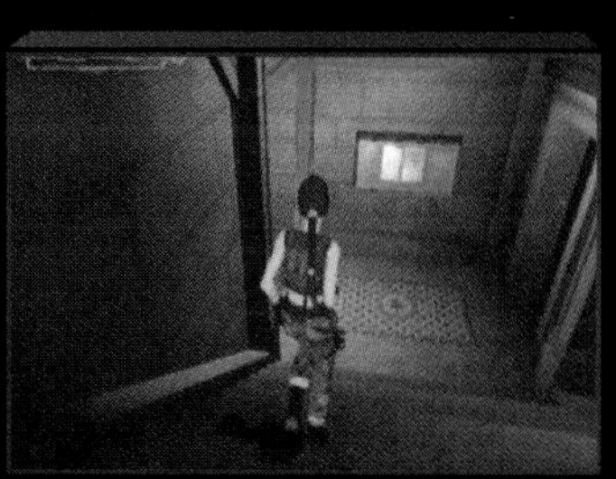

Head down the stairs. There's a small gallery, but there's nothing in there except a museum guard. There's no need to fight him.

Go through the doors at the bottom of the stairs to reach the entrance to the archaeological dig site. Open the metal double doors to begin the next chapter of Lara's adventure.

The Archaeological Dig

The location of anomalous findings underneath the Louvre has been turned into a full-fledged archaeological excavation. Work has progressed steadily, and a deep fissure has been painstakingly cleared of dirt and debris. With the dig currently closed, and with minimal security, you can explore the surface for clues. You're looking for two Ancient Symbol Tracings, after which you should descend into the main pit to hunt for clues on opening the archaic locking mechanism. There are four symbols to locate and line up on the ancient lock itself. Once you achieve this, the past civilization reveals its entrance, and you are free to investigate the tomb.

ENTITIES ENCOUNTERED
- Museum Guard
- Gendarme Security (x3)

CRITICAL ITEMS TO LOCATE
- First Ancient Symbol Tracing
- Second Ancient Symbol Tracing

AVAILABLE UPGRADES
- There are no available upgrades in this area.

Stepping away from the Louvre's security doors, enter this dank and deserted basement. Fortunately, the mesh door is open. Step forward.

Ignore the area to the left, pass the small digger, and run around the right side of the sandy ground. You see a large excavation hole and a gap in the perimeter fencing. Don't go there yet, though.

Your movements disturb a security attendant who barks, "You're under arrest!" in French. Disable him and take his K2 Impactor, then investigate the porta-cabin from where he appeared.

Inside the porta-cabin are a number of air-conditioning units that keep the temperature at the dig constant. Activate the air conditioning so that any elevator devices you interact with later have a better chance of working. Now exit.

Draw your weapon and continue around the dig site surface until you reach a tent with computers reading telemetry data. Out comes a guard wearing a heavy jacket. Deal with him at once, then pick up the M-V9 he drops.

Check out the pair of double doors to the right of the tent. Run between the two corrugated walls of iron and push open the doors to enter an excavation area.

When you reach the makeshift desk with the computer equipment, maneuver the scanner to the first Ancient Symbol, then check the left printer. On the tray is a piece of paper. Pick it up and check your Inventory. This is the First Ancient Symbol Tracing. It is an unknown glyph, found with the giant scanner ahead of you.

NOTE **You can activate the remote controls next to the printer and view the infrared materials detector that's currently scanning this room. Maneuver the scanner around, point at the ground, and uncover artifacts buried in the stone and sand below. The First Symbol is in the top-left corner of the dig area. The scanner only works when you switch on the air conditioning and power in the first cabin.**

When you've finished scanning, return to the main dig site surface and run right, past the computer tent and into the porta-cabin next to it. There's a door to open. Head inside; there's nothing of note around the far end of the structure.

This porta-cabin was used to research data and weigh samples. Look for a piece of paper lying on the fax machine above the file cabinet. This is the Second Ancient Symbol Tracing. The glyph is a dot with a circle around it.

The second tracing is a circular symbol and the first looks like an inverted "G." The second symbol also appears on the wall. With these two papers in your backpack, step out of the porta-cabin and draw your weapon once more.

Another guard has been alerted to your presence. Once you deal with him, pick up his M-V9 pistol, and run toward the entrance to this level, stopping at the gap in the mesh fence.

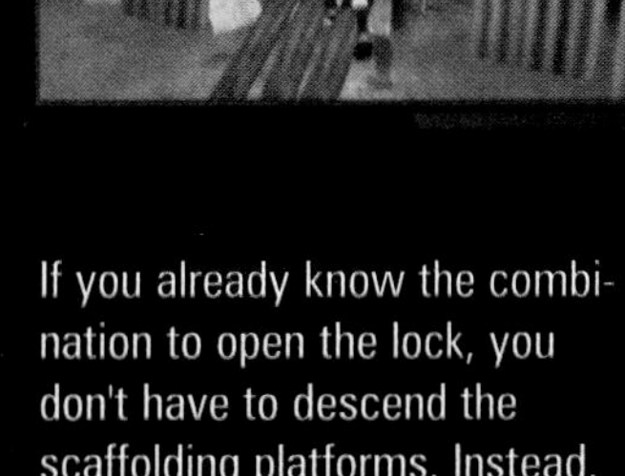

There's a yellow ladder. Drop onto the scaffolding below, and descend to the base of the pit. There are a number of ways to go down here—the route described is the quickest and safest, although there are two shortcuts to take.

If you already know the combination to open the lock, you don't have to descend the scaffolding platforms. Instead, you can leap to the jutting stone pedestal under either side of the stone archway.

The leap from the right side of the scaffold to the ledge above the rock wall is an alternate route. It takes longer, as you must shimmy across the underside of the arch. Make sure you run and leap early, over the railing, if you want to land these jumps.

Head along the left side of the scaffolding planks, turn the two corners, and clamber down the yellow ladder to the next series of scaffold platforms. By now you've spotted a spinning circular device embedded in the far wall.

Head toward this device. Walk around the ladder, around the corner, pass under the ladder, and stop by the gap in the planks next to the blue barrel.

Although you can leap across, continue around, and clamber down the yellow ladder, it is faster to drop off the edge near the barrel, cling onto it, and drop past a second plank to the bottom scaffolding area, above the excavated ground. By now, you should have heard the radio chatter and seen gunfire in the pit below.

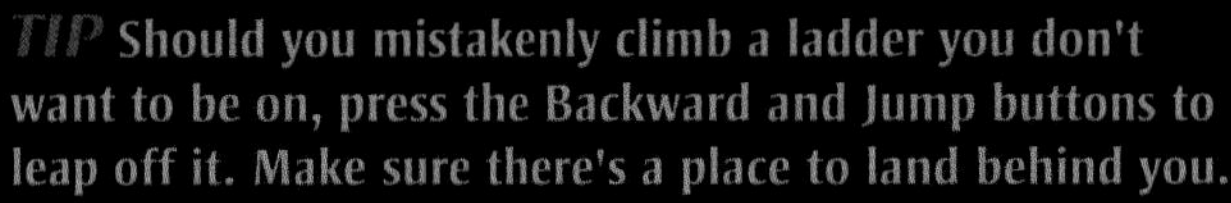

TIP Should you mistakenly climb a ladder you don't want to be on, press the Backward and Jump buttons to leap off it. Make sure there's a place to land behind you.

There is a final guard in heavy padding down here. Shoot at him from one of the scaffolding ledges above. You can engage him in close combat—but you might not live.

Run left, locating the orange battery power unit, and clamber down the nearby ladder to the excavation floor. There are various machine parts, rubble, wheelbarrows, and a hardhat area of little interest. Head to the lit area.

There has been some feverish deciphering going on at a computer table. On an easel rests a sketch of the locking mechanism currently whirring above you. Study the board.

There are four "locking wheels." The unlocking symbols for the outer and inner ones have been deciphered. They are a crescent and an insect (possibly a scarab beetle). Remember these two symbols.

Accessing the mechanism is the tricky part. It is five stories up from your current location, and the only way to reach it is to ascend the rock wall near the two wheelbarrows.

Regain your grip strength halfway up the wall by dropping onto the small platform, then continue up to the rock ledge underneath the stone archway. This is one of the ledges you could have leapt to from the top of the scaffold. Save your game.

Now stand under the archway and leap up. Lara grabs the underside of the archway and swings across the span of the arch. Pull the camera behind her, and don't stop.

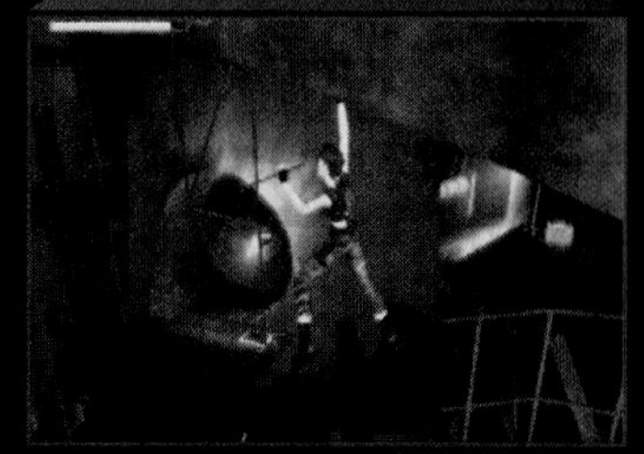

You drop onto the ledge on the opposite span of the archway. Turn around and look at the rotating lock mechanism from here.

TIP **If you're feeling reckless, try a running jump from this ledge. Point directly at the scaffold near the mechanism, and grab it as you hit the scaffold poles and drop. Pull yourself onto the wooden platform. You've executed an impressive shortcut. When you want to move to the opening you unlock, leap and grab the stone ledge under the arch. It is difficult (save your game), but not impossible.**

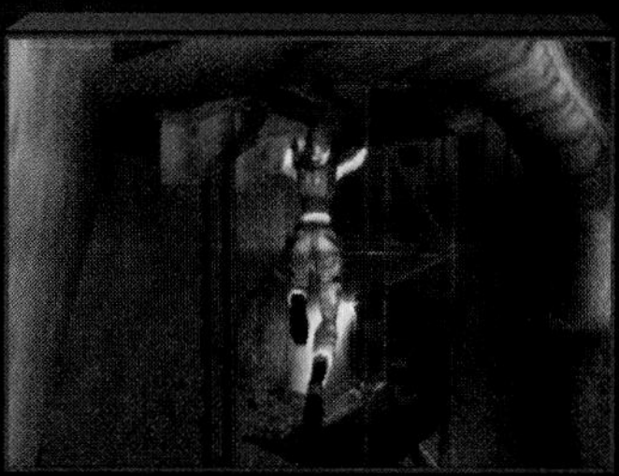

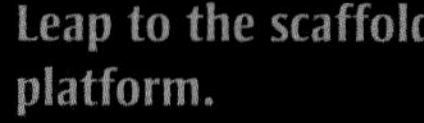

Leap to the scaffold platform.

Leap back to the archway ledge.

The proper way to reach the mechanism is to pull yourself up from the ledge to the wooden platform, then vault onto the top of the archway. Make a right turn, run across the top of the archway bridge to the middle, then make a left turn.

Cross the planks and investigate a round hole in the earth ahead. It looks like a door, but you cant' open it. This area is your final destination at the dig.

Walk to the planks near the archway bridge, and locate the lever that powers the cargo elevator. Pull the lever, and the elevator descends to the level of the planks near the locking mechanism. (Note: this only works if you turned the air conditioning on at the first cabin.) Return to the ledge under the arch.

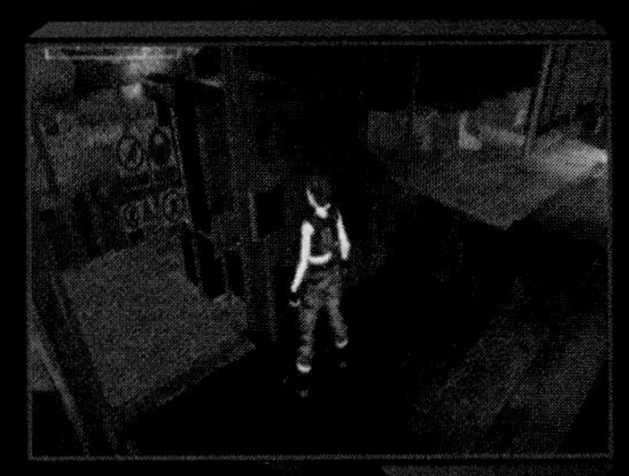

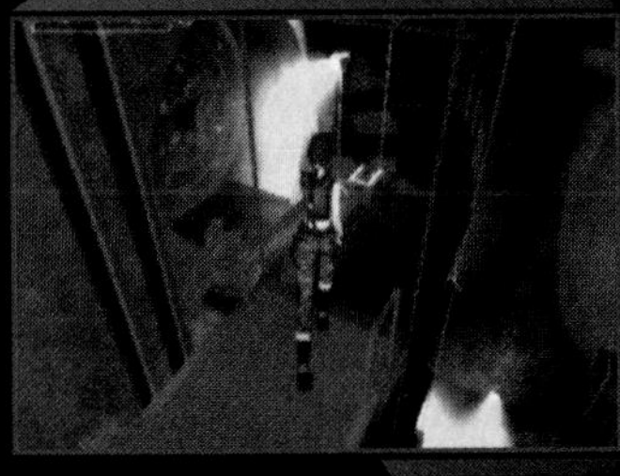

Leap from the ledge to the elevator platform, then walk onto the scaffold. Look at the whirring lock in front of you. There are four separate sections spinning independently of each other. Each has eight symbols on it.

Stop the whirring, then rotate each section so the appropriate symbol lines up with the rectangular iron bar at "nine o'clock" on the device. Move to the "pointer" on the mechanism and pull it down. All four sections rotate at once. Rotate one at a time.

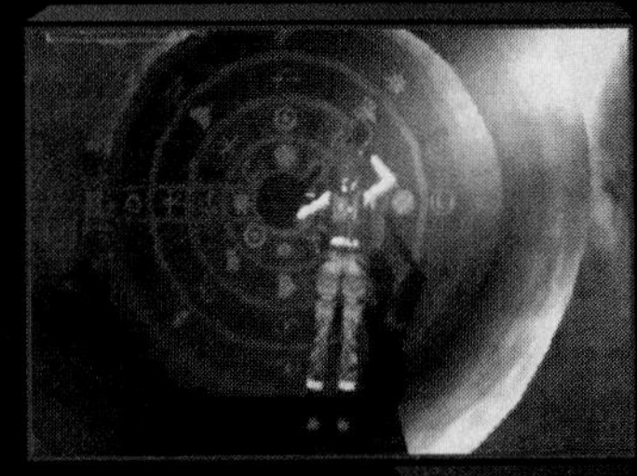

There are four long levers to the right of the mechanism that achieve this effect. Run there now. All the levers are in the "on position," and each relates to a section. Lever #1 turns the outer section on and off. Levers #2 and #3 turn the second and third sections on and off, respectively. Finally, lever #4 (far right) turns the inner section on and off.

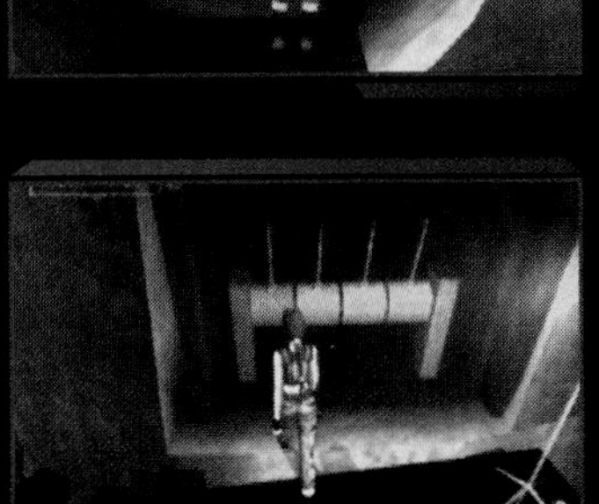

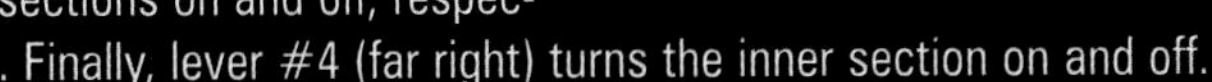

Stop and turn each section independently, starting with the outer one. Ignore the first lever. Now pull levers 2, 3, and 4 to the lower position. Run back to the mechanism.

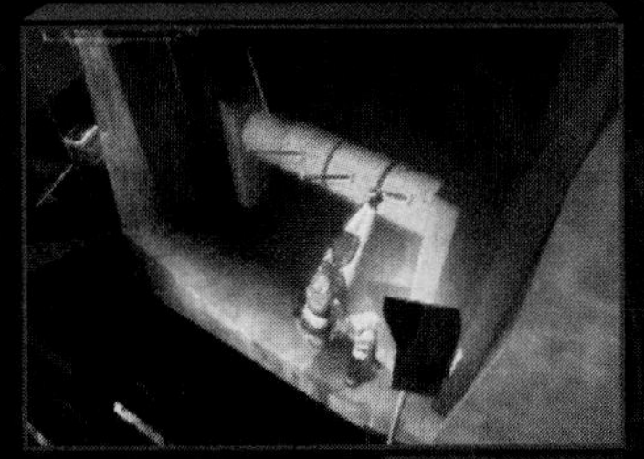

Move the pointer. Only the outer section moves. Continue to pull the pointer until the crescent shape lines up with the rectangular bar. Now run back to the levers. Pull lever #1 to the "off" position.

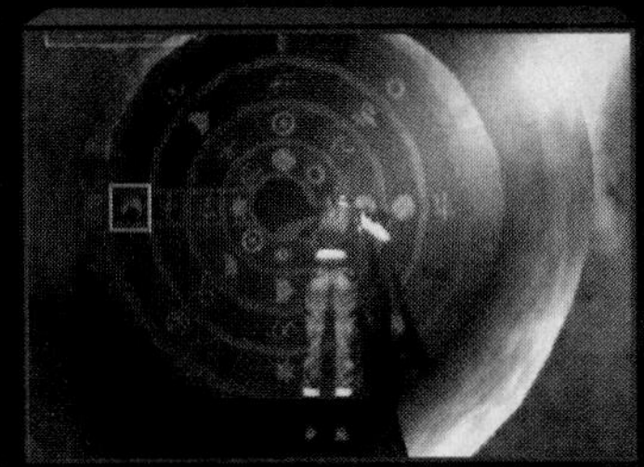

Now pull lever #2 only. Run back to the mechanism. Pull the pointer until the "inverted G" symbol lines up with the rectangular bar. Check your inventory to make sure the symbols are correct (as other symbols on the mechanism look similar).

Head to the levers. Pull lever #2 to the "off" position. Now pull lever #3, return to the mechanism, pull the pointer, and rotate the third section until the dot and circle symbol lines up in the metal rectangle. One more to go.

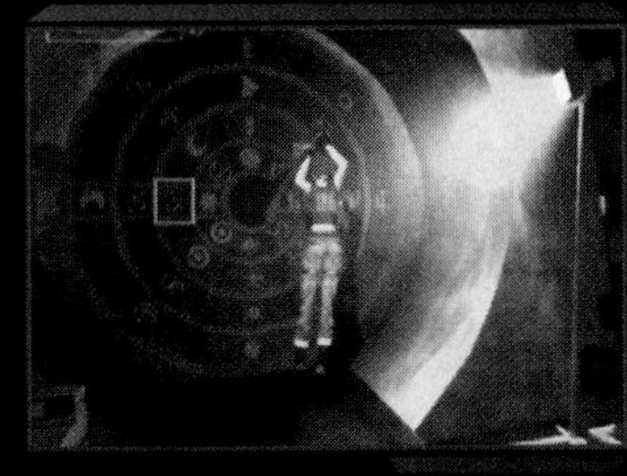

Move to the levers for the last time. Pull lever #3 to the "off" position. Now pull lever #4, head back, and pull the pointer until the inner section lines up the insect symbol with the metal rectangle. Check the screenshot. That's the unlocking code.

As soon as you're finished, the mechanism grinds to life, maneuvering dozens of metal rods and retracting the entrance "floor" in the circular pit at the top of the excavation. The entrance to the Tomb of Ancients is now open.

Save your game and move onto the elevator platform. Leap to the ledge under the arch, climb on the wooden ledge, then up onto the arched bridge. Run across the bridge, turn left, and move into the now-open entrance.

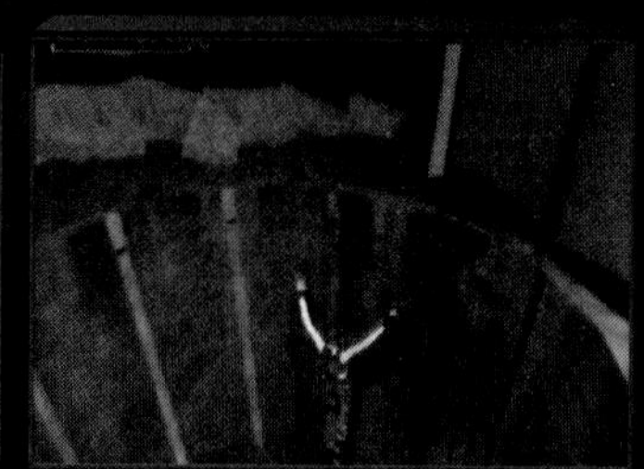

There's a gaping hole in front of you. Run and jump into it, or fall and hang off the edge of the circular pit. You are now about to enter the Tomb of Ancients, where traps will test your very sanity.

Tomb of Ancients

This gigantic, cylindrical sinkhole with ancient walls and carvings will test your mettle. You must climb down the walls, ensure your jumping is accurate, and access two laborious sets of jutting wall ledges in your quest to pull two levers, the last of which opens a grating at the base of the chamber. Once in here, it is a short jog to the Hall of Seasons. Ignore the broken bridge as you descend, and save before every jump. Finally, you'll return to this area when you make your escape. So remember where you came in; it'll save your life.

ENTITIES ENCOUNTERED

- Bat
- The Knight

CRITICAL ITEMS TO LOCATE

- V-Packer Shotgun

AVAILABLE UPGRADES

- **Upgrade Kick Door/Wall: Lower Body Level 5**
  A swift kick to a door below the main chamber allows access to the Hall of Seasons.

You land on an area of rock below the elaborate door, unable to leap back to the dig. Run along the tunnel until you reach the edge of it. Peer down to see a wooden beam below.

TIP **Even if you are sure of your jumping, hanging, and dropping capabilities, you should still save your game after each leap. Some require precise lining up and maneuvering. Others are simply devilishly difficult. You have been warned.**

Hang off the tunnel edge, land on and hang off the beam, then drop onto the sandy ground below. Don't leap from the upper tunnel entrance, as you'll hurt yourself.

Walk to the edge of the cave opening, and drop so you're hanging from it. If you press the Backward button now, instead of falling, you shimmy down the craggy rock face, finding nooks to hold onto. Continue climbing down this cliff wall, even as it overhangs.

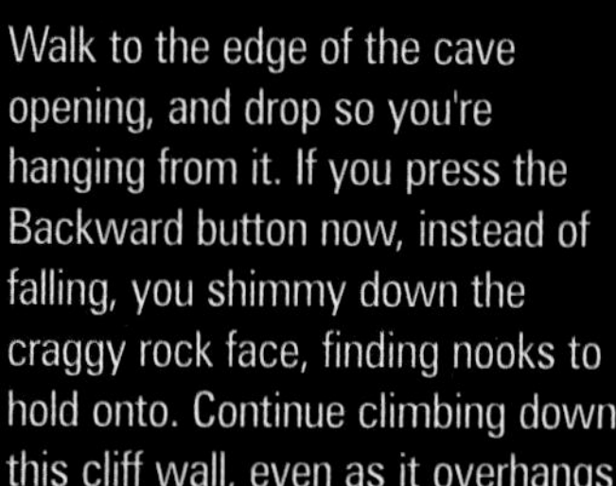

Head to the cave entrance ahead of you, and gaze at the gigantic cylindrical hole you must descend. As the camera sweeps past the bats, you see two portions of a broken bridge, with the wreckage strewn about the bottom. The base of this structure is where you're headed.

Move down as the cliff continues to hang over. When it straightens to a vertical wall, you can drop to a small, stone ledge at the base of the cliff face. Turn and look left when you reach the ledge.

TIP Your path isn't always a series of jumps and grabs. There are certain points where you should look for textured cliff walls that can take your weight as you climb down them. If you're stuck, look around for a wall to shimmy along.

To the left of the green stone ledge you're on is a wooden support beam. Stop for a moment, bring out your ranged weapon for choice, and down a pesky bat. Now execute a regular jump from the back of the ledge, then grab that beam. Don't jump from the front edge, or you'll overshoot.

Don't hop (Walk, then Jump) either, as you won't have time to grab the beam. Once you're on this beam, look down. There's a broken bridge and ornate archway below you.

Do not fall from this ledge to the broken bridge, as the drop kills you. Instead, look left at the cave entrance on the exterior wall. Save your game, then run from the end of the beam, turn, and leap at the entrance at full speed.

Once on the cave ground, follow it around to a natural sinkhole in the floor. Dangle from the ground, drop on the natural step, walk and drop onto the next step, turn 180 degrees, and fall off the final step. Don't fall and miss any steps or you'll wound yourself.

You emerge from the ornate archway on the broken bridge span you saw earlier. There's a sealed door behind you. Look left.

NOTE **Don't go to the other side of the bridge. It is almost impossible to leap the gap between the two portions of the bridge. And if you do make it across, there is nothing of interest except a locked stone door and a locked trapdoor on the floor in front of it. This is where you'll exit this area; ignore it for now.**

Move to the left balcony on the left side of the bridge between the door and the lantern. If you peer over the edge, you see a gargoyle below. That's the area to aim for, although it is a deadly jump if you're not precise with your timing.

There are three ways to descend from the bridge to the lower ground, and each is dangerous. Save your game, then attempt one of the following.

Descending the Bridge Method #1

This method involves vaulting over the balcony, dropping past the ledge and gargoyle, and landing on the rock platform below. You'll lose half your health if you hit a wall to halt your drop on the way down, but you'll make it. If you miss everything, you will expire in a crumpled heap.

Descending the Bridge Method #2

Try a running jump a couple of meters behind the balcony so you sail over it, then land on the gargoyle. You can then dangle from the ledge and drop to the rock platform. However, the chances of an overshoot, or of slipping off the gargoyle are high.

Descending the Bridge Method #3

The simplest method is to get as close to the doorway as possible, vault over the balcony so you're falling right next to the wall, and land on a tiny lip. Dangle off the lip, drop onto the rock platform, and count your blessings. You can achieve the same effect if you leap over the balcony at the wall, hit it, then slide down to the lip.

This rock platform reaches a dead end. View the lever in the square alcove on the opposite wall (that's where you need to go), then look for the brick-patterned rock below you.

Dangle off the rock, then shimmy down, continuing as the rock wall slopes into an alcove. Climb into the alcove, then drop to the ledge below. There's nowhere to leap to from this area. Turn and look to the left area of the ledge.

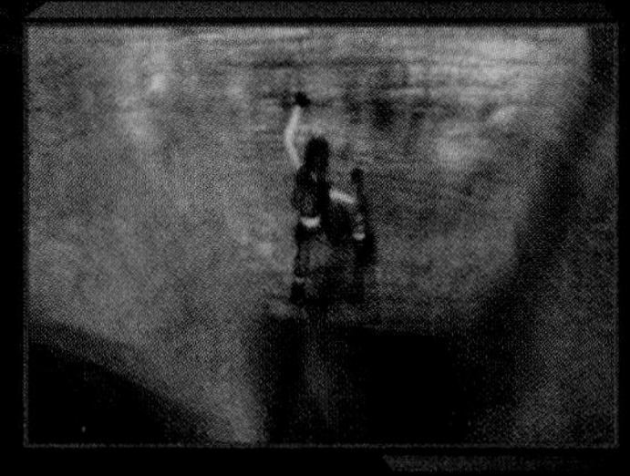

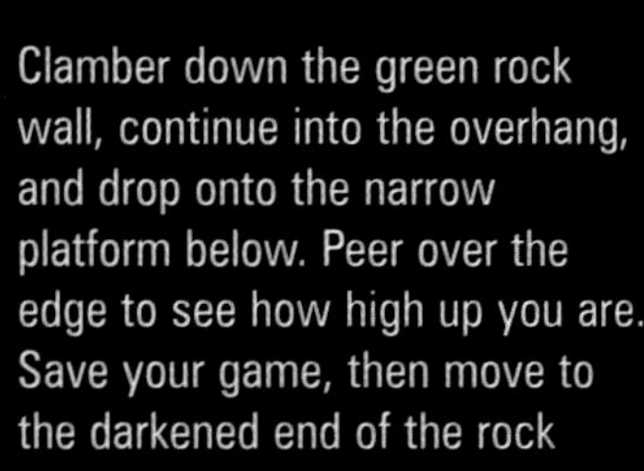

The climbable wall continues to the left and wraps around the rock formation. To ensure you reach the next area without losing your grip, jump from the left side of the alcove and shimmy around the corners of this rock outcropping, heading to the green rock area.

Clamber down the green rock wall, continue into the overhang, and drop onto the narrow platform below. Peer over the edge to see how high up you are. Save your game, then move to the darkened end of the rock platform.

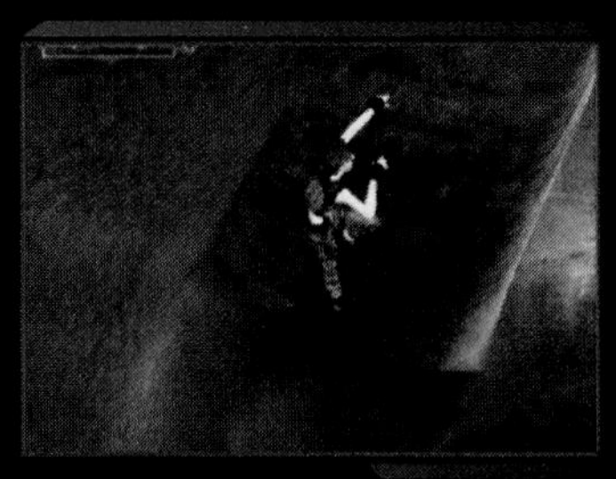

Ahead is a wooden support buttress. The jump is tricky. Take a couple of steps back from the edge, then regular jump, landing on the buttress. A running jump sends you over the buttress, and a walking jump is too short.

Once you're standing on the wooden support, move to the wall and pull the lever jutting out of the wall. A series of stone platforms rumbles out of the wall below you. These giant steps descend to the ground below.

TIP **Save your game before each and every jump to minimize anguish and backtracking.**

Jumping to step #1 is easy. Just walk, then hop to the platform without any hassle. Make a regular jump to step #2. Reach out and grab the step if you fall short. Take a couple of steps before you leap.

Leap to step #3 by running and jumping. The step is higher, so you can land on top of, or hit it and slide down it, ending in an Action button grab. Pull yourself up and onto the platform.

The next step is below you, but you cannot reach it by hanging off the platform. (You'll fall past it to your death). Instead, leap at the wall above the step and slide down onto it, or hop from the back of the upper step.

TIP **When you're jumping to a step and think you'll overshoot, leap at the wall directly above the step, slam against it, then drop and land on the step. There's no damage, and no overshooting.**

The next step (#5) is also below the one you're on, but this is a longer drop. Jump into the wall above the platform, and a slide down onto it. When you land, turn and look right.

There's damage to be had if you drop from this platform, so leap to step #6 using a hop (Walk and Jump buttons). The platform is closer than you think, and you'll sail over it if you attempt a regular or running jump. Dangle and drop onto the ground.

You've finally made it to the base of this gigantic tomb. There's no reason to inspect this area, especially since there's something carrying a flaming sword on the far side of this arena. Ignore the trapdoor (it is still locked), and avoid the Knight.

Run to the small gap in the wall, duck, and crawl under it into a tiny alcove. There is a lever here. When you pull it, the six steps retract, and eleven more appear. These lead back up the circular wall to a torch-lit alcove with a lever in it. You saw this earlier.

Your new adversary is deadly. Arcane magic prevents the Knight from dying, so avoid those sword swings. Blast it with weapons until it falls, which gives you time to escape before it regenerates.

Run past the Knight to the top of the debris mound. Grab and pull yourself up the first new step. Save your game. Once on top of the step, move to the edge nearest the next step and hop, then grab the step and pull yourself up.

TIP **Again, jumping at the wall, sliding down onto the platform, and avoiding the risk of real jumping maneuvers is the best way to ascend these steps.**

From step #2 to #3, take a running jump, then stop as you land on the third platform. Grab the step if you fall short. Once on step #3, walk to the edge, jump, and grab step #4 above you.

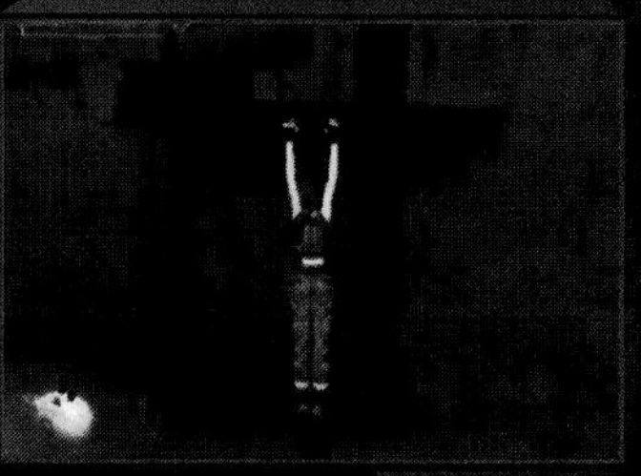

A running jump is required from step #4 to #5, but stop before you fall off the far side. Attempt the same move from step #5 to #6, except grab the platform as you hit the side of it. Pull yourself up onto step #6 and turn around.

Execute the same move from step #6 to #7; try the running jump, then grab and haul yourself onto the platform. Walk to the edge of step #7, then jump straight up and grab step #8, clambering onto this jutting platform.

The next jump is tricky. Jump, but point yourself toward the wall so you come up short, then grab step #9 and pull yourself up. Running jumps and hopping cause you to come up too long or short. Now look to your final two steps.

For step #9 to #10 hop, then grab the platform as you fall, maneuvering yourself onto it. Finally, try a running jump at the last step (#11), grab the platform, and haul yourself onto the torch-lit step.

Turn left, clamber into the alcove, and pull that switch. No more steps appear, but the trapdoor at the base of the tomb falls open. You must now descend the steps.

Save your game, climb down to the step, turn right, and survey the next two steps (#10 and #9). Try a running jump and bypass #10 completely (remember to grab step #9), or jump into the wall and slide down to step #10.

If you land on step #10, hop to #9. Now point yourself so you jump from a standstill, hit the wall, and land on step #8. Simply drop from step #8 to #7, directly underneath you.

From step #7 to #6, walk to the edge and hop to it, then turn 180 degrees and survey the final five steps. Move to the far edge of step #6, turn so you face the wall above step #5, and hop into it, sliding onto the step itself.

Although it looks farther away, a simple hop from step #5 to #4 is all that's required. Now look down and walk off this step, landing on step #3. Hop to step #2, hop to step #1, and finally land on the debris below. Your workout is almost complete.

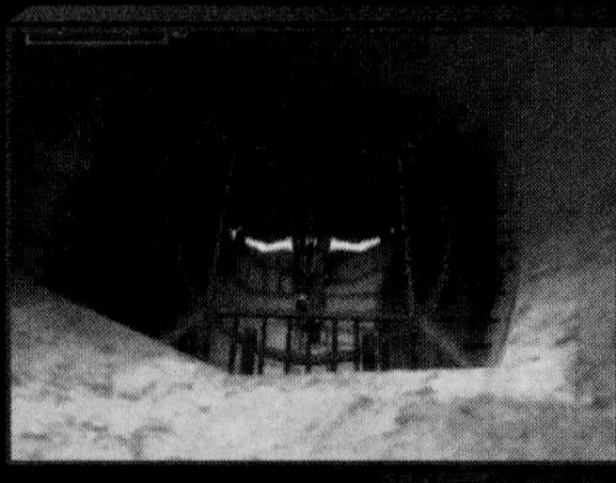

Avoid the Knight, move to the open trapdoor, and fall through to the ground below. You do not return here until this series of levels is complete. Run down the heat-filled passage, and at the mine junction, make a right.

You come to an iron door. Kick it open and strengthen Lara's legs at the same time (Upgrade Kick Door/Wall: Lower Body Level 5). The blocked area beyond holds a discarded V-Packer shotgun and two sets of V-Packer Standard Cartridges (a total of four boxes).

After making the shotgun your weapon of choice, return to the junction and make a right. Run down the tunnel to a second metal door on your right. With your new leg strength, kick open this door. Too weak? Then retrace your steps to the other door and open that first.

You appear in a long corridor. Stride over the ground mosaic, ignoring the two sealed doors, and step through the doorway ahead of you. Uh-oh! The door above slams down behind you.

You're left in a long, arched chamber. On either side of you are darts springing out of traps in the walls. These inflict glancing damage if you're hit. You can make out a door at the far end of this narrow corridor. It is barred.

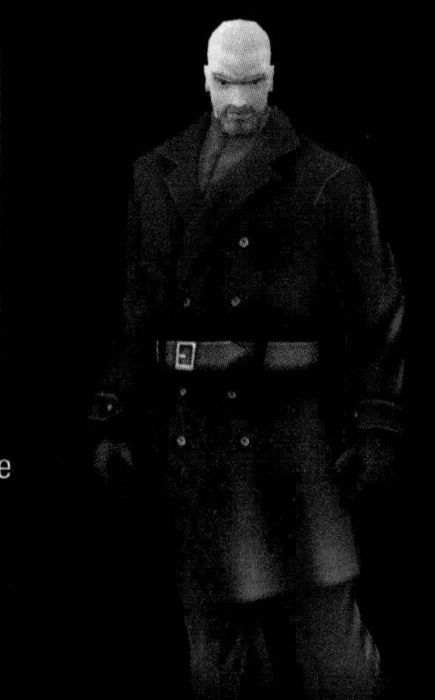

This trapped hallway requires you to stay at the entrance, turn right, and pull a lever. This raises the bars on the doorway ahead, but also commences a nasty spike-thrusting trap at each of the three archways. Also, the doorway seals after 15 seconds. Save your game before you pull the lever.

As soon as you pull the lever, turn and run toward the first archway spike trap and leap early, sailing over it. Precisely time this jump, or you'll be hit by the spike. Continue the run, leaping over the second spike, the third spike, and through the doorway.

The doorway seals behind you. Walk into a corridor with a large wooden door at the end. Open the door, stride through into an identical chamber, then breathe a sigh of relief. You've located the fabled Hall of Seasons.

The Hall of Seasons

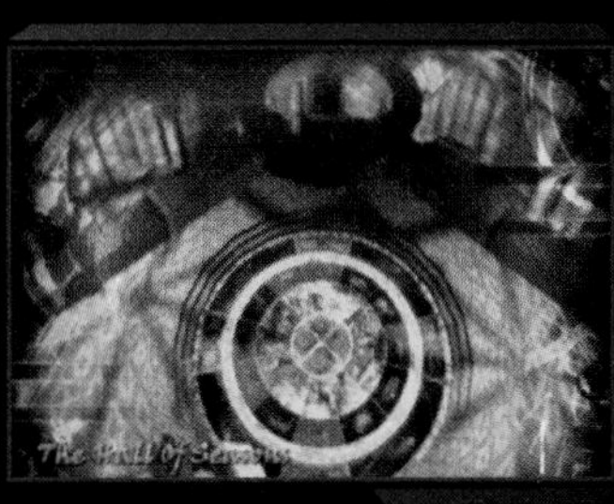

This is a gigantic hub, and you return here many times. Initially, you're inside a circular hall. Unlock each of the sets of doors surrounding you, and you end up in one of four elemental chambers. Your job is to locate four elemental crystals (one from each chamber), attach them to various parts of the furnace, release moving columns in the main hall, and climb to the roof of the hall, where a bizarre brother guards an Obscura Painting. If you choose the wrong door, you fall into the dungeon. In the dungeon, you negotiate many traps until you find an elevator back to the circular hall, or if you've already located all four crystals, the entrance to the furnace.

ENTITIES ENCOUNTERED

- The Knight (x4)
- Brother Obscura

CRITICAL ITEMS TO LOCATE

- Fire Crystal
- Earth Crystal
- Air Crystal
- Water Crystal
- Obscura Painting #1

AVAILABLE UPGRADES

- **Upgrade Grip: Upper Body Level 7**
  Lara can scale steep overhangs with ease after this workout.

Enter the Hall of Seasons. Investigate the rubble fallen from the structure above.

Your main area of interest is the central calendar on the floor of the hall. It details the signs of the zodiac, coupled with the months in Latin, and the four seasons in golden foot plates. Medieval scenes signify each month in question.

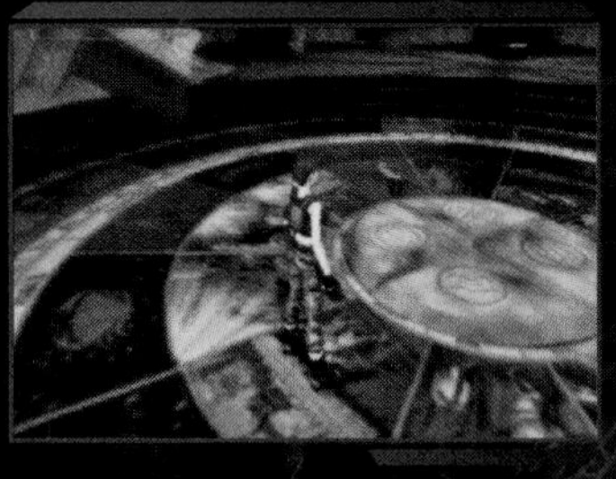

There's little time to marvel at this contraption, as a Knight is trotting in to swipe at you. Ignore or temporarily pulverize this beast, then look to the golden foot plates below. Each has a symbol on the ground relating to an element.

The element of earth is a stone-shaped glyph with a line under it.

The element of fire is a sunburst-shaped glyph.

The air element is a glyph of three lines ending in hooks.

The element of water is a glyph of three wavy lines.

Many doors surround you, twelve of which have a glyph sign above them. If you step on one of the golden foot plates, the three doors closest to the golden foot plate open.

When the doors open, avoid the Knight and enter one of the doors. You'll find yourself in a short corridor leading to a lever. Above the lever is a second glyph. This glyph is the one you should look at to solve this puzzle. The glyph above the lever and the glyph on the golden footplate you stepped on should match.

Pull the lever. The gate or door blocking your way raises, allowing you access to one of four different elemental chambers.

These chambers are Neptune's Hall, Wrath of the Beast, The Sanctuary of Flame, and The Breath of Hades. Collect a crystal from each to access the upper floors of the hall.

If you chose the wrong door and pulled the lever, the floor crumbles and you fall into a dark tunnel. Follow the tunnel to a slope and slide down it. See "The Basement of Traps" section for details on how to get back to the Hall of Seasons.

TIP **If you pulled the wrong lever, you have a split-second to attempt a sideways jump away from the opening below you, so you can stay on the ground floor of this hall and try again. Jumping and landing to the side works in all sections, but is very difficult!**

Entering Neptune's Hall: Water

Stand on the water glyph, then enter the left doorway. Inside is the matching water glyph.

Entering Wrath of the Beast: Earth

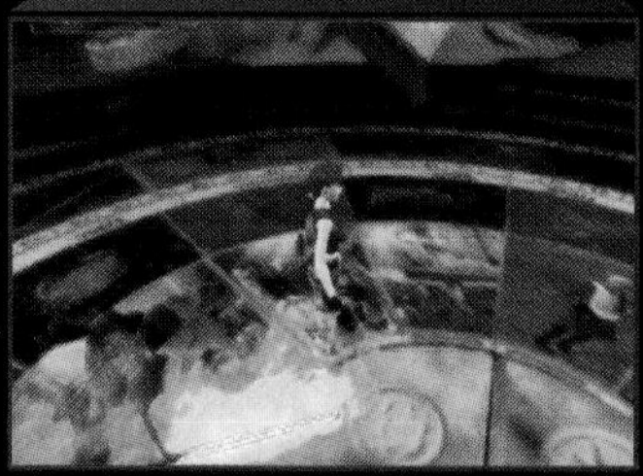

Stand on the earth glyph, then enter the middle doorway. Inside is the matching earth glyph.

Entering The Sanctuary of Flame: Fire

Stand on the fire glyph, then enter the right doorway. Inside is the matching fire glyph.

NOTE **Walkthroughs for each elemental chamber are covered later in this section.**

Entering The Breath of Hades: Air

Stand on the air glyph, then enter the right doorway. Inside is the matching air glyph.

TIP **If you succeed in opening the portcullis inside the left or right corridor, run straight through to the door leading to the elemental chamber. Don't pull the lever in the middle section out of curiosity, unless you want to drop into the basement instead.**

The Basement of Traps

If you pulled the wrong lever, then you appear in one of four entrances. Pick up the Large Health Pack, then head into the circular tunnel, as there are two areas to investigate. The hazards described in this portion of the walkthrough begin from the entrance where you appear if you stood on the water floor plate.

The instruments of torture described in this portion of the walkthrough appear as if you are running counterclockwise around this circular basement. That means at the entrance you turn right. When you enter this section, you see a large, spiked harvester on your left. Run right, and it follows you on the rails.

Step to the far left or right of the passage (before the lava pit), and let this infernal contraption roll past you without harming you, jumping the pointy spikes. Make a running jump across the lava pit. Save your game first.

Once safely over the lava pit, run around the curved corridor until you reach a door on your left. It is the only door on the inside of this circular tunnel, and it leads to the furnace deep under the Hall of Seasons. Do not enter here until you have all four element crystals.

Continue past the furnace until you come to six wall spikes shooting out of the wall. Four are on the right wall, two on the left one. Walk around each point as it protrudes, or leap over the hole before the spike shoots out. Don't stray to the edges or you'll fall into a strip of lava.

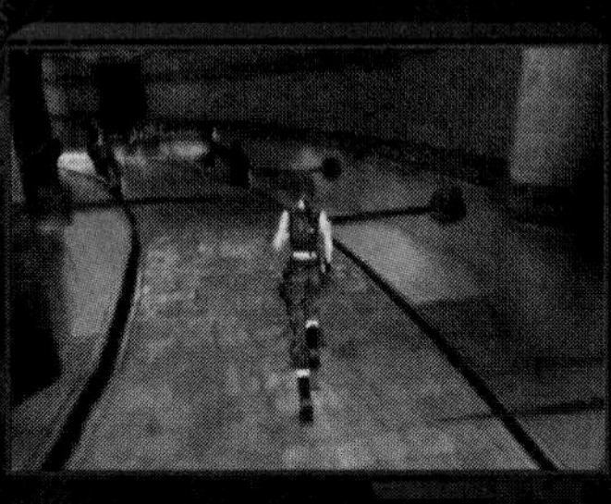

Continue to a doorway on your right. This is another entrance (if you failed to enter the elemental chamber associated with air). Parked to one side of the door is the spiked harvester. Run around it, then jump across another lava pit (cling to the wall if you fall short).

Jump around the right side of the lava pit, as there are another two running along both walls. This means you must keep to the right. Just beware of the retracting blade on the wall, which spins horizontally, then vertically. Nasty.

Avoid the blade by running straight under it before it forms properly. Or Commando Crawl to avoid the spinning blade. Ducking and regular crawling get you minced. Continue past the end of the inner wall lava pit.

If you're searching for a way up to the Hall of Seasons (after accidentally falling down here, or when you switch the furnace on), check out the exit to your right. This outer doorway leads to an elevator. We're continuing on with our hazard check, however.

Pass another entrance on your right (where you end up if you choose the incorrect doorway when treading on the fire floor plate), move between the descending spike arms, and watch for the metal protrusions sticking out of the ground. When you near them, they split into four knives.

Run around these four traps, then watch the next trap. Three curved scythes whip the corridor in front of them. One is from the ceiling, while the other two come out of the walls. To avoid being sliced, wait for them to swing, hug one wall, and leap over them as they retract. Keep moving.

Stay away from the stone block that falls from the ceiling, then lifts up again. Moving under the block as it ascends is the best way to avoid it. Now execute a running leap across the lava pit, and you're back at the initial entrance area.

Exiting the Basement of Traps

You can enter the furnace after collecting all four of the elemental crystals, so it is best to ignore it until your inventory has been stocked with them.

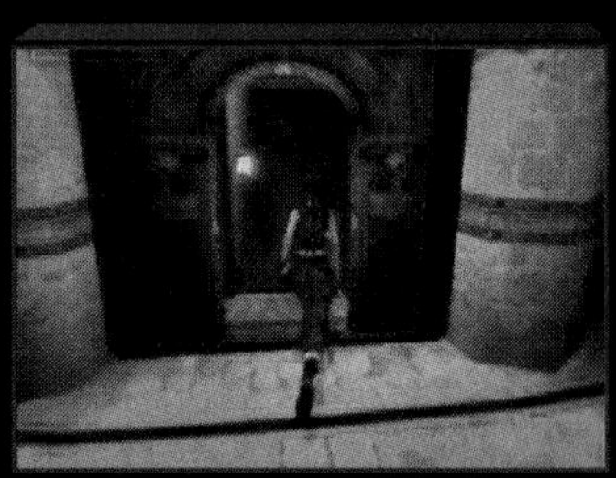

The proper exit to the Hall of Seasons is the door leading to the rope elevator on the outer wall. Move into the elevator and pull the rope. Once you finish, pull the rope a second time to reach the appropriate floor.

You appear at a door; open it and jog through the connecting corridor to the Hall of Seasons.

Follow the notes outlined previously for entering each elemental chamber. These can be accessed in any order you like, but are presented here in order of difficulty. Save often. First, access Neptune's Hall by treading on the water floor pad and entering the left door.

You return to the Hall of Seasons a total of five times (not including trips to the basement or furnace, which are part of the hall). You return after each elemental crystal has been obtained, and again to escape after an encounter with Brother Obscura.

Neptune's Hall

Neptune's Hall consists of an underwater search for the Water Crystal, which is embedded in a rock column at the center of a water-filled chamber. Initially, the chamber needs to be filled with water, or you'll dive and land on tile. Negotiating a Knight, you find a smaller passage to swim down, locate a lever to fill the water, then return to the entrance chamber to dive into the central area. A quick search for a second lever occurs, after which a swim through a maze of rock tunnels lands you under the central gate. After pocketing the crystal, you swim down to pull a final lever, unlocking the circular door parts, and swim back to the initial chamber to return to the Hall of Seasons.

ENTITIES ENCOUNTERED
- The Knight

CRITICAL ITEMS TO LOCATE
- Water Crystal

AVAILABLE UPGRADES
- There are no available upgrades in this area.

Although the initial passageway is lit by a number of torches, there's only swimming to contend with. First, run around the four pillars. Don't drop into the hole in the central area of the passage, or you'll land with a sickening thud in the large chamber below.

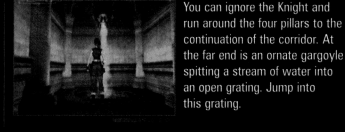

You can ignore the Knight and run around the four pillars to the continuation of the corridor. At the far end is an ornate gargoyle spitting a stream of water into an open grating. Jump into this grating.

This chamber must be filled with water before you can high dive. First, nullify the Knight that's conjuring fireballs at you. Engage him in combat near the hole, then push him in. You destroy him and won't need to worry about him later.

Dive downward. You only have a limited air supply, so follow the route exactly. Pass the broken grating cover, down through the hole, and into a large underwater hallway with a checkered floor.

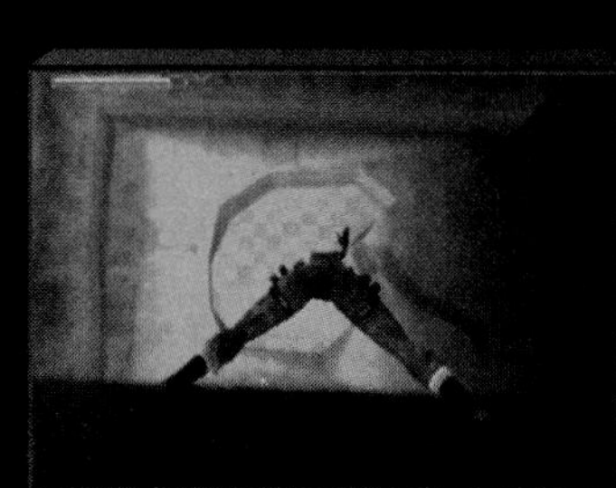

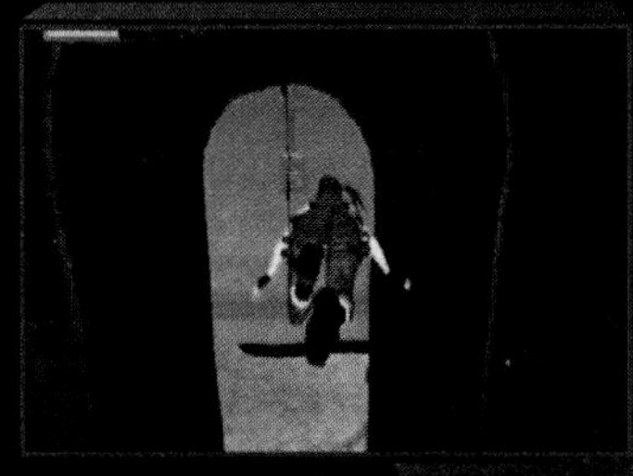

Swim upward so you can see the far wall (the taller one that is open rather than the smaller one blocked by a lock). Wait for the trap blades to swing, and slowly rotate back into position, then dart through.

Beyond the trap blades is a small antechamber with a lever on the wall. Grab and pull the lever. This raises the water level in the central chamber You're still on the same breath of air, so quickly exit the antechamber.

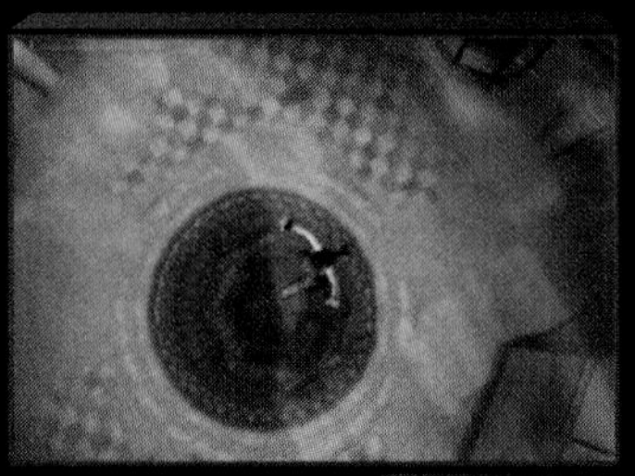

Locate the hole in the hall ceiling and paddle up through it, past the grating, and surface at the gargoyle fountain. Use the Action button to pull yourself out of the water, then run to the four columns and hole in the initial corridor.

Leap into the central chamber, now filled with water. Below you is a circular door mechanism. Below this door is the Water Crystal.

Return to the surface for air, then swim underwater. Look for the locked door with the demon-head gargoyle above it. Swim to the right of that, looking for a mound of sand with plants growing out of it.

To the left of this mound is a gap in the stonework. Swim through to an antechamber, and locate the lever above and to the left. Pull it, and the giant tubes surrounding the main chamber spill out more water.

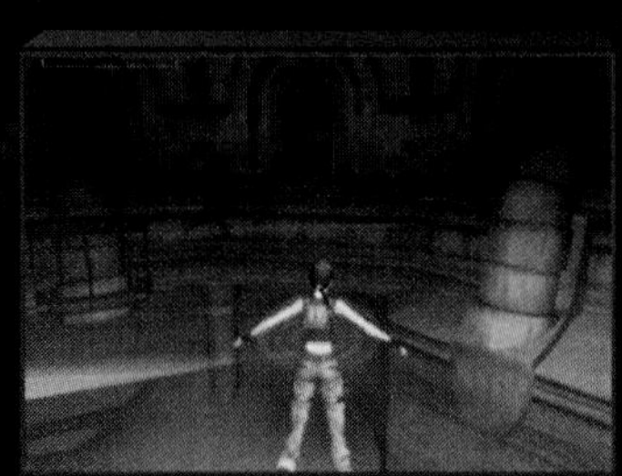

This raises the water level so you can swim back to the circular chamber and clamber onto the narrow ledge surrounding the large pool. There are five arched doorways that are now accessible. All but one lead to dead ends.

Head for the archway with an orange tinge of light emanating from it. Run through this archway and make a left. You pass an archaic light, heading for a square hole in the ground.

The hole is full of water. Save your game, then plunge right in, swimming up slightly as you reach a tunnel below. Now swim down this underwater tunnel. A third of the way along, you see the ornate arched arrows of the central chamber casting a shadow against the right wall, right near a Large Health Pack.

Continue to another square shaft in the ground, and dive again. When you exit into a farther underwater tunnel, grab a Large Health Pack, then stop and look behind you. There is a grating with a piece missing. Swim through the gap in the grating to a small pocket of air. You need this.

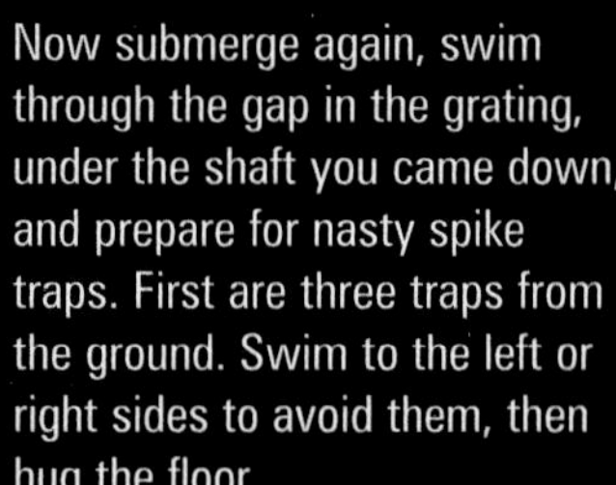

Now submerge again, swim through the gap in the grating, under the shaft you came down, and prepare for nasty spike traps. First are three traps from the ground. Swim to the left or right sides to avoid them, then hug the floor.

Hugging the floor means you swim under three spikes jabbing you from the ceiling. If you're hit by one, you expire, so keep alert. Finally, there are two sets of spikes, one from the bottom and one from the side. Stay in the lower left or right corner of the tunnel.

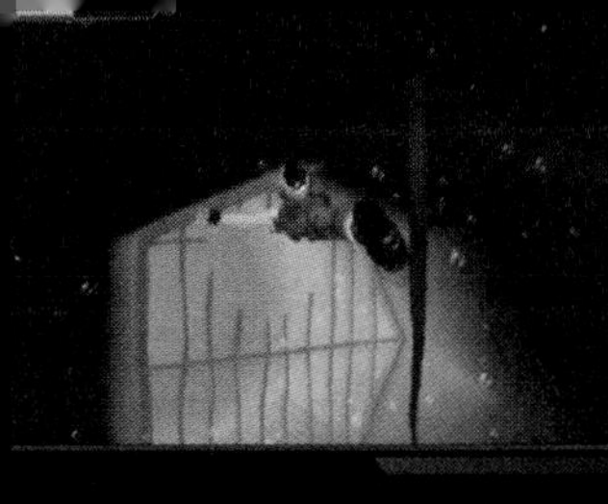

Swim through the gap in the grating, and wait for the star shape of spikes to appear. Swim through the gap between two spikes before they retract, and finally head through the gap in the grating. At the end of this tunnel is a shaft to your left.

Swim along it to find yourself underneath the door mechanism. There's no time (or air) to investigate this. Dive to the rock column under the center of the door, and locate the blue stone. This is the Water Crystal.

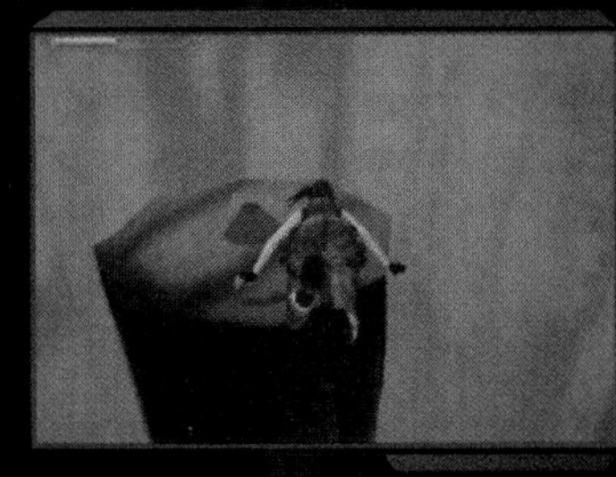

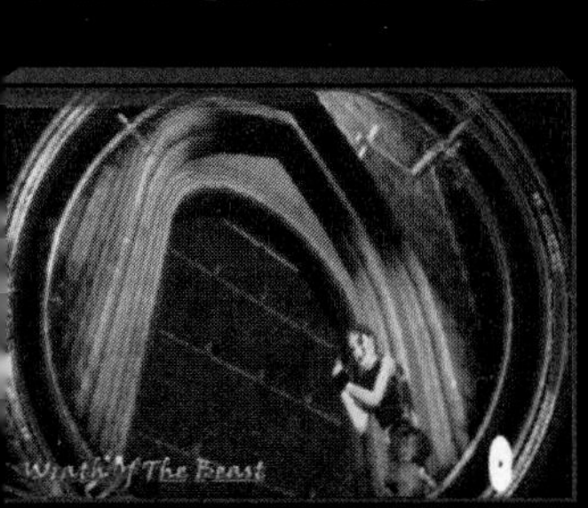

Pocket it. The door mechanism released when you took the crystal, so swim upward, through the open door mechanism, and take a breath.

Return to the murky column sides to locate and pull a lever, releasing the ornate door lock below the demon-head gargoyle carving. Surface in the large central chamber, then swim through the now-open door.

You appear inside the checkered-floor hallway, where you first found a lever. Ignore the lever, head up through the hole in the ceiling, and up to the gargoyle fountain. Clamber out of the grating hole, run back around the four columns, and head back to the Hall of Seasons.

Follow the notes outlined previously for entering The Wrath of the Beast. Tread on the earth floor pad and pull the middle lever.

Wrath of the Beast

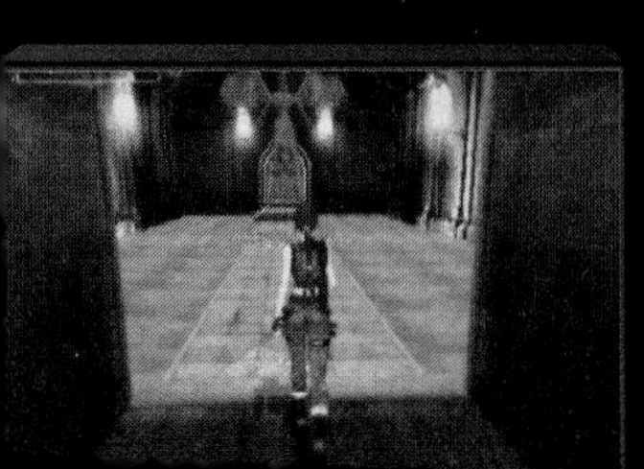

This level consists of unsteady platforms above bottomless fissures. What looks to be an empty hallway is transformed into a series of craggy platforms, which fall away as you land on them (some of them before you land on them). Follow the pattern of platforms around and to the other side of the precipitous gap, then claim the Earth Crystal. The floor reforms, but three Knights appear and should be thwarted so you can pull two levers on opposite walls to release the exit door. Flee this beastly area and never speak of it again.

ENTITIES ENCOUNTERED

- The Knight (x3)

CRITICAL ITEMS TO LOCATE

- Earth Crystal

AVAILABLE UPGRADES

- There are no available upgrades in this area.

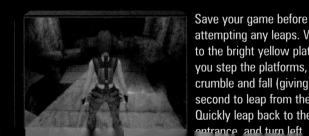

Enter through the wooden door and you watch as the flat and easily accessible hallway turns into a series of fissures and unstable ledges. The demonic statue crumbles, and an earthquake devours the hallway.

Save your game before attempting any leaps. Walk down to the bright yellow platform. As you step the platforms, they crumble and fall (giving you a second to leap from them or die). Quickly leap back to the entrance, and turn left.

Drop down onto the green platforms that are fixed to the side walls, and go around them to the corner. Turn right, then walk forward until you drop onto a green rock area. Don't jump to this platform. Once here, hop to the long thin platform ahead. Don't overshoot, as the adjacent rock beyond it is unstable.

Once you're on this long thin platform, run along it until you reach the gap, leap it, and land on a rock jutting out of the opposite wall. Save your game! Once you reach this wall area, turn left and check out the long thin plinth. This can be edged across with your back to the wall, or leapt with one quick bound.

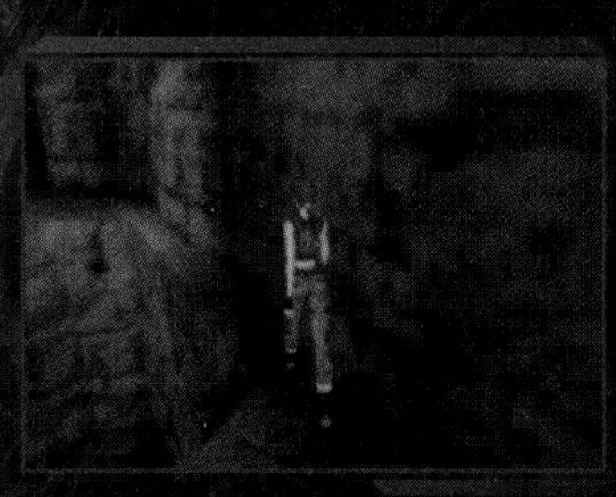

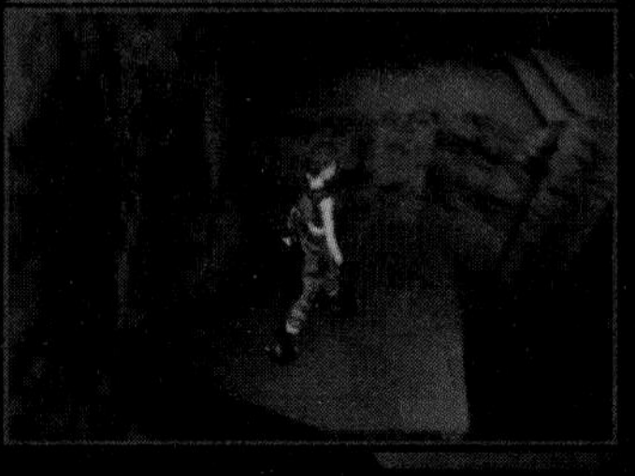

Now comes the tricky part! Turn left, and run left slightly onto the crumbling platform ahead, leaping onto the central platform just as the one behind you falls. This central section is also unsafe, so as you land, turn 90 degrees to your right, and leap again.

You'll land on another unsafe rock on the opposite wall. Sidejump immediately, making sure you land facing the wall, or you plummet to your death. Land on the crumbling platform, then turn 90 degrees right and jump again onto the last rock piece. This one doesn't fall. When you're done, leap to the corner.

Save your game, then turn right and execute a running jump to the upper ledges. Cling to the ledge, pull up, and run and leap again. Pull yourself up, leap, and grab one more time before both platforms vanish. Now clamber onto the sturdy, yellow platform.

Turn and look right to see a curved pathway leading to a large door. Save your game, then run along the right edge of the falling platforms (the left ledges fall earlier). Reach the gap and leap over it. The remaining platforms in this area crumble.

Don't leap too early or you'll fall short of the solid ground ahead, as well as the steps leading up to a great supply of V-Packer Cartridges, and a slot device holding the Earth Crystal. Take it, and the ground behind you rises up to fit together in a series of pentagons.

Step onto the platform, and draw a weapon, as three flames form ahead of you. Each is a Knight. Down a couple of them , then move to the left or right side of the hallway and pull on a lever. Repeat the process at the other side.

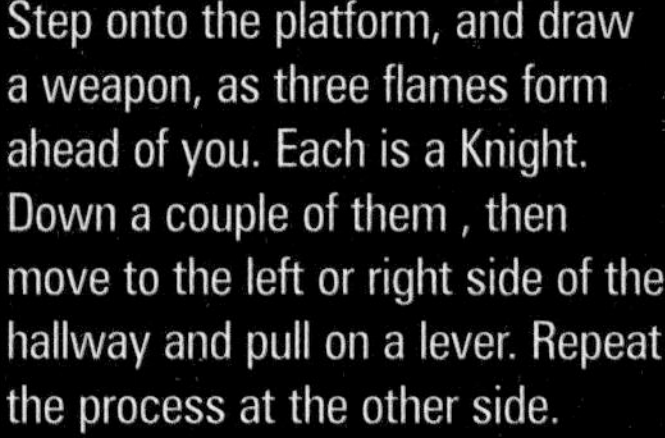

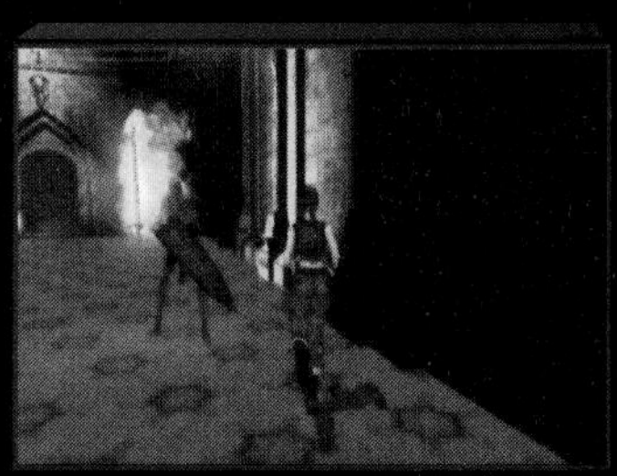

Do not fall into the maelstrom, as it spells instant death. Instead, struggle to open the exit door. It is easier to down two of the Knights, then attempt the lever; otherwise, you'll be blasted by their fire attacks. If you're doused in fire, run to one of the two water cascades over the entrances, and snuff the flames. Head through the open door, back to the Hall of Seasons.

Follow the notes outlined previously for entering The Sanctuary of Fire. Tread on the fire floor pad and pull the right lever.

The Sanctuary of Fire

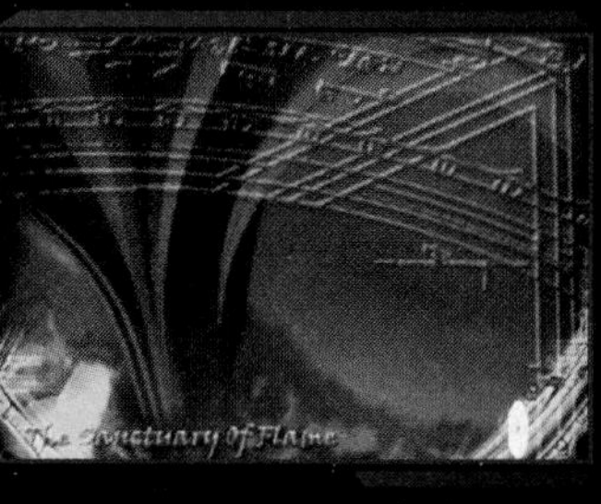

This lava-filled chamber is bristling with deadly hazards. After dropping down the steps and avoiding the channels of lava, you must hop across a series of pentagonal platforms (some of which are booby-trapped) without slipping, falling short, or jumping in the wrong direction. If you do, you'll be bathing in molten rock before you expire. If you reach the other side, take the Fire Crystal and head onto a series of floating platforms. Again, some fall away or shoot up into the ceiling. Finally, on the stepped area, escape this horrific place and pocket that well-earned crystal.

ENTITIES ENCOUNTERED
- There are no enemies in this area.

CRITICAL ITEMS TO LOCATE
- Fire Crystal

AVAILABLE UPGRADES
- There are no available upgrades in this area.

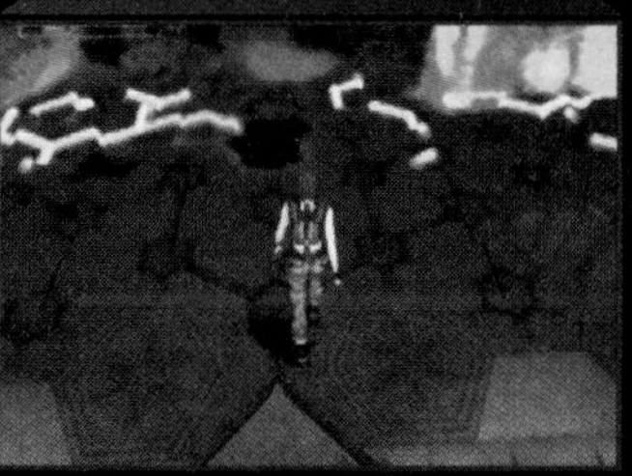

As you enter this chamber, you notice two intertwined snake carvings on either side of the entrance wall. These spill lava down channels. Wait for the lava to disperse, then save your game. Carefully tread on the blocks.

Wait for any landing fireballs to hit the ground and dissipate, then head down the steps to the right. Avoid the red blocks near the spouting lava, as these shake and explode into the air. Walk until you reach the edge of the lake of fire.

Head to the edge of the main cluster of blocks, and try a running jump on the trio of blocks ahead of you.

When you land on this trio of blocks, do not stand on the one farthest from you; it shoots into the air (carrying you to a fiery demise if you're on it). Instead, move to the block to the right side, and make a running leap to the duo of blocks ahead of you.

Leap to the two blocks ahead, but watch out as the nearer one starts to sink into the lava—quickly move onto the left block. Ignore the block to your right, and the two on your left side; all three sink when you land on them.

Instead, execute a running jump to the cluster of blocks at the end of this lake, and run over them and onto the safety of the steps. Do this at once, as the initial block sinks, and the last block shoots high into the sky. Run to the top of the steps.

Pass under the scowling gargoyle head and pry the Fire Crystal from its mount in the archway alcove. Save your game, turn around, and take a deep breath—you have to return over the lake of fire, and this time it's harder.

As you run down the steps, platforms grow out of the molten mire to aid you. Step onto the first block, and hop onto the first floating platform. Leap to the right and use two standard jumps.

Don't head left up the series of five platforms; it ends in a platform high above a central line of blocks. Drop instead to here (you need a mixture of hopping and jumping to reach the upper platform). Otherwise, try one last standard jump from the third right-side platform.

Now on the line of blocks, don't stand on the ascending far one. Instead, look left and right to see two more sets of platforms forming. Don't head right, as the middle of these right-side platforms sinks when you stand on them. Instead, look left and jump.

Use a standing jump (not a hop) to reach the trio of platforms, and don't overshoot. Move to the far one and hop to the single platform ahead of you. Now hop again to the single block, and back onto the initial block area. Save your game, and leave this hideous place through the door you came in, back to the Hall of Seasons.

Back in the Hall of Seasons, enter The Breath of Hades by stepping on the air floor pad and pulling the right lever.

The Breath of Hades

If you thought jumping across The Sanctuary of Fire was difficult, prepare for further frustration. There's some swaying and narrow columns that need pinpoint accuracy to land on. Progression over this series of ledges is further impeded by wind from numerous directions, courtesy of stone dragon heads that can blow you off course if you're jumping, or even standing on the swaying stalk platforms. Be forward thinking and check the wall to the right of your starting location for a lever that raises the portcullis on the other side of the gap, or you won't be able to reach the Air Crystal. With the final crystal in your grasp, return across the airy crevasse, and enter the Hall of Seasons to slot each of the four elements in the furnace beneath the main hall.

ENTITIES ENCOUNTERED
- There are no enemies in this area.

CRITICAL ITEMS TO LOCATE
- Air Crystal

AVAILABLE UPGRADES
- There are no available upgrades in this area.

As you step into this frightful chamber, you see there are ten stone dragon heads lining the left, right, and far walls. They randomly blow out smoke, one at a time, with no discernable pattern.

If you're hit by a blast of this smoke, you're knocked off the tiny stalk-like column you're resting on (or jumping to), making this leaping extra treacherous. Peer into the gloom at the back of this room.

A portcullis bars the way to the holder with the final crystal on it, and you don't want to waste time leaping over this crevasse more times than is absolutely necessary. Find a way to raise the portcullis.

Locate the section of darker wall bricks, and push them just as you would a crate. They disappear into the wall, and the entire section is shoved inwards, revealing a hidden alcove with two clips inside. At the end is a lever. Pull it.

This opens the barred portcullis. Now head to the edge of the crevasse, and save your game. Wait for the smoke from the nearest dragons to pass, and hop to the first column in the middle of the crevasse area.

You can also move to the left area and try a standing jump to a column slightly farther away on the left side of the crevasse. From here, hop forward to another column, and again to a third column along the left side of the pit. As you land on the third column, a rumbling occurs.

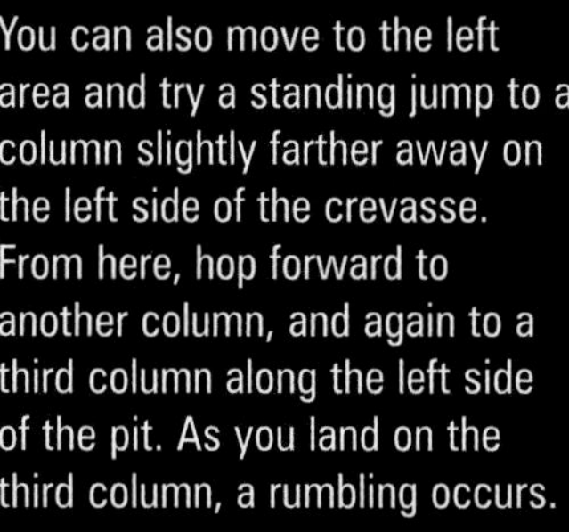

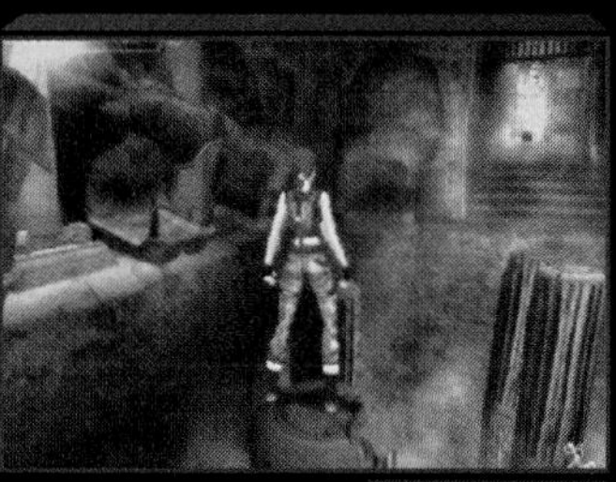

The dragon head to your left (the third from the foreground when you enter the room) rumbles back, revealing a Large Health Pack and two V-Packer Cartridges under its jaw. This is a purely optional item to grab. Now jump (don't hop) onto the alcove and claim your prize.

Stand on the edge of the dragon alcove and jump to the column nearest you, then attempt a running jump off the column to the second platform nearest to the far side of the pit. This is possible, but incredibly difficult.

If you're taking the normal route, all movement to the second-to-last platform is achieved by hopping. Judge each leap, as some require you to wait until the columns are farther apart, and you may need to leap from the edge farther from your target so you don't overshoot.

When you're on the second to last column, attempt a running jump over the last column and land on the solid, stone surface. Run up the steps (you did remember to release the portcullis, didn't you?) and grab the Air Crystal. Now to retrace your steps.

Save your game. Run down the left side (if you're facing the entrance) and try a strong running jump to the fourth column, ignoring the first three. This is easier than hopping over the first three.

Now hop to the next column, then the second to last column nearest the exit. From here, you can turn around and leap. Press Backward and Jump to back-flip onto the stairs, then exit this chamber. All four crystals are yours. Head out the door.

Returning to the Dig Site

Activating the Furnace

Run back into the main Hall of Seasons, and move to the central floor pads.

Now that you have all four of the crystals, access the basement traps area of the Hall of Seasons. Purposefully choose an incorrect lever, fall into the basement, and head to the door on the inner wall.

This leads down a spiral staircase. At the bottom is a door which opens to reveal a lever. Pull it to reveal a set of straight steps leading to a circular furnace area. Make a left turn, jogging along a curved, wooden platform.

At the left side of this is a small platform leading to a valve in the wall. This is part of the device to power the furnace, waiting for a crystal to activate it. Turn the valve here, near the stone glyph for Air.

Now locate the three other holders for the remaining crystals. Descend to the ground area using the ladder near the entrance door. Move down the rungs onto the wooden platform below the upper one.

TIP Want to show off? Dangle from the upper, curved platform and drop off it. Now stab the Action button and grab hold of the lower, curved platform. This saves time climbing down ladders. Don't dangle and drop off this lower platform, though; you'll fall into lava.

Climb down the lower platform ladder and onto the base of the furnace. A lone Knight thwarts you, but he is easily outrun. Locate the ladder against the outer area of this structure and climb it before the Knight catches up to you.

At the top of the ladder is a valve for the furnace. This is where you turn the valve associated with the fire crystal. Because the furnace has a series of traps set off after all valves are turned, come back here later. For now, turn the valve, or run around this wooden ledge next to the furnace.

You are looking for a chain spanning the furnace. Grab the chain and shimmy along it to the jutting wooden ledge on the outer side of this chamber. When you're above it, drop and run toward the ladder.

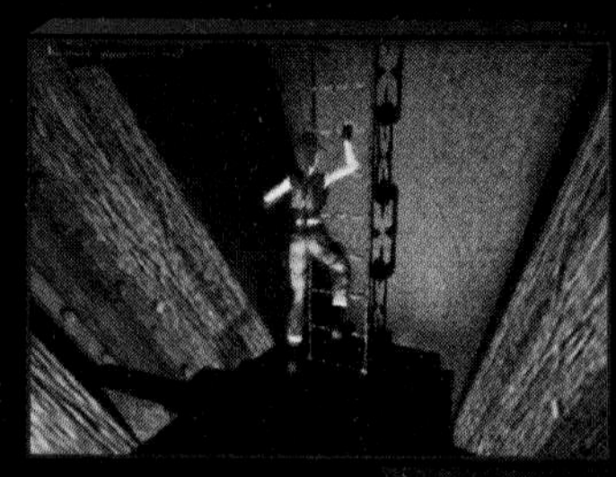

Climb the ladder adjacent to the vertical chain until you reach the top of it. Back-flip off onto a wooden ledge on the upper area, above the wooden ledge and chain. Now turn and run around the small, wooden platform to the ladder and climb it.

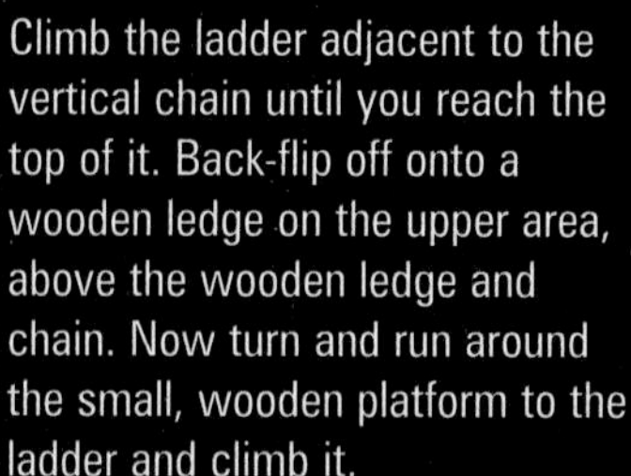

Shimmy off the right side of the ladder to the small uppermost platform, and turn right. The giant pipe connecting the outer wall to the furnace (and supplying fuel to four platforms in the Hall of Seasons) needs a valve turning . The Earth Crystal helped you reach this point.

Climb down the ladder to the small, wooden platform, but do not descend the second ladder near the giant chain. Instead, turn and look at the furnace. There is an upper, circular platform. Execute a running jump to it.

Run around this platform until you spot another chain, this one leading to a high, wooden platform you haven't visited yet. Shimmy across to the platform, drop onto it, then turn left and run to the base of the ladder. Climb it to a tiny, upper alcove.

Once atop the alcove, turn right and locate the valve in the wall. You hear a creaking noise from below and the sound of water gushing into the furnace. The furnace door has opened and the entire structure is activating!

You can drop from the alcove or climb down the ladder to the platform below. Shimmy across the chain to the upper circle platform of the furnace. From here, dangle off the platform, drop and press Action to catch the lower platform, then pull yourself up here.

Pay close attention to the rotating blades nearby and leap to the left of them, across the wooden circle platform, to the curved platform near the way you came in. A running jump makes it here (stretch out to grab the edge of the platform).

Save your game, move to the rope elevator entrance (in the outer wall of the basement of traps), and utilize it to ascend two floors to the main Hall of Seasons. Head through the doors and you appear near the rubble. Something has happened.

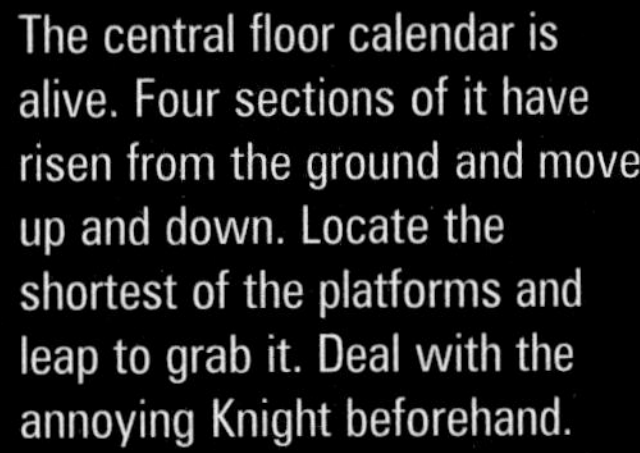

The central floor calendar is alive. Four sections of it have risen from the ground and move up and down. Locate the shortest of the platforms and leap to grab it. Deal with the annoying Knight beforehand.

Now run to the open furnace door and around to the final valve. Ignore this if you already turned it. If you didn't, you can avoid the swinging blades that have activated. An incredible grinding sound is heard as the furnace roars to life. Unfortunately, it also sets off a number of thrashing metal traps throughout this chamber. Time to go.

Climb down the ladder to the base level and crawl under the rotating blades, or wait for one to pass, and run after it before it circles and catches you. Run to the ladder and climb two floors of curved, wooden platforms to the exit.

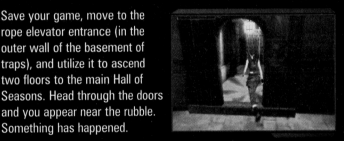

TIP **If you want to stay off the floor, climb the rubble and make a running jump at the column to your right. Land on it, then continue to jump and climb.**

Wait for your platform to ascend and the one to your right to descend. When they are at equal height, make a standing jump to the next one. Repeat this two more times until you reach the highest (fourth) column. Stand on this as it ascends.

At the platform's highest point, jump and grab the edge of the circular support with the four girders protruding from it. Pull yourself onto the circular girder, turn left, and run to the flat girder on this structure. Run along it.

You've made it to the lower balcony of the Hall of Seasons. Continue upward. Jump or vault over the balcony, then turn right. If you turn left, you jog to a barred wall that you cannot pass. Ignore the left area.

As you begin your run, an alcove in the outer wall shatters, and a Knight appears from it. Ignore it and continue your jogging. Run around the inside of the hole in the balcony.

Run under and around the staircase. Ignore the bars in front of you (this is where you'd end up if you took the left turn after the girder) and instead climb the stairs. If you want extra speed, jump the steps five at a time.

Once at the top, there is a sealed arch in front of you, a locked door to your right, and an entrance to the upper balcony on your left. Run into the upper balcony, make a left, and jog around the upper balcony quickly.

You can't enter the upper balcony and turn right, as there's a dangerous gap that you cannot leap. However, when you reach the other side of the gap (after running around the balcony and dodging the Knights), check the wall to the left of the hole. It can be climbed.

Shimmy up the wall, then move diagonally upward and right, heading for the narrow ledge near the fallen rock wall. Continue until you're above the ledge lip, then drop. Turn and pull the lever. The locked door atop the stairs creaks open.

Don't leap to the stairs entrance from here—you'll fall. Instead, climb down to the upper balcony the way you came, run around the upper balcony, back through the entrance, and through the raised door.

You find yourself at a dead end with V-Packer cartridges to pick up. However, there is a patch of darkened wall to push. Hold the Action button and shove the wall section into a small hidden passage with a Large Health Pack in it.

Lara feels stronger; she has just increased her grip (Upgrade Grip: Upper Body Level 7). She can now hang longer while climbing or monkey-swinging. This is important, as you must exit this ancient place with haste.

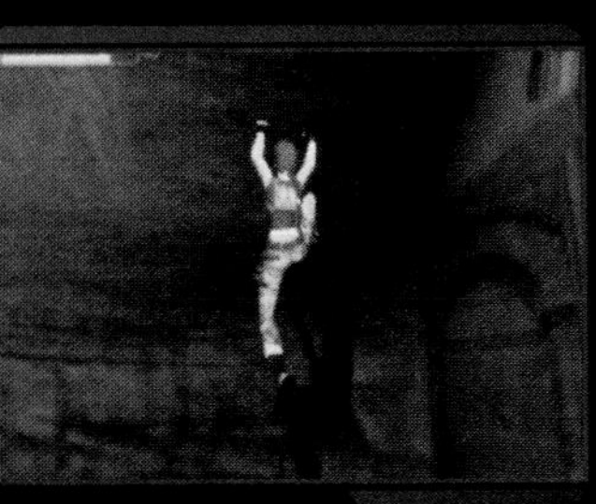

Retrace your steps back around the upper balcony to the lever. From the narrow ledge, wall climb upward, but this time keep going. Do not climb this wall prior to Lara's upgrade, or you won't have the strength to complete it.

Lara climbs, hangs, and climbs up an overhang, then grabs the rock roof, spins around, and continues to climb. Once she's monkey-swinging, look for a small ledge for her to move to (on the left rock wall) so she can regain her strength.

Don't continue without this rest. Cling to the roof, and follow the seam of the rock so you aren't spending time hanging around—you need every second. Climb up the overhang and continue up, into the roof structure.

Quickly move to the side and drop onto the circular roof chamber. Run to the door, and it opens. Dash into the narrow corridor with the T-junction at the end. To the right is a locked door.

To the left is a staircase. Climb the stairs, and as you ascend, a door opens at the top. This leads to a ancient altar, where the bodies of certain Obscura experiments were kept and rituals were performed. Lara steps past the statues.

Reading the Latin inscription on the sarcophagus, Lara translates it to mean "through the spirit of the keeper beholds the truth." It seems that the "keeper" has already shown himself. A hooded, floating, monk-like figure appears in the chamber.

Brother Obscura

Draw your weapon (the shotgun is ideal for this battle) and take a defensive stance. Brother Obscura has taken a dislike to your presence here and will float about you, readying himself for a charge, which damages you.

Before Brother Obscura has a chance to swoop in on you, blast him with your shotgun. The force of the attack backs him up. Alas, he comes back just as strong. It seems Brother Obscura suffers the same immortal fate as the Knights.

You cannot defeat Brother Obscura, only ward him off for a few seconds. When you achieve this, scan the statues surrounding the sarcophagus for a shining blue light. Sheath your weapon and run to this light immediately.

Press Action at the light, and you can take Obscura Painting #1 from the statue. Wait too long, and the painting randomly moves to another statue, and Brother Obscura attacks again. Once the painting is in your possession, flee.

Head out of the altar room and down the steps. Something isn't right—there is waist-deep water at the bottom of the steps. Taking the picture triggered an ancient trap, and the entire tomb is filling with water. Move quickly through to the door that opens.

You appear inside the Tomb of Ancients. Slosh forward through the water, and the corridor you're in completely fill up. Look at the hole in the roof of the tunnel, and swim through as fast as you can. Exit through an open trapdoor.

You appear out on the opposite side of the broken bridge. Ignore the sealed door behind you—swim into the now-underwater cylindrical cavern, and swim upward.

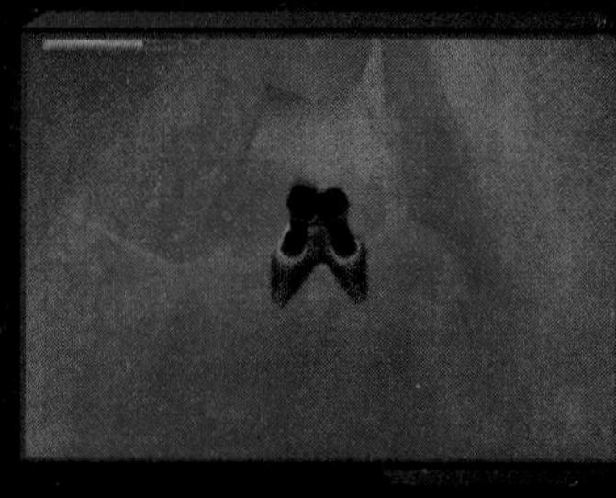

Point yourself forward and up, but don't head for the small hole. That's not the exit cave; it is farther up toward the ceiling. If you're running out of breath, swim to the air hole at the very top, grabbing the Health Bandages on the ledge while you're at it. Swim into the upper cave hole, past the wooden beam, and into the entrance to the tomb.

You appear outside of the digging area, emerging from a secret exit. Run to the crate next to the mesh wall, climb onto it and over the wall, then turn and enter the large double security doors. Time to investigate this painting inside the Louvre.

Galleries Under Siege

Back in the Louvre, there seems to be something strange about the Obscura Painting you obtained. A quick trip back to the x-ray machine inside the art gallery helps you find out what it is. Alas, your progress has been tracked by a paramilitary organization known as the Agency, headed by a threatening Prussian named Gundersen. Agency troops storm the Louvre, spreading poison gas throughout the gallery. While fighting these assailants, you must ascend to the x-ray room, obtain the Respirator, x-ray the painting, and descend through the unlocked door. Once in the lower gallery, you're surprised by the appearance of the motorcyclist who's been watching you from the shadows for longer than you know.

ENTITIES ENCOUNTERED

- Museum Guard
- Gendarme Security (x2)
- Agency Soldier (x9)
- Marten Gundersen
- Kurtis Trent
- Louis Bouchard
- Bouchard's Bodyguard

CRITICAL ITEMS TO LOCATE

- Respirator

AVAILABLE UPGRADES

- **Upgrade Dash Enable: Lower Body Level 6**
  Locating the Respirators allows Lara the luxury of sprinting.

With the authorities now fully aware of your infiltration, you must take the Obscura Painting to the x-ray chamber near Carvier's office. Run past the bright lights illuminating the entrance to the dig.

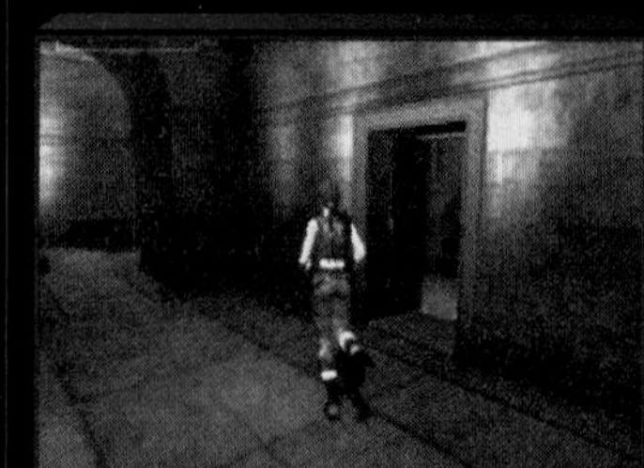

Head up the wide staircase, and at the top of the steps, turn left. To the right lies a dead-end chamber containing a stack of boxes. Once in the left portion of the connecting corridor, dash for the open double doors on the right wall.

Ignore the remainder of this passage. Jog up the staircase, make a right turn, and follow the stairs upward. As you make a second right turn, draw your preferred weapon or ready your fists.

Aim at the incoming security guard, or launch a volley of non-lethal flurries into him. Once he collapses to the ground, collect the Vector-R35 Clip he drops. The chamber he was guarding is of little interest.

Instead, continue up the stairs, past the information board, and up another flight. You witness a stealth infiltration of the Louvre. Teams of soldiers wearing military-grade combat suits with respirators flood the main areas with gas, knocking out the guard.

Rappelling from the air ducts, Marten Gundersen arrives. These soldiers are working for the Agency. Gundersen barks orders: "Synch to sector A9! Fan out and keep low! Maintain radio silence! You have your targets! Move out!" This looks like trouble.

You disturb another guard at the top of the staircase, between the two bull statues. Beat down the museum guard and collect another Vector-R35 clip. Enter the corridor to the door around the left corner. The gas is seeping through. Save your game.

As you open the door, you see that the chamber is filled with noxious gas. There are gas masks in the area next to the x-ray machine, so race there as soon as possible. First, though, there's a guard to handle at the door to your left.

Press the Stealth button and silently edge forward toward the guard. Press Action to grab him about the neck and bring him to the ground. This doesn't attract any nearby guards and allows you to grab his Mag Vega machine gun.

Walk through the door he was guarding (the display chamber you're in leads to a sealed door) and run toward the exit at the other end of the room.

On the way, you meet a second Agency special forces soldier. Introduce him to your Mag Vega (or any other weapon), then stoop to pick the Mag Vega ammo he drops when he crumples. If you have time, you can retrace your steps to the previous room.

There are two more special forces soldiers here who can be taken out, and their ammunition collected. However, a wiser move is to run toward the far end of the display corridor, past the rope the soldiers rappelled on, and into the entrance chamber.

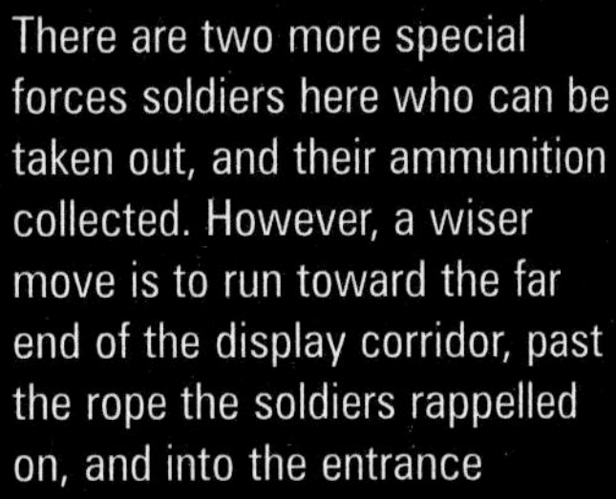

There is only one exit, to your left through the open door (the others are sealed, with the one ahead of you lit by a red warning light). This leads to the corridor and the metal staircase you descended after entering Carvier's office. At the base of the stairs, gun down the waiting Agency goon.

Climb the staircase with haste; you don't have much air left. Keep going until you reach the top, then open the door that leads to the narrow corridor with Carvier's office at the far end. Ignore the door on your left, and take the door to your right.

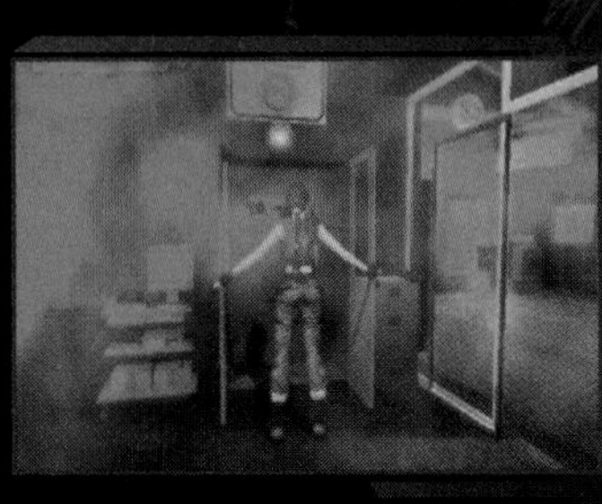

You can run into the art restoration room without the soldier running from the far end of the corridor attacking you. Run into the room, through the two glass doors, and claim the Respirator. All this running strengthens Lara's legs (Upgrade Dash: Lower Body Level 6).

Inspect your inventory, and place the Respirator onto your face. Lara can now run (using the Sprint button) for short periods of time. Test this out in a moment, but first, tackle the soldier firing at you. Blast or beat him to the ground, and take his Mag Vega ammunition.

You've already ransacked Carvier's office and the room next to it, so head back into the room with the gas masks and inspect the x-ray computer. Take the Obscura Painting #1 and insert it into the x-ray machine. The results are shocking.

With this newfound information pocketed, it's time to leave. Exit the x-ray room, run down the corridor, open the door to the metal staircase, and jog down the steps. Turn left along the corridor, until you reach the entrance chamber.

Just as you leave for the metal stairs, the red light above the double doors in this room switches off, and the door unlocks. You can now enter this doorway and secure the chamber beyond. This is the room with the ancient rugs lining the walls. Draw your weapon.

Tackle the Agency soldier rappelling from above, and collect any Mag Vega ammunition he drops. Once he's been subdued, keep your weapon primed and tackle two more soldiers on the stairs by the large Greek statue. Then descend the stairs.

Turn left at the base of the main stairs, then run down the narrow set of steps to the connecting corridor below. Turn right and enter the open doorway. The other side of this corridor is empty, save for the sealed door. Once through, make a left turn.

Lara is startled by a surprise attack. Whistling through the air is an unknown discus-type device (actually an ancient weapon known as the Chirugai) that narrowly misses her. She is then ambushed by the mysterious motorcyclist.

The man known as Kurtis Trent, disarms Lara, but she manages to palm a ceremonial Shard. They stare at each other, then Kurtis escapes. Lara begins to pursue him just as Gundersen arrives on the scene.

The Agency power-player orders his underling to fire, strafing a display cabinet as Lara runs for safety. As she makes a break for the fire escape, the Chirugai returns to Trent's grasp, and he uses it to dislodge a giant gong. Both Lara and Trent dive through the door.

A hapless Agency goon is crushed at the door by the rolling gong, and the path is blocked. Gundersen is upset. Back on the fire escape, Trent executes an impressive acrobatic maneuver and disappears from view. Lara runs down the stairs after him.

Appearing outside the Louvre in a deserted alley, Lara spies Trent lying comatose on the ground. As she inspects him, she's struck from behind by an Agency soldier. Through her flickering eyelids, she spies a strange figure (Bouchard's body guard) striding away.

Regaining consciousness, and with Trent nowhere to be found, Lara rendezvouses with Bouchard, and they ride in his car to Werner Von Croy's apartment. With her discovery of identical occult markings on the walls of the apartment and the Obscura Painting, Lara needs to solve a few riddles.

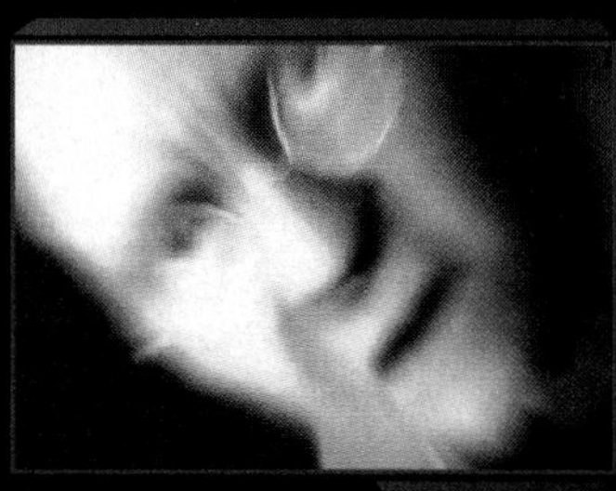

Tearing apart the police cordon tape, Lara relives the death of Von Croy in her mind's eye. Ritual markings splatter the wall. Lara steps on a picture of her and Werner. The death of Von Croy is played over. This time, the professor is agitated at the shadows.

Out strides a man with a strange glove-like device strapped to his hand. One swipe sends Lara sprawling into the wall. Now she remembers—she didn't kill Von Croy. She is innocent. She must locate the deviant responsible.

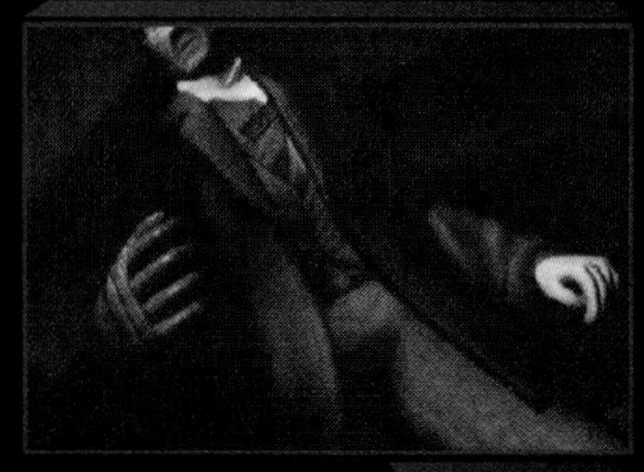

Von Croy's Apartment

Returning to Von Croy's apartment is a cathartic experience for Lara, as she ponders the murder of the professor and realizes who is responsible. There's no time to blame anyone, as the double-crossing Bouchard has left you a present in the form of a madman known as the Cleaner. Clock him in a series of fraught battles throughout the apartment complex as you avoid both his bullets and the numerous laser trip wires he leaves behind. After stamping out this mercenary, you realize you can trust no one. You must follow the scene of the Monstrum crimes to the capital of the Czech Republic, Prague.

ENTITIES ENCOUNTERED
- The Cleaner
- Louis Bouchard

CRITICAL ITEMS TO LOCATE
- Jackal Walking Stick
- Rigg 09 Pistol

AVAILABLE UPGRADES
- **Upgrade Kick Door/Wall: Lower Body Level 7**
  A swift kick to a door behind the spiral stairs allows access upstairs and through a fire door.

The Cleaner is hiding, waiting for you to make a mistake. Grab the Rigg 09 pistol and three sets of ammo from the floor to the right of the sofa, or bring out your weapon of choice (the V-Packer shotgun is excellent) and prepare for battle. Sometimes the Cleaner appears only after you have searched the apartment for ammunition.

NOTE Don't try to escape. If you flee the apartment without dishing damage to the Cleaner, an inescapable "Z"-shaped trip wire blocks your path. It's only deactivated after the Cleaner leaves the area.

Take cover behind the sofa, the wall column to the right of it, or the wall column on your left. Wait for the Cleaner to shoot a burst of machine gun fire, then dart out and blast him with your gun. Hand-to-hand combat is unwise and suicidal.

You can move in on the Cleaner by running around the sofa (or left column) and diving into the open office adjacent to the kitchen (there's two more ammo clips here). Plug away at your assailant until he makes a move from the kitchen. He runs either to the dining room table opposite the office…

...or the sofa where you began your fight. As he darts out, make run into the kitchen for cover, then fire your preferred weapon on him after he lets off a round. Continue to strike him, bob back into cover, and hit him again. After the fight, take the two Rigg Clips from the kitchen island.

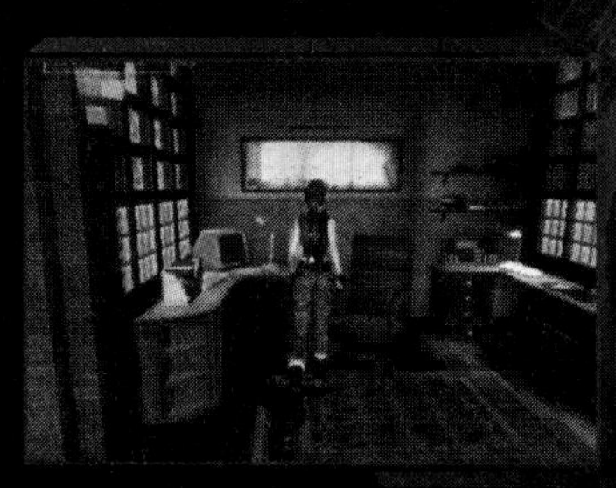

After five or six good takedown shots, the heavily armored Cleaner moves from the sofas and through the exit door. Don't follow him yet—he will be back later. Instead, look around Von Croy's apartment. Start with the Rigg Clip behind the dining room table.

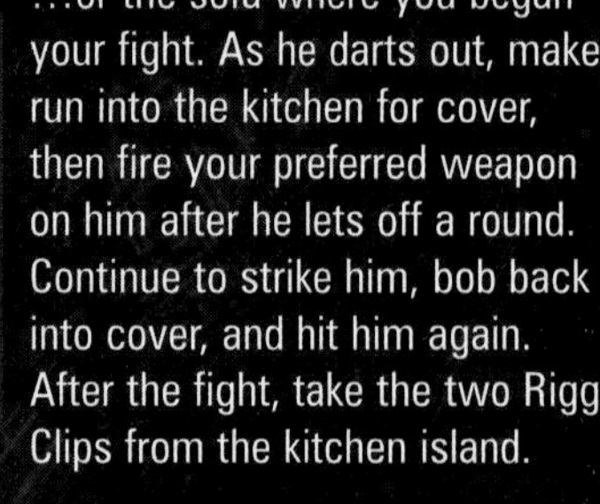

There's the Jackal Walking Stick near your starting point, and arcane literature on the Sanglyph and Lux Veritatis in Von Croy's study. All three items are added to your Notebook. Move around the spiral staircase (don't climb that yet) and check out the door behind it, in the corner near the Health Bandages.

Kick it open to check the other side, which is a small hallway and stairs to the left. Fortunately, that boot strengthens Lara considerably, granting her extra leg power (Upgrade Kick Door/Wall: Lower Body Level 7). Pick up the two Rigg ammo on the sideboard and on the floor, then head up the stairs.

Up the stairs is a bathroom. A Rigg 09 Clip is in the left corner, and a small Health Pack is near the shower. Turn left and head up the steps to another door. Kick it open to enter Von Croy's spacious bedroom.

There are two Rigg Clips on the floor, another by the bed, and another Rigg Clip and a Large Health Pack inside the closet. Head down the spiral stairs to the kitchen. If you ascended the stairs, the door to the bathroom wouldn't be accessible—you must kick open the hallway door below. If you started this area without ranged weaponry, the Cleaner appears now.

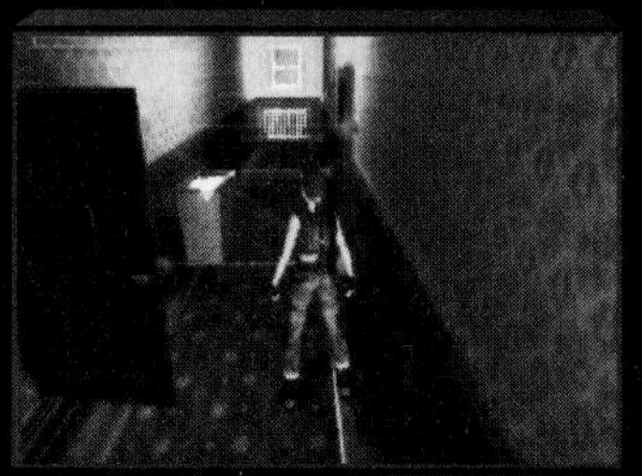

Time to leave. Pass under the ransacked bookcase doorway, make a left turn, and head out of the apartment and into the building. By the door with the police caution tape that you ripped open earlier, be careful. Turn left to see trip wires spread along the corridor.

The backwards "Z" pattern of the trip wires impedes your progress; it seems the Cleaner is more cunning than previously thought. Turn around and move along the corridor toward the red fire door. You must have upgraded your kick to open it.

Behind the red door is a landing with a Small Health Pack and a Rigg Clip. Don't step any farther into this area; another series of trip wires rigged to explosives halts you dead in your path. Return to the main corridor.

The wall with the two doors isn't of interest—only the open door on your right (or left if you didn't access the fire door). Head through this door to a rummaged room with papers scattered everywhere. Take a Rigg Clip from the papers. Save your game and draw your weapon; the Cleaner is near.

As you round the left corner, you'll see an item behind an upturned sofa to the left. As you pick up the Rigg 09 Clip, the Cleaner shoots a man-sized hole in the plaster and destroys the wall. React to this ambush by leaping and shooting around the room, seeking cover behind the sofa and entrance wall.

The Cleaner drops his machine gun in favor of two pistols. Blast him about four times until he's badly wounded and staggers away through an open door in the adjacent hall. Heal, then step through the wall opening the Cleaner created. Pick up his dropped Viper SMG near the hole, plus the two Viper SMG Clips and Chocolate Bar on the covered table behind you.

The closed door is locked, but the open one allows you to enter the main corridor, on the other side of the "Z" trip wires. Turn and view the remainder of the corridor. There are deviously positioned wires to navigate with skill and timing. Save the game.

The three laser wires are easy to avoid. Execute a Commando Crawl under the first, and continue under the second and third. Stand up and peer around the corner. The landing looks safe enough—until it is destroyed by remote.

Intense fire is enveloping the landing ahead, so ignore this area and head down the steps. Almost immediately, there is a gap in the staircase. Jump this gap to avoid setting yourself on fire. All the other areas of this landing are either dangerous or dead ends. Turn left, then drop down this hole.

When you land on the staircase below, turn around and walk up the three steps, then turn and check out the lower floor corridor. It looks the same as the one you just came from until you make a left turn. Head there after descending to the tile floor and taking the two Rigg 09 Clips and Large Health Pack from under the stairs and the nearby table.

Save your progress. Deactivated trip wires are laid in front of you. Simply hop through them—they have a one-second timer and then form a "Z" shape preventing backtracking, but you won't be hurt if you move before they activate. Take the Rigg Clip from the corridor in front of you, then run, aiming at the alcove on the left.

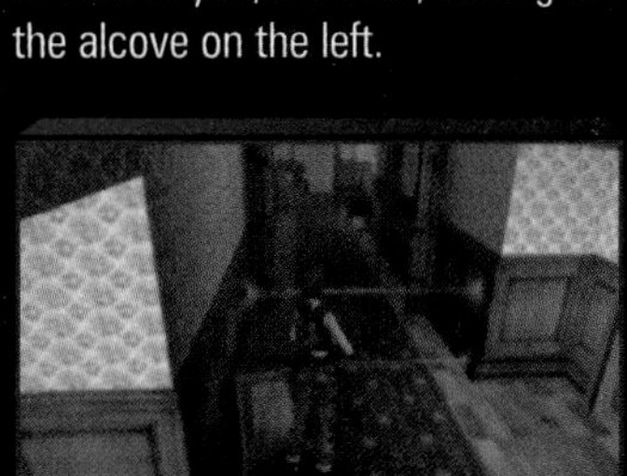

Reposition yourself in the corridor, then dive to the doorway alcove ahead and to the right as the Cleaner takes potshots at you from the end of this passage. Stay here and don't get shot by the Cleaner. Look at the set of three trip wires, all blinking in front of you.

There is one, low-level trip wire that remains on constantly. The other three sets of wires blink off and on in order, starting with the ones next to you, then the ones halfway down this passage (above the one constant wire), and the set nearest the Cleaner. Put away your weapon and save your game!

As soon as the trip wires furthest from you (the third set) switch on, run and jump over the single middle trip wire, then land in the left doorway alcove. Bring out the Cleaner's Viper SMG, and strafe him until he staggers back and falls down the stairs. You can faintly hear a phone ringing.

The phone is still ringing when you reach the defeated Cleaner. Bouchard is on the line. "Is she dead, yet?" croaks Bouchard, "We have to get back to Prague!" The double-crosser is about to be paid back for his dealings with the Agency.

Lara answers the phone, leaving the Frenchman sweaty and nervous. Taking a pass card from the Cleaner's body, Lara detonates the remaining explosives with his timer and unlocks his SUV. It is time to visit Prague.

The Monstrum Crimescene

After Lara's adventures on the streets of Paris and underneath the Louvre, her quest takes her to Prague. Despite the chilly weather, she's in hot pursuit of Louis Bouchard, whose "Cleaner" didn't manage to tidy up his loose ends in Von Croy's apartment. Along the way, she hopes to find Mathias Vasiley, who's also hunting for the Obscura Paintings.

Lara's not the only person who's traveled from France to the Czech Republic recently—the Monstrum has preceded her and murdered Vasiley in his apartment. All the doors are locked, and policemen patrol the crime scene. Lara must enter Vasiley's apartment through the sewers and unlock the secret of the fifth engraving, which leads to the final Obscura Painting.

ENTITIES ENCOUNTERED

- Luddick, a reporter
- Czech policemen (x2)
- Rottweiler
- Louis Bouchard

CRITICAL ITEMS TO LOCATE

- Vasiley Full Fax
- Last Obscura Engraving
- Cellar Key

AVAILABLE UPGRADES

- **Upgrade Shoulder Barge: Upper Body Level 8** By pulling a chest of drawers in Vasiley's apartment, Lara increases her upper-body strength.

Upon arriving in Prague, head toward Luddick, the reporter standing next to the red car. He's covering the Monstrum story. If Lara has enough Euros in her pocket, he's willing to share some dossiers about the Monstrum killings and provide Lara with information about Eckhardt.

NOTE **Don't worry if you don't have the cash. This information is not essential, and you can pick it up from other sources as you go.**

According to Luddick, Vasiley was more than an art dealer, he was also involved with the Mafia. He found something that the Mafia wanted, and when he tried to hold on to it, the Monstrum took him out. All of the evidence was taken to the Strahov, the center of Mafia operations in Prague. Luddick's crude "dossier" is nothing more than a grainy photo of Bouchard and Eckhardt. Lara tells him who Bouchard is, and Luddick tells her that he thinks Eckhardt is the Mafia's top dog. Eckhardt and the other five major Mafia figures have met up at the Strahov. Luddick can get Lara into the Strahov, but he needs to work his contacts a bit.

TIP **To get the maximum amount of information from Luddick, make the following choices when in dialogue with him:**

- **"The one you're watching? With police tape all round it."**
- **"I gather Vasiley was some kind of an art dealer."**
- **"How could you possibly know that?"**
- **"Keep talking till the money runs out."**
- **"All of them?"**

After speaking with Luddick, go down the nearby alley and take out the policeman at the end of it. It's possible to sneak up on him in Stealth mode, but it's difficult. Instead, draw your pistol and shoot him from a distance.

Head out of the alley, and toward the courtyard. Run to the opposite corner from where you started. There's a policeman here; sneak past him or take him out.

Walk down either of the two alleys in this corner of the courtyard; they join behind the building. There's another policeman and a Rottweiler back here, so move carefully and keep a weapon ready.

Once you're rid of the policeman and Rottweiler, stand near the steaming sewer grate, press the Action button, and drop through into the sewers.

Walk down the sewer tunnel and take the first right. Continue along the ledge of the sewer until you come to the hole in the sewer wall. Walk through that hole and into the basement of Vasiley's apartment.

Go through the open door and up the stairs.

At the top of the stairs, walk forward until a cutscene starts. Lara sees Bouchard rummaging through Vasiley's papers. She sneaks up on him and puts a gun to his head. As he slowly turns around, she pistol-whips him and knocks him out. Lara handcuffs Bouchard to the radiator. When the cutscene is over, press Action to speak with him.

NOTE **To get the most out of your conversation with Bouchard, make the following choices during conversation with him.**

- *"A psycho, huh?"*
- *"The Cabal? Not the Mafia?"*
- *"I found Vasiley's faxes, and four Obscura Engravings he sent to Von Croy."*
- *"Killed like Vasiley, you mean! Why does Eckhardt do that to the bodies, Bouchard? And what does he want the Paintings for?"*
- *"A Lux Veritatis vault!"*

Eckhardt ordered Bouchard to kill Lara in Paris. She was a "loose end" that he wanted tied up. Eckhardt was responsible for killing Bouchard's men and injuring Arnaud. Not only is Eckhardt a monster, he is the Monstrum.

Bouchard had to take a painting from the Louvre and bring it to the Strahov in Prague on Eckhardt's behalf. Eckhardt is protected by the Cabal, a mysterious group based in Prague. The Cabal is far older and more dangerous than the Mafia, which it uses as a front for its activities. Anyone who asks too many questions disappears, like Von Croy.

Von Croy was hired to find the Obscura Painting in the Louvre, but he figured out too much of the Cabal's plan and got in touch with Vasiley in Prague. They exchanged information, and Vasiley sent Von Croy four of the Obscura Engravings, but he kept one from Von Croy. The Obscura Engravings contain encoded maps of the locations of the Obscura Paintings, and Von Croy used one of them to find the Louvre Obscura Painting.

However, the Cabal intercepted Von Croy and Vasiley's faxes, which meant that it no longer needed Von Croy's services. He and Vasiley became liabilities that Eckhardt was eager to eliminate.

Bouchard doesn't know why Eckhardt wants the Obscura Paintings, but he knows that it has something to do with reviving the Cubiculum Nephili, a.k.a. the Sleeper, the last of the extinct Nephilim race. Eckhardt thinks he can use the Sleeper to breed the Nephilim back from extinction.

The final Obscura Engraving shows the location of the Vault of Trophies, one of the last Lux Veritatis strongholds. Eckhardt desperately wants to get into it. The Lux Veritatis rounded up all five Obscura Paintings in the late 1400s and hid them in the vault; the final Obscura Painting is almost certainly in that vault. The only thing Bouchard knows about the vault is that it's beneath the Strahov.

Lara decides to have a look around Vasiley's apartment for the fifth Obscura Engraving. When Bouchard asks Lara if she's going to leave him cuffed to the radiator, she replies that she is. Bouchard's been moving around too much for her tastes.

Once the conversation is over and you regain control of Lara, head through the door opposite Bouchard to search for the fifth Obscura Engraving.

In the great hall beyond the door, climb the spiral staircase to the second story landing.

Walk across the landing to find a bluish-green chest of drawers. Pull or push it to enhance Lara's Upper-Body Strength Upper Body 8.

NOTE **This strength upgrade allows you to pull the chains on the scaffolding around the stained glass window.**

Return to the scaffolding above the spiral staircase, then jump and pull yourself up along its various levels until you reach the top.

Once you reach the top of the scaffolding, turn and face the large stained glass window opposite the door you came through. Walk carefully to the end of the scaffolding and jump to the section directly in front of you.

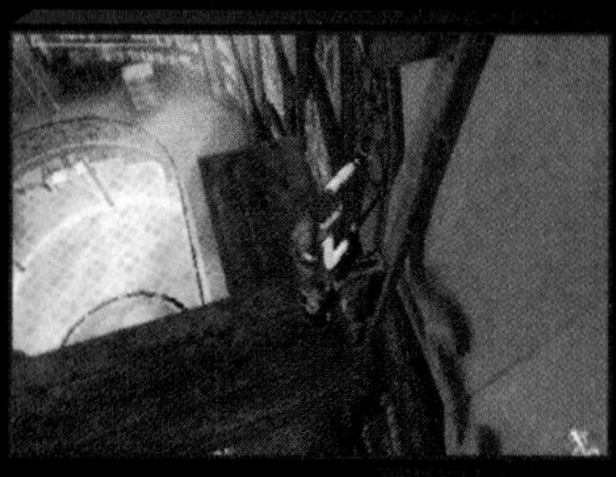

Approach the chain at the end of this scaffolding and press Action to pull it. Note that pulling the chain angles the central, circular pane in the stained glass window toward the ground. Pull it twice more (three times total) so that the window reflects a beam of light at the design on the floor of the room.

TIP **If you accidentally pull the chain too many times, you can angle the window back up by pulling on the chain on the other side of the stained glass window, above the chest of drawers you pulled.**

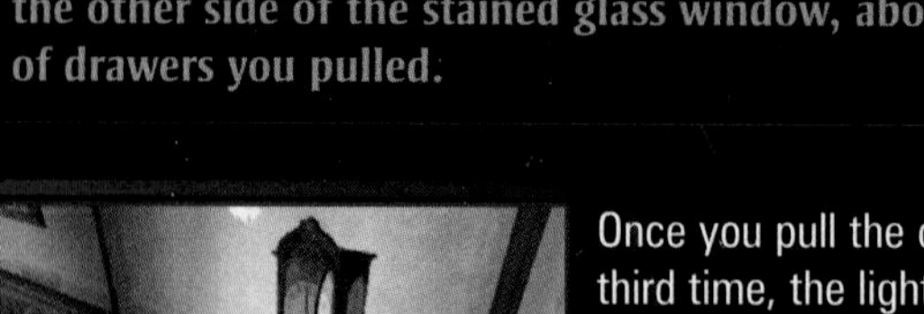

Once you pull the chain for the third time, the light hits the Roman numeral "III" on the design on the floor. This causes the face of the nearby grandfather clock to pop open. Climb down the scaffolding and descend the spiral staircase.

Approach the grandfather clock near the door through which you entered the hall, and press Action to see a close-up view of the clock face.

Press Action repeatedly to move the clock hands to three o'clock, just as the beam of light on the "III" indicated.

This activates a secret mechanism that transforms the insignia on the floor into a spiral staircase leading into a hidden office below the hall. Go down the stairs—and don't fall off.

Pick up the piece of paper on the floor in front of the desk; this is the Vasiley Full Fax. The fax is addressed to Mlle. Carvier and refers her to a website (SHADOWHISTORIES.PR). There's also a five-digit code for accessing restricted information: 31597.

By coincidence, there's a numeric keypad next to the large painting behind the desk. Press Action near the keypad and enter 3-1-5-9-7.

This slides the painting back and reveals a hidden alcove with the Last Obscura Engraving in it. Grab the Last Obscura Engraving and walk back up the stairs.

CAUTION Be careful not to run up the stairs too quickly and fall off the end. It's a silly mistake, but it's easy to make.

Return to the room where you left Bouchard, only to find that he is gone. There's no sign of his handcuffs either. Exit the room and walk down the hall.

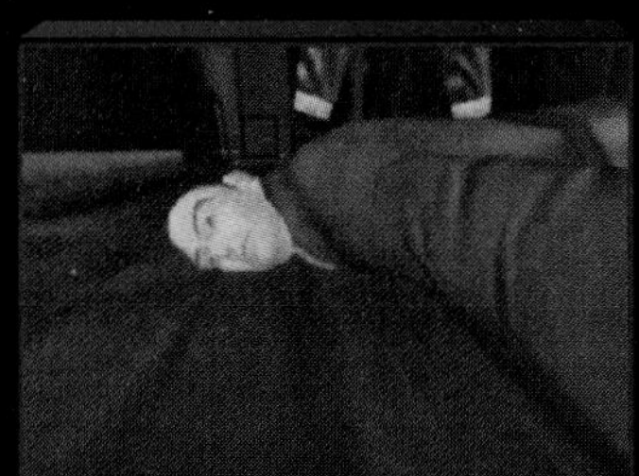

As she walks down the hall, Lara hears a sound from behind a door. She shoulders it open, and Bouchard's lifeless body falls out. There's no hope for him, and there's no immediate danger to Lara. Pick up the Cellar Key from Bouchard's corpse.

Go back down the stairs that lead to the basement of Vasiley's apartment, and open the red door with the Cellar Key to leave the apartment.

Luddick waits outside of the cellar entrance to Vasiley's apartment. Speak to him, and he agrees to give Lara the code to the Strahov Fortress, her next destination. In exchange, he wants the whole story—the events in Paris and whatever happens in Prague. Lara agrees, and Luddick gives her a low-level pass code that will get her into the complex. He even agrees to give her a ride to the fortress, but that's as far as he's willing to go.

Strahov Fortress

After discovering the Last Obscura Engraving at the Monstrum Crimescene, Lara accepts assistance from a Czech reporter, Luddick. He provides her with a low-level entry code to the Strahov Fortress, a multipurpose industrial facility used as a headquarters by the mysterious Cabal.

Lara's goal is to descend through the many levels of the Strahov Fortress. In this section, she must stealthily take out several Agency soldiers, find two different security passes, shut off the power to the defense systems, and make it to the Bio-Research Facility.

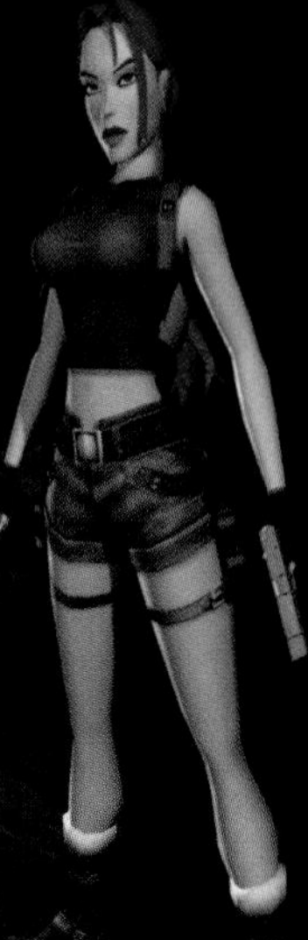

ENTITIES ENCOUNTERED

- Agency Soldiers (x11)
- Rottweilers (x2)
- Luddick
- Eckhardt

CRITICAL ITEMS TO LOCATE

- Strahov Low Security Pass
- Strahov High Security Pass
- Scorpion X

AVAILABLE UPGRADES

- **Upgrade Push Object: Lower Body Level 8**
  By rearranging a pile of crates in the saw room, Lara buffs up her legs and can push a pair of stacked crates to a valve that she must turn to shut off the gas in the area.

Lara's adventure begins at the entrance to the fortress's loading bay. Walk straight ahead from the start of the level to find a Large Health Pack in an open trailer. The camera angle prevents you from seeing it when you're close, so look for the "grab" icon in the lower-right corner of the screen.

Once you have the Large Health Pack, approach the metal door to activate an electromagnetic crane in the rafters of the loading bay. The crane swoops down and latches on to a trailer.

NOTE **You must reach the other side of the loading bay. There are two ways to do it—riding a trailer or making a few tough jumps. We recommend the former method.**

Method #1: Riding the Trailer

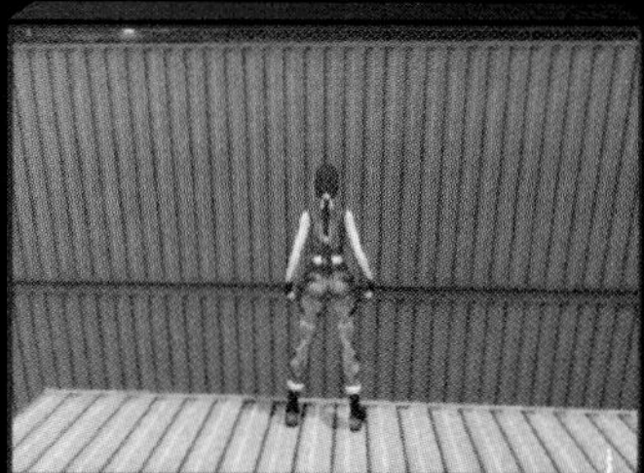

Climb onto the adjacent trailer, wait for the crane to lift it, and jump to the stacked trailers under the one that the crane just lifted.

Turn and face the trailer that the crane is carrying, and wait for the crane to stop moving for a second. The crane's trailer is now within a running jump of the trailer you're on. Run toward the trailer, jump, and press Action to grab the edge.

Ride the trailer as it crosses over the wall between the two sections of the loading bay. Climb off when the crane sets it down on the ground.

Method #2: Tricky Jumping

CAUTION This is *not* the recommended method for reaching the other side of the loading bay—only use it if you fail to leap onto the crane trailer.

Jump onto the stacked trailers , and face the opposite direction from the crane.

Make a running jump toward the white air-conditioning unit with the chain-link fence around it. Press Action in midair to grab the lip of the fence. Pull yourself to the top of the AC unit.

Turn to Lara's right to face the other half of the loading bay. Stand at the edge of the AC unit, jump, and press Action to grab the edge of the wall separating the two halves of the loading bay.

Hop over to the adjacent catwalk and drop onto the catwalk below the nearby ladder.

Walk in Stealth mode until you come to the ladder at the end. Climb the ladder to reach another catwalk.

Walk along this catwalk in Stealth mode until you come to yet another ladder, the end of which is broken off. Climb down the broken ladder, and drop off the end of it to land on a stack of wooden crates.

TIP **Staying in Stealth mode keeps the soldiers from hearing your footfalls, but if you're caught in their flashlight beams, they'll attack with machine guns blazing.**

Regardless of which method you use to reach the other side of the loading bay, you must sneak very carefully around two Agency soldiers patrolling the floor and a third soldier in a small booth. Take out the two patrolling soldiers. Use Stealth attacks if possible.

TIP **You can climb into some of the large, steel pipes to hide from soldiers and get a safe view of the loading bay.**

Once you've taken the two patrolling soldiers out, sneak into the small booth to dispose of the third soldier. Be sure to grab the third soldier's Strahov Low Security Pass after eliminating him.

NOTE **Most of the Agency soldiers leave behind 30-round 9mm Mag Vega Clips when you take them out. These slot nicely into the Mag Vega you took off of the Agency soldier eliminated in the Louvre, guaranteeing you virtually unlimited ammo. Be sure to grab as many clips as you can.**

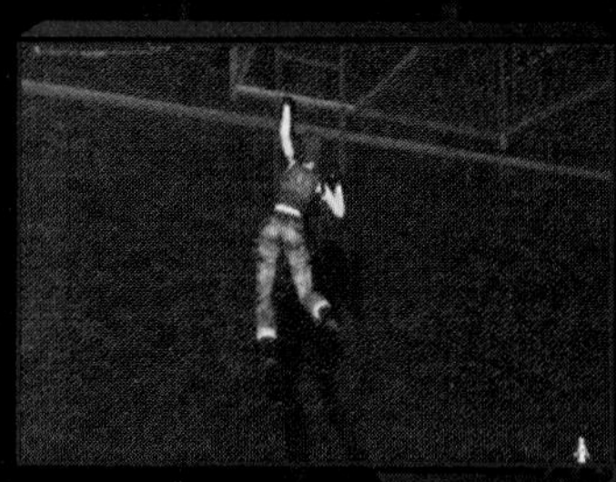

Once you have the Strahov Low Security Pass, climb back onto the stacked crates underneath the broken ladder that you dropped from (if you used method #2 to reach the other side of the loading bay). Climb all the way up the ladder to reach the metal catwalk.

Walk to the left end of the catwalk (as you face the ladder) to find a green door. Go through this door and press Action on the card reader inside to use the Strahov Low Security Pass and open the door to the garage.

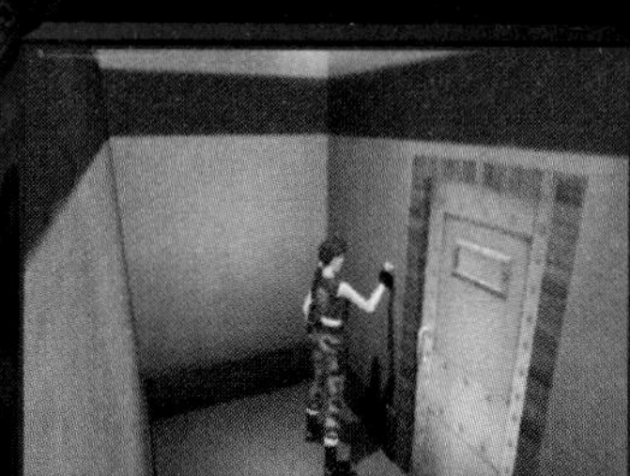

NOTE **There's another door leading to the garage at the end of this catwalk, but you'll likely be detected if you use it.**

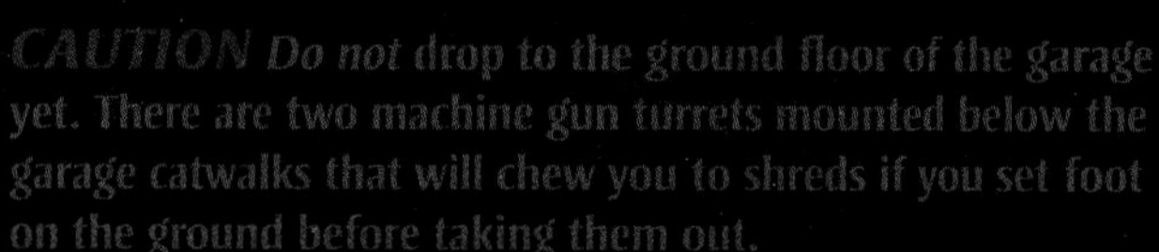

CAUTION *Do not* drop to the ground floor of the garage yet. There are two machine gun turrets mounted below the garage catwalks that will chew you to shreds if you set foot on the ground before taking them out.

There are three soldiers on this catwalk. It's extremely tough to take them out without being hurt, but you must get rid of all three of them. We advise sneaking in Stealth mode with a weapon drawn. Take the soldiers out from behind with a stealth attack if possible—if not, just do it quickly.

Walk all the way around the catwalk after taking out the three soldiers, and climb the ladder at the other end of it.

Enter the control booth at the top of the ladder and get rid of the soldier inside. Press Action near the control panel to activate the electromagnetic crane in the garage.

Climb down the ladder to the garage, and walk around the catwalk until you come to the long ladder leading into the rafters of the garage. Climb all the way up this ladder.

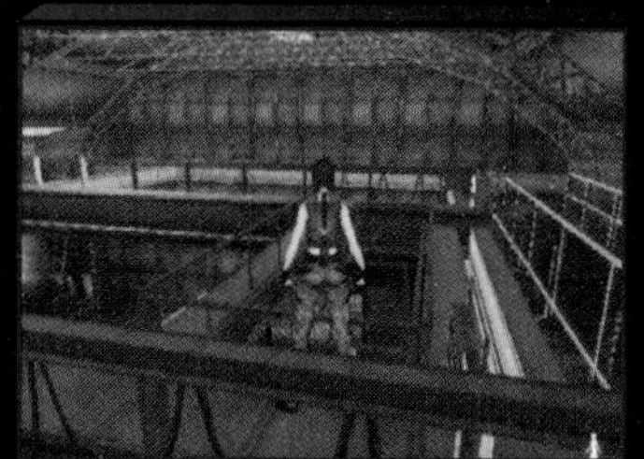

Walk along the catwalk in the rafters of the garage to reach the stairs leading down to the electromagnetic crane's control booth.

As you approach the door to the crane control booth, you see a cutscene of Lara using the crane to smash the two machine gun turrets on the rafters below.

With the machine gun turrets out of the picture, you can now safely set foot on the floor of the garage. To reach it, climb back down the last ladder you ascended, walk along the catwalk until you're above a tractor trailer truck, hang from the railing, and drop onto the truck.

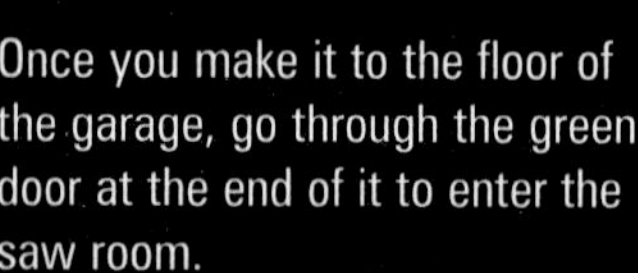

Once you make it to the floor of the garage, go through the green door at the end of it to enter the saw room.

Most of the passageways in the saw room are sealed with glowing blue security lasers. Don't walk into them, unless you want to die.

There's only one area in the saw room that's not sealed off by security lasers—the area with the giant saw itself. To reach it, climb onto the stack of crates near the locked gate.

Unfortunately, there's gas shooting out of overhead vents that prevents Lara from jumping across. To reach the valve that shuts off the gas, you need to first earn a lower body strength upgrade, which you do by pushing the stacked crates around.

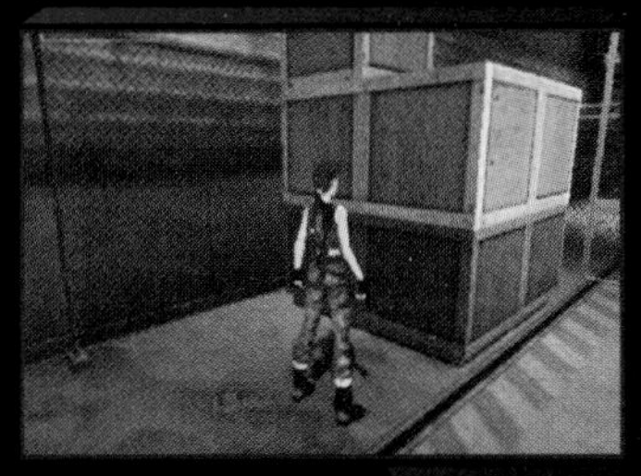

Your ultimate goal is to get the highest crate in the corner between the wall and the barbed-wire fence. To do that, you need to position a line of crates in the level below it so that they lead right into that corner. And to do *that*, you need to push the three loose crates on the floor into position so that you can move the next highest level of crates onto them.

It sounds rather confusing (and, let's face it, it is), but all you really need to do is pull and push two crates along the floor so that they're between the stacked crates and the floor.

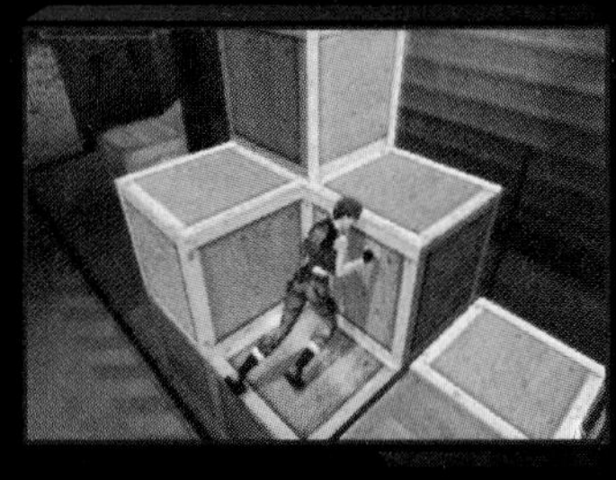

Then, when you have the lowest crates in position, pull and push the next highest level of crates on top of them so that you can slide the highest crate right into the corner where the fence meets the wall. Presto! Instant strength upgrade!

Now return to the center of the room and pull the two stacked crates across the hall and up to the air conditioning unit mounted on the wall.

Climb up onto the crates, and from there, climb up onto the A/C unit. This lets you reach the valve, and turning the valve shuts off the gas.

With the gas shut off, return to the stack of crates, stand at the edge of the highest crate, and jump over the locked gate, into the area with the giant saw.

There are two Rottweilers in this area. Take them out quickly.

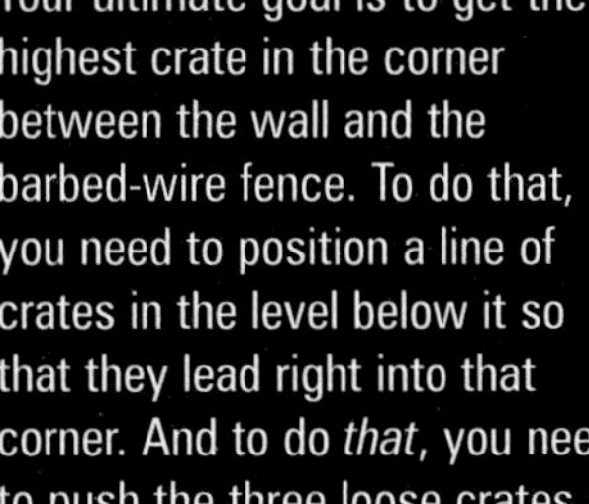

Once you've gotten rid of your canine problem and investigated the saw area, climb the ladder near the locked fence to reach the saw controls.

Stand at the saw controls and press Action to activate the saw, which starts cutting through the slab but bounces off the stone and severs an overhead air duct.

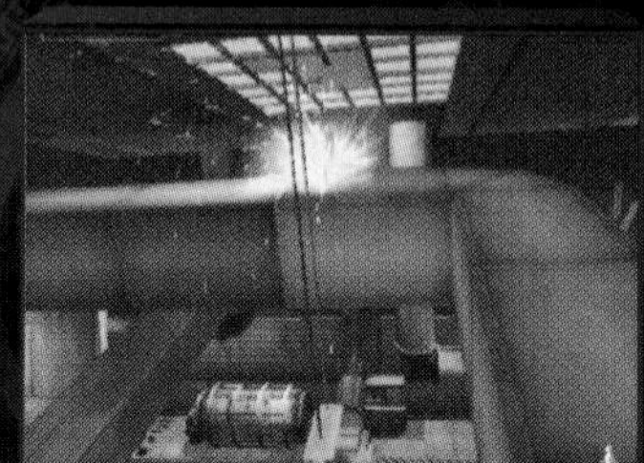

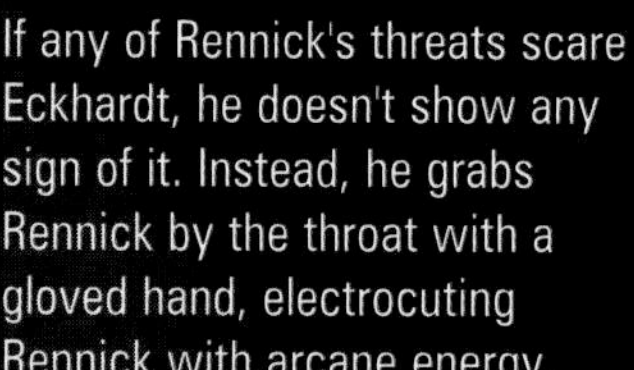

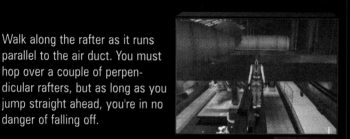

After the saw cuts the air duct, stand to the left of the saw controls and jump up to grab a rafter above the controls. Pull yourself onto the rafter.

Walk along the rafter as it runs parallel to the air duct. You must hop over a couple of perpendicular rafters, but as long as you jump straight ahead, you're in no danger of falling off.

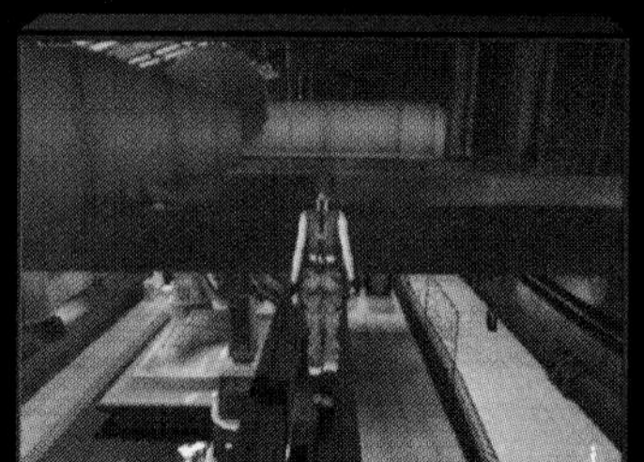

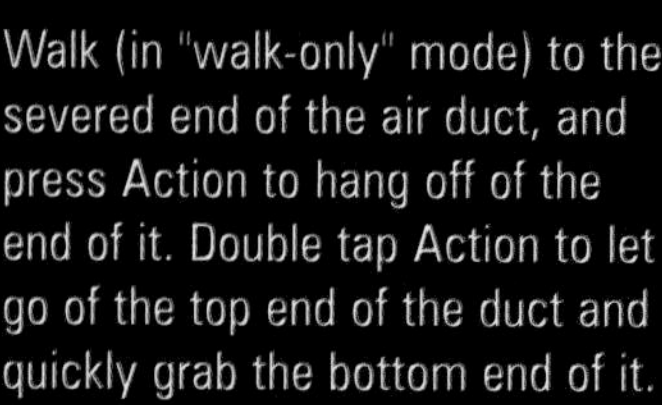

Once you reach the severed part of the air duct, face the duct, back up a couple of steps, and jump on top of it.

Walk (in "walk-only" mode) to the severed end of the air duct, and press Action to hang off of the end of it. Double tap Action to let go of the top end of the duct and quickly grab the bottom end of it.

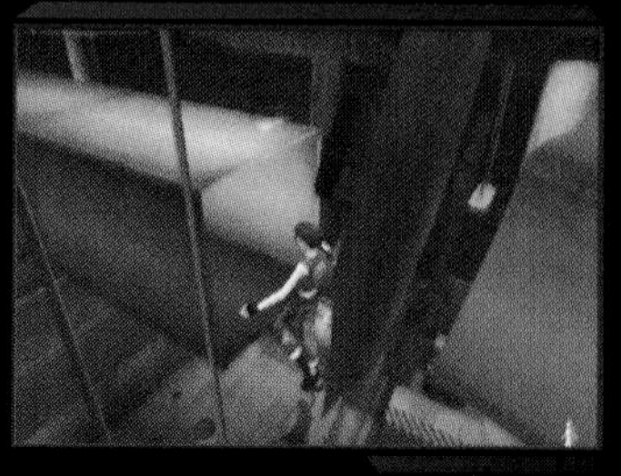

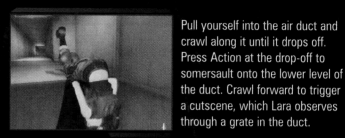

Pull yourself into the air duct and crawl along it until it drops off. Press Action at the drop-off to somersault onto the lower level of the duct. Crawl forward to trigger a cutscene, which Lara observes through a grate in the duct.

One of Eckhardt's henchmen hauls Rennick into an interrogation room and throws him roughly into a chair. Rennick frantically tries to convince Eckhardt not to harm him, claiming that his paper knows where he's gone and will reveal the files Rennick has kept on Eckhardt.

If any of Rennick's threats scare Eckhardt, he doesn't show any sign of it. Instead, he grabs Rennick by the throat with a gloved hand, electrocuting Rennick with arcane energy.

As Eckhardt murders Rennick, a mysterious sign draws itself on the wall of the interrogation room.

Once he's finished off Rennick, Eckhardt casually tosses the reporter's charred body into a chair and exits the interrogation room.

When you regain control of Lara, crawl to the end of the air duct and drop out of it onto a stack of tires.

There's an Agency soldier at the end of the air duct. Take him out silently from behind. He drops the Strahov High Security Pass.

After taking out the soldier, head toward the door to the fortress's power room (in the opposite direction from the series of laser trip wires that stretches across the hallway).

Use the Strahov High Security Pass to unlock the door and enter the power room. Take out the Agency soldier on the other side of the door quickly.

Move around the power room in Stealth mode. There are two soldiers in the back who are alerted to your presence if you make too much noise.

Approach the controls at the front of the power room to automatically turn off the power to the fortress's security systems. While looking at the power diagram, Lara asks herself what in the fortress could require so much power to operate? Her question is answered in the following cutscene.

In a different part of the Strahov Fortress, a soldier frantically presses buttons on a control panel as the lights around a research area turn off one by one. In the center of the research area is what appears to be a holding cell, the door of which has been ripped off of its hinges.

An emergency hatch seals shut, locking out two other soldiers in the research area. Panicked, they pound on the glass of the first soldier's control booth, to no avail—they are quickly killed by some sort of hideous creature.

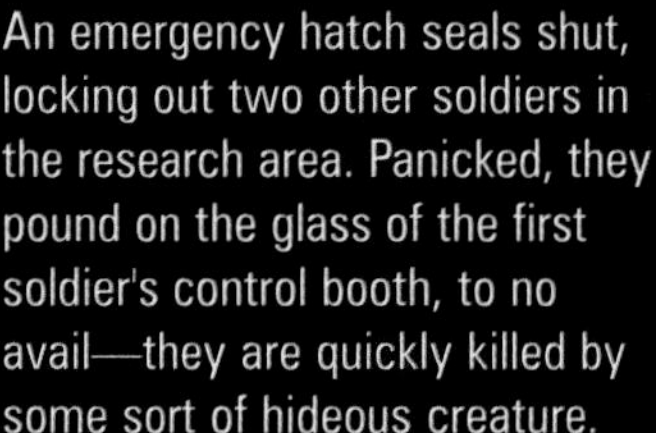

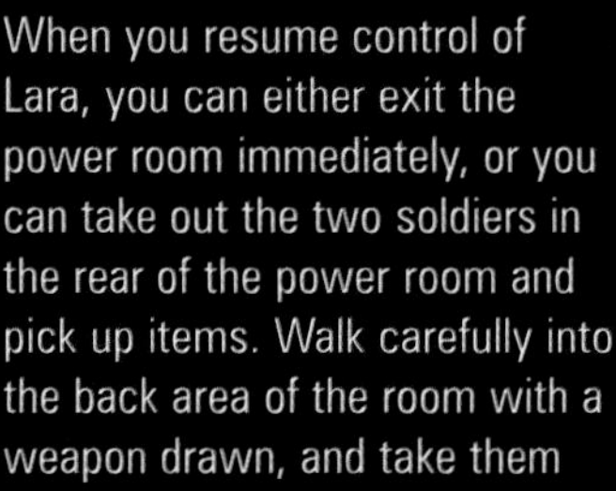

After slaughtering the soldiers, the creature crawls on top of its former cell and lets out an unearthly growl. What has the Cabal been doing down here?

When you resume control of Lara, you can either exit the power room immediately, or you can take out the two soldiers in the rear of the power room and pick up items. Walk carefully into the back area of the room with a weapon drawn, and take them out before they can resist.

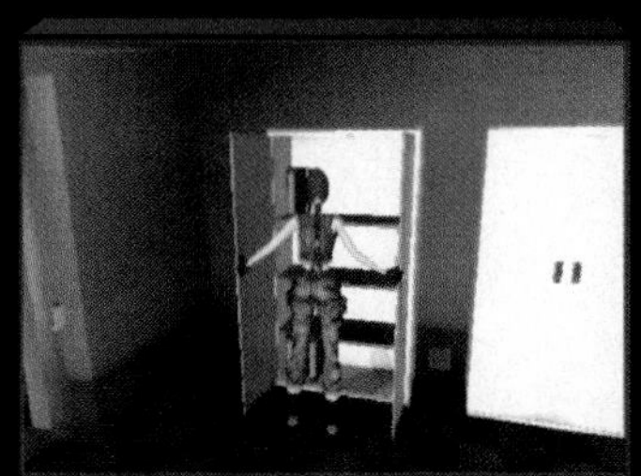

There's a Candy Bar and a Mag Vega Clip on the soldiers' table, and two Scorpion X Clips in the large, white cabinets near the door. Add in the two Mag Vega Clips that the soldiers leave behind, and you've scored quite a haul in this area.

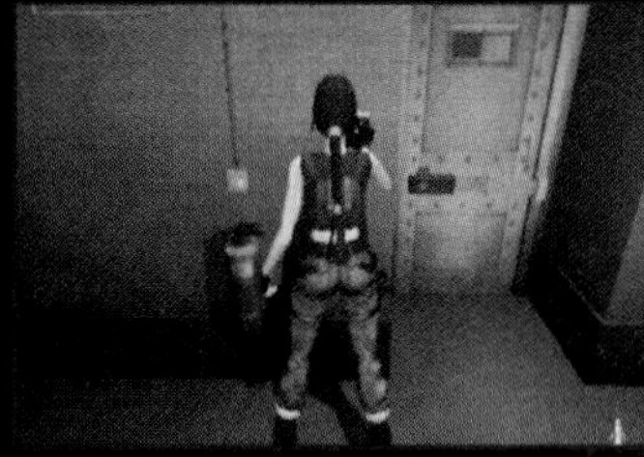

Shutting off the power to the fortress's defense systems lowers all of the blue laser barriers that sealed off most of the Fortress, including the entrance to the interrogation room where Rennick was murdered. Backtrack to the area near the air duct exit to find the interrogation room entrance. Unlock it using the Strahov High Security Pass.

There's nothing you can do for Rennick, but there is a Scorpion X pistol near his body that you can pick up.

Open the white cabinet behind Rennick to find a pack of Health Bandages, handy for dressing those battlefield wounds.

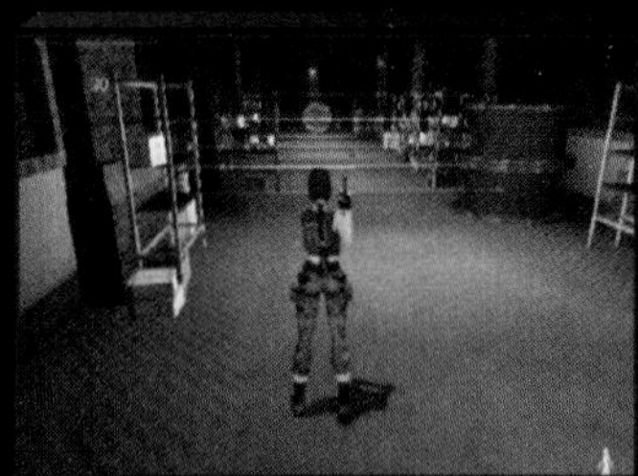

The only thing left to do in this area is to reach the door to the Bio-Research Facility. Exit the interrogation room and face the hallway with the red and yellow laser trip wires.

This is a nasty hallway—crossing a laser trip wire can kill you instantly, and there are also three mines that bounce into the air and explode at chest height when you draw near. To make it down the hallway, you must commando crawl (hold the Duck button and the Stealth button while moving forward) and stay as far away from the mines as possible. As long as you slalom around the mines and don't stand up until you're well past the laser trip wires, you should be fine.

But wait! There's an easier way! Aim and shoot at the red pressurized canister near the giant spool of cable to send the cable rolling down the hallway, activating the trip wires and mines, while you remain at a safe distance.

On the other side of the laser trip wires is the main part of the saw room, with all of the blue laser security fences deactivated. The door to the Bio-Research Facility is a green door with a card reader next to it. Use the Strahov High Security Pass to unlock the door, and go through to proceed to the Bio-Research Facility.

The Bio-Research Facility

Moving into the Bio-Research facility, Lara experiences more of the horrors that await mankind if the Cabal succeeds. After talking to Muller, Lara checks a fountain to find an exit, then deals with two abominations in a gestation chamber before climbing along a pipe to unlock the drain under a pod. Once through the maze of balconies in the subsequent room, she faces an intelligent tree—or at least the remains of one. Finally, she ascends a giant series of balconies, witnesses a horrific demise, and secures three Botanical Access Cards before exiting.

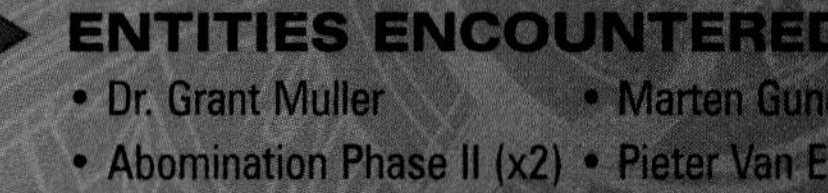

ENTITIES ENCOUNTERED

- Dr. Grant Muller
- Abomination Phase II (x2)
- Abomination Grub (x8)
- Leviathan
- Cabal Soldier (x5)
- Tendril Trunk
- Marten Gundersen
- Pieter Van Eckhardt
- Kristina Boaz
- Carnivorous Horror
- Kurtis Trent

CRITICAL ITEMS TO LOCATE

- Botanical Low Access Pass
- Botanical Medium Access Pass
- Botanical High Access Pass

AVAILABLE UPGRADES

- **Upgrade Jump: Lower Body Level 9**
  A leap across a gap in the largest greenhouse area allows Lara to make even longer jumps.

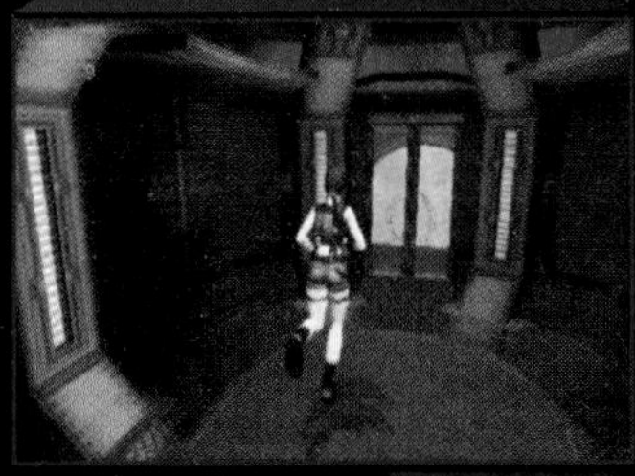

Stepping out of the elevator and into an antechamber, you see a gigantic hothouse teeming with life ahead of you. Walk forward, toward the pair of ornate doors, and step into the heat.

Beyond the doors is a giant greenhouse brimming with genetically manipulated plants of all shapes and sizes—but mainly the huge kind. Cordoned off in the middle of the chamber are four planting beds.

These beds contain the most vicious flora, an affront to Mother Nature. In the center of the quadrangle is a fountain (where large butterflies often congregate). There are three stone gargoyles peering out of this pedestal fountain.

Two of the gargoyles spill water out of their mouths and into the shallow fountain pool. A third is not spouting water.

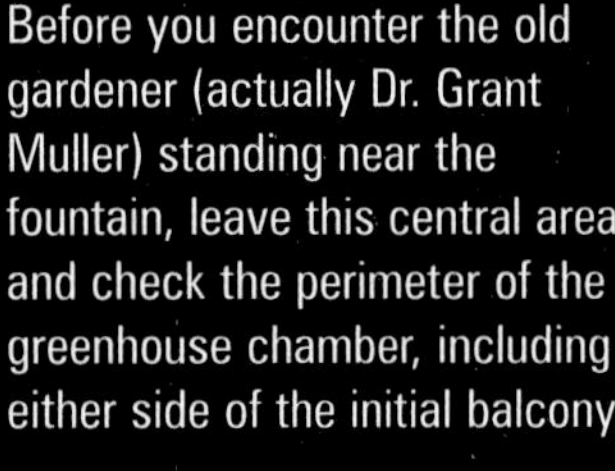

Before you encounter the old gardener (actually Dr. Grant Muller) standing near the fountain, leave this central area and check the perimeter of the greenhouse chamber, including either side of the initial balcony.

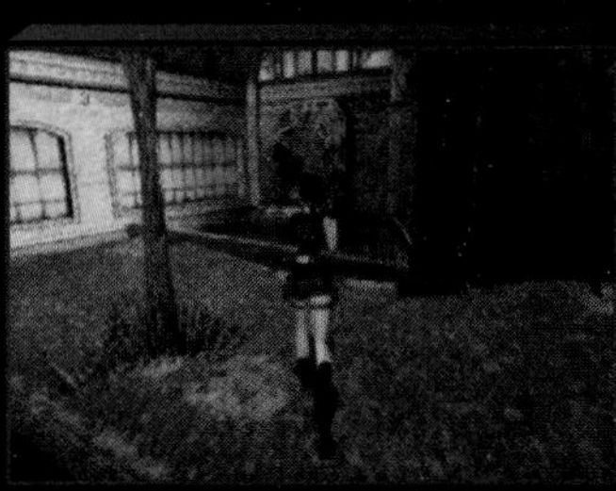

On either side of the steps you descended from the entrance are two gargoyle heads—one in each corner. They are identical to the smaller pedestal heads in the fountain.

Check the sides of the greenhouse; you can run along (or on) thin planter beds, some of which have yielded their crops of seemingly carnivorous plants. Head to the far left end of the area and stoop to pick up the Viper SMG Ammo as a tendril swipes at you. Just what is going on, here?

At the far end of the garden are a few examples of a new subspecies of fly-trapping flora, the *Dioaea muscipula Giganticus*. These plants have spiky stems (don't run into them) and will whip you if you venture too close. Other nearby plants wheeze a gas that can choke you. Behind the left side plants are three more Viper SMG Clips.

When you've finished exploring, move to the center of the chamber to encounter Dr. Grant Muller. He is tending to his "brethren" and is surprised to see you. "Intruders don't last long in Strahov!" he informs Lara.

Lara wants to know what Muller is up to. He tells Lara of the Cabal—the new order of life on earth. Scoffing, Lara then learns that the order of the Cabal controls everything in Prague, and that arcane experiments by the Cabal leader, Pieter Van Eckhardt, have resulted in immortality for all.

Muller then reveals that the Cabal plans to restore an ancient race of giants known as the Nephilim. To this end, the Cubiculum Nephili (prototype of the final specimen) has been created.

The vital essences of this creature have been extracted to breed pure Nephilim, not the abominations that currently stalk the dark corners of Strahov Fortress—the Proto-Nephilim. Muller ends his vision of the future with a quick insecticide blast to Lara's face.

When you regain your composure, don't attempt to chase Dr. Muller. Instead, inspect the central fountain you checked out earlier. It seems that the gargoyle head without the water streaming from it can be manipulated. Pull it back.

One of the gargoyle heads shifts back from its base, into a secret corridor. Run from the center of the garden toward the far right corner (if you're looking back at the entrance).

Run in to the corridor and look for areas of interest. You find one almost immediately; there is an opening in the right side wall. Enter it.

You are now in a small antechamber with a wayward plant growing in it and a ladder jutting upward. Climb the ladder to a short, curved balcony. On the wall next to another balcony is a lever. Pull the lever after collecting two more Viper SMG Clips.

The security door to the exit of this chamber unlocks. You can now leave the greenhouse by dropping from the balcony or climbing down the ladder, entering the small corridor tunnel and emerging back into the main hothouse.

Once in the courtyard, ignore the steps to the balcony that leads back to the area you started from (don't get confused, as the two sides of the room look alike). Instead, run up the central steps to the red-tile balcony and open the security door (with the two "rivet" locks).

Step inside the cramped connecting chamber. Take a couple of steps forward and you'll spot an identical door to the one you just unlocked. Fortunately, there is a large, yellow unlock button next to the door. Press it, and the door opens.

Surveying the large incubation chamber ahead of her, Lara spies something stirring in the fluid. Two abominations break free from its confines and begin to thrash about! Time to strap on those guns.

Quickly run down the steps or vault over the gallery to the floor of the chamber. As you approach the creatures, remember they have no qualms about ripping you limb from limb.

Keep shooting them until they both slump into a heap. Use any of your ranged weapons, as its swinging, claw-like appendages deal a lot of damage.

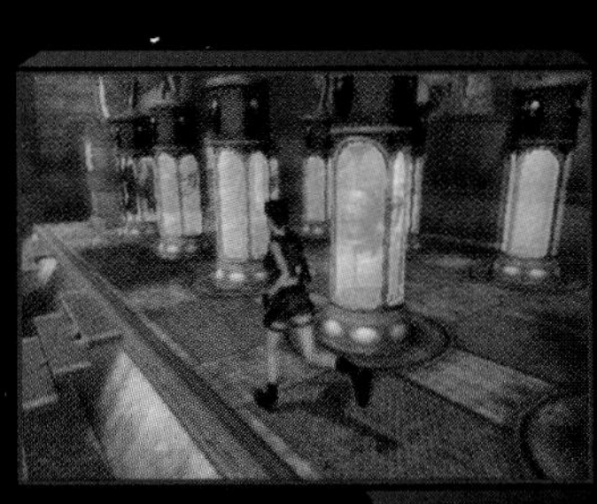

The sheer size of this area makes combat straightforward, as you always have space to run. Once combat is over, you can inspect the remaining incubation chambers. They hold a variety of revolting grub specimens. Check the underground on the other side of the left entrance steps down one narrow stretch for Health Bandages.

The security door at the far end of the structure is firmly sealed. Out of the corner of your eye, you may see movement on the upper side balconies. To exit, you must take an alternate route. But where to go?

The answer lies above you. View the scaffold structure feeding the incubation chambers; there are two ladders on either end. There must be some sort of incubation control up there. Alas, the ladders are old and don't reach down nearly far enough.

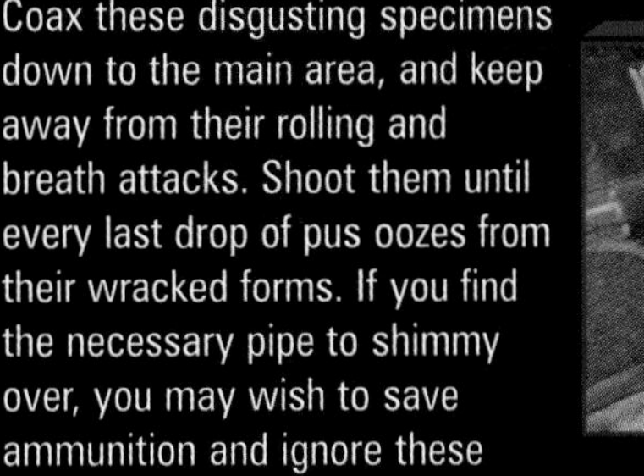

Instead, head to the left upper side balcony. The other one (if you're looking from the entrance door) yields nothing of interest. However, four chutes along each wall randomly deposit Abomination Grubs that scuttle towards you and attack!

Coax these disgusting specimens down to the main area, and keep away from their rolling and breath attacks. Shoot them until every last drop of pus oozes from their wracked forms. If you find the necessary pipe to shimmy over, you may wish to save ammunition and ignore these critters. They keep coming!

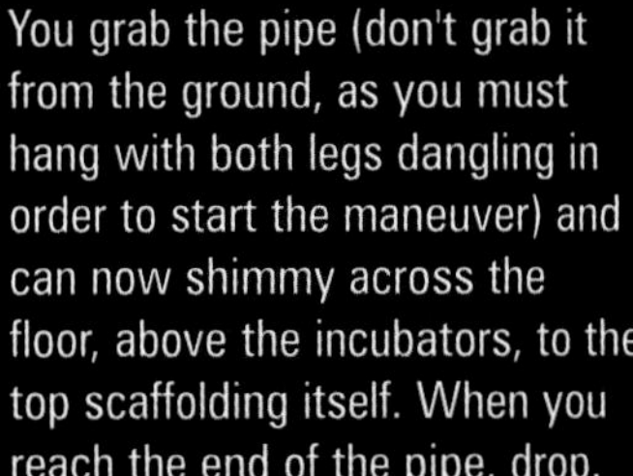

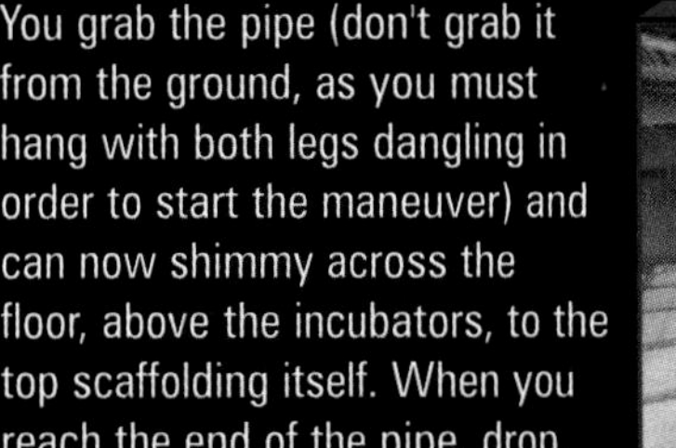

When you regain composure, visit the left balcony, which sports a pipe running along the underside of the ceiling support buttress (check the far end for an ammo clip). It is half-hidden by a large fern, and under a Mag Vega Clip. Pick up the clip, reach this pipe, and jump vertically.

You grab the pipe (don't grab it from the ground, as you must hang with both legs dangling in order to start the maneuver) and can now shimmy across the floor, above the incubators, to the top scaffolding itself. When you reach the end of the pipe, drop.

You land on a partially collapsed walkway. In your next couple of moves, always remember to stay on the tile-like platform. Don't venture onto the sloping incubator tubes or you'll slide off. Your first plan of action is to visit the end of the platform.

Here you find a valve. Turn the valve on so the incubator fluids drain from the end incubator units, where the abomination attacked you. Run along the platform sections hopping over the two broken areas halfway across.

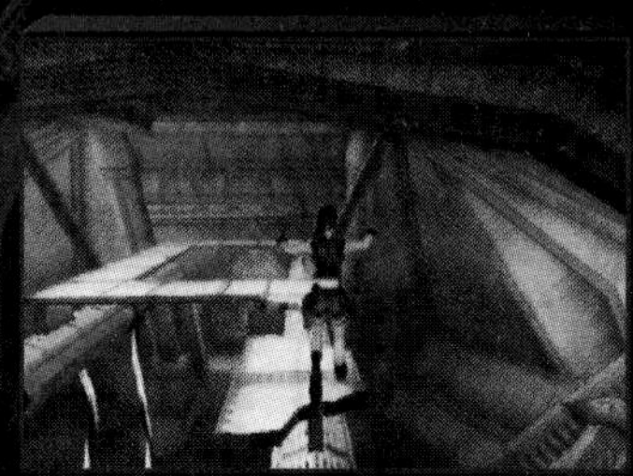

Continue to the other end of the platform to a second valve and turn it. The incubator with the smashed glass has a false bottom. This releases, revealing a chute heading straight down. You have now located the exit from this chamber. There are still a few Grubs slithering around on the ground however (a total of eight appear in three different colors).

Now to get down. Your first option is to climb down the ladder from either end of the incubation chamber. Once you can't descend any farther, you'll have to drop to the ground. You lose half your health if you try this, so be aware that it could end in your demise.

The other method is to return to the area of the platform with the pipe above it, and leap onto it before shimmying back down to the upper side balcony. From here, run back down to the main incubator, find the one with the false bottom, and leap in after ignoring or defeating the second abomination.

You fall through the tube and land in a large underground vat filled with fluids. Swim to the surface, then grab the side of the structure and haul yourself out of it. This chamber holds little of interest.

Venture through the doorway with the lantern above it, and into a water reservoir, where liquids from the entire facility are routed through two massive pumps above you. Ahead is a ladder bolted to a wall, with a door at the top.

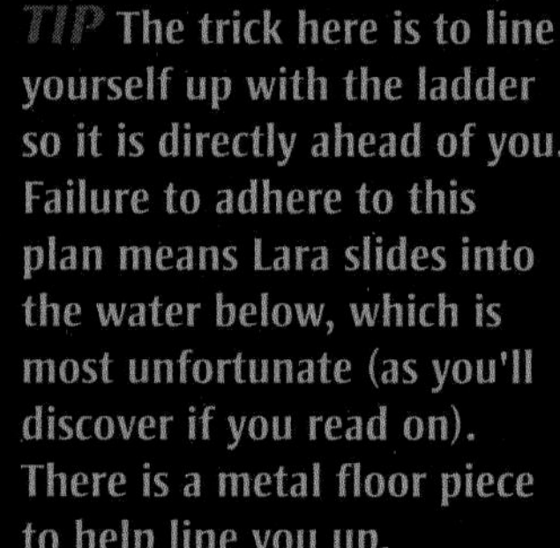

You cannot see it, but the area in front of you is sloping. If you stand there for any reason, you start to slide and have only milliseconds to react. Use the camera to view this area before you start wandering around. Save your game here.

TIP **The trick here is to line yourself up with the ladder so it is directly ahead of you. Failure to adhere to this plan means Lara slides into the water below, which is most unfortunate (as you'll discover if you read on). There is a metal floor piece to help line you up.**

Run and jump from the tip of the sloping area, or from halfway down the slope, leaping toward the ladder and pressing Action to grab hold of it. Now pull yourself onto the ladder, climb it to the top, take the Small Health Pack, and open the door.

▶ WATER TORTURE

Did you slip and fall into the water? Lara's shrieks stir a dangerous killing machine, the Leviathan. Seething with tendrils, this beast from the deep has no qualms about destroying you.

This beast cannot be harmed, and you need luck and a strong pair of lungs to outfox it. Wait until it loses interest in you, then swim through the open grating and make an almost immediate right turn, moving quickly to grab the ladder ahead.

This ladder leads to the next room you'd appear in if you had negotiated the jump properly, and the walkthrough mentions the two locations where you can swim to (terrible underwater attacks notwithstanding). The other ladder is a swim to the left, in the middle of the pool. You'll be shot by a soldier if you attempt the shorter, right turn. Run the gauntlet to the farther ladder instead.

Assuming you didn't fall, open the door at the top of the ladder and enter the connecting tunnel. Air seeps through crumbling pipes as you run right, down a corridor, left, up some stairs, and to another blue door. Open it.

Just before the door is a notice reading "Bio-Dome. Level 3 Security Only." At least you know where you are. Step through into a large, long chamber with multiple balconies stretching into the distance. Below is a pool of water. This is where you'd end up if you'd fallen instead of grabbing the ladder.

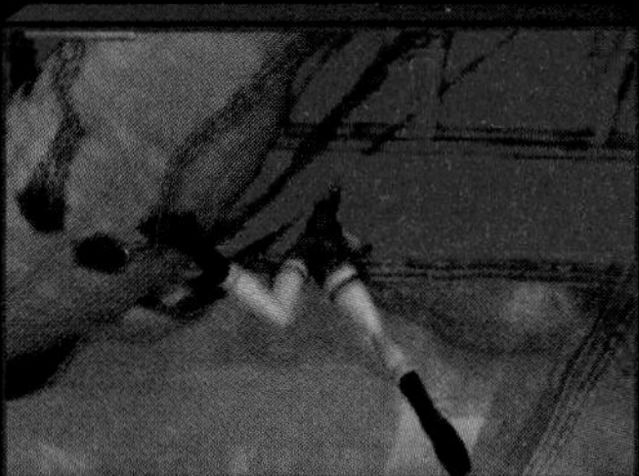

To avoid any unnecessary drops into the water (and an audience with the Leviathan), heed the following strategy. It saves a lot of needless running.

Start by equipping your favorite weapon and running along the initial walkway. Turn right, then left, and leap over the gap, or check the stairs below. Depending on where you entered this area, in either of these areas ahead, or directly under the doorway entrance is one patrolling Cabal soldier in a biohazard suit. Shoot or knock him with your fists into the pool below.

Once this soldier has fallen, jump back to the initial walkway and take the left path. There is a junction where the gantry-way continues to the right, or onward along the edge of the pool itself.

Move toward the left edge of the room, next to the water. If you haven't yet spotted the mutation in the pool, it is visible here and can even be shot at (just in case you accidentally fall into the pool later). Bullets simply zing off its hardened hide.

Walk to the end of the lower gantry. Carefully jump to and land on the middle of the pipe (don't slide to the right); walk to the end, stooping to pick up a Viper SMG Clip. Turn the valve and the compressed air seeping along the upper, right wall will stop.

This is important later in your room maneuvering. For now, though, move back onto the main gantry, up the steps, and head left instead of continuing upward. Then run down the other set of stairs (you accessed these already if the Cabal soldier was patrolling the grassy area below the starting walkway).

You end up underneath the starting walkway near some overgrown ferns and a ladder to the right (this is where you'd appear from the water if you had swum to this area and turned right). The ladder is unimportant—check out the ivy in the left corner.

TIP **If you don't want to go to all the hassle of "stair walking," you can simply vault over the railing from the initial walkway and land on this grassy area without any problems. Don't forget to turn the valve off, though.**

The ivy takes your weight and can be climbed. Continue upward and head diagonally up and right, around the brickwork in the corner, shimmying to the side. Don't head back to the starting walkway. Instead, continue heading straight up the ivy.

This eventually allows you to haul yourself onto an upper ledge. There is a door with a light above it and a ladder. The door is firmly sealed and cannot be entered. The ladder leads to your next area of interest.

Climb the ladder to an upper walkway. Carefully walk (don't fall off the sides) to the end of the gantry, turn left, and pull the lever. At the other end of the structure, a moving platform comes to life.

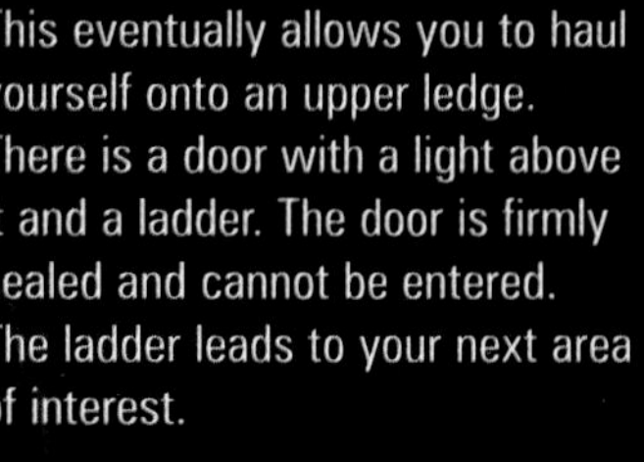

The platform moves along a metallic coupling until it reaches a short-circuited portion, then stops. It then moves back to the gantry. It is much too far away to contemplate reaching. Descend.

The reason for summoning the erratically moving platform isn't apparent yet, but it will be soon. Move to the initial walkway and leap over the gap in it. To the left is a walkway leading to a ladder and an upper planting bed full of strange and scary-looking flora with a Mag Vega, Viper SMG Clip, and Health Bandages.

You needn't investigate this area at all. Inside, look for the narrow metal ledge near the left turn in the walkway. Hug the wall and sidestep along this platform. You can dangle and shimmy across if you wish.

At the end of the narrow ledge is a pipe bolted to the wall. Pressurized steam prevents you from holding on to it, unless of course you turned the valve of the large pipe across from you (this was covered earlier). With no steam, climb up.

TIP If you're feeling reckless and don't want all that backtracking, you can leap from the walkway, missing the railing, and hitting the wall, then slide down to the lower gantry. Turn off the steam. But beware the loss of health required for the landing, though.

Climb the pipe until it disappears into the wall under narrow ledge. Grab this ledge and shimmy to the left. This may take several attempts. Continue left along the ledge until you reach a small walkway.

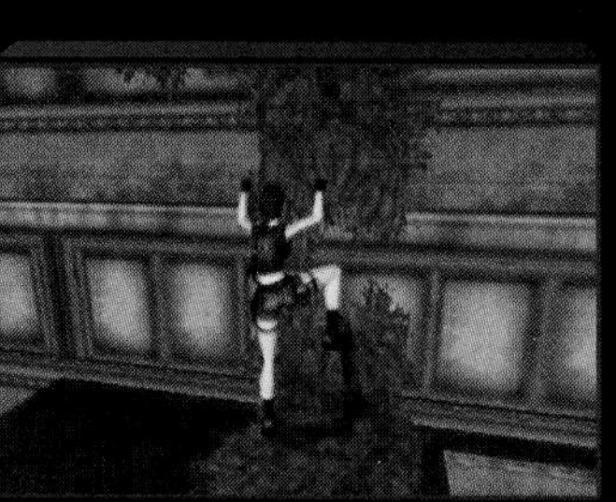

This walkway is covered in moss and ivy. If you turn and look up and around, you see that the ivy is growing across the roof. Up ahead of you is the upper gantry and short-circuited moving platform (this is vital to the next step—make sure you moved the platform here).

Climb the ivy, straight to the top, until Lara turns and faces left. Then move her left until she reaches the main coupling in the middle of the ceiling. With your remaining strength, turn her to the right.

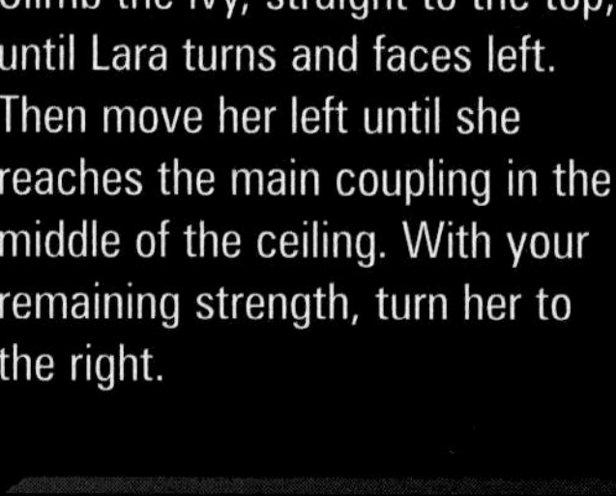

Shimmy so she runs out of grip strength just when she's blocked by a cross-beam. She drops and lands on the moving platform. If you aren't far enough, or don't move to the corner where the coupling and cross-beam meet, prepare for splashdown.

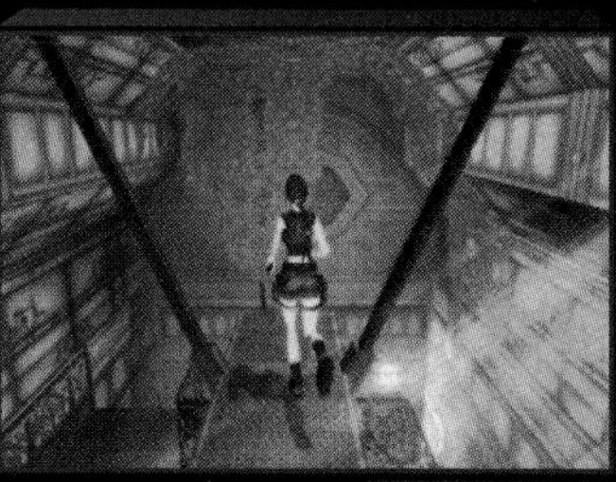

From the moving platform, walk onto the upper gantry. This ends in a ladder that you should immediately climb down. Now on an L-shaped (and all-new) walkway, move around it to another ladder, and descend this one.

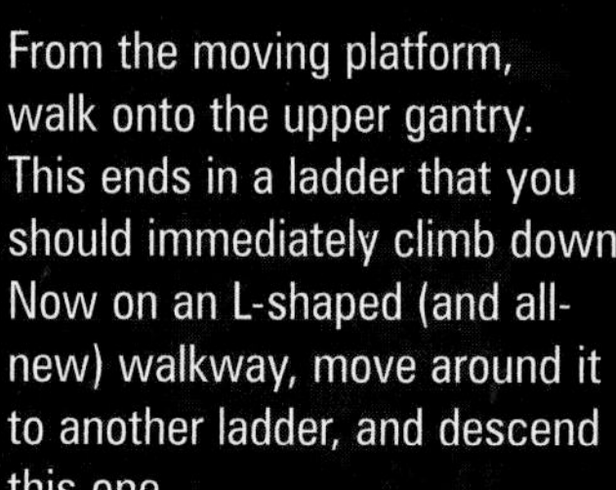

You can execute a back-flip off this ladder, landing on the final walkway. Run to the yellow wall switch and press it firmly. This releases the security door and lets you through this room's exit. Step inside and activate a second door switch.

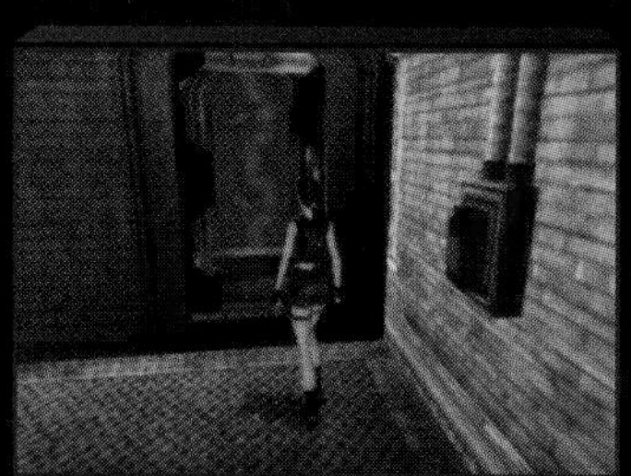

This switch opens an adjacent door leading to a curved walkway. As you run around the corner, a giant tendril wraps around a pair of double doors, firmly sealing them. The tendril, unpleasant and pustule-ridden as it is, is attached to something even more unpleasant.

It seems this giant trunk has rudimentary intelligence and has been instructed to guard this door. Either vault over the railing or clamber down the ladder into the courtyard below. Look for the set of iron stairs after grabbing the Mag Vega Clip below the walkway.

The stairs lead to a giant sprinkler system and potting shed. A feed pipe sprouts from the wall adjacent to the tree that enters the trunk. Perhaps this is the source of the plant's flexibility and strength.

On the window side of the balcony potting shed are two low cupboards which appear to be empty. Inspect these, but ignore the table next to them. Your main focus should be the piping behind you.

There are a total of five valves set against the wall; turning three of them activates a feed pipe that floods a small vat and pumps different types of feed into the tendril trunk next to the door. A combination of feed types will relax the unusually taut weed.

The answer to this conundrum does not lie in arbitrarily turning on and off different valves. There's a list of approved mixtures pinned to the wall to the left of the quintet of valves.

Take a moment to study the four pieces of paper pinned to the wall. To view all four diagrams, push the table obscuring the bottom one to the side. Now you can read the charts. They have the different valve names (represented by symbols) pointing to the trunk.

The diagram with the large, red "X" through it is the one to release the plant's freakish grip on the door. Although it's partly obscured by the first diagram, you can make out lines from valve 1, 2, and 4.

NOTE **Did you simply turn on all the valves, or turn the wrong ones? Wait for the feed to drain and start again.**

The pipes are represented by the symbols that look like a "Y", a "+", and a bell shape (1, 2, and 4 respectively). Turn these three valves (and these three only), and watch as the vat fills up with yellow liquid. Nothing happens until you pull the release lever at the vat.

When the correct mixture of feed is transmitted through the pipe, the tendril trunk shudders and points upward, then dangles from its central trunk with a feeble shake. All the smaller tendril pieces shrivel into the trunk, and it releases its iron grip on the door.

You may now pass through the double doors into a connecting chamber and push open a pair of larger, blue doors. A slumped body is sprawled near a plant on a high walkway. You see a gigantic greenhouse structure as the camera pans away.

This chamber is far larger, and patrolled by more guards, than any you've previously been in. Save your game and begin your exploration. There are four floors of walkways to ascend as you search this body for information.

The ground floor is vast and menacing, and can be explored in any manner you wish. However, follow the directions ahead to ensure success. Start by running along the stone pathway.

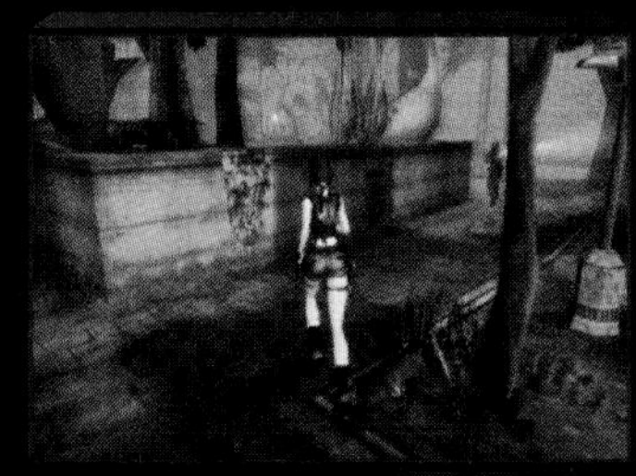

Pause at the junction and turn right. Sprint past the heat lamp, along the side of a raised bed with numerous carnivorous plants in it, and continue along the pathway as it curves left. As you round the corner, equip your weapon.

Ahead of you is a Cabal soldier with a flashlight. Take him out. There's no one else nearby, allowing you to strike him down with ease. Take his Botanical Access Card.

Follow the pathway as it passes a green pool of water, then curves right into a doorway. This is where the soldier's patrol route began. As you enter this area, you see a door ahead of you that is firmly locked with three security code locks.

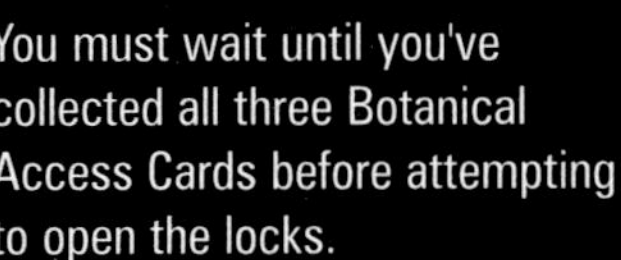

You must wait until you've collected all three Botanical Access Cards before attempting to open the locks.

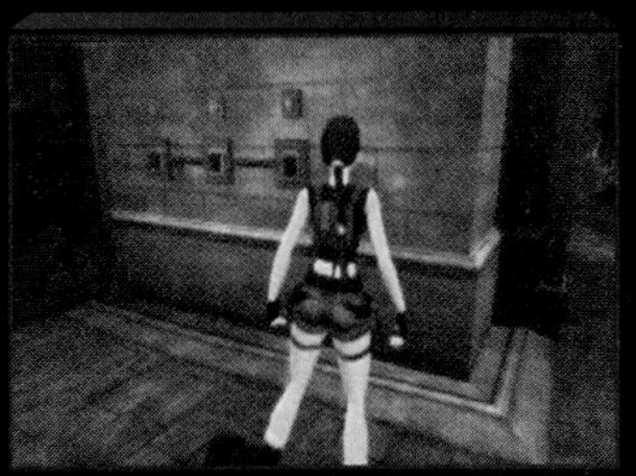

Return to the ground floor, ignoring the green water (there's little here of interest). Instead, travel around the pathway to the initial junction, and take the other route. This leads to a plant-filled area on your left, full of disgusting mutations.

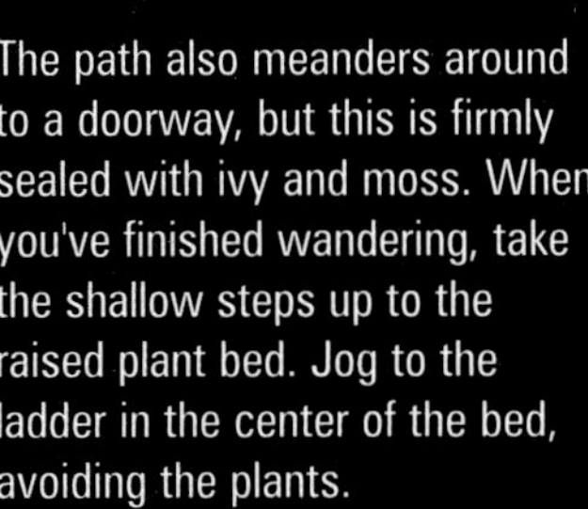

The path also meanders around to a doorway, but this is firmly sealed with ivy and moss. When you've finished wandering, take the shallow steps up to the raised plant bed. Jog to the ladder in the center of the bed, avoiding the plants.

Climb the ladder to the first floor of a series of balconies. When you reach the junction at the wall, you can turn left or right. Don't bother heading right yet, as this path ends with a right turn and a collapsed section of walkway you cannot cross yet.

Instead, turn left and begin to sprint along the balcony. At the far end of the walkway is a set of iron stairs heading upward. Ascend them, then turn and ascend the next set of steps. When you reach the top, you're on the second floor of balconies.

Immediately to your left is an iron trellis with a locked door in the center of it. No matter how hard you try, you cannot jump around it. It seems this area is out of bounds. However, there is a gap in the fence ahead of you, leading to a greenhouse roof.

Make a standing jump from the middle of the walkway, over the gap in the fence, and onto the flat portion of the greenhouse roof. If you over- or undershoot, you'll land on the sloping glass roof area, slide, then fall into the green pond below.

If this occurs, try to grab the lip of the gutter before you fall, shimmy over so you can actually land in the water, drop, and retrace your steps back to this point. Alternatively, drop onto the wider lip, walk to the corner, and take the Health Bandages before you swim. Save your game first.

Assuming you land safely on the flat roof section, turn and look right, down at the smaller flat roof section. You must jump to reach this area next. Execute a standing jump from the middle of the first flat roof to the second.

Move quickly, or you'll attract the attention of the Cabal soldier on the walkway above and behind you (past the door you couldn't open). Shrug off his machine gun fire if need be, then walk to the edge of the second flat roof, and hop to the third.

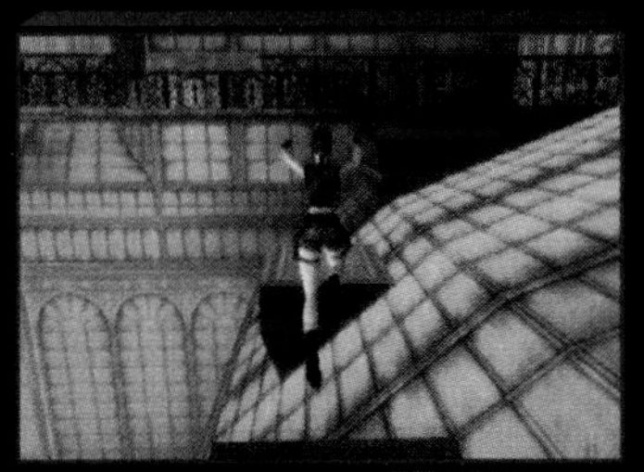

There doesn't seem to be anywhere left to leap until you check the walkway ahead and slightly to your left. Take a running jump at the gap in the railing, and press Action to grab the walkway and haul yourself onto the balcony.

Run forward toward the "roundabout" balcony, where a suspended plant bed holds a flourishing display of evil flora. Move directly to the other side of the structure, and you see the balcony continues to a small gap. Your running tremors cause the balcony to crumble.

This results in a much wider gap as falling metal crashes to the ground. You don't have the leg strength to make this jump. Instead, turn and view the side exit to this roundabout, as well as the incoming Cabal soldier running to intercept you. Bring out your big guns.

Take out the guard, then continue along the walkway (the ledge that crumbled is still too dangerous to attempt). You find yourself at a second junction. Make a left turn and run to the trellis door you couldn't access.

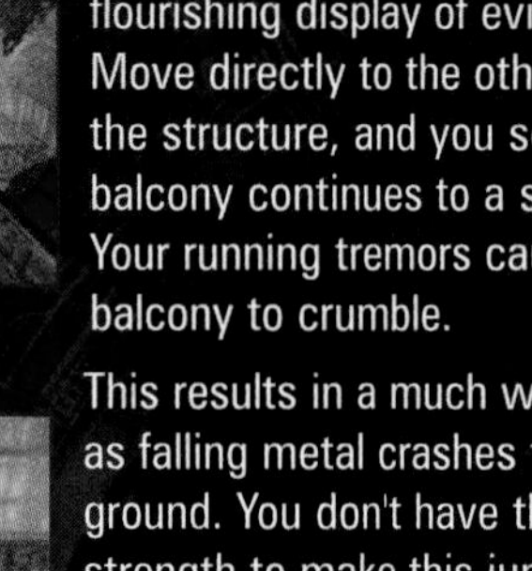

TIP **Open the trellis door so that if you incorrectly time your jumps and fall (but survive), you can head straight back into this section without leaping the greenhouse roof again.**

Make a right turn at the junction, or head back from the previously barred doorway. Follow the balcony as it meanders ahead, left, and left again, hugging the exterior wall. You see a staircase to the right as you turn, but this cannot be accessed.

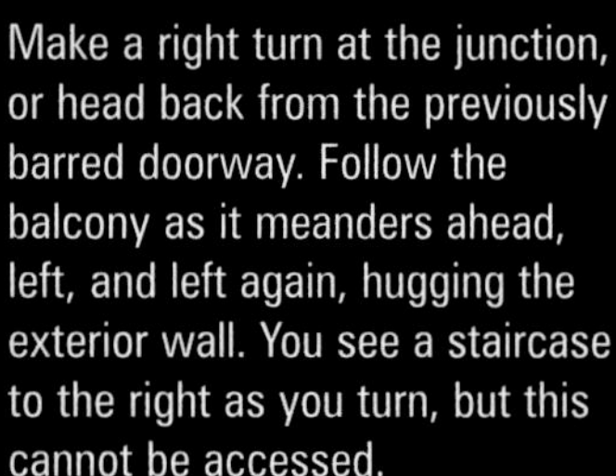

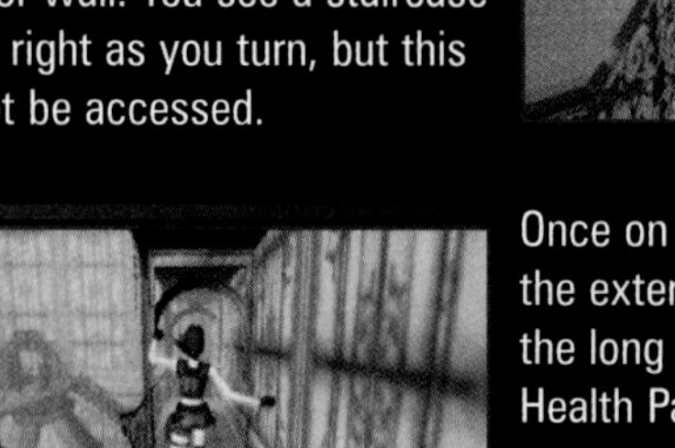

Once on the stretch of corridor by the exterior wall, look ahead at the long gap with the Large Health Pack at the far end. This area tests your leg strength. Hit the Sprint button, then leap over the gap. Land on the other side—don't fall into the gap.

NOTE **Miss the jump and land short? You fall onto a small and previously unexplored piece of balcony under the walkways above. Vault over a railing and land on a walkway underneath (don't fall onto the ground, or you'll suffer damage).**

Lara's jump to the Large Health Pack, and back again, causes her strength to increase (Upgrade Jump: Lower Body Level 9). Perhaps now she can attempt the leap across the unstable ledge. Sprint back to the "roundabout" section where the bridge fell.

Save your game, sprint to the gap, then launch yourself with a long jump. Land on the other side, and ignore the Cabal soldier patrolling the lower, right-hand section if you haven't investigated it yet (this is only possible after the leg upgrade).

Turn left and begin to ascend the stairs (these are the ones you saw earlier, just before the first long jump). Continue around, watching out for the curved corner with the gap that you can accidentally fall through (the plant is growing out of it). Retrace your steps if this happens.

The time has come to ascend to the very top of this gargantuan greenhouse. Sprint along the long walkway to the very end. Once at the railings, you notice some ivy to your right. Grab hold and climb it, then shimmy to the right, and right again onto a broken upper walkway.

Pull yourself onto the walkway and survey the scenery. Ahead of you is the slumped body of a dead Cabal soldier. If you peer off to the right, you can just make out an upper platform. You have no method of reaching it, though.

Viewing the upper, circular balcony from her location, Lara watches Muller keying information into a central computer with limited results. Gundersen strides into view. Apparently, the power is out throughout the facility. Eckhardt then appears.

Eckhardt is understandably worried that everything in the facility is locked down and hopes that "nothing is loose." Muller and Gundersen agree, but one of the scientists, Kristina Boaz, hurries onto the balcony to inform Eckhardt of some rather troubling news.

She didn't destroy the Proto-Nephilim. Gundersen is both surprised and disgusted, and he leaves to personally oversee this problem. It appears, however, that the beast cannot be destroyed without a particular ceremonial Shard, so this mistake isn't Boaz's fault.

This excuse isn't acceptable to Eckhardt, who beckons Muller over and instructs him to set one of his creations on the hapless Boaz. Descending from the ceiling is a carnivorous horror that devours the screaming scientist whole. "This mess must be sorted out at once!" bellows Eckhardt as they leave the balcony.

Once the shock has subsided, remove yourself from this area as quickly as possible. Run along the walkway to the fallen form of the decaying guard, and obtain the Botanical High Access Card from the corpse.

Now comes the laborious process of descending the structure you just climbed. Start by vaulting off the far end of the walkway onto the lower walkway, then descend the steps to the gap you previously leapt over. Once at the "roundabout," head for the trellis door.

Exit the trellis door, head down the two flights of stairs, along the walkway, and stop at the junction. Don't descend to the ground just yet, as you only have two of the three necessary Botanical Access Cards. Run ahead, around the corner, to the gap over the entrance ground.

You couldn't reach this before. Now with a sprint and upgrade, you can sail over the gap, run up the steps, and engage the final Cabal soldier. When the guard falls, stoop to claim the last Botanical Access Card. Excellent.

You see a ladder descending from this section, but it stops high above the ground (meaning you couldn't have reached this area earlier). Hang and drop from the lowest part of the walkway. Now check your Inventory. Have you acquired the three Botanical Access Cards from the three guards? Then head for the exit.

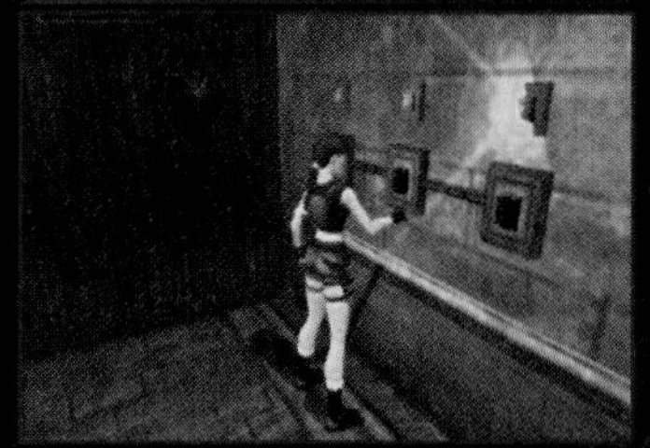

Head for the far right corner of the ground floor (when standing by the entrance). Enter the doorway and turn to the set of three security locks. One may already be flashing. Press the other two buttons.

The dead guard's card unlocks the left lock. The card from the guard on the small, lower-level balcony opens the middle lock. The ground floor guard's card opens the right lock. With all three lock buttons pressed, the door in front of you now opens.

You can now descend a set of stairs that ends in an entrance to an underground mesh walkway. Before you speed across this walkway, stop for a moment and look to your left. A set of steps descends under the mesh walkway to a mist-filled under-chamber.

Move along the chamber under the mesh walkway to find it deserted, except for a small, square hole in the floor. Upon closer inspection, you see it's filled with water. Take a deep breath and dive right in. After a small, U-shaped tunnel, you emerge in a storage room.

Climb onto the ledge next to the water, and observe the two crates nearby. Pull the smaller of the two crates along the wall twice. Keep the box next to the wall, but don't pull it all the way to the end. Position it under a hole in the mesh platform above you.

Clamber onto the box, then jump and grab the lip of the opening to pull yourself up and onto the mesh platform. Ahead is a door that is firmly jammed and cannot be accessed. Instead, turn left and ransack the three lockers.

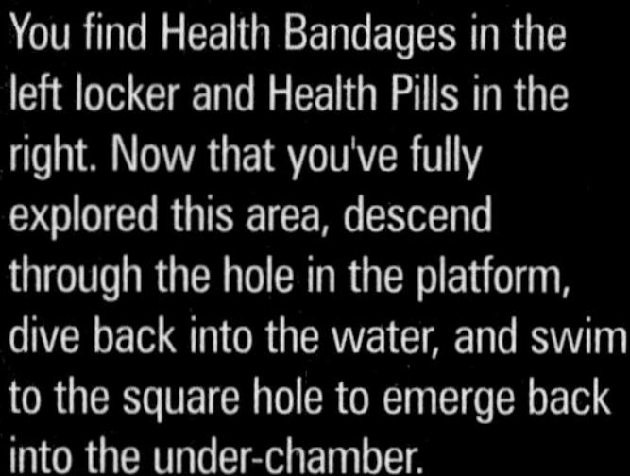

You find Health Bandages in the left locker and Health Pills in the right. Now that you've fully explored this area, descend through the hole in the platform, dive back into the water, and swim to the square hole to emerge back into the under-chamber.

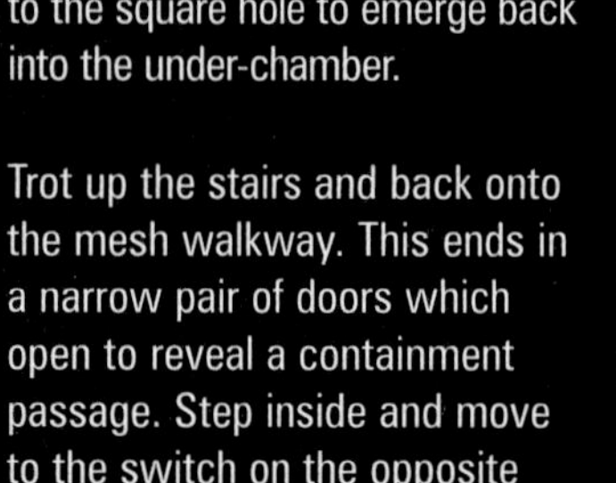

Trot up the stairs and back onto the mesh walkway. This ends in a narrow pair of doors which open to reveal a containment passage. Step inside and move to the switch on the opposite wall. Press this, and the door to your left opens. Step through.

You appear in a small connecting chamber. In front of you is a security door that is firmly sealed. Look instead for another narrow pair of doors leading to a second containment passage. Step through into the chamber, heading for the switch.

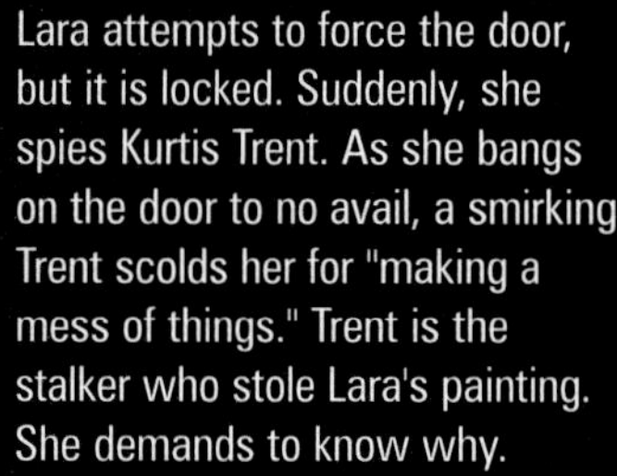

Lara attempts to force the door, but it is locked. Suddenly, she spies Kurtis Trent. As she bangs on the door to no avail, a smirking Trent scolds her for "making a mess of things." Trent is the stalker who stole Lara's painting. She demands to know why.

Trent has little time for explanations; he's more concerned with turning on the power to the fortress. He also feels that Lara has "caused enough problems," and remarks, "It is safer if you stay in one place." In turn, Lara reveals the Shard she has picked up from the Louvre.

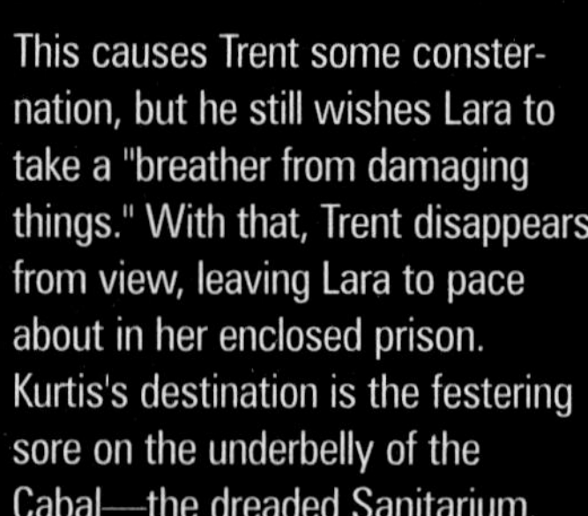

This causes Trent some consternation, but he still wishes Lara to take a "breather from damaging things." With that, Trent disappears from view, leaving Lara to pace about in her enclosed prison. Kurtis's destination is the festering sore on the underbelly of the Cabal—the dreaded Sanitarium.

Sanitarium

Kurtis Trent is your playable character in the Sanitarium and Maximum Containment Area of the Strahov Fortress. After his ambush of the voluptuous Miss Croft in the preceding chapter, it's hard to tell if Kurtis is on your side or not. But there's no time to ponder the question—you've got to get him through the lower levels of the Strahov Fortress in one piece.

Kurtis's adventures in the Sanitarium involve finding items (such as security passes) to solve puzzles and unlocking the entrance to the Maximum Containment Area. Along the way, Kurtis displays his psychic talents, including his Farsee ability that lets him peer around corners and look through locked doors. Also, every time you see a five-digit number, remember it—you must open several numeric keypad locks.

The majority of the enemy creatures are Sanitarium Zombies, laboratory subjects who have been exposed to experiments for so long that they no longer pass as human. Even though the Sanitarium Zombies do minimal damage, put them out of their misery. Kurtis comes loaded with hundreds of bullets for his custom Boran X pistol, so you may as well use it.

ENTITIES ENCOUNTERED

- Sanitarium Zombies (x13)
- Agency Soldier
- Proto-Nephilim

CRITICAL ITEMS TO LOCATE

- Farsee Code 06289
- Strahov Assistant's Pass

AVAILABLE UPGRADES

- You play as Kurtis Trent in this level, and Kurtis does not have the ability to upgrade his physical strength.

TRENT'S TRICKS

Kurtis Trent has some psychic abilities that Lara Croft lacks. They kick in automatically when you need them, so there's no need to activate them yourself. Kurtis has the power to telekinetically move objects without touching them, and he also has a Farsee ability that lets him view areas that he can't physically reach.

Despite his mental powers, Kurtis is physically less impressive than Lara. He cannot upgrade his upper- or lower-body strength, and he's slower to stand up from a crouch. He also lacks a Stealth mode, so he can't do a Commando Crawl. Aside from these quirks, Kurtis has an identical control scheme to Lara's.

Walk to the edge of the long, cylindrical shaft in front of you and press Action to hang from the edge .

Press Action twice quickly. The first press releases Kurtis's grip on the ledge, and the second press prepares him to grab the next ledge below him. If you do it right, you'll snag the next ledge without plummeting to an untimely demise.

After reaching the second ledge safely, drop from that one and catch the ledge below it, then repeat the move twice more to drop past the ledges. Pull yourself onto this rust-colored ledge, grab the Health Pills, then return to the edge and drop to the next one.

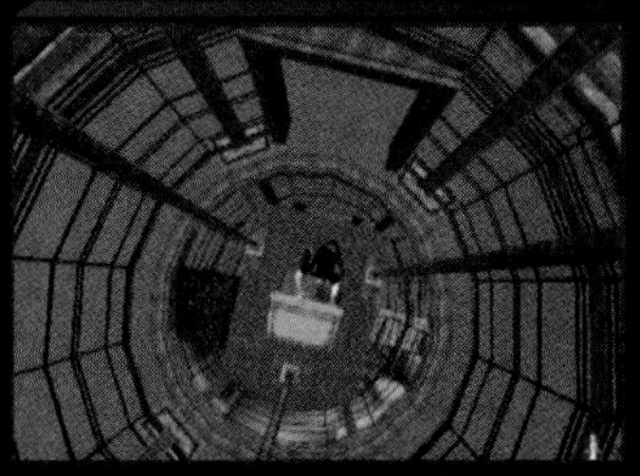

Drop off this ledge and land near a metal hatch in the floor of the shaft. Press Action near the hatch to open it, then drop through the hatch.

Climb down the nearby ladder to reach a platform just below you.

From the platform at the bottom of the first ladder, climb down another ladder that leads to another metal platform far below you.

Walk to the end of the platform, and face the shaft in the center of the room and the overhead platform directly in front of you. Jump forward and press Action in midair to grab the edge of the platform and pull yourself onto it.

Go through the double doors at the end of the platform to enter the Sanitarium.

At the entrance to the Sanitarium is a reception area and a steel gate that blocks the wards from the outside world. You see a Sanitarium Zombie as it thrashes toward you from the other side of the gate. Shoot it through the gate, then open the door to the gate.

TIP Although Kurtis has plenty of ammo, you can conserve it by holding your fire until you can see the whites of the Zombies' dead eyes. The closer you are when you fire, the fewer bullets it takes to kill the Zombies. Since the Zombies do little damage, you can afford to get close to them.

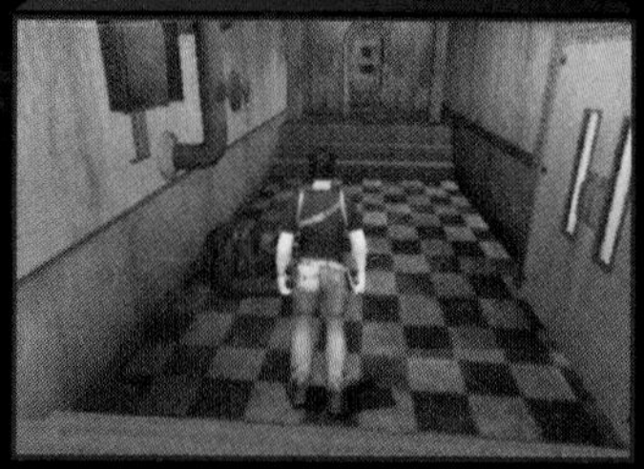

Go through the gate and walk down the hallway beyond it. There's a dead Agency soldier in the hallway and a clip of Boran X ammo lying next to him. Approach the Boran X ammo to pick it up, and you trigger the following cutscene.

Another Agency soldier clings to life at the end of the hallway, but not for long—a bestial claw grabs the soldier and pulls him down the hallway.

Kurtis runs into the hallway, but the soldier and beast have vanished, and only a dangling grate to an air vent betrays the creature's escape route.

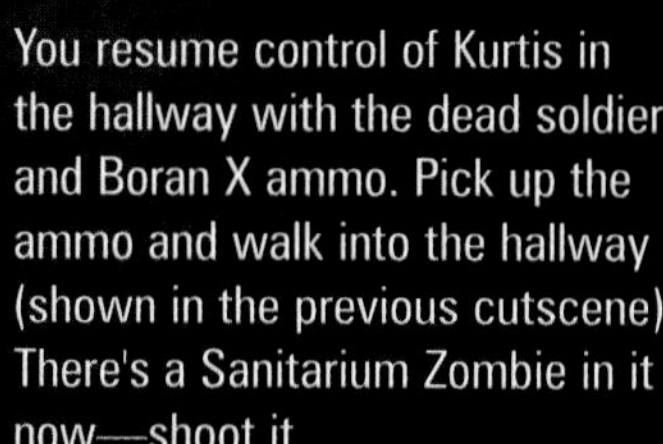

You resume control of Kurtis in the hallway with the dead soldier and Boran X ammo. Pick up the ammo and walk into the hallway (shown in the previous cutscene). There's a Sanitarium Zombie in it now—shoot it.

TIP To avoid being surprised by enemies, always walk into rooms and around corners with your trusty Boran X drawn. Since you automatically target any hostile creatures if your weapon is drawn, you'll never be caught unaware.

There's a cell with an open door at the end of this hallway. Go into the cell to find a docile Sanitarium Zombie. Put that pistol away and talk to him to learn that the creature that dragged off the soldier is called a Proto-nephilim, a.k.a. "the screamer" and "Black Angel." It's on the loose and killing everything that moves. The Sanitarium inmates were used as food for the beast, but when Lara shut down the power in the Strahov Fortress level, it started munching on Agency soldiers.

The Zombie used to be the Turkish truck driver who brought Eckhardt's "Sleeper" to the Strahov Fortress. The driver was locked in the Sanitarium with the Proto-Nephilim. He thinks he'll be safe in his cell. Kurtis advises him to keep the door locked and, in a moment of tenderness, doesn't shoot him in the head

There's nothing else to do around here except return to the hallway and approach the locked gate at the end of it. To the left of the gate is the first of several numeric keypad locks in the Sanitarium. But what's the code?

Fortunately, Kurtis's Farsee ability kicks in as you approach the door. He gets a red-tinted glimpse of the areas beyond the gate, including a desk that has a slip of paper with a five-digit code on it, 06289.

NOTE **After the Farsee cutscene, Kurtis has a new "item" in his Inventory, Farsee Code 06289. It's not so much an actual item as it is a convenient way to remember the number that Kurtis saw in his Farsee vision.**

When the Farsee vision ends, enter 0-6-2-8-9 into the numeric keypad. The gate unlocks.

Go through the open gate with your pistol drawn, and Kurtis targets a Sanitarium Zombie in a hallway beyond another gate. Pick it off from the other side of the gate if you wish (although the range limits your accuracy), and the wounded Zombie flees.

Open the gate and go through it, finishing off the Sanitarium Zombie if you didn't get him from the other side of the gate. At the end of the hallway is another gate. Open it and proceed into the next hallway.

The next hallway has white double doors at the end of it and an open room containing an orange-clad Sanitarium Zombie. Take out the Zombie and go through the double doors to the Sanitarium cafeteria.

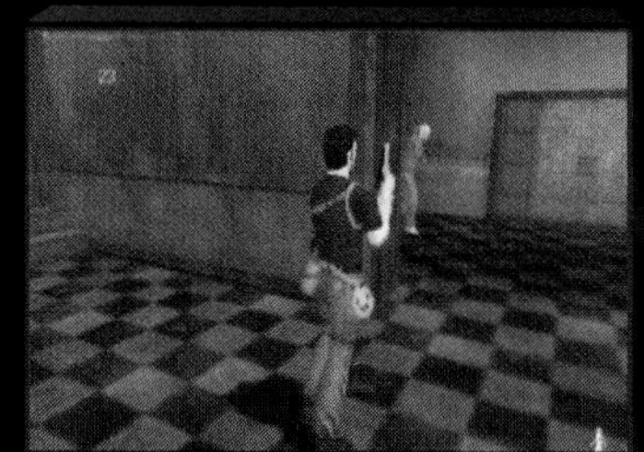

The cafeteria is just to the side of a long, curving hallway. There are four Sanitarium Zombies in the area. Walk down the hallway and kill all four Zombies as you go.

Halfway down the hallway, across from the cafeteria, is a set of double doors with the number 38471 next to them. Remember that number, and continue down the hallway, guns blazing.

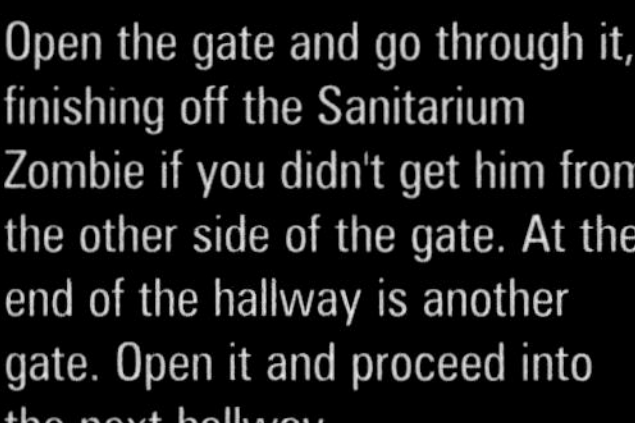

At the end of the hallway is a handicapped-accessible ramp leading to a set of white double doors. Go through these doors.

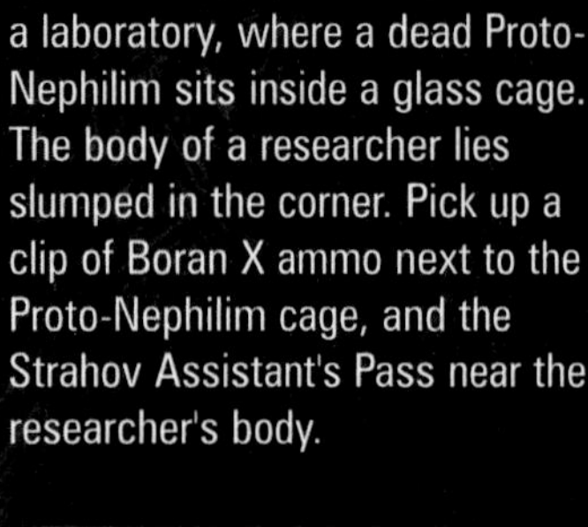

The white double doors lead into a laboratory, where a dead Proto-Nephilim sits inside a glass cage. The body of a researcher lies slumped in the corner. Pick up a clip of Boran X ammo next to the Proto-Nephilim cage, and the Strahov Assistant's Pass near the researcher's body.

Once you have both items, backtrack down the long, curved hallway until you come to the cafeteria. There's another Sanitarium Zombie inside the cafeteria kitchen, but you can't get to him. However, you can pick up Boran X ammo and a Chocolate Bar from the floor of the cafeteria.

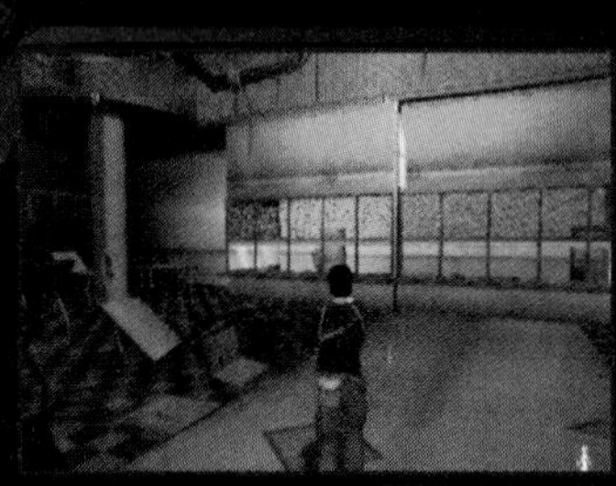

NOTE **You can enter the open cells on either side of the long, curved hallway, but there's nothing of interest in any of them.**

Once you have both items, walk to the far right corner of the cafeteria (as you face the kitchen) to find a locked door and a card reader. Press Action near the card reader to use the Strahov Assistant's Pass and unlock the door.

Go through the door, past the stairs, and into the kitchen. Take out the Sanitarium Zombie there.

Return to the stairs you just passed, and climb them to reach a catwalk above the floor of the cafeteria.

Walk counterclockwise around the catwalk, but watch out—there's a gap in it. Walk to the edge of the gap, jump forward, and press Action in midair to grab the edge of the other side of the gap. Pull yourself up and keep going around the catwalk.

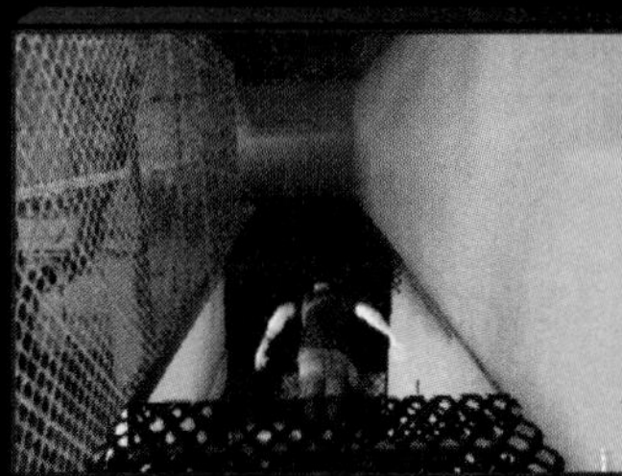

At the other end of the catwalk, you find a control console. Press Action next to it, and you can enter a code on a numeric keypad. Enter the number you saw next to the locked double doors across from the cafeteria (3-8-4-7-1) to unlock those doors.

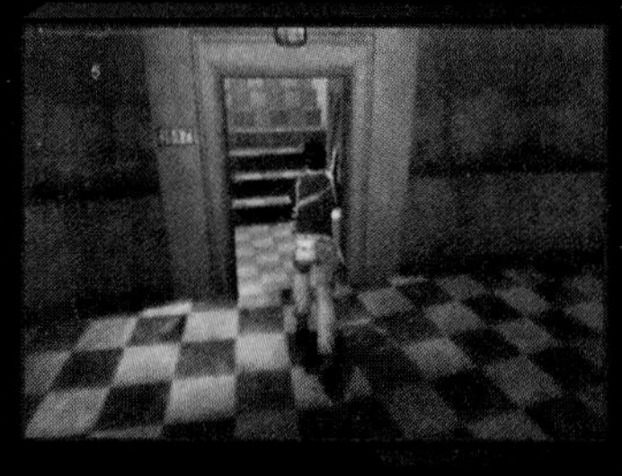

Now backtrack until you're back on the floor of the cafeteria. You can take the stairs from the catwalk, or drop through the gap in the catwalk into the kitchen.

Once back in the cafeteria, head through the now-unlocked double doors. Go down the short hallway beyond them, and enter the white door at the end of it to trigger the following cutscene.

The Proto-Nephilim is at it again. This time, he pops out of a ventilation duct and chomps on a scientist studying the corpse of a Sanitarium Mutant. What's a Sanitarium Mutant, you ask? You're about to find out.

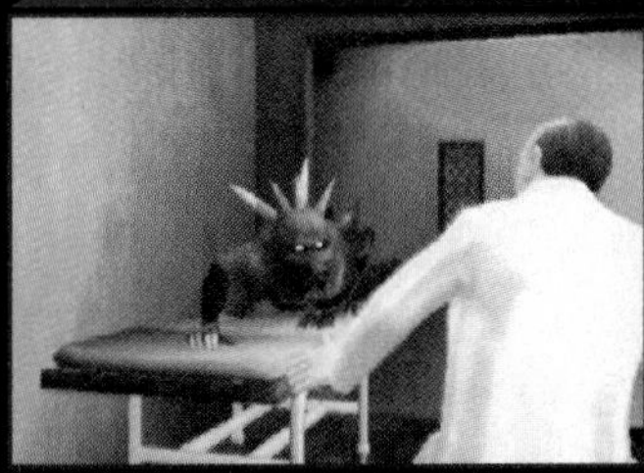

You resume control of Kurtis near the locked doors to the lab. Run around the corner and encounter one to three Sanitarium Zombies. Destroy them.

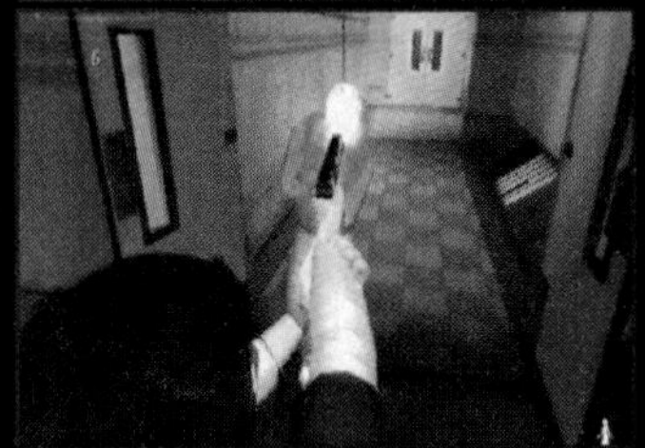

At the end of the corridor is a floor-level ventilation duct. Press Action near it to remove the cover, then crawl inside.

After a short crawl, you come to an area where Kurtis can stand up; the duct continues overhead. Leap up, grab the edge of the continuation of the duct, pull yourself into it, and keep crawling forward.

The duct ends in the lab where you saw the Proto-Nephilim consume its latest snack. Drop into the lab to find that the Proto-Nephilim has once again escaped with its meal.

The only thing you can do in the lab is remove the cover to another floor-level ventilation duct. That clever Proto-Nephilim must have escaped through it and somehow replaced the cover—from the other side of the duct.

Crawl into the duct and jump to grab the edge of the duct as it continues overhead. Keep crawling through it until you reach the end, and a cutscene plays.

The Proto-Nephilim snacks on an Agency soldier on the other side of a ventilation fan; there's no sign of the scientist it attacked earlier. The Proto-Nephilim catches sight of Kurtis, and instead of attacking him as it has everything else, it flees.

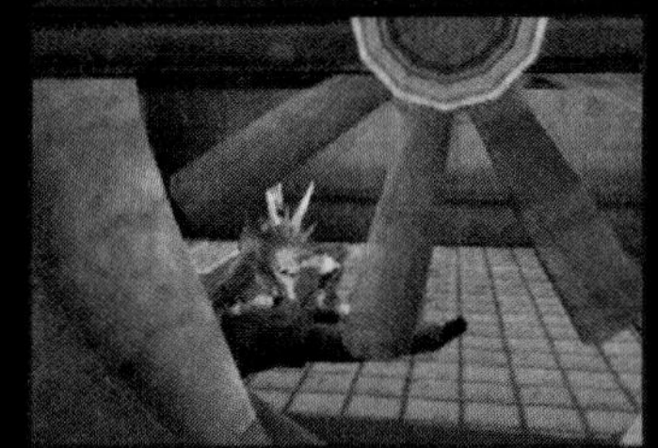

When the cutscene ends, drop into the room. You can't walk or crawl past the fan, but there is a broken ladder leading to a small platform. Unfortunately, you can't climb it. What to do?

Draw your pistol, stand in a corner as far from the fan as possible, and shoot the pressurized canisters near the fan until they explode.

This causes the broken ladder to fall over, and you can now jump and grab the edge of the platform. Pull yourself up and activate the switch that shuts off the fan.

Don't forget to grab the Boran X ammo lying on the floor next to the fan.

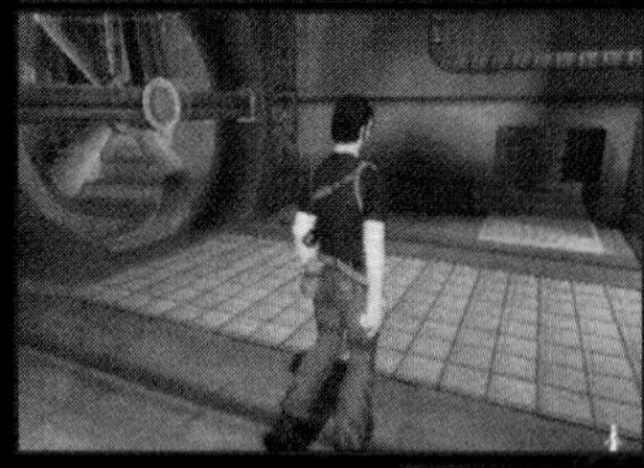

With the fan stopped, crawl underneath it and into the hallway beyond it. There's another ventilation duct here that you need to crawl into.

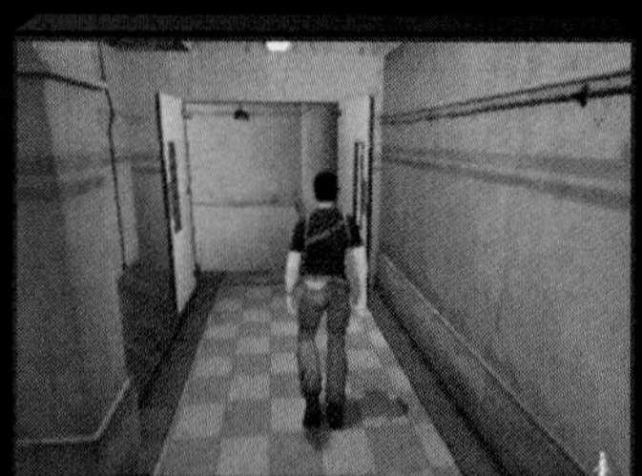

From the end of the duct, take a right and walk through the open double doors and into the Maximum Containment Area.

Maximum Containment Area

As if the Sanitarium wasn't creepy enough, Kurtis's journey through the Maximum Containment Area takes him closer to the defective Proto-Nephilim holding cell. Most of the enemies in the Maximum Containment Area are Sanitarium Mutants—think Sanitarium Zombies plus Proto-Nephilim DNA. They're fast and nasty customers, so don't spare the bullets.

Kurtis's ultimate goal is to reach the Proto-Nephilim's lair and kill it. To do so, he must find a variety of keys and codes to unlock doors—and, of course, chew through a lot of ammo.

ENTITIES ENCOUNTERED
- Proto-Nephilim
- Sanitarium Mutant (x5)
- Agency Soldier

CRITICAL ITEMS TO LOCATE
- Farsee Code 17068
- Sanitarium Low Access Pass
- Sanitarium Medium Access Pass

AVAILABLE UPGRADES
- Kurtis has no available upgrades.

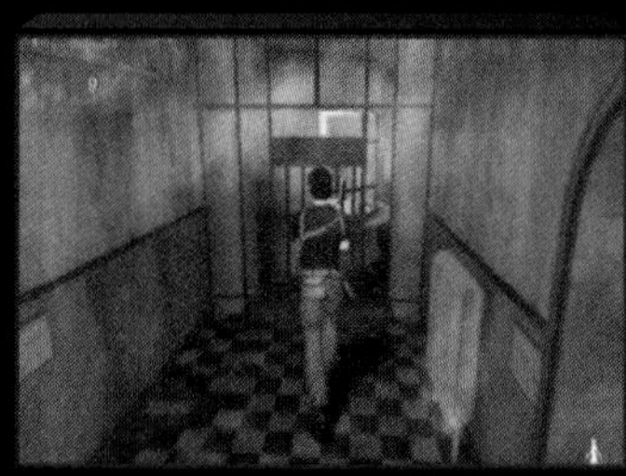

From the entrance to the Maximum Containment Area, head straight down the hallway and through the metal gate at the end.

From the other side of the gate, you can go straight through another gate, left through the security office door, or right to a pool of bubbling, green water.

Go into the office first, through the green door left of the metal gate. There's another numeric keypad in here. You haven't found another code yet, so there's no need to use it. But keep it in mind. Leave the office.

Now head down the hallway with the bubbling green water at the end of it. The water is poisonous and will eat away your health energy if you land in it, so jump up and shimmy along the wires that run down the right wall. Get back across the pool the same way.

Finally, open the gate near the security office to enter another cell-lined corridor, and go through the double doors at the end of it.

At the four-way intersection beyond the double doors, take a right and hug the left wall as you walk down the hallway.

As Kurtis passes the second cell door on his left, his Farsee ability is automatically triggered. He gets a glimpse of the scene inside of the cell, which includes the corpse of a Sanitarium Zombie with the number 17068 on its back.

NOTE **This gives Kurtis the Farsee Code 17068. It's not actually an item, but you can view it in your Inventory to remind yourself of the code.**

Return to the security office near the beginning of the Maximum Containment Area, and enter 1-7-0-6-8 into the numeric keypad to unlock the two cell doors you just walked past.

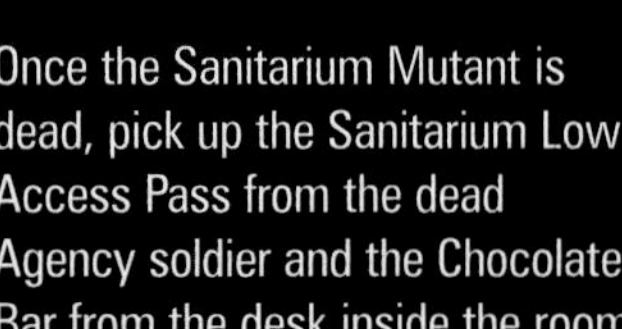

Return to the cell door where Kurtis had his Farsee vision and enter the cell. Walk inside, but immediately back away from the door and aim your pistol toward it to shoot the Sanitarium Mutant that tries to barge in. Hammer the Action button as fast as you can to fill them with lead.

Once the Sanitarium Mutant is dead, pick up the Sanitarium Low Access Pass from the dead Agency soldier and the Chocolate Bar from the desk inside the room.

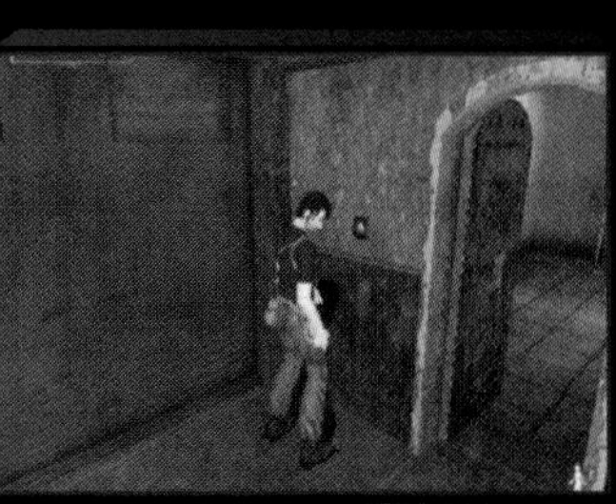

Walk out of that room, take a left, and follow the corridor to a huge, metal shutter with a blinking card reader to the right of it. Use the Sanitarium Low Access Pass on the card reader to open the shutter.

CAUTION **Watch out. Opening the giant, metal shutter releases two more Sanitarium Mutants. Keep your Boran X ready.**

In an open cell near a set of locked double doors with a red light above them, you find a clip of Boran X ammo sitting on a satchel on a bed.

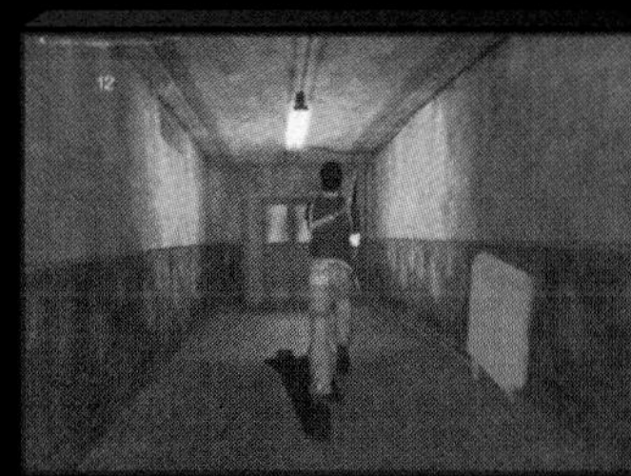

Next to the aforementioned cell is a long, sloping corridor with a door at the end. Go through that door to enter the next area.

Take an immediate right after going through the door, walk down the corridor, and take your first left to enter a lab. A cutscene follows.

The Proto-Nephilim runs past Kurtis without attacking him, then runs down the hall and under a half-shut steel door.

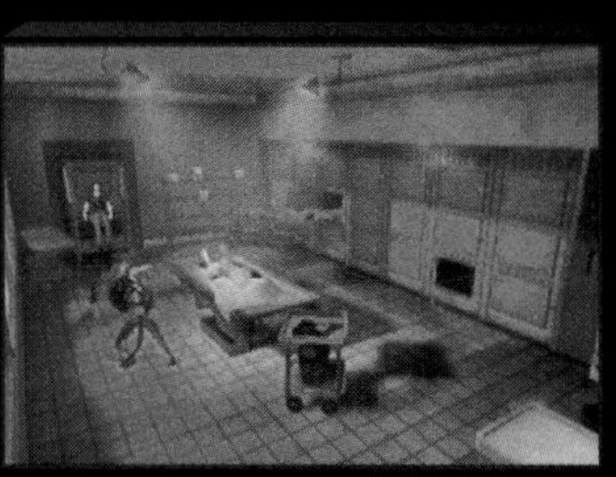

Don't chase the Proto-Nephilim immediately; a Sanitarium Mutant busts into the lab. Shoot them, exit the lab, take a right, and continue walking along the hall.

CAUTION There are two more Sanitarium Mutants somewhere in the hallway—keep your finger on the trigger.

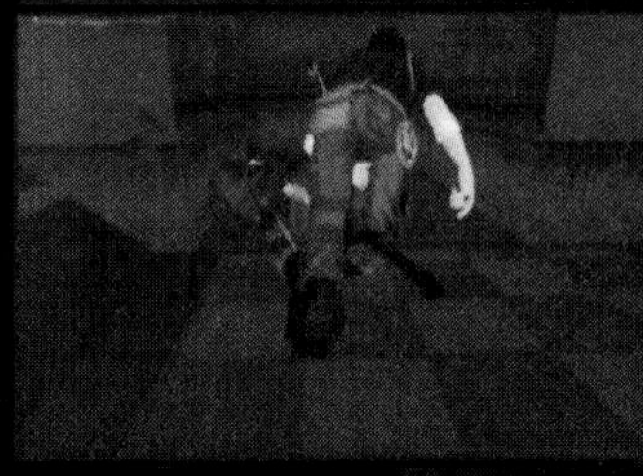

Approach the half-closed steel door and crawl under it. You'll tread over the body of an unlucky Agency soldier who was the Proto-Nephilim's last meal.

Head down the spiral stairs beyond the half-closed steel door. At the bottom of the stairs is a black-and-white-tiled hallway.

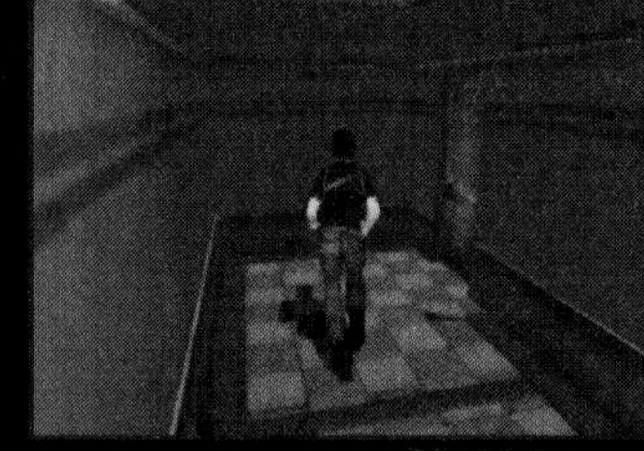

Run down the hallway until you come to the steel door that leads to the Proto-Nephilim chamber area, which you first saw when Lara shut off the power in the Strahov Fortress.

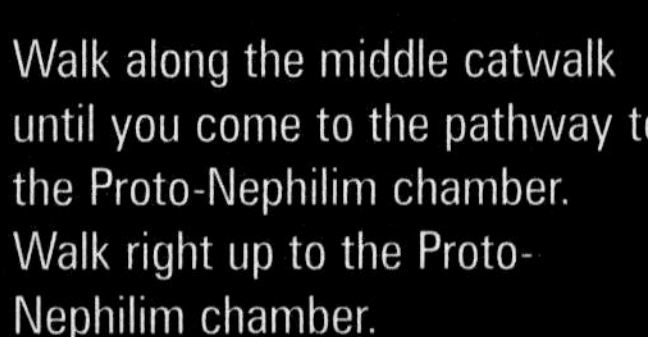

Run along the lower catwalk of the Proto-Nephilim chamber area until you find a ladder leading up to the middle catwalk. Climb it.

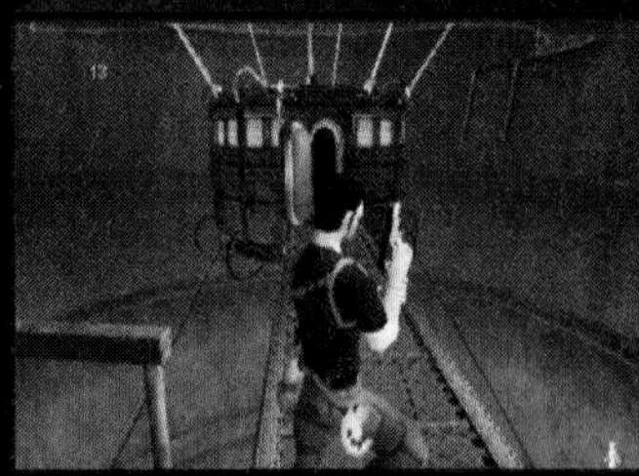

Walk along the middle catwalk until you come to the pathway to the Proto-Nephilim chamber. Walk right up to the Proto-Nephilim chamber.

Jump and grab the edge of the roof of the chamber and pull yourself up to it. Walk along the roof and face the broken section of the upper catwalk.

Stand at the edge of the Proto-Nephilim chamber and jump forward toward the upper catwalk. Press Action immediately after jumping to grab the edge of the catwalk, then pull yourself up to it.

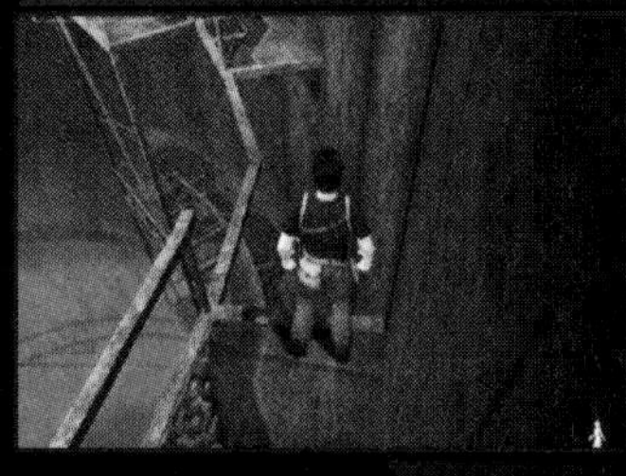

There's a gap in the upper catwalk. Walk to the edge of the gap, jump forward across it, and press Action to grab the edge of the other side of the catwalk.

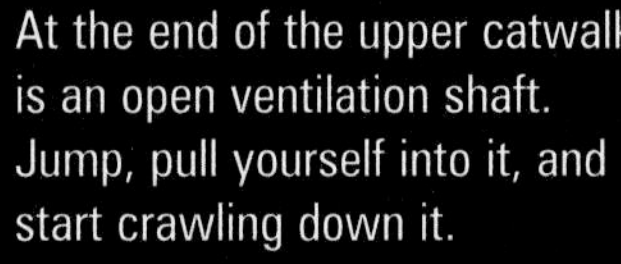

At the end of the upper catwalk is an open ventilation shaft. Jump, pull yourself into it, and start crawling down it.

Although there are a couple of drop-offs and some intersections, there is literally only one path you can take through the duct. Wrong turns are blocked with grates.

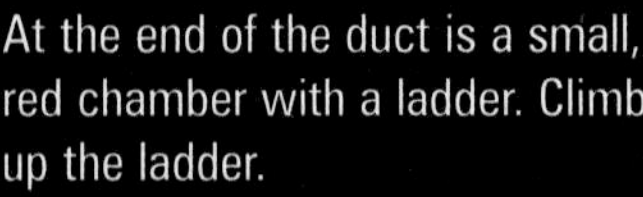

At the end of the duct is a small, red chamber with a ladder. Climb up the ladder.

At the top of the ladder are the mutilated corpses of two Agency soldiers and the Sanitarium Medium Access Pass. Pick up the pass.

Press the button to the right of the hallway leading out of the room to open the door at the end of it.

Before leaving, pick up the Chocolate Bar on the floor of the room. You're heading toward the boss fight against the Proto-Nephilim, so you need all the healing items you can get.

When you're ready, walk down the hallway through the door you just opened. You're back in the area near the half-closed steel door and the last lab you saw. At the first intersection, take a left and follow the hallway as it turns.

At the end of the hallway, you find a locked door and a blinking card reader. Press Action near the card reader to use the Sanitarium Medium Access Pass and open the door. Go through the door to begin the boss fight against Proto-Nephilim.

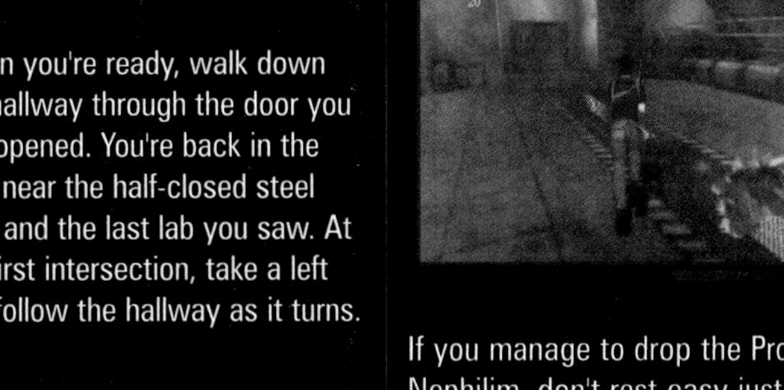

In the cutscene that precedes the fight, the Proto-Nephilim finally stops running from Kurtis and starts stalking him. It almost pounces on Kurtis, but Kurtis telekinetically lowers a giant, steel shutter, preventing the Proto-Nephilim from attacking him. The Proto-Nephilim's a crafty devil, however, and it sneaks in through a ventilation duct. The fight is on.

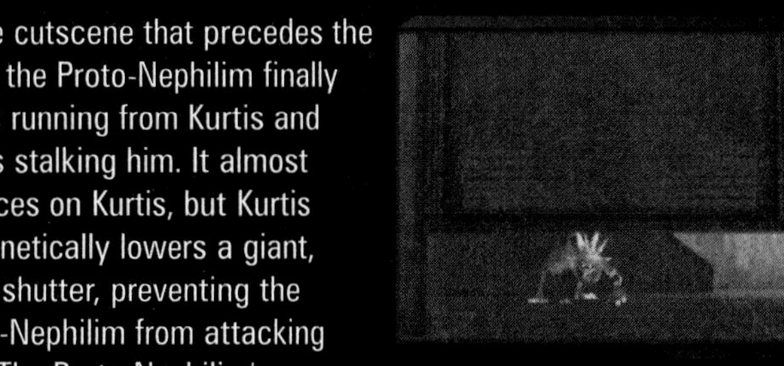

There's a very simple pattern to this boss fight. All you have to do is keep moving in circles with your Boran X drawn. The Proto-Nephilim lurks on the ceiling and drops to the floor to attack.

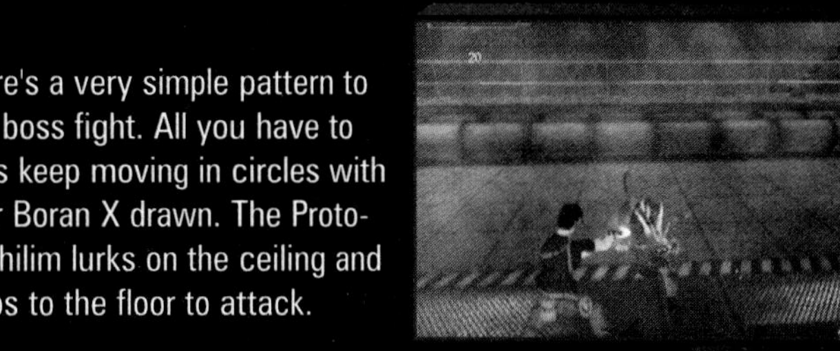

TIP If you keep running, it won't land on you, and if your gun is drawn, you'll automatically target the Proto-Nephilim. The Proto-Nephilim always growls just before dropping from the ceiling.

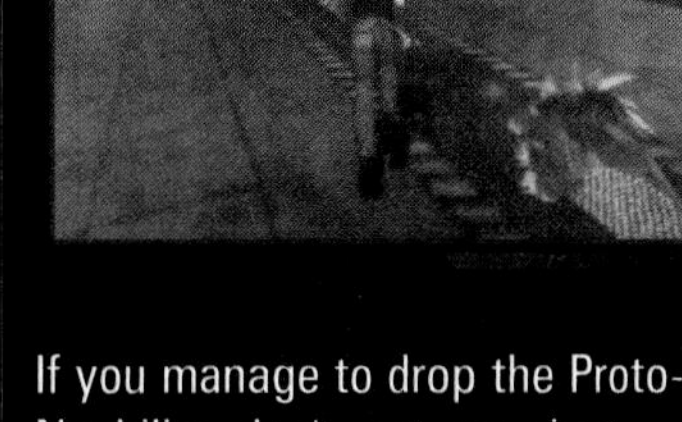

Continue running circles around the Proto-Nephilim while firing at it like a madman. Eventually, it falls over or runs back to the ceiling and drops on you again.

If you manage to drop the Proto-Nephilim, don't rest easy just yet—it gets back up and runs back to the ceiling to drop on you again.

TIP There's an unlimited supply of Boran X ammo on the floor; pick it up when the Proto-Nephilim retreats the ceiling or plays dead. There's also a Large Health Pack in here as well.

Repeat the attack pattern, running in circles and shooting at the Proto-Nephilim, until you drop it fourth times. At that point, run up to it, and you see a cutscene of Kurtis plunging the crystal Shard into the beast, killing it.

Once you've killed the Proto-Nephilim, pull the big switch at the end of the room to open a secret chamber and free Lara Croft.

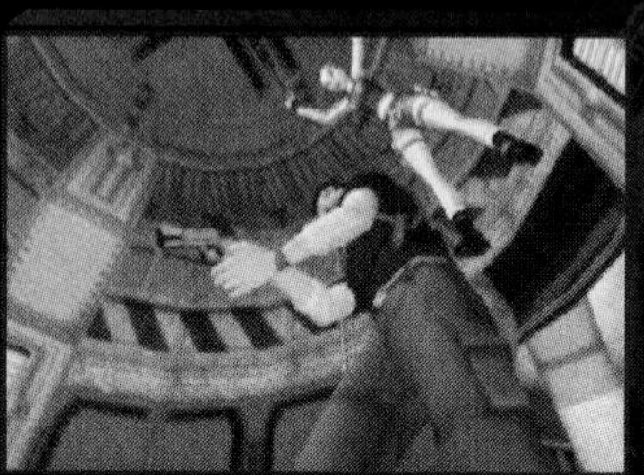

Lara, however, has already managed to free herself, and she hides in the ceiling of her prison chamber as Kurtis cautiously walks in, gun drawn. Jumping down, she kicks the gun from his hand, draws one of her own, and fires—at a Sanitarium Mutant directly behind Kurtis.

Lara and Kurtis formally introduce themselves, and Lara throws Kurtis up against the wall to disarm him. When asked about the Obscura Painting, Kurtis apologizes, saying it went AWOL at the Louvre.

Kurtis tells Lara that he and Eckhardt have business that only one of them is going to walk away from. Lara confides that her beef with Eckhardt is also personal.

Kurtis tells Lara that Eckhardt plans to use the five Obscura Paintings to revive an ancient evil called the Sleeper and revive the extinct Nephilim race. To do that, he's been collecting alchemically transmuted elements from the bodies of the victims he's murdered. Eckhardt is the original Black Alchemist, and he's very close to finding the last Obscura Painting.

As he speaks, Kurtis shows off his telekinetic ability by mentally lifting a weapon and spinning it around the two of them, as Lara keeps her pistol trained on Kurtis.

Kurtis says that the last Obscura Painting is hidden in a Lux Veritatis vault beneath the Strahov. To destroy the paintings, Kurtis needs the Shard that Lara picked up at the Louvre. Lara says that there should be three of the Periapt Shards, to which Kurtis responds that Eckhardt has the last one. It's the only thing that can destroy him permanently, so he keeps it safe.

The Shards are ancient weapons of the Lux Veritatis. Two of them were entrusted to Kurtis's father, whom Eckhardt murdered in order to prevent them from falling into Kurtis's hands. Obviously, the plan didn't work, and now Kurtis wants revenge.

Convinced of his integrity, Lara suggests that they work together. She gives Kurtis her Shard, and Kurtis tells her that Eckhardt must be stabbed with all three Shards to be destroyed. Lara suggests that Kurtis go after the third Shard while she recovers and destroys the last Obscura Painting. Kurtis knows that Eckhardt keeps the Shard in his old alchemy lab in the lower regions of the Strahov. Lara sees on the fifth Obscura Engraving that the Obscura Painting is hidden in something called the Vault of Trophies, which has an underwater entrance.

The scene shifts to Gundersen and Eckhardt in conversation. How did Lara get the Obscura Engraving and the map, asks Gunderson. Eckhardt doesn't know, nor does he care. The Cabal has been unsuccessful so far in its efforts to open the Vault of Trophies, so perhaps Lara's talents will succeed where theirs failed. Regardless, he suggests that they prepare for Kurtis's imminent arrival. Eckhardt doesn't believe that Lara is capable of destroying the final Obscura Painting. Is he right? There's only one way to tell for sure.

Aquatic Research Area

After sneaking past a handful of motion-sensing machine-gun turrets, you need to restore power to the aquatic labs while dodging a Leviathan. Only once Lara has explored all of the secrets of the deep will the biggest secret of them all reveal itself—the entrance to the Vault of Trophies, where the final Obscura Painting is rumored to be hidden in the Lux Veritatis vault.

ENTITIES ENCOUNTERED

- Leviathan
- Agency Soldier

CRITICAL ITEMS TO LOCATE

- None

AVAILABLE UPGRADES

- **Upgrade Grip: Upper Body Level 9**
  By preparing a cartload of raw chum for Leviathan, Lara works those biceps and earns an upgrade that lets her shimmy farther along ledges.

From the start of the level, press the big, yellow button in front of you to open a door.

You enter the next area on a catwalk. There's a ladder at the end of it that leads down. Unfortunately, there are two motion-sensitive machine-gun turrets on the floor that destroy you if you get too close to them.

Instead of climbing down the ladder, hang from the edge of the catwalk near where you entered the room, then drop from there to the floor. You're too far away from the nearest machine gun to trigger its motion sensor.

Duck and crawl while holding the Stealth button to Commando Crawl along the wall opposite the machine-gun turrets. Crawl through a hole in the support beam to reach a valve.

Stand up near the valve, and press Action to turn it and release a blue fog into the room. Wait a few seconds for the room to fill up. The fog completely nullifies the machine guns' sensors, rendering them harmless.

With the machine guns disarmed, side-jump over the obstacles to the right of the valve, and climb onto the pipe on the far wall.

Climb up the pipe, shimmy right at the cross-shaped intersection of pipe, and climb the next vertical pipe to the right.

You reach a ledge. Shimmy right along the ledge until you can pull yourself up. Walk to the platform below the ledge and drop onto it.

Go down the hallway leading from the platform. Near the end, you find a monitor for the security camera in the next part of the hallway. Use it to see that there are volatile chemicals stored near a blinking light, as well as another machine-gun turret near the chemicals.

Walk halfway down the next section of hallway, and aim at the blinking light near the machine-gun turret at the end. Shoot the chemicals near the light without stepping within range of the machine gun.

Pop enough caps into the pressurized containers near the blinking light, and they explode, taking out the turret as well.

Walk casually past the wrecked machine-gun turret and climb the ladder beyond it.

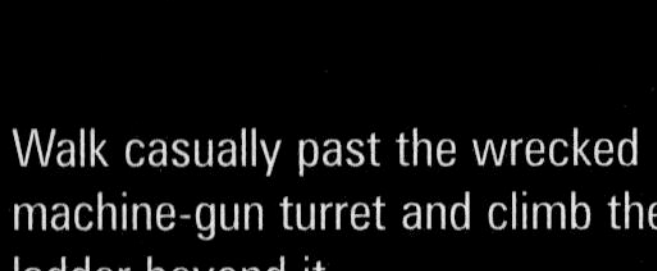

Follow the hallway to pass through a set of thick steel doors and enter the Aquatic Research Area proper.

Walk past the doors as you enter the research area, and a console directly in front of you flickers, indicating that the research area's power levels are dangerously low.

Walk counterclockwise around the catwalks of the Aquatic Research Facility until you see a smashed observation window under the water near you. You also see a vicious shark hybrid called Leviathan.

CAUTION The Leviathan can't attack you unless you enter the water, but if it hurts you even once, it kills you instantly. Stay out of the water unless there's a barricade between you and the beast.

Dive into the water and swim through the broken observation window. You're protected from the Leviathan by a wire-mesh wall under the water.

There's a switch on the wall inside the observation area. Pull it to restore half power to the Aquatic Research Facility.

This also opens a door on the surface of the research facility.

Swim through the yellow-and-black stripped tunnel opposite the power switch and follow it into the underwater room beyond.

When you enter the underwater room, swim up and through another passageway lined with yellow-and-black stripes. Swim through the hole in the ceiling just beyond it.

This brings you back to the surface. Pull yourself out of the water and walk along the pathway into a dry room. There's a Small Health Pack here.

Press the yellow button near the steel door to open it. Go through it and follow the hallway to return to the main part of the Underwater Research Area.]

The door that opened is on the opposite side of the research area from the smashed observation window. It sits directly above an intact observation window. Head over to it.

Press the large, yellow button at the end of the hallway beyond the door to open the thick steel door next to it.

Pull the switch to the right of the elevator door at the end of the room beyond the thick steel door you just opened. This restores power to the elevator and calls it to your level.

Push the yellow button to the left of the elevator door to activate a security camera elsewhere in the Aquatic Research Area (it's actually in the room that the elevator runs down to).

Enter the elevator and push the button inside of it to ride down to the observation area below the water.

Exit the elevator and head to the door in the steamy room you saw through the security camera.

The door opens automatically. Go through it to find another switch, and pull the switch to restore full power to the Aquatic Research Facility.

Once you've restored power to the facility, backtrack to the surface by riding the elevator back up.

When you return to the surface, you see a quick cutscene of some changes that restoring the power has made to the facility. Power now runs to two switches in two different rooms high above the catwalk, and a hatch opens above a previously blocked ladder. Visit the switches in the order they were shown.

High above the center of the Aquatic Research Facility is the mechanism designed to feed Leviathan. Perhaps if you could offer him a snack, he'd stop trying to munch on you.

Starting at the catwalk near the entrance to the facility, run clockwise and follow the stairs and catwalks as they lead to the high platform in the center of the facility.

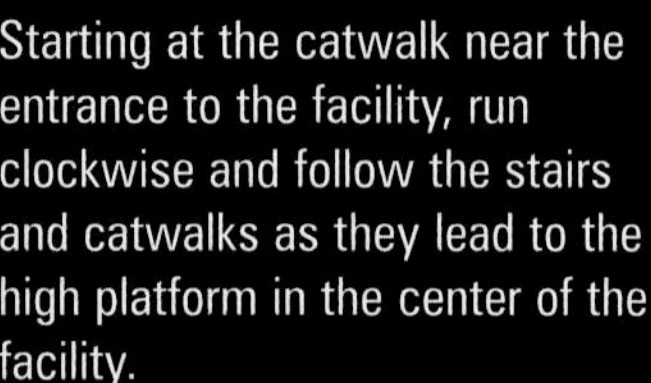

In the center of the feeding platform is a cart on a lift. Pull the cart off the lift so that it rests on the conveyor in front of it on the catwalk. You may need to push it from behind to fully seat it on the conveyor.

Once the cart is on the dark square, push the nearby yellow button to activate the conveyor and move the cart to the end of the catwalk.

Now pull or push the cart into the room at the end of the catwalk. Position the cart so that it's directly under the chum dispenser.

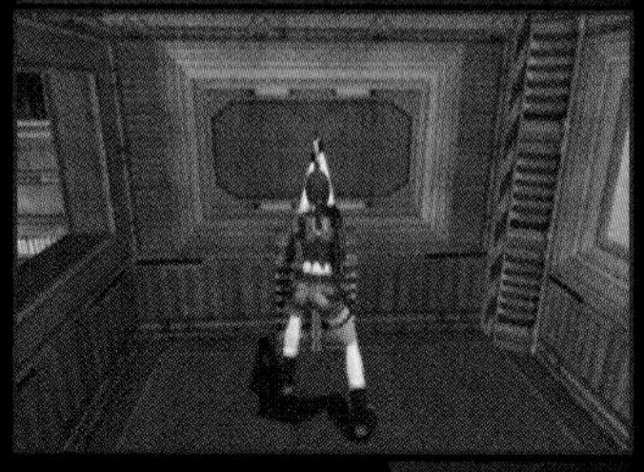

Pull the lever at the other end of the room to send a generous serving of chum into the cart.

With the cart filled, pull it back onto the conveyor on the catwalk. Lara's upper-body strength increases (Upgrade Grip: Upper Body Level 9). She can climb and shimmy longer.

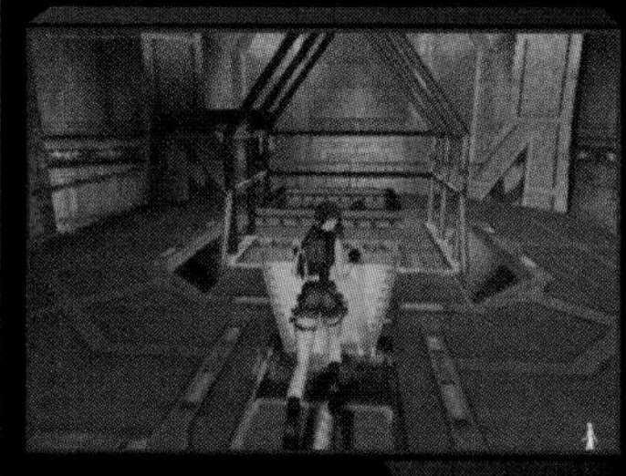

Push the yellow button to send the cart back to the other end of the catwalk, then push it back onto the lift. Now you have to figure out how to drop the lift into the water.

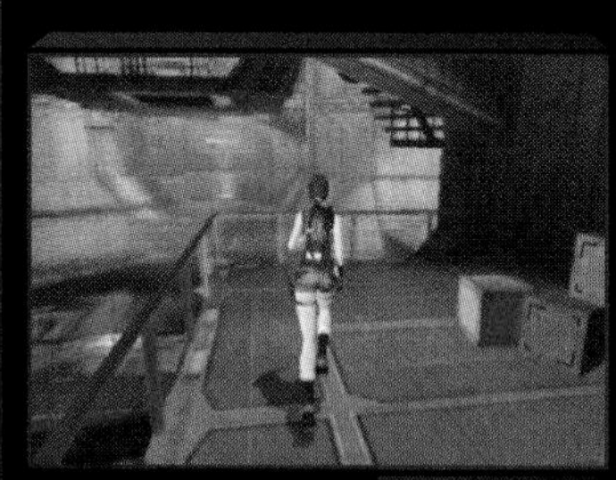

Backtrack to the entrance of the Aquatic Research Facility. Then run counterclockwise around the catwalks. Reach a platform with a pile of crates and a ladder leading up into an observation room. The top of the ladder was blocked by a trapdoor, but restoring the power removed the trap.

Climb up the ladder to enter the observation room. You can press Action near either of the two white consoles to the right to activate security monitors. The monitors show the center of the bottom of the pool and a room with wetsuits in it.

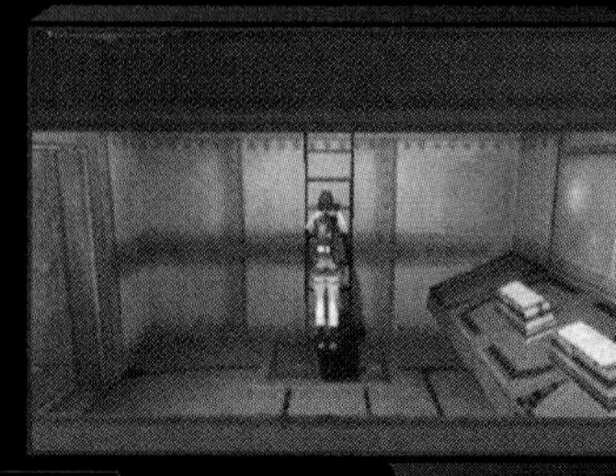

NOTE **The security-monitor images let you know what you must do after feeding Leviathan.**

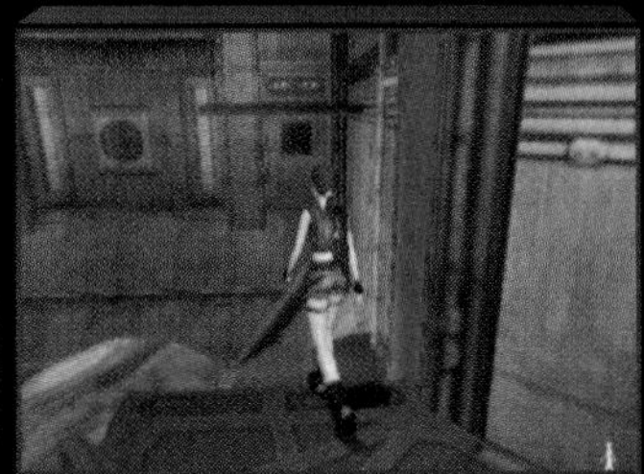

Walk out of the observation room along the catwalk, and walk to the end of the broken catwalk.

CAUTION **If you get here and Lara says that the ledge above her is too far to reach, then you haven't properly upgraded her strength. You can't complete this part of the Aquatic Research Facility until you get the strength upgrade from filling the feeding cart with chum.**

Climb the pipe on the wall, moving to a horizontal pipe in order to reach another vertical pipe next to the top of the first vertical pipe.

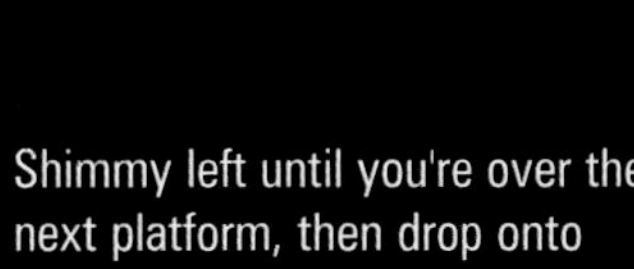

Climb the second vertical pipe and shimmy onto the ledge to the left of the top of it.

Shimmy left until you're over the next platform, then drop onto that platform.

Press the yellow button to summon a moving platform to your current location. Step onto it quickly, as it returns to the other side after a very short stop on your side.

Walk toward the giant hatch, which opens automatically.

Take a left after the giant hatch to find a switch at the end of the room. Pull the switch.

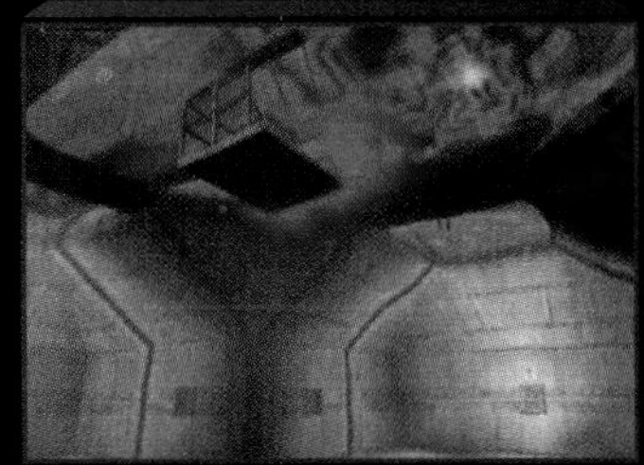

The switch lowers the cart of chum into the water. Leviathan wastes no time in chowing down on it. And now that he's fed, he doesn't want to make a meal out of Lara anymore.

Return to the entrance of the room you're in right now, press the yellow button on the wall opposite the entrance hatch, and go through the door that opens when you do so.

There's another door at the end of a short hallway. Press the nearby yellow button to open it, and have a weapon drawn when you do.

On the other side of the door is an Agency soldier. Take him out before he knows what's happening.

In the cabinets on either side of the entrance are a Mag Vega Clip and a Viper SMG Clip. Pick them both up and backtrack to the entrance to the Aquatic Research Area.

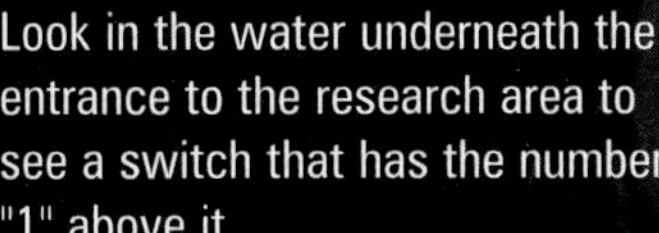

Look in the water underneath the entrance to the research area to see a switch that has the number "1" above it.

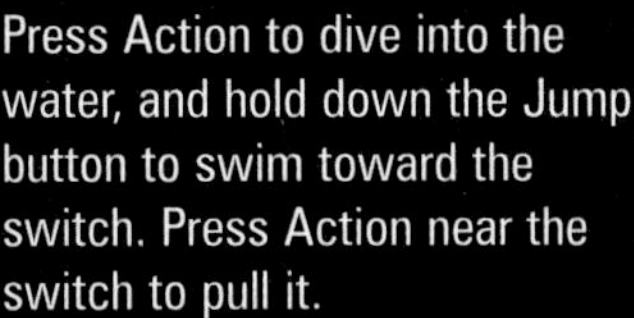

Press Action to dive into the water, and hold down the Jump button to swim toward the switch. Press Action near the switch to pull it.

This opens a door at the bottom of the research area's central pool.

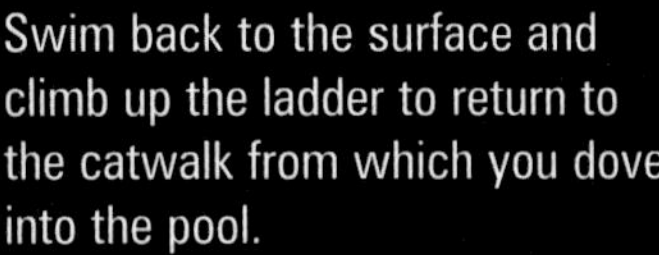

Swim back to the surface and climb up the ladder to return to the catwalk from which you dove into the pool.

Directly across the pool from switch #1 is a tunnel labeled "2." Take breath of air and swim into this tunnel.

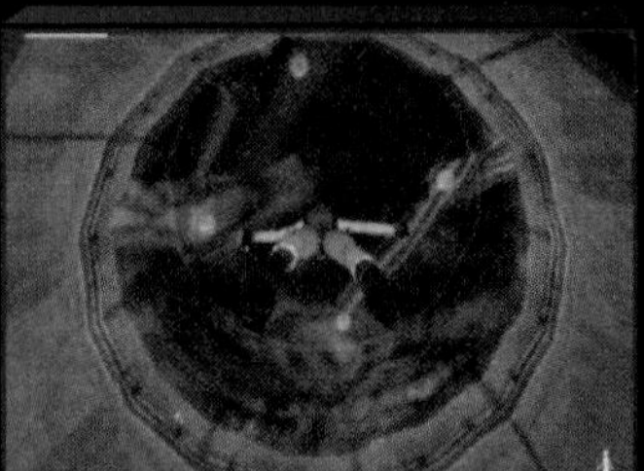

The aquatic tunnel bends upward. Follow it up to trigger the following cutscene.

Lara swims to the surface at the end of the tunnel to find a closet full of wetsuits. She slips out of her current outfit and into one of them, equipping herself properly for the underwater entrance to the Vault of Trophies.

Lara then presses a yellow button that floods the chamber with water, and the cutscene ends.

Before swimming out to the main pool of the Aquatic Research Area, pull switch #2 near the wetsuit closet to open the passage to the Vault of Trophies.

Swim back into the main pool of the Aquatic Research Area, and paddle through the now-open passage to the Vault of Trophies in the middle of the floor of the pool.

Vault of Trophies

Lara's marine adventures aren't over yet. From the Aquatic Research Area, she swims through an underwater maze to the entrance of the Vault of Trophies. After a bit of puzzle solving that literally takes her breath away, she enters the vault, indulges in a bit of nerve-wracking platform jumping, and faces two indestructible Fire Knights trying to get the fifth and final Obscura Painting. It's all in a day's work for the world's most famous tomb raider, even if she's not technically raiding tombs.

ENTITIES ENCOUNTERED
- Fire Knight (x2)

CRITICAL ITEMS TO LOCATE
- Last Obscura Painting

AVAILABLE UPGRADES
- **Upgrade Pull Chain: Upper Body Level 10**
  Pull the rusted lever in the area of the vault near the Fire Knights to beef up Lara's arm strength. This lets her pull the chain that raises the nearby tapestry.

From the start of the Vault of Trophies, swim along the tunnel, and watch out for the spikes that protrude from the walls.

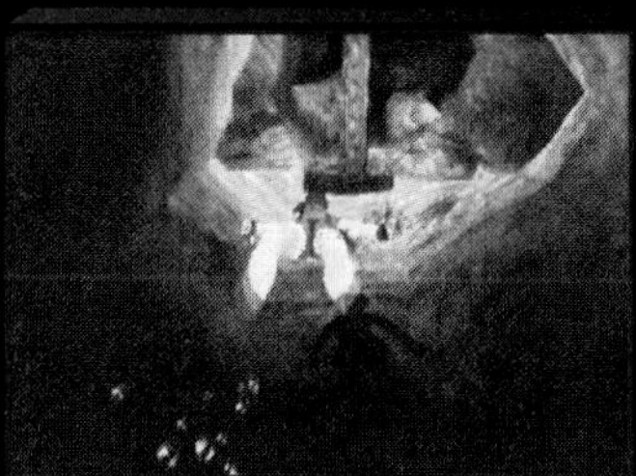

At the first intersection in the tunnel, turn right and keep swimming until you have to turn right or left. Turn left.

Swim to the top of the first intersection to grab a breath of air before continuing. All of the intersections in this first area of the vault have air pockets above them, so use them.

At the next intersection, take a right and you arrive to a small, air-filled chamber. Take a deep breath and dive back into the water.

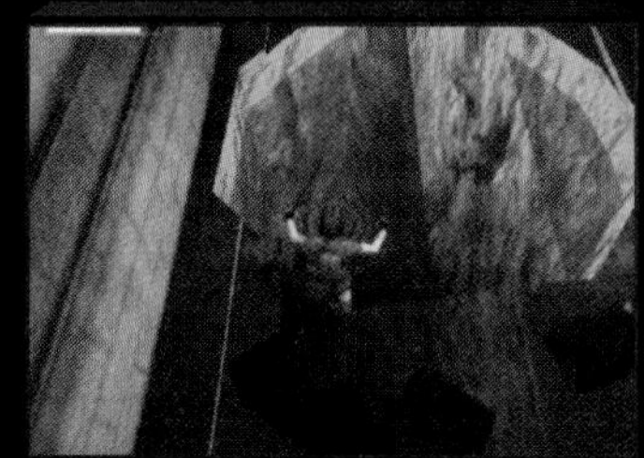

At the first intersection, continue past another set of spikes, and take a left at the next intersection. You're swimming against the current.

When you see the gap in the left wall, swim into it.

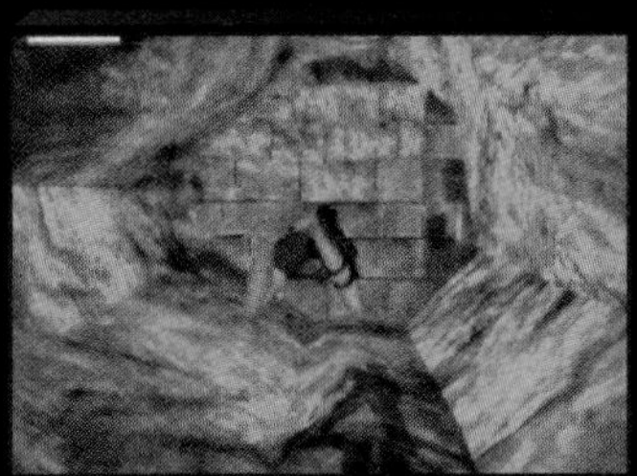

From the air-filled chamber, swim through two intersections to reach a brick wall. Press Action near the wall to kick it down and swim into a large chamber with eight statues of knights in it.

Each of the eight statues has a name written on the back of its pedestal, and there's a chain behind each statue. A mural on the wall shows two dueling knights with the letters "L" and "V" above them.

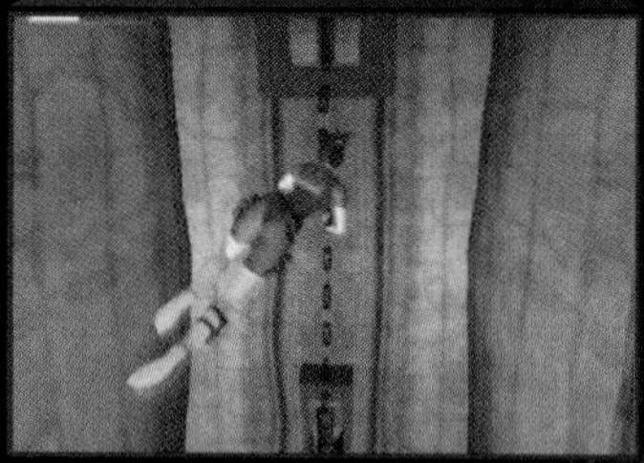

There are only two knight statues whose names begin with those letters: Vasiley and Limoux. Pull the chains behind those statues to move them forward.

CAUTION You probably won't have enough breath to find the Vasiley and Limoux statues and pull their chains. Double back to the air-filled chamber after moving the first statue to make sure that you don't run out of air.

Once both statues' chains are pulled, a magical bolt of energy rises from their swords and strikes the center of the chamber's roof, revealing a passage leading up.

Swim through the passage to reach a chamber filled with sweet air, and continue to the next part of the Vault of Trophies.

At the entrance to the vault cavern, Lara strips off her wetsuit, changing back into her usual raiding clothes.

Run down the cavern pathway until you see the large, crushing block fall from the ceiling on a chain. Sprint under it when it raises to get past it.

At the end of the cavern is a switch. Pull it to cause several small, stone platforms to appear over the yawning chasm ahead of you.

CAUTION There's some frustrating jumps ahead. Save frequently (after every successful jump).

When you land on the platform, all of the other platforms except the two in front of you crumble in the abyss. Jump to any platform that's in the row closest to you.

TIP To jump onto the tiny platform, stand one step back from the edge of the chasm, face the platform, and hop onto it by holding the Walk button as you tap the Jump button.

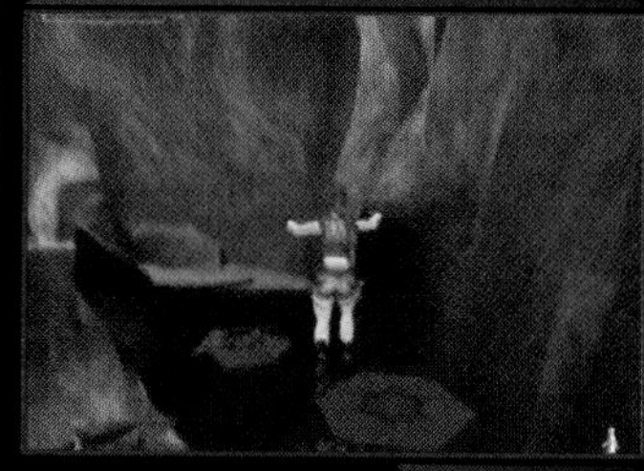

Even if you land safely, the platform's going to crumble out from under you in three seconds.

Stand in the center of the platform you're on and hop toward one of the two visible platforms in front of you. You'll notice that when you land on it, two more platforms appear in front of that one, just like when you landed on the first platform.

In this way, keep jumping across the invisible platforms until you reach the plateau in the center of the chasm, which is visible and does not crumble out from under you.

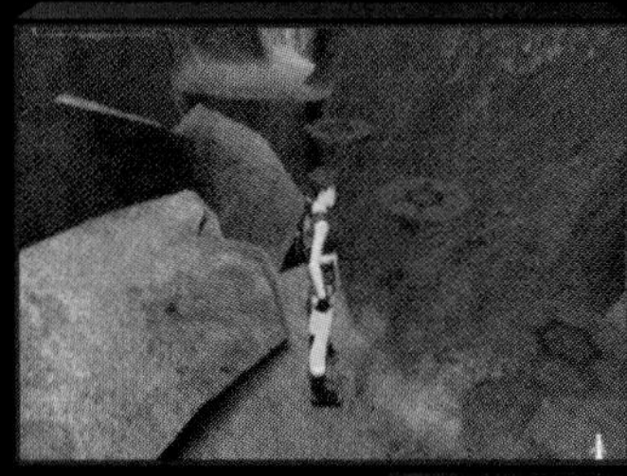

From the plateau above the center of the chasm, hop across the three small platforms leading to the other side of the cavern.

TIP Hold the Walk button and tap the Jump button to ensure that you don't overshoot the platforms. Fortunately, these don't crumble out from under you, so take your time lining up your jumps.

Walk down the tunnel at the other side of the chasm to enter the Vault of Trophies proper.

There are two Fire Knights in the Vault of Trophies. Like other Knights, Fire Knights can never be permanently destroyed. You can knock them down, but they get back up in 15 seconds. They attack with flaming swords if you're near them and with fireballs if you're at a distance.

The Fire Knights also carry shields that deflect your attacks. To hurt them, wait for them to lunge at you with their swords, dodge the strikes, and shoot them in the back. The V-Packer shotgun is excellent for taking them out.

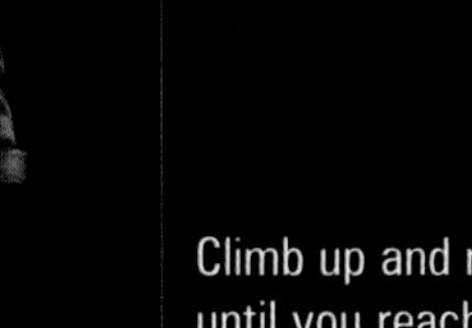

TIP Keep both Fire Knights in front of you at all times to avoid being hit from behind by one while fighting the other.

Knock both Fire Knights down, then run to the lever to the right of the giant fireplace at one end of the vault.

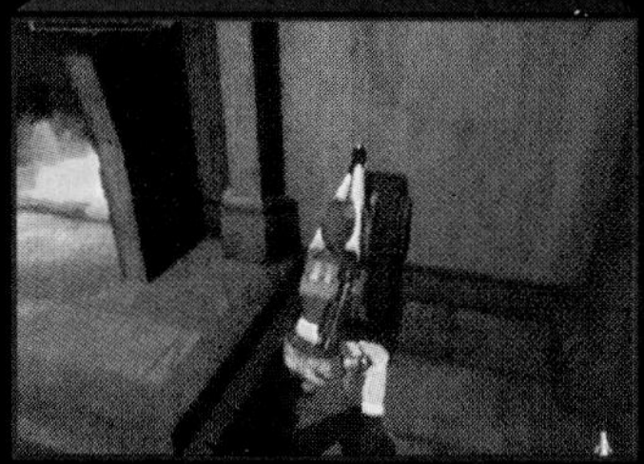

Pulling the lever increases Lara's upper-body strength (Upgrade Pull Chain: Upper Body Level 10) and slides a bookcase that conceals some Health Bandages. Pick them up.

If the Fire Knights are getting up, knock them back down. Run to the chain next to the giant tapestry at the opposite side of the room from the fireplace.

With her latest strength upgrade, Lara can pull the chain and raise the tapestry, revealing a scalable surface behind it.

As soon as the tapestry is up, run to the wall behind it and start climbing. If you're quick, you can get above the heads of the Fire Knights before they can attack, which keeps you safely out of harm's way for the moment.

Climb up and right along the wall until you reach a ledge that you can shimmy on.

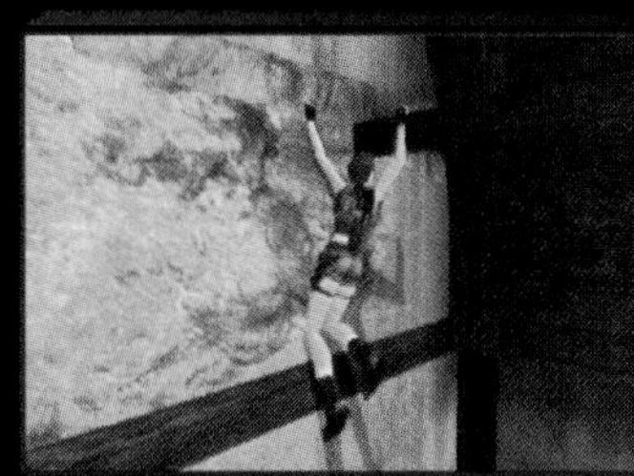

Pull yourself onto the ledge and turn around to face a metal grate in front of you. Jump straight onto the platform.

Stand in the center of the platform and face the fireplace at the other end of the room. Jump up to grab the underside of a grated catwalk over your head.

Monkey swing down the catwalk until you reach the chandelier in the middle of the room.

Drop onto the chandelier to trigger another sliding bookcase near the fireplace. Jump to grab the catwalk overhead, and monkey swing back to the platform you started from.

Jump onto the ledge next to the tapestry wall, hang from it, and drop to the ground. Watch out for the Fire Knights waiting for you—sprint toward the bookcase you just moved.

The Last Obscura Painting is behind the bookcase. Picking it up shuts off the fire in the fireplace.

Run to the fireplace and crawl through the tunnel behind it to escape the Fire Knights.

Stand up and go through the door beyond the fireplace to find the entrance to another underwater tunnel.

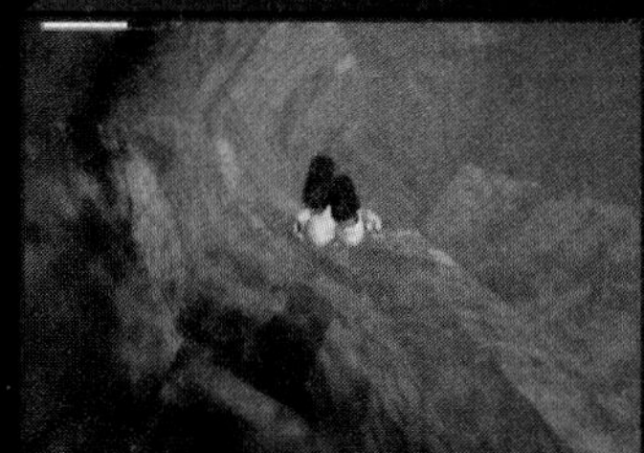

Dive into the pool and swim ahead to an intersection—go right.

Keep swimming until you come to an intersection. Head right at the intersection to reach the end of the Vault of Trophies.

Boaz Returns

When last we saw Kristina Boaz, she was fed to Dr. Muller's Carnivorous Horror as punishment for keeping the Proto-Nephilim alive. You'd think that being devoured by a giant polyp with teeth would finish most people off, but not Boaz. Instead, she wound up melding with the Carnivorous Horror and was locked away by Eckhardt for a special occasion—and that occasion is now.

ENTITIES ENCOUNTERED
- Eckhardt
- Gundersen
- Boaz

CRITICAL ITEMS TO LOCATE
- None

AVAILABLE UPGRADES
- You play as Kurtis Trent in this section, and Kurtis does not have the ability to upgrade his physical strength.

Lara makes it past oxygen-depriving underwater tunnels, vicious traps, and invincible Fire Knights, only to pop out of the water right in front of Eckhardt.

Eckhardt, Gundersen, and Muller have Kurtis as their prisoner, and Eckhardt tells Lara that she and Kurtis may leave if she gives him the Last Obscura Painting.

Eckhardt raises a floor out of the water, putting Lara on solid footing—and cutting off her underwater escape route. She tosses Eckhardt the painting, and Eckhardt kicks Kurtis down to her.

You didn't expect Eckhardt to keep his promise, did you? He introduces Lara and Kurtis to the new-and-improved version of Kristina Boaz, a freakish hybrid of her previous human body and the Carnivorous Horror.

But Eckhardt isn't done, yet. As a consequence of Muller's failures, Eckhardt tosses him into the arena as well, and Boaz gobbles him up.

Kurtis gives Lara a boost out of the arena, augmenting it with a telekinetic push. He tosses her his two Shards and says he'll deal with Boaz.

For the first part of this fight, Boaz remains in her Carnivorous Horror form. Although she's large and unwieldy, Boaz moves quickly and attacks with her claws. Shoot her several times in the face to get her to lob toxic globs of green goo at you.

Dodge the green globs and strafe around to the side of her. On either side of Boaz are two green pods from which she fires the green globs. Shoot each of them repeatedly to destroy them. Only shoot at the pods that are launching green globs, as

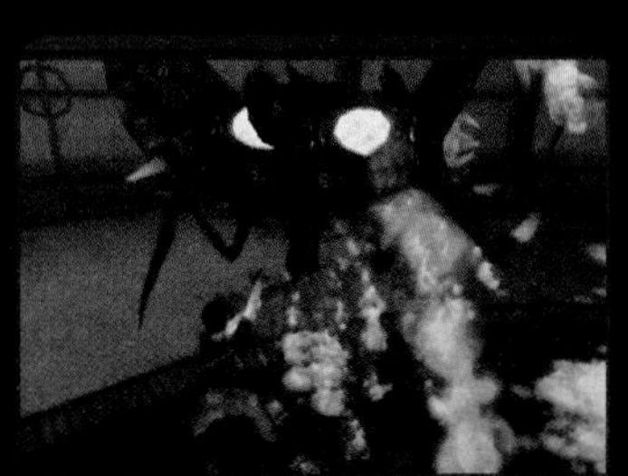

NOTE **You can only shoot the pods when Boaz is hurling the green globs at you. If she stops firing them, move around in front of her and shoot her in the face several times to get her to lob the green globs again.**

TIP **If you're not able to target the correct pods, press the Switch Target button to aim for an intact pod.**

Once all four pods are destroyed, Boaz drops to the ground—but the fight isn't over yet! Boaz crawls out of the Carnivorous Horror carcass sporting a pair of insectoid wings on her back. Time for round two!

TIP **If you're low on ammo, there's a Boran X ammo on the floor of the arena. It doesn't disappear when you pick it up, so you can grab clip after clip—while dodging Boaz's attacks, of course!**

In her humanoid form, Boaz is much faster and maneuverable. She attacks with her razor-sharp talons when close to Kurtis, and with a bioelectric blast of lighting when she's at a distance.

Although Boaz is more dangerous in her second form, your strategy should remain the same—keep dodging and pumping bullets into her.

Eventually, your bullets do the trick, and the lifeless Boaz drops to the floor. Well, maybe it's not quite lifeless.

Kurtis makes the crucial mistake of turning his back on his enemy. With her dying breath, Boaz impales him on her claw.

Kurtis throws his bladed disk at Boaz, decapitating her, but the damage has been done. The screen fades to black as blood seeps from Kurtis's wound.

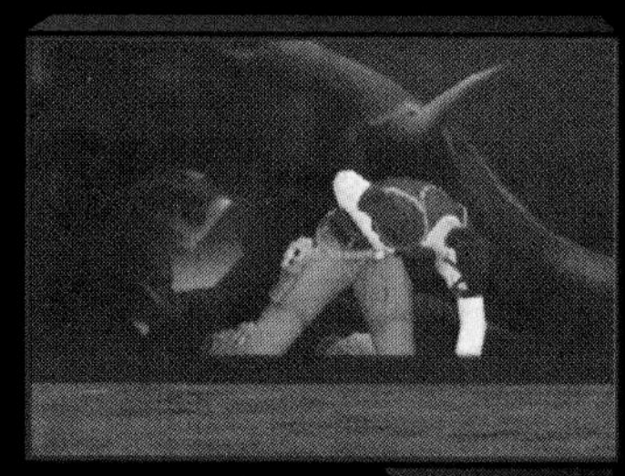

The Lost Domain

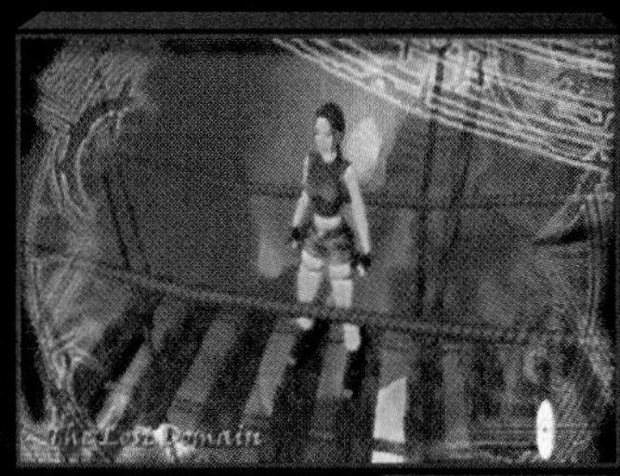

Miss Croft must traverse three treacherous tunnels in order to reach the hated Eckhardt's laboratory. Although the initial chamber structure seems confusing, it's actually quite simple once you realize how to negotiate each area. You must merely leap across a series of rocky platforms above instant lava death, upgrade your lower body for one last time, pass quickly through a dark tunnel, and emerge into a large and crumbling cavern with a trap-filled door at one end. The trap must be deactivated before you can cross the last series of tiny ledges and reach the entrance door. This level takes minutes to complete, but only after hours of trial and error.

ENTITIES ENCOUNTERED

- There are no entities encountered in this area.

CRITICAL ITEMS TO LOCATE

- There are no critical items to locate in this area.

AVAILABLE UPGRADES

- **Upgrade Jump: Lower Body Level 10**
  A series of precise jumps enables Lara to sprint and jump, thus allowing her to exit the middle chamber.

Lara starts by sliding down the tunnel entrance. You cannot return from whence you came, so move forward through the reddish gloom to the first cave junction. The path continues ahead and right.

Check out the area ahead of you. The tunnel opens into a narrow cavern with a nasty drop below, a series of rock platforms to reach, and a nearby lever. When you activate the lever, a door at the far end of the cavern creaks open.

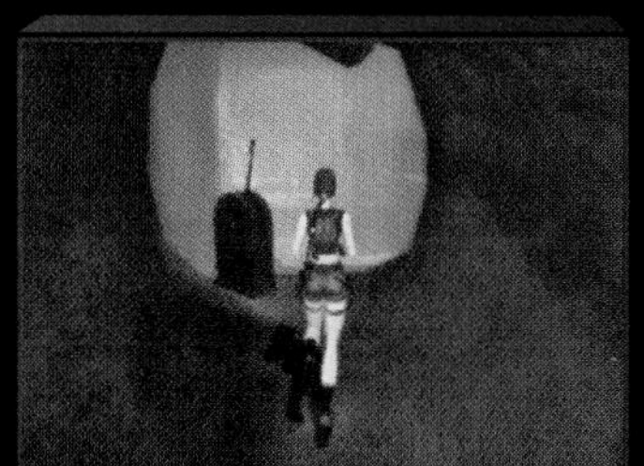

The door closes 13 seconds later, leaving you trapped in this cave. You don't have the necessary strength to bound across the three rock platforms, and shimmying along the sides of the level takes far too long.

It is impossible to continue in this direction. Return to the cave junction and take the right (or left if you're returning from the gray cavern) entrance. You jog past a barred opening with an unobtainable Large Health Pack resting behind it.

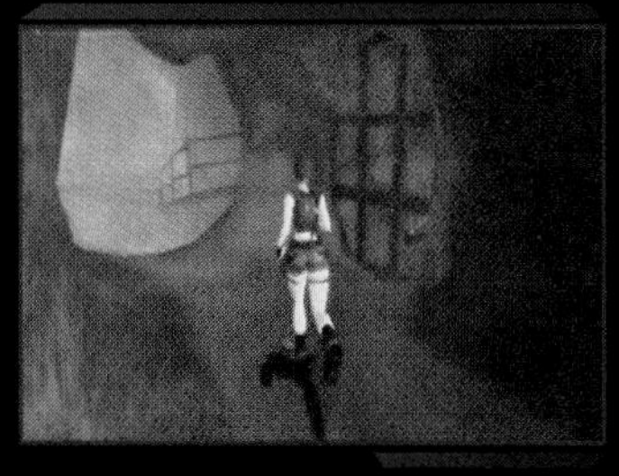

Move to the opening of the first tunnel and peer into the heat haze. You see a rickety wooden platform to your right and ahead a slope to a gap with molten lava beneath it. Save your game.

Step forward onto the sloping ground; you automatically start to skid. You have a second to jump before you drop off the end of the slide and down to a nasty demise. Leap and land on the collection of rock platforms ahead of you.

Gingerly walk across the rock formations until you reach the third one. You can see a lever at the end of this tunnel. That's where you're headed, but there's one last rock platform.

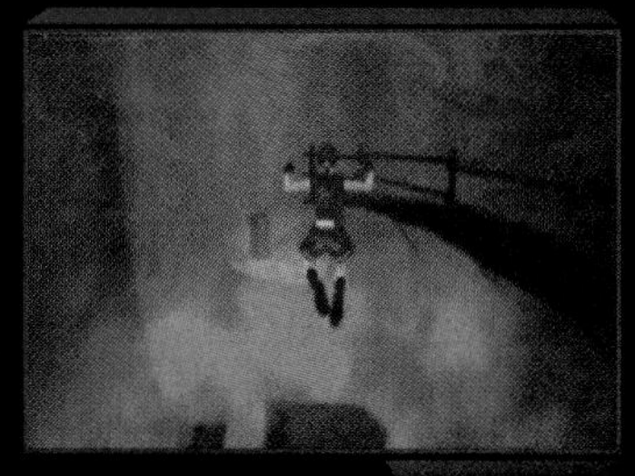

Walk to the edge of the platform, then hop to the small rock ledge. Don't perform a running or standing jump, or you'll fly over the ledge to your death—it's nearer than it looks. Once on this ledge, look around you. There's a tiny ledge to your left.

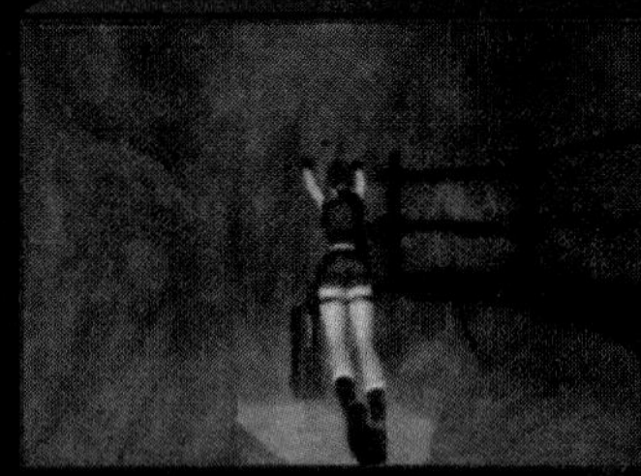

Ignore the tiny ledge for now, and instead perform a standing jump toward the outcrop with the lever on it. Outstretch your hands just in case you fail to reach the outcrop. As Lara reaches the lever, she remarks that her legs are stronger.

Congratulations, you've upgraded Lara to her buffest level possible (Upgrade Jump: Lower Body Level 10). With this ultimate athletic power, you can now sprint and leap huge distances like never before. Move and pull the lever next to you.

This raises the barred gate at the entrance to the tunnel, allowing you to access the Large Health Pack. Turn and walk into the edge of the wooden walkway (don't jump up or you won't grab it), and begin to cross back the way you came.

TIP Use the wooden walkway to return to the main corridor, and definitely *do not* try leaping back across the rock platforms. The final slope at the cavern mouth cannot be accessed, although you can slide down backwards and back-flip to the central rocks for fun.

Step off the wooden walkway, round the corner, and stoop to collect the Large Health Pack before moving under the open barred gate. At the junction, make a right and move to the long, gray cavern. Before you pull the lever, save your game.

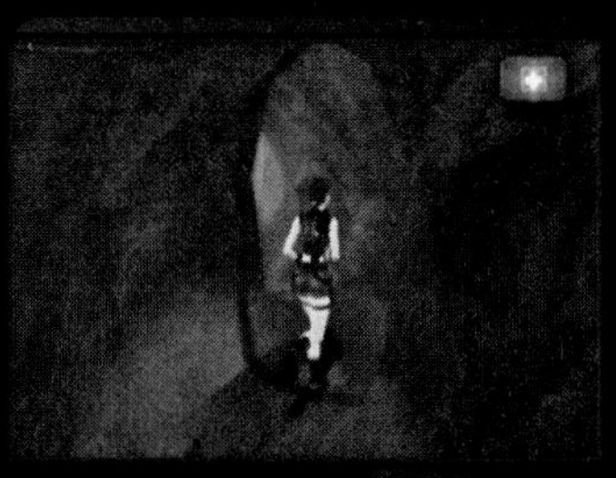

The following section details the two ways to complete this chamber—one correct, and one incorrect. You may wish to shimmy and discover this entire cavern the incorrect way and prcatice your jumping, or simply jump three times and skid under the closing door (the correct way).

Navigating the Gray Cavern: The Incorrect Way

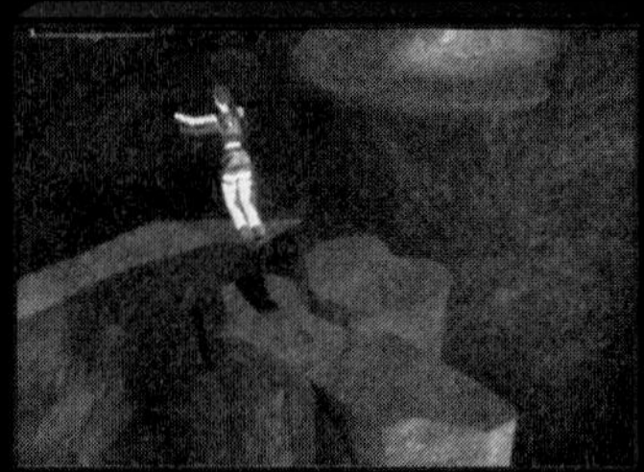

Before you realize that the lever opening the door is on a time release, you can optionally begin a spot of spelunking. Drop from the cave mouth to the collection of stone platforms in front of you. Then move to the right wall ledge.

Hop across the gap to the wall ledge, moving toward the far end of it until there is no more ground, then jump to grab a crack in the wall. Shimmy across this crack to the first set of rock platforms, or try a standard jump from the ledge.

Run left into a small cave mouth. Follow this small passage right, and right again; you appear at the second set of platforms. Hop across to land on them.

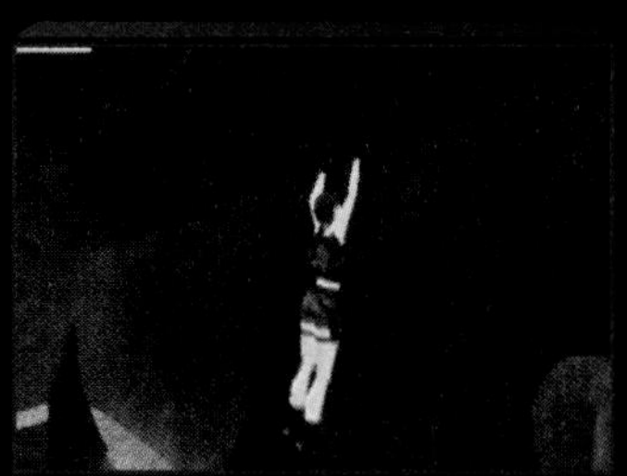

From here, move carefully onto the lip of the right-hand ledge, jump vertically, grab the crack above, and quickly shimmy left. You have just enough grip strength to make it to the final exit ledge. However, the door closed minutes ago. Follow the correct method after upgrading yourself.

Navigating the Gray Cavern: The Correct Way

Move to the lever and pull it back until the grated gate at the far end of the chamber opens. Run backward a little ways and start sprinting to the edge of the cavern mouth, leaping to execute a sailing sprint jump.

Position yourself so you don't steer through the air, or you'll have problems continuing your leaping. When you land on the first island of rock platforms, ideally at the near end, continue the sprint and jump again almost immediately. This is possible.

TIP **Problems leaping in one continuous sprint? Then stop on the first island, quickly retreat back to the near end of the structure, and begin another sprint and jump.**

Continue from the first to the second clump of rock platforms, sailing through the air to land precisely on the far set of platforms. From here, ignore the left cavern opening and the right narrow ledge, and sprint to a final platform.

Once through the door, you hear it closing behind you—there's no turning back now. Move through the connecting tunnel until the passageway opens into a giant cavern with lava spilling over rocks.

You can just make out an archway at the far end of the chamber. This is where you're headed, but only after you remove the torches from the two statues guarding the arch, deactivating a trap. If you want to explore the area and practice your jumping, thus activating the trap, heed the following section.

NOTE **The easiest way through this area is to deactivate the Cowled Cutter. Follow the advice in "How to Deactivate" for the easiest method out of here.**

The Cowled Cutter: How to Activate

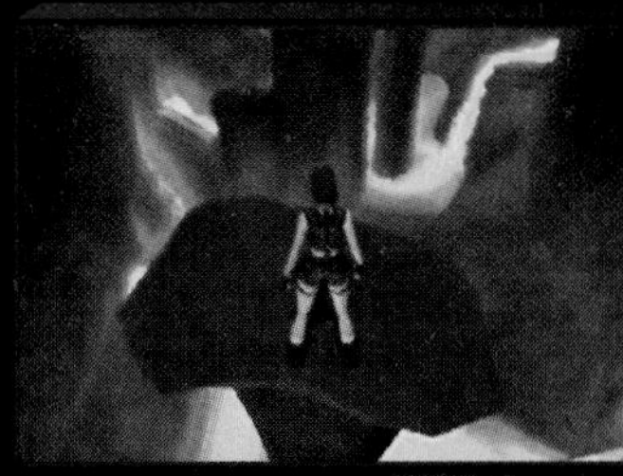

Ignore the ladder and ledge to your left, and press the Walk button to stroll to the edge of the rocky outcrop you're on. There's a gap, and a huge gout of flame roars upward. Hop to the platform in front of you.

This large ledge is lower than the initial outcrop. From here, reverse to the back of the ledge, line yourself up with the small platform in front and slightly left of you, and perform a standard jump. Hopping doesn't reach quite far enough, and running and jumping overshoots.

From here, turn slightly right to line yourself up with the group of rock platforms ahead of you, and make a standing jump over to them. As you land, another blast of fire rockets upward. Wait for it to dissipate, then turn left.

Ignore the single platform to your right, and instead simply make a standard jump to the next group of flat rocks. Once there, ignore the small rock platform to the right, very close to the group you're on, and leap to the larger platform ahead.

You're very close to the steps and the archway. Hop over the small separation between the next two rock platforms and land on the final rock. From here, you can jump onto the steps. However, before you leap, you may spot a square groove cut into the stairs themselves.

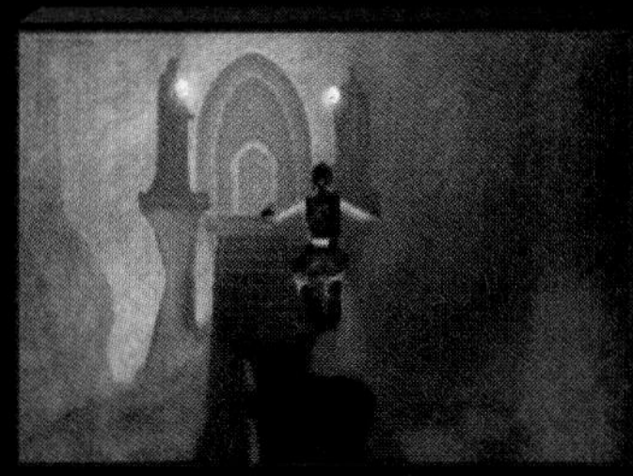

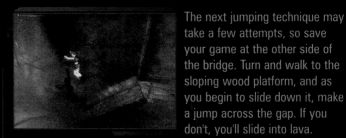

This is a running mechanism for a nasty trap. Land on the steps (with the two statues still conjuring fire from their hands), and a horizontal harvester scythe (known as the Cowled Cutter) springs up and moves quickly at you. You will die if you are struck by it. Immediately back-flip onto the rock in order to save yourself. You'll now have to backtrack, and follow the advice in the following section, to deactivate the cutter and leave the area.

The Cowled Cutter: How to Deactivate

NOTE **Deactivating the Cowled Cutter is the only way to escape this infernal zone, but you miss out on much of the leaping from platform to platform.**

From your initial outcrop of rock, make a running jump toward the ledge on the left wall. You see that there is an old, wooden ladder to climb once you reach this area.

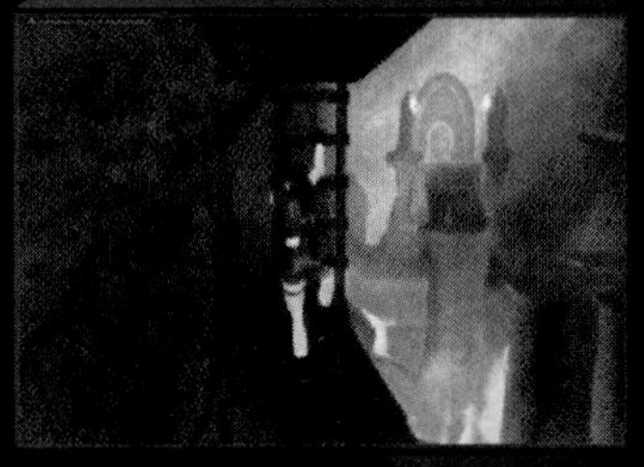

Once you reach the top of the ladder, step onto a tiny, wooden platform and get a great view of the turbulent lava below. Turn around, grab the next wooden ladder fixed to the rock wall, and clamber to the topmost platform.

Turn around and see a dilapidated rope bridge creaking in the heat. This is easier to cross than you might think—a running jump with some steering gets you to the other side with minimum fuss. You don't need to stretch and grab the other side.

The next jumping technique may take a few attempts, so save your game at the other side of the bridge. Turn and walk to the sloping wood platform, and as you begin to slide down it, make a jump across the gap. If you don't, you'll slide into lava.

During the jump, hit Action to grab the small ledge ahead of you. Make sure you grab this ledge, or you'll have to retrace your steps to the broken bridge. Once on the wooden ledge, pull the lever. The fire in both the statues' hands snuffs out.

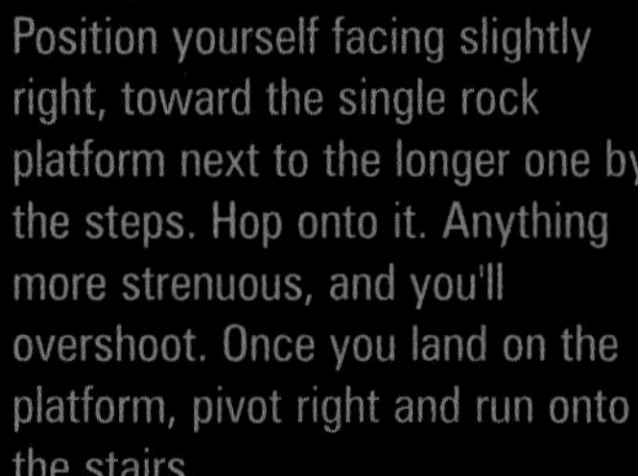

The trap is now deactivated. Hang off the wooden ledge, drop onto the rock platform near the wall (you land on it and don't need to grab for it), then walk to the edge of the platform to peer down on the final group of rock platforms below.

Position yourself facing slightly right, toward the single rock platform next to the longer one by the steps. Hop onto it. Anything more strenuous, and you'll overshoot. Once you land on the platform, pivot right and run onto the stairs.

Run to the large archway with the imposing seal of the Cabal on it. As you approach it, the door is etched with fire around the seal, splitting it in half. The fire recedes, and the door rumbles open. You are now entering the lair of the madman Eckhardt himself.

Eckhardt's Lab

After a short but scary slide through a nasty spike trap, you emerge inside a medieval torture chamber masquerading as Pieter Van Eckhardt's underground lair. Amid the bubbling concoctions and two pools of acid, there are two Knights to engage, and three separate Alchemic Phials to obtain. Fix the purified oxygen vials to large incubation devices to turn the circular pool of liquid into harmless water. Only then can you dive into it, secure the Shard, and slide into Eckhardt's main chamber for a final audience with the madman himself...as well as the being known as the Sleeper.

ENTITIES ENCOUNTERED

- The Knight (x2)
- Pieter Van Eckhardt
- Pieter Van Eckhardt Clone
- The Sleeper

CRITICAL ITEMS TO LOCATE

- Alchemic Phial #1
- Alchemic Phial #2
- Alchemic Phial #3
- Shard
- Eckhardt's Glove

AVAILABLE UPGRADES

- None: Lara is now at maximum upgrade level.

With the door bearing the Cabal seal firmly shut behind you, the tunnel ahead is your only way forward. It is imperative to save your game at this point, before you reach the descending slope. Once you begin to slide, move to the left wall of the tunnel.

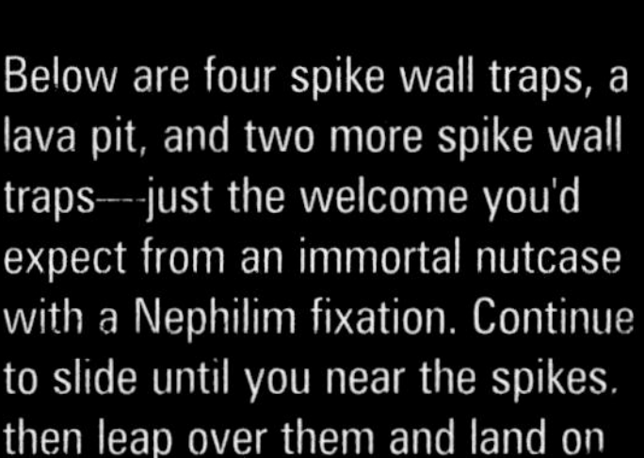

Below are four spike wall traps, a lava pit, and two more spike wall traps—just the welcome you'd expect from an immortal nutcase with a Nephilim fixation. Continue to slide until you near the spikes, then leap over them and land on the ledge.

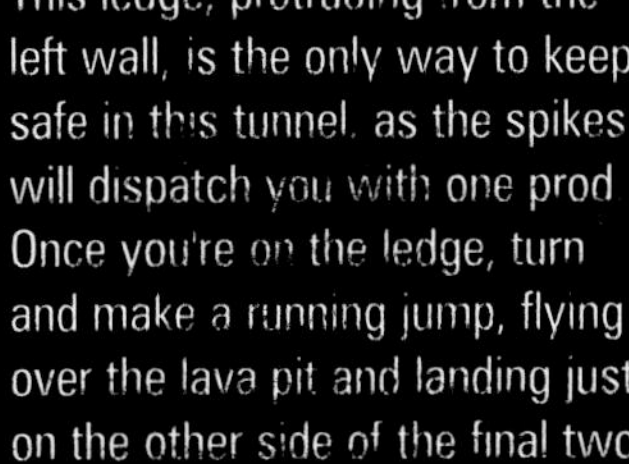

This ledge, protruding from the left wall, is the only way to keep safe in this tunnel, as the spikes will dispatch you with one prod. Once you're on the ledge, turn and make a running jump, flying over the lava pit and landing just on the other side of the final two spikes.

Run to the edge of the corridor and through the pointed archway into Eckhardt's laboratory itself. The madman isn't here at the moment, but he's left a little welcoming committee in the form of two Knights.

From a cursory inspection of the chamber, it appears to be full of arcane devices, pits, and traps—plus incubation channels to purify the acid in the water of a circular pool to the right of the main laboratory. Diving into this liquid now results in a quick and agonizing demise.

This puzzle takes some working out, but it hinges on purifying the acid in the pool. For this to happen, you must locate three Alchemic Phials scattered around this room, and slot them into the appropriate wall mounting.

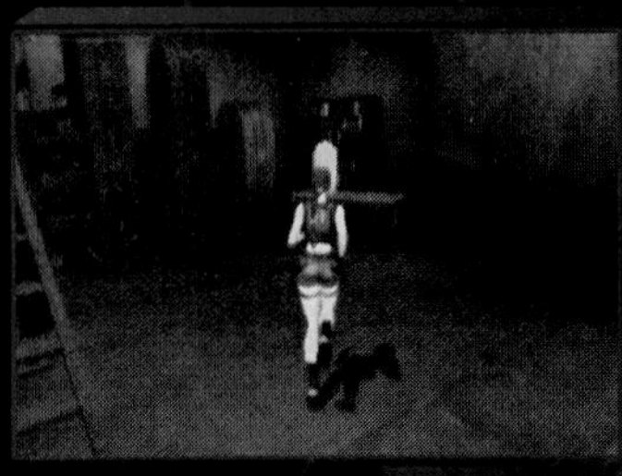

Start by running left and up the first set of steps to the upper "throne" area. Jog around the right side of the structure and the table to a small desk. The table holds Alchemic Phial #1. Under the raised floor to your left is a Small Health Pack. Nab that, too!

Now is the time to open the trapdoor. Pull the lever and watch as the trapdoor grinds open. The lever is now useless, so walk to the edge and peer into the pit. Only drop into this pit after you have lowered the cage.

TIP There's nothing more satisfying than frying a Knight in acid, and there are two methods to try. One involves coaxing the two Knights to the empty area of ground near the trapdoor, then running back to pull the lever just as the Knights turn around. The other is to shoot both Knights so they collapse on the trapdoor, then open it.

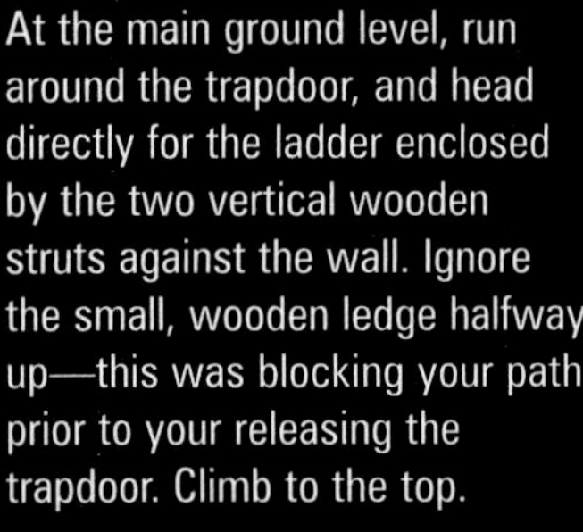

At the main ground level, run around the trapdoor, and head directly for the ladder enclosed by the two vertical wooden struts against the wall. Ignore the small, wooden ledge halfway up—this was blocking your path prior to your releasing the trapdoor. Climb to the top.

You find yourself on a narrow walkway that surrounds the entire chamber. On the other side is a ladder broken halfway down (ignore this). Over the raised throne area is an upper incubation device. Take Alchemic Phial #1 and slot it into this circular holder.

Ignore the slightly unnerving seismic tremor, save your game, and note that the phial fit into this device. It does not fit into the other two devices (the one directly below you, and the other one near the circular pool). Run around to the ladder you ascended.

Instead of heading back to the ground, you should be on the lookout for the two remaining phials. View the cage and see one of the phials inside. Reach the cage by running and jumping off the upper walkway, and landing on the top of the cage itself.

The cage is sturdy except for an opening at one side (the side nearest the circular pool). Step on this and you fall through to the cage floor below. Walk carefully to the phial and take it. This is Alchemic Phial #2. Save your game just before you pick it up.

As soon as you pick up the phial, the cage starts to shake and lowers itself to the trapdoor pit below. The cage descends until it is submerged completely in acid.

As the cage descends, run to the opposite side of the cage from where you took the phial. Climb up the side of it, turn left or right at the top, and pull yourself out.

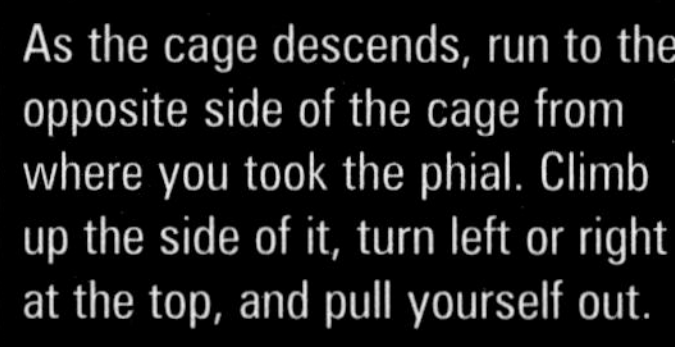

You still have time to climb out and either jump to safety or ride the cage down to the acid. As long as you're on top of the cage, you will be standing above the acid. Don't fall down the gaps around the cage, or into the cage opening, though.

Before you drop into the pit of acid, you should plant the next Alchemic Phial on the incubation device. This device is located directly underneath the first one, at the top of some rickety stairs on the raised area of ground. Slot it in and save your game.

Now drop into the acid pit, taking care to land on the sturdy part of the cage, not the opening. Patches of dark mud line the walls around you. These aren't of interest to you yet, however.

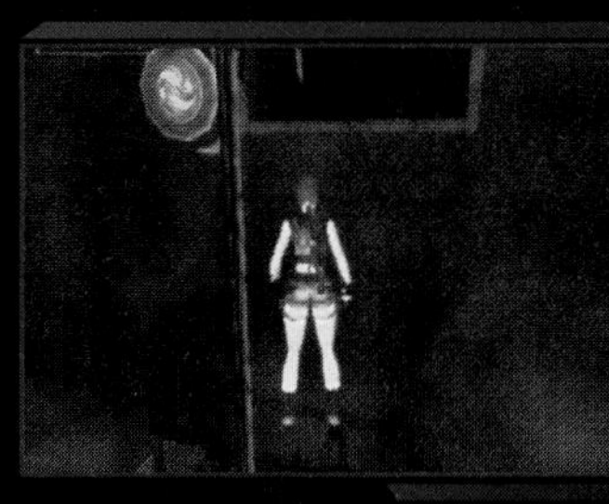

Peer inside the rectangular hole in the wall underneath the lever. Something is shining inside. Leap and grab the lower lip of the hole; pull yourself up and into the hole, pressing Duck to crouch. Maneuver on all fours toward the object.

This is the final phial. Grab Alchemic Phial #3 and back out of the hole, hanging on the lower lip of the hole and landing on the cage again. Now there's the small matter of getting out of this pit.

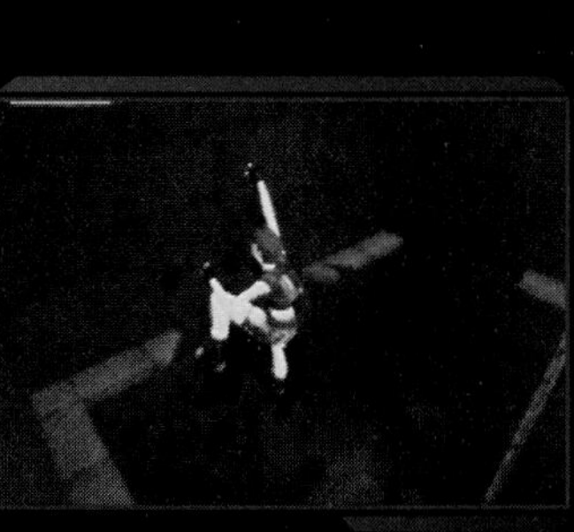

The plan is straightforward. Save your game, then turn and line yourself up with any of the patches of mud sprayed on the walls. Leap and press Action to grab the mud. Do this quickly—if you're too slow, you'll fall and dissolve in the acid below if you drop into the open hatch.

Now comes the impressive part. Clamber up the mud until you reach as far as you can, just below the lip of the ground. You can't grab this, so back-flip off the mud, landing on the ground behind you.

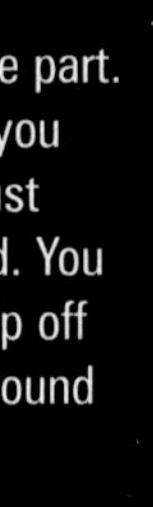

Now move toward the smaller antechamber housing the circular pool. This is the first time you need to enter this area. Jump over the pool of acid and land next to the circular incubation device. Place the final Alchemic Phial here.

After another seismic shock, a stream of white liquid streams along the filtration channel in the center of this chamber. The liquid falls into the circular pool, changing the chemical composition of the water so the acid is removed.

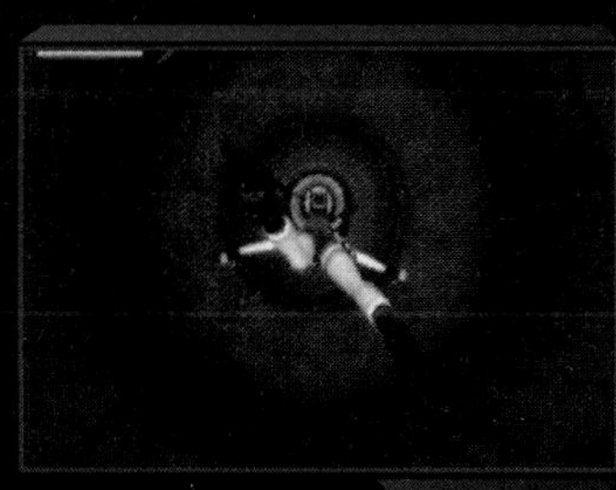

Back-flip or swan dive into this circular pool, and swim down to the submerged altar. Resting on the altar is a crystal Shard. Pick it up, and the window overlooking the rock path in the main chamber opens.

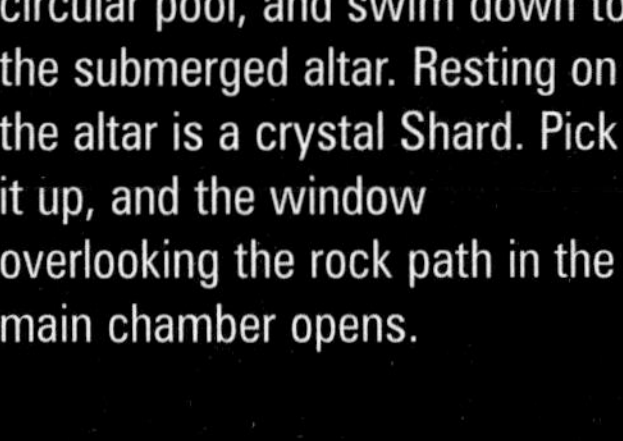

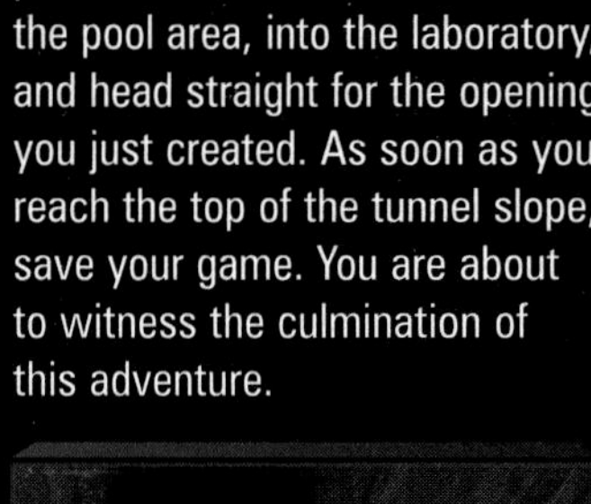

Swim back to the surface of the pool and climb out. Run out of the pool area, into the laboratory, and head straight for the opening you just created. As soon as you reach the top of the tunnel slope, save your game. You are about to witness the culmination of this adventure.

Step into the tunnel and you slide all the way to the bottom. Steering doesn't help you. When you reach the base of this tunnel, ignore the path you came down, and instead open the large, wood door in front of you.

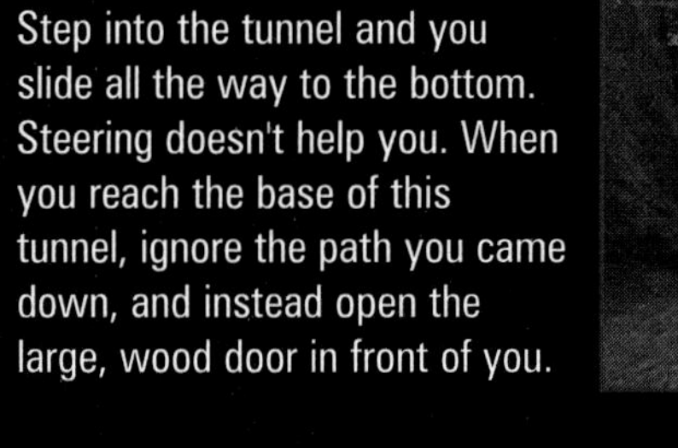

You appear inside an unbelievably vast subterranean chamber. Take a moment to gaze around. There are three circular balconies and what appears to be a white entity strapped to a focusing device. Eckhardt is running around the base.

Eckhardt places a series of metal objects inside a welding device to meld them into a Glove of power. Electromagnetic sparks swarm about his roaring form as he grows in strength. Above him, a metallic embryonic chamber opens. The Sleeper descends.

Lara's zinging bullets have their desired effect. "Still alive, Miss Croft?" queries Eckhardt as he prepares to harvest her body parts to revive the sleeping Nephilim. Lara scoffs at his arrogance. He is nothing but a cheap grave robber.

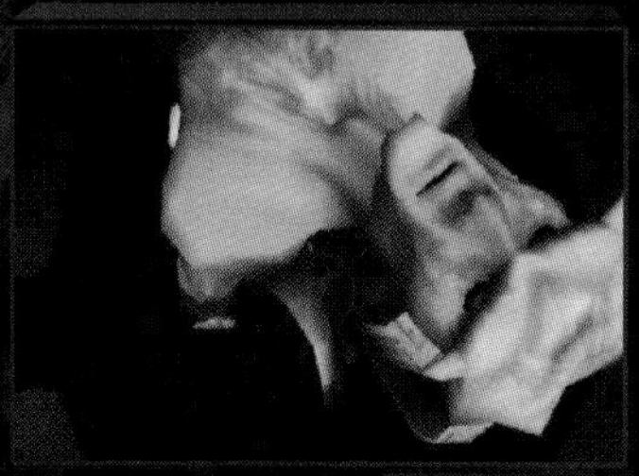

To wake the Sleeper, Lara must die, just as the Lux Veritatis were hunted down and dispatched. Eckhardt is temporarily taken aback as Lara produces the Shard, which is glowing in power. Eckhardt has made up his mind, lands on the ground, and prepares for the final battle.

Pieter Van Eckhardt

As soon as Eckhardt has finished his rambling diatribe, he turns and aims at you, brandishing his Glove and forming a ball of light or fire. He then launches an arc of fire or lightning blast directly at you. Jump left or right, leaping early to avoid being struck.

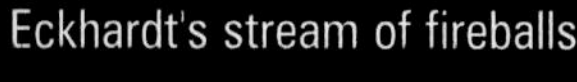

Eckhardt's stream of fireballs.

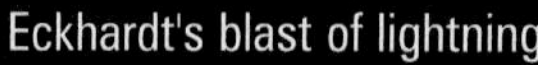

Eckhardt's blast of lightning.

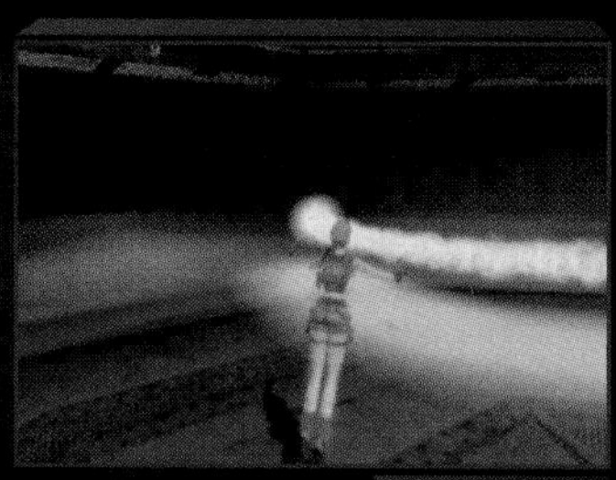

It is not possible to blast Eckhardt while he is summoning his power, as he is temporarily impervious to your bullets. Quickly avoid his succession of attacks from the center of the great chamber.

Once inside the four gantry supports, Eckhardt raises a force field, preventing you from escaping. Turn and thwart the attacks of the madman.

Eckhardt jogs around the perimeter of the arena, pausing between each support to launch a fire or lightning attack. Jump over, or quickly retreat to avoid these blasts, then wait as Eckhardt leaps onto an upper platform.

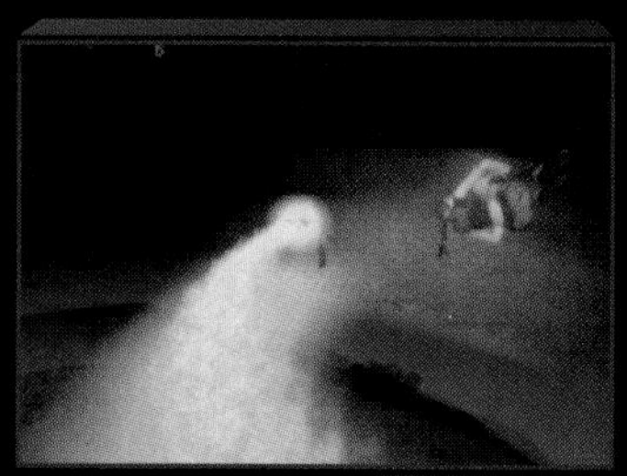

He immediately drops back down, then spends the next 20 seconds running around the outer edge of the gantry supports, creating three clones of himself!

Destroy these weaker Eckhardts as they move toward you. Let rip with every weapon you possess; try the V-Packer or machine gun.

Once the three clones have moved into the center of the chamber, they morph into Eckhardt. He launches either a fireball array or a series of lightning strikes. These attacks also inflict a seismic ground pound.

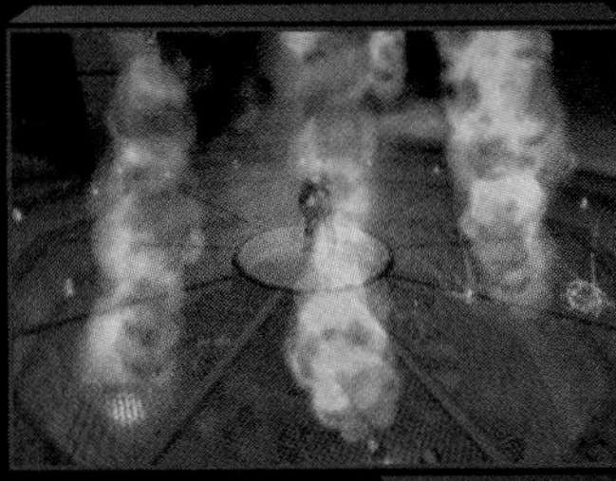

Eckhardt's fire ball array.

Eckhardt's bolt lightning strike.

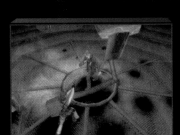

Eckhardt's seismic disturbance.

These attacks are deadly and all-encompassing. Fortunately, you can study the patterns and tell where the strikes are about to hit. Move between the incoming blasts, whether fire or lightning, and beware of falling rocks and masonry.

NOTE **As soon as you see the tips of the shadows from each attack, move between the shadows to avoid being struck. Do not stop shooting at the morphing clones.**

The best time to strike Eckhardt is just after he launches one of his attacks. Blast him repeatedly, at as close a range as you can muster, continuously peppering him with bullets until he falls to his knees.

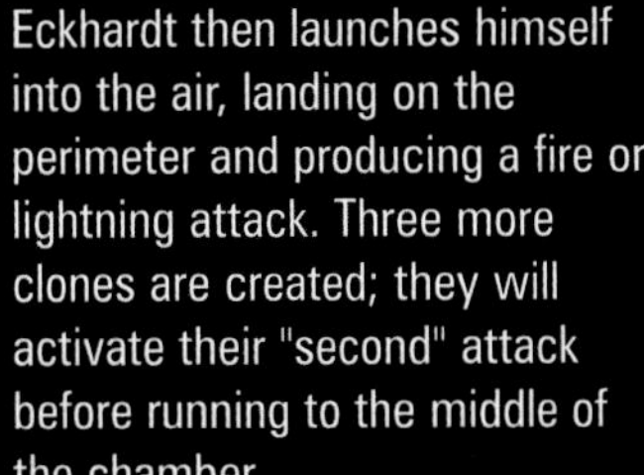

Once fallen, Lara runs up to Eckhardt and strikes him with one of the three ceremonial Shards.

Eckhardt then launches himself into the air, landing on the perimeter and producing a fire or lightning attack. Three more clones are created; they will activate their "second" attack before running to the middle of the chamber.

After the second attack, pop caps into Eckhardt until he stumbles to his knees for a second time. Lara will produce Shard number two, stabbing it into Eckhardt.

The pattern of attacks continues in the same manner as before, with an outer fireball or lightning barrage, a clone-creating jog around the perimeter, the clones congregating in the middle of the arena, and alternate fire and lightning strikes.

Bring Eckhardt to his knees for a third and final time. As Lara reached for the last Shard, it is taken from her by...Joachim Karel! Karel, it seems, is the real mastermind behind the Cabal, and an actual Nephilim himself!

Karel is also a shapeshifter, which explains why Eckhardt killed Von Croy, who was undertaking a mission on his behalf, and why Bouchard's bodyguard could take the form of a Cabal soldier. It was Karel in Eckhardt's form both times!

Lara is now offered a new path—to join with Karel and take on a new order of the world. With her immense power as a Nephilim, there would be no end to the power she and Karel could command!

Karel plunges the final Shard into Eckhardt's blackened skull, and Eckhardt slumps against one of the gantry support columns. Karel now turns on Croft. If she will not join him, he will enjoy vanquishing her!

Joachim Karel

Karel circles Lara, floating in a green aura of power, and thrusting forward with a continuous barrage of energy blasts designed to knock you off your feet. Learn their timing (one is launched about every five seconds), and leap before it strikes you.

Ignore Karel's frightening form, but dodge the single balls of energy he creates. Now complete the remaining objectives. You may find yourself under fire as you ascend, but ascend you must!

At this point, the slumped Eckhardt gives up a final and vital object: Eckhardt's Glove. Pick up this powerful item; the force field has been removed and you can exit the center of the room and jog around the supports.

One of the supports has a button on it. Press it while you have Eckhardt's Glove in your possession, and two ladders descend from above. Climb to the first level, and at the top, run left around the platform.

Ascend the ladder joining the first and second gantry platforms. Once on top of the gantry, survey the scenery. There is a third floor and the Sleeper above you.

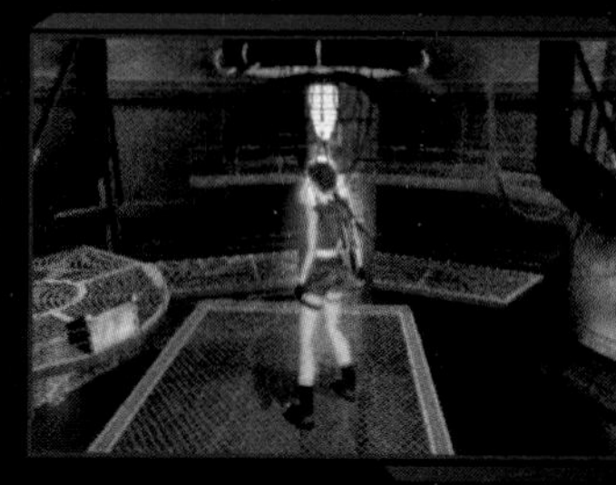

Move toward the gantry support with the ladder riveted to it and climb to the top-most gantry platform, now at the same level as the Nephilim specimen. Once you reach this area, move to the jutting platform over the middle of the gantry. Leap off it, straight at the Sleeper!

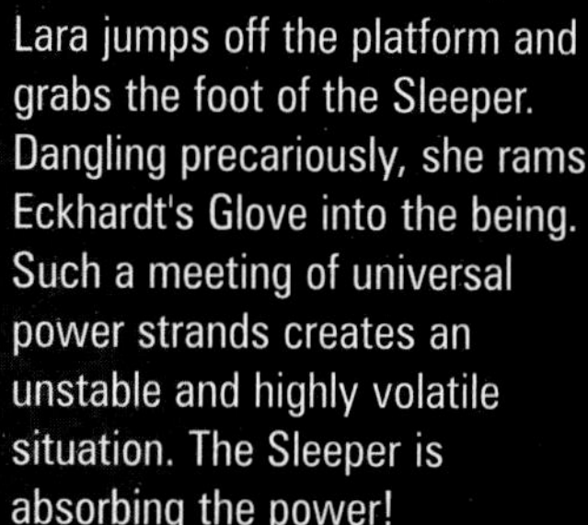

Lara jumps off the platform and grabs the foot of the Sleeper. Dangling precariously, she rams Eckhardt's Glove into the being. Such a meeting of universal power strands creates an unstable and highly volatile situation. The Sleeper is absorbing the power!

Shattering its bracings, the Sleeper dissolves into white light. Sending out shooting bands of incredible energy, Joachim Karel is flooded in this matter. The entire Sleeper chamber buckles and tears. Congratulations, Miss Croft!

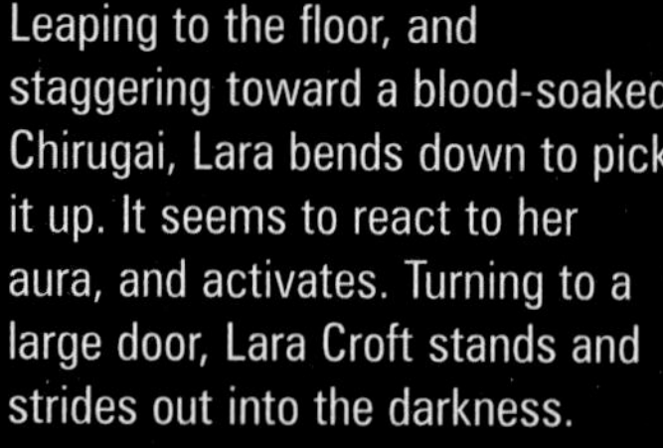

Leaping to the floor, and staggering toward a blood-soaked Chirugai, Lara bends down to pick it up. It seems to react to her aura, and activates. Turning to a large door, Lara Croft stands and strides out into the darkness.

Lara's Notebook

This section details the notation and studies undertaken by Miss Lara Croft during her excursion into the unknown. In addition, material from the writings of Professor Werner Von Croy have also been uncovered and are presented for the first time in their unabridged form. Please note that the wretched condition of the pages, and damage to the paper itself, means that some of the entries may be in a misplaced order.

Entry #1

Find Bouchard

Entry #2

Check out Eckhardt

Entry #3

Eckhardt–client. Be wary!

Entry #4

Louis Bouchard. useful contact. Purchased handgun. Discretion assured.

Entry #5

Get to the Louvre and find Werner's Painting.

Entry #6

Find items to pawn for cash.

Entry #7

Buy health items

Entry #8

Find Cafe Metro in Place d Arcade.

Entry #9

Find Bouchard's club Le Serpent Rouge.

Entry #10

Find Bouchard's new premises (Le Serpent Rouge closed down).

Entry #11

Find Bernard, ex-Janitor at the club

Entry #12

Contact cafe owner Pierre, ex-barman at the club.

Entry #13

Retrieve the Box at Serpent Rouge. In broken lighting rig.

Entry #14

Check out the stranger asking for Bouchard.

Entry #15

Contact Francine. 17 Rue Dominique. Code 0536

Entry #16

Find Bouchard's Doorman.

Entry #17

Deliver passports to Daniel Rennes, pawnbroker—Rue St. Mark and Cours la Seine.

Entry #18

Get into the Louvre.

Entry #19

Locate Carvier's office. Need security pass to reach the archaeological dig.

Entry #20

Get access to the archaeological dig at the second buttress.

Entry #21

X-Ray the Obscura Painting.

Entry #22

Check out von Croy's apartment for four missing Obscura Engravings.

Entry #23

Check on Mathias Vasiley in Prague.

Entry #24

The wrathful sentinels guard the hall within.

Entry #25

ULTRICES ATRIUM CUSTODIUNT.

Entry #26

Through the spirit of the keeper behold the truth.

Entry #27

ULTRA VIGIL & UMBRAM, ECCE VERITAS.

Entry #28

Go to Prague.

Entry #29

Look for 5th Obscura Engraving at Mathias Vasiley's premises.

Entry #30

Get into the Strahov.

Entry #31

Get Strahov entry code from Luddick.

Entry #32

Locate the vault of Trophies in the oldest part of the Strahov. Last Painting there.

Entry #33

Check the premises for a hidden area.

Entry #34

The three Periapts joined together to burn (or glow) with righteous light to confine evil.

Entry #35

TRES PERIAPTI CONUINCTI CUM IUSTITIAE IGNE MALA CINGUNT.

Entry #36

Find the security control room.

Entry #37

Gain access to the Biodome.

Entry #38

Shut down power to clear a route through the Biodome to the vault of Trophies.

Entry #39

Find Eckhardt's old lab. We need that third Periapt Shard.

Entry #40

Find aqua gear.

Entry #41

Rearrange the statues. They are the key.

Entry #42

FRATRIBUS COLLATES IANUAE PATENT.

Entry #43

The brothers reunited see the gates thrown open.

Entry #44

use all three Shards to destroy Eckhardt.

Entry #45

use the Glove to destroy the Sleeper.

Professor Werner Von Croy's Notebook

Entry #46

Terrified to go out. Monstrum terrorising the streets.

Entry #47

Tried contacting Lara again in London. No response. Still not forgiven me for Egypt.

Entry #48

Obscura Paintings: Five 15th century works of black alchemic magic. All lost, hidden by the Lux Veritatis.

Entry #49

Five Obscura Engravings: Drawn copies of the Paintings. Contain encrypted maps of each Painting's location?

Entry #50

Mathias Vasiley in Prague. Has sent me four Obscura Engravings. He kept the fifth Engraving back. Wants more money.

Entry #51

Deciphered the encrypted map in Vasiley's Engravings. One of the Paintings is beneath the Louvre. Where the latest archaeological digs are.

Entry #52

Carvier says she has a security pass for the digs in her office.

Entry #53

A metallic symbol is hidden beneath surface of each Painting. Check with Carvier about X-Ray facilities in Louvre?

Entry #54

Lux Veritatis—Light of Truth. A secret 12th century Order of warrior monks who hid the Obscura Paintings in the 1400s.

Entry #55

Said to possess the three Periapt Shards, artifacts of power, crystalline shards shaped like spearheads, weapons of light. !!??

Entry #56

Lux Veritatis try to suppress the Cabal of the Black Alchemist from the 1300s onwards.

Entry #57

Lux Veritatis—links to Nephilim???

Entry #58

Nephilim from ENOCHIAN gospels. Cursed hybrid offspring of angels and humans. Exterminated in biblical times.

Entry #59

Related prophecy. Through the Golden Lion the Nephilim will enslave the sons of man and inherit the Earth.

Entry #60

The Sleeper, or Cubiculum Nephili—literally sleeping cask or chamber. Thought to be the last intact specimen of the Nephilim race. Supposedly buried in Anatolia, TURKEY.

Entry #61

The Sanglyph—some artifact of alchemic power? Linked to the Black Alchemist in 1400s. Details scarce.

Entry #62

The two missing symbols are hidden close by the buttress.

Entry #63

The Lux Veritatis Order was said to possess weapons of light—the three Periapt Shards. These were looted from ancient underground cities in ancient Turkey.

Entry #64

The Lux Veritatis were said to have destroyed the last of the Nephilim Sleepers or Cubiculum Nephili.

Notes from the Brotherhood of the Lux Veritatis

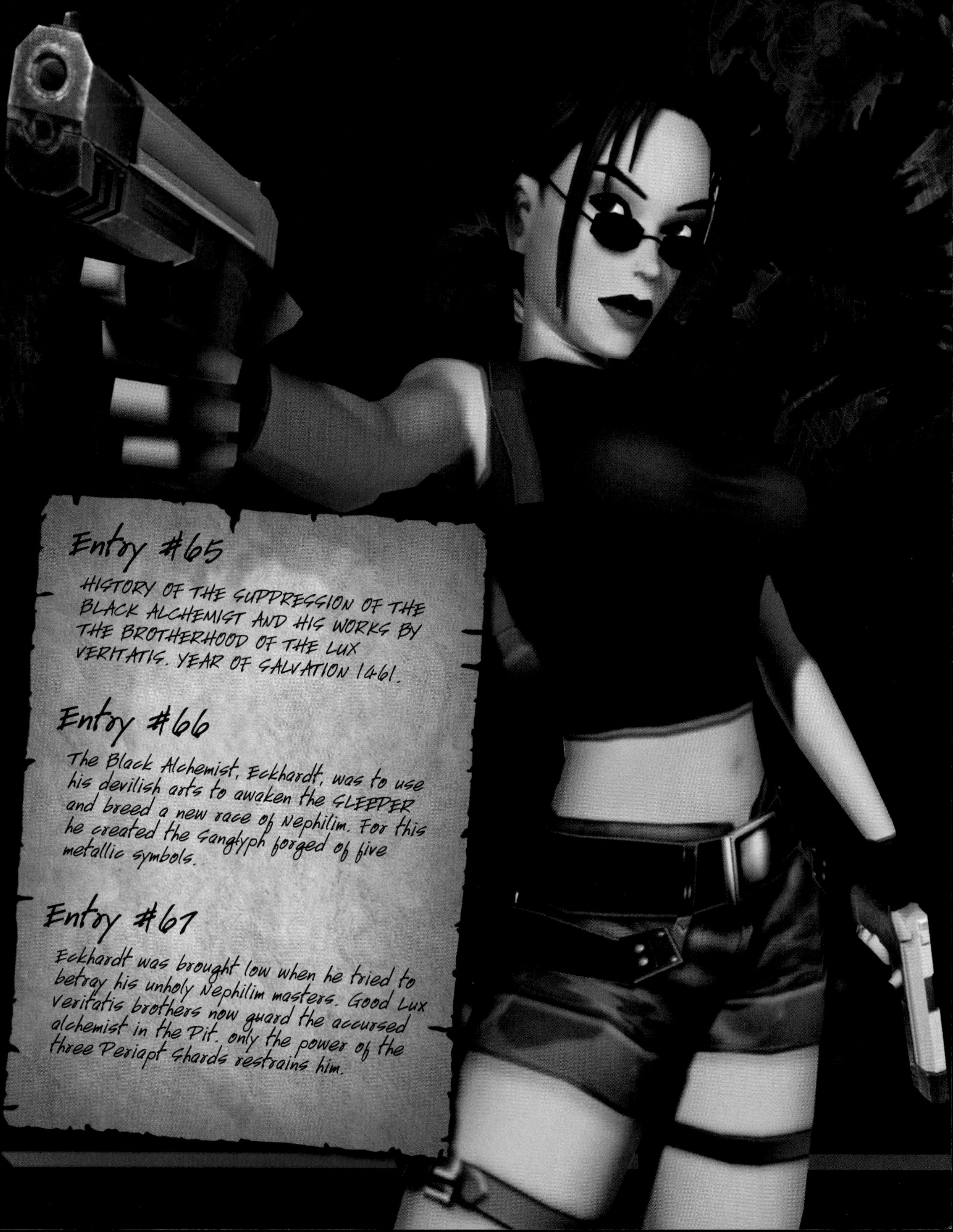

Entry #65

HISTORY OF THE SUPPRESSION OF THE BLACK ALCHEMIST AND HIS WORKS BY THE BROTHERHOOD OF THE LUX VERITATIS. YEAR OF SALVATION 1461.

Entry #66

The Black Alchemist, Eckhardt, was to use his devilish arts to awaken the SLEEPER and breed a new race of Nephilim. For this he created the Sanglyph forged of five metallic symbols.

Entry #67

Eckhardt was brought low when he tried to betray his unholy Nephilim masters. Good Lux veritatis brothers now guard the accursed alchemist in the Pit. only the power of the three Periapt Shards restrains him.

Entry #68

Autumn 1345, Prague. Have 100 summers to prepare for the revivifying of the Nephilim bloodline. And the reward for my labours will be immortality.

Entry #69

1425. By the means of human sacrifice the Sanglyph is complete! Have today cast the Nephilim metals into five symbols of power.

Entry #70

The Glove, attuned in like fashion is almost complete. With it I shall harvest those essences necessary for the Sleeper's awakening. By the Glove and Sanglyph combined shall bestir the Sleeper to my bidding.

Entry #71

My every attempt to extract Nephilim essences have come to naught. I need the true cask of the Sleeper. It must be found!

Entry #72

The thrice cursed Shard of the Lux Veritatis maggots I have placed beyond reach. With it hidden none will stand against me.

Entry #73

Get the Great Engine working.

Lara's Upgrade Chart

Perhaps the most important part of Lara's continued evolution throughout her expedition is her strength training regime. Lara begins her game with both her upper-and lower-body strength at level 1. Throughout her adventure, when Lara must upgrade to continue. All of the examples (including areas where you have a choice of when to upgrade) are shown in the following section.

Building the Upper Body

Area: Parisian Back Streets

Upgrade Type: Grip

Level: 2

Remarks: A brief wrestle with a Crowbar to open a padlocked roof hut results in increased arm strength—perfect for hanging and shimmying.

Area: Derelict Apartments

Upgrade Type: Push Object

Level: 3

Remarks: After using a little legwork and pushing power to maneuver a crate at the top of the stairs, Lara can now shoulder barge certain doors open.

Area: Parisian Ghettos (two alternates)

Upgrade Type: Shoulder Barge

Level: 4

Remarks: This upper-body upgrade can be acquired by pulling a lever in Le Serpent Rouge's garage, or by shouldering down a mausoleum door in St. Aicard's Graveyard.

Area: Louvre Storm Drains

Upgrade Type: Turn Valve

Level: 5

Remarks: After halting the rotation of a propeller fan, Lara can then build her body into a valve-turning machine.

Area: Louvre Galleries

Upgrade Type: Shoulder Barge

Level: 6

Remarks: After shimmying along a high wire, Lara's upper body is stronger than ever. She can now shoulder through heavier doors.

Area: The Hall of Seasons

Upgrade Type: Grip

Level: 7

Remarks: Lara can scale steep overhangs with ease after this wall-push workout at the top floor of the hall.

Area: Monstrum Crime Scene

Upgrade Type: Shoulder Barge

Level: 8

Remarks: By pulling a chest of drawers in Vasiley's apartment, Lara increases her upper-body strength.

Area: Aquatic Research Area

Upgrade Type: Grip

Level: 9

Remarks: By preparing a cartload of raw chum for Leviathan, Lara works those biceps and earns an upgrade that lets her shimmy farther along ledges.

Area: Vault of Trophies

Upgrade Type: Pull Chain

Level: 10

Remarks: Near the end of the Vault of Trophies, Lara winds up in a room with two Knights and a large tapestry. Pull the large lever near the fireplace to earn this strength upgrade, which lets Lara pull the chain that raises the tapestry.

Building the Lower Body

Area: Industrial Roof Tops

Upgrade Type: Jump

Level: 2

Remarks: Pushing a large crate with a generator inside it allows Lara to leap farther.

Area: Parisian Ghettos

Upgrade Type: Jump (two alternates)

Level: 2

Remarks: You can increase Lara's leg strength by pulling a crate in Le Serpent Rouge, or by pushing the stone altar in St. Aicard's Church.

Area: Parisian Ghettos

Upgrade Type: Kick Door/Wall

Level: 3

Remarks: When Lara kicks down the catwalk bridge in the rafters of Le Serpent Rouge, her leg strength is increased.

Area: Louvre Galleries

Upgrade Type: Push Object

Level: 4

Remarks: Lara pumps up her arm strength by pushing a small display case near the Mona Lisa. This gives her the strength to move a larger case in the same gallery.

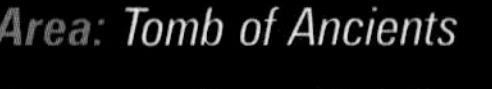

Area: Tomb of Ancients

Upgrade Type: Kick Door/Wall

Level: 5

Remarks: A swift kick to a door below the main chamber allows access to the Hall of Seasons.

Area: Galleries Under Siege

Upgrade Type: Dash Enable

Level: 6

Remarks: Locating the Respirator allows Lara the luxury of sprinting.

Area: Von Croy's Apartment

Upgrade Type: Kick Door/Wall

Level: 7

Remarks: A swift kick to a door behind the spiral stairs allows access upstairs and through a fire door.

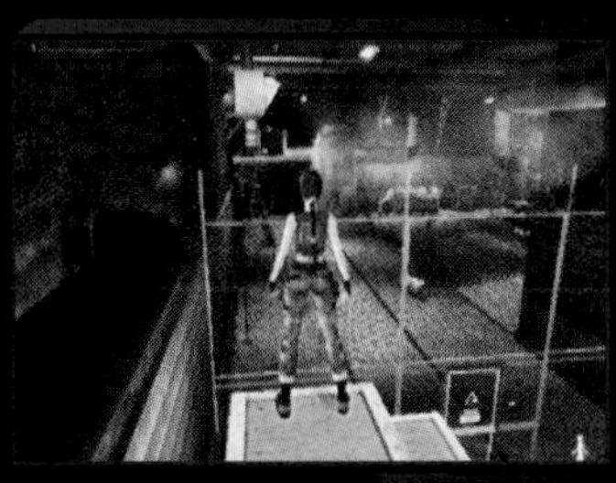

Area: Strahov Fortress

Upgrade Type: Push Object

Level: 8

Remarks: After rearranging the stacked crates so that the highest one is next to the saw room's fence, Lara becomes strong enough to push two stacked crates at once.

Area: Bio-Research Facility

Upgrade Type: Jump

Level: 9

Remarks: A leap across a large gap in the largest greenhouse area allows Lara to make even longer jumps.

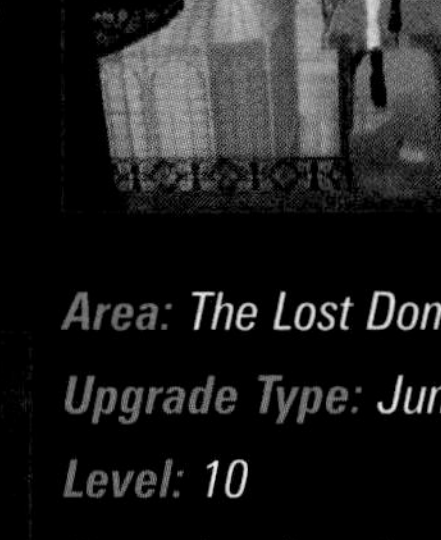

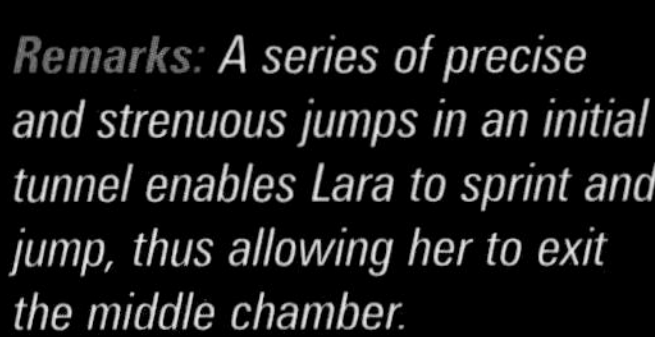

Area: The Lost Domain

Upgrade Type: Jump

Level: 10

Remarks: A series of precise and strenuous jumps in an initial tunnel enables Lara to sprint and jump, thus allowing her to exit the middle chamber.